CALL THE BRIEFING!

Call the Briefing!

BUSH AND REAGAN,

SAM AND HELEN:

A DECADE WITH

PRESIDENTS AND

THE PRESS

Marlin Fitzwater

ADAMS MEDIA CORPORATION
Holbrook, Massachusetts

Published by Adams Media Corporation
260 Center Street, Holbrook, MA 02343
by arrangement with Times Books, a division of Random House, Inc.

ISBN: 1-55850-637-3

Printed in the United States of America.

J   I   H   G   F   E   D   C   B   A

Library of Congress Cataloging-in-Publication Data
Fitzwater, Marlin.
Call the briefing : Bush and Reagan, Sam and Helen; a decade with presidents and the press
/ Marlin Fitzwater. — 1st ed.
p.   cm.
Includes index.
ISBN 1-55850-637-3 (pb)
1. Reagan, Ronald—Relations with journalists. 2. Bush, George, 1924– —Relations with
journalists. 3. Donaldson, Sam. 4. Thomas, Helen, 1920– . 5. Fitzwater, Marlin.
6. Presidents—United States—Staff—Biography. 7. Press and politics—United States.
8. United States—Politics and government—1981–1989. 9. United States—Politics
and government—1989–1993. I. Title.
E877.2..F58   1996
973.927'092—dc20
[B]   96–24059
CIP

COVER PHOTO: The White House.

This book is available at quantity discounts for bulk purchases.
For information, call 1-800-872-5627 (in Massachusetts, 617-767-8100).

Visit our home page at http://www.adamsmedia.com

FOR
BRADLEY,
COURTNEY,
MELINDA

Preface

Political life at the White House is played out on scales grand and small, among foreign heads of state, presidents, staff, family, and the press; and all the relationships are personal. Often at the nexus of these relationships, directing traffic and explaining the rules, is the president's press secretary. For nearly a decade, 1983–93, I struggled with the minidramas of daily White House life, from the table-pounding meetings that ended the cold war to the daily press briefings where reporters and presidents argued over words and motives. This book is about the personal relationships that are unique to the White House, unique to the adversarial nature of the press and the presidency, and of course unique to the great personalities that guided America out of the cold war period. It's not a definitive history or a journalistic report on the period. Indeed, I don't even touch on two of the most successful undertakings of the Bush administration: the Panama invasion and the Persian Gulf War. Books by Colin Powell, James A. Baker III, and President Bush deal with these accomplishments in great detail. Rather, it's my method to dwell on a few major events from this time that show the blend of personalities in the White House, how they influenced national life, how the media fit in, and the fragility of life as a spokesman.

In many ways this is a family portrait. The press who cover the president daily, much to their own consternation, are significant family members. Although I am harsh with some of them, I love them all, as I would eccentric aunts or combative uncles. We work together, within steps of each other, within seconds of the Oval Office, and within earshot of the world. Yet we conduct private inner wars to submerge the personal and policy conflicts that drive us. It is a world of personal strategies in which everyone has a plan for dealing with everyone else. No wonder it burns people up. But it is also very exciting, adrenaline producing, and intellectually addictive. I hope to give you the flavor of that private world.

Historical study also suggests that every White House, every president, somehow becomes a metaphor for the times. Perhaps the times shape the man, like Hoover, or the man shapes the times, like Roosevelt. But in most cases, we can look at them and know America. I believe Ronald Reagan and George Bush guided and reflected their times quite well, particularly the cold war and its aftermath. Historians will chronicle and judge their exact roles. I have tried to include only enough description to catch the immediacy, the fears, the personalities, and tensions that drove the White House during this period.

Summit meetings between Soviet and U.S. leaders in the 1980s attracted the world's attention, drawing thousands of reporters. The White House planned for every eventuality. Nuclear war was at stake. Fearing and hating communism was an industry. School kids practiced civil defense. Ronald Reagan was elected to fight the red menace. But when the cold war ended, Americans blotted it out of their thinking like a board game suddenly outgrown, and today people can hardly recall its pervasive effect on society. In a very few years, one president had scared the Soviets into economic collapse and another was welcoming Russia into the international community. This book is also about the tenor of those events, the delicacy of words in international relations, the role of a presidential spokesman, and how the cold war dictated so much of White House and press relations.

Finally, the press are always with me, a permanent part of the equation. Press secretaries do not make policy, nor does the press. But together we make a difference at the margin. Together we are an appendage to the presidency that ties the daily deliberations of government to the American people. I am proud of that role and of my media family. We are a curious and strange lot. Even as White House colleagues tried to goad me into privately criticizing the press for their political beliefs, I had trouble doing it, feeling instead that reporters are complex personalities who generally have reasons for writing insane stories. Reporters resent being labeled conservative or liberal. Yet inside the White House, the president's staff puts every reporter in one of those groups. Politicians see things politically. Also, it's easier to accept criticism if you see the reporter as an ideological critic rather than a personal one. We had a lot of critics.

I set out to write about Presidents Reagan and Bush, who had been the focal points of my life for ten years. But after four months of staring at the computer, I realized that the real focal point had been the briefing room and all the psychological wars I had waged there. I also found I enjoyed writing about, and examining my relationships with, all those reporters who had spent years trying to decipher me. The one quality that sets journalists apart from almost everyone else is their intense belief in the value of journalism. I'm glad I started as a journalist, and I came to know the best of the lot in the White House press corps. I hope that respect comes through in this book.

The impact of Ronald Reagan and George Bush on my life cannot be calculated. In the twilight of my years, when the memories of exotic places and momentous decisions will have vanished, I will still feel the sense of grace, dignity, and honor that these two men brought to my being. They will walk beside me forever.

Shortchanged in this book are my loyal staff, who for six years cheered me up, pulled me down, dragged me out, and carried me around. They also taught me that the human capacity to learn, to retain knowledge, and to use it wisely is unlimited—and the process of doing this is among the most rewarding of life's endeavors. They all deserve my gratitude. Special thanks to Bob Barnett, who convinced others I could write this book; Roman Popadiuk, Leslie Arsht, and Trudy Bryan, who read my manuscript and challenged my ideas; and Christopher Tuttle and Kathy Jeavons, who were invaluable organizers and researchers. I thought I could easily write this book in a year, but it took eighteen months. After staring at my computer for weeks and visualizing 400 blank pages, I called Peter Osnos, my editor at Random House, in total desperation. He said, "Just do it three pages at a time." That was the key, and I appreciate his wisdom and support.

Contents

CALL THE BRIEFING!

CHAPTER ONE

The Lions

The White House press corps gathers every morning like a pride of lions. It snarls and growls, sleeps and creeps, and occasionally loves, but it is always hungry. And although containing the most gentle-looking of creatures, it can be aroused to anger with the slightest provocation. After six years and over 850 briefings as press secretary to Presidents Reagan and Bush, I cautiously crept into the White House briefing room on January 20, 1993, to say good-bye.

Even on this last day, I would not avoid the preparation. "What do they want to know?" I asked my deputy, Laura Melillo.

"The usual. Why did you lose? Who did you kill? And is the president bitter?" she said.

"No, really. I'm going to the pressroom for one last conversation. Do you think they will be kind? Will they say they liked me? Will Helen be civil?" I asked, mostly serious. Even after all these years, ten in the White House, I still wanted their approval.

I also wanted to win on this last day, to give the press a professional readout on the president's morning activities, to be congenial and to say good-bye with dignity and style. Every day was a contest of wills, of psychology, of preparation, of debating skills. I wanted to hang this last day on my wall, a trophy of my victory over the press. I wanted one last win that I would always remember, like Björn Borg on his knees at Wimbledon with the cup held high over his head. I knew I would never forget this day.

"They will want to know what the president and first lady did all morning. Last visit to the Oval Office," Laura said. "Last comments.

Notes left behind? Any Iraqi leftovers? Will they leave by helicopter? Who's on *Air Force One* to Houston?"

"OK," I said. "I know those. What about attitudes? Anybody mad, besides David Kennerly? I wouldn't let him in the press pool. He always wants special favors because he was President Ford's photographer, but it's not fair to the regulars. I won't do it. Goddamn it, fairness has been my hallmark for six years, and I won't change today."

"He'll be mad," she said. "He'll say, 'What difference does it make on the last day?'"

"Well, it matters to me. It matters to the regular photographers who hang around here all day and get nothing. They're good guys. I won't do it."

"OK," Laura said, recognizing my outraged anger from years of studying my moods. "Don't worry about it. Chill out. Just go down there and be friendly, as you always are, Max Marlin Fitzwater." Laura always said my full name when she wanted to soften me up; she'd bat her eyelashes and smile a little too cutely, so I would know that she cared about me and cared that I said the right things to the press. She was a wonderful, warm woman of twenty-eight whom I had hired six years earlier. She had short black hair like Liza Minnelli, large black eyes that danced with amusement, and a smile that said love, not the sexual kind, but the human kind that lets you know she is always in your corner. Press secretaries always need someone in their corner. Someone to pull them out of the lions' cage.

This book is about those battles—a decade of contests between two presidents and the White House press corps. The press secretary to the president stands between the opposing forces, explaining, cajoling, begging, sometimes pushing both sides toward a better understanding of each other. It is a war of wits, both funny and sad, and it is intensely personal. This is also a story of those relationships, and how the White House works.

"All right," I said confidently, "I'm ready. Let's go say good-bye." I entered the briefing room, with its fifty seats silently empty, a couple of photographers asleep in row three, but with a bustle of activity rumbling just beyond the back row. That was the work area where the computers and typewriters were located, where the print reporters gathered to discuss their stories, where the wire service desks were always full and humming.

"This is good," I thought, "I'll get past the briefing seats without getting trapped. If one reporter stops me, and if I talk, the others will come running. That signals excitement, or news. I want to keep it calm. Keep the lions calm." So I walked quickly into the back work space, hoping to arrive before they could all stand or jump up. If I could get in their midst, and strike a totally relaxed pose, maybe they would stay relaxed. I would know in an instant.

I reached the wire service desks, stopped, and rested my arm on a nearby computer ledge, acting as if this might be the laziest moment of my life. Several reporters turned their heads toward my arrival. There was a general stirring as each one judged the situation. A couple moved slowly for their notebooks, wanting to be ready. One left her pad on the desk, wanting to be cool in case I had nothing to say. A television reporter, James Alan Miklaszewski, emerged from the back of the room, from booths belonging to each of the big television networks, and walked toward me. He was moving slowly, not arousing too much curiosity, and not shouting questions. This was another good sign that no controversies had popped up in the morning. No one had made any derogatory remarks about the president. President-elect Clinton had not appeared in public. There were no "urgents," to use the wire service word for a big story being urgently moved on their tickers. I relaxed.

Helen Thomas emerged from the United Press International booth and moved to her usual stakeout position at my elbow. The group parted slightly so Helen could get through. For some, it was respect for her age, or the fact that she was always on the job even though UPI had almost no clients, or that she could smell a story two days before anyone else in the room. Others moved simply because they didn't want to be embarrassed if she decided to push them out of the way. She deserved respect on all counts.

"Hi, Helen," I said. "What's happening?"

"What's happening?" she exclaimed. "That's my line. What's happening with you? What's the president doing? Has he said goodbye to the help?"

Helen has an interesting way of belittling press secretaries, indeed anyone. I'm sure she honed the technique over decades of having to suffer fools and hapless bureaucrats, of fending off White House staff trying to ingratiate themselves. She does it without any change of expression. I watched her closely, watched the soft folds in her face that might signal a facetious attitude, or a twitch of the eye that might soften the encounter, or a forehead line that might move ever so slightly to break the tension. But none of those signals appeared. It was a studied hardness, meant to give serious purpose in a situation that called for levity.

There is not a dent in Helen's game. She has played it a thousand times, with Jody Powell and Larry Speakes, with Ron Ziegler and Pierre Salinger. She has faced them all down with that shrill harshness that transforms her soul and her appearance into a molten volcano. And when she is in this trancelike personality, there is only one adequate response: deadly seriousness, abject humility, total sobriety.

When I saw the signs and heard her words on this historic morning, I immediately reacted. My mind sent a red-alert signal to every nerve of my body that said, "Play the game." I looked her squarely in the eye, ignoring all those around me, reporters and staff alike. They knew my fear. They were waiting to see how I would respond, if I was up to the challenge, if I could diffuse the situation, if I could ignore the personal slap and rise above the insult, if I could take the guff while making my point for the president. So many others had failed. Even I had fallen. But it was the last day of a ten-year run. It was a final test from the great one, the Jackie Gleason of correspondents, the woman who has asked every question and heard every lie a dozen times over, the woman who integrated the men's world of Washington journalism, the woman who broke more stories than anyone alive. And I was honored. She was testing me. She was giving me one last shot and, by God, I would win. I would play the game to the very last moment as well as any press secretary had ever played it.

I knew she would explode if I tried to be funny. "This is not funny," she would say.

"You're not through yet," she said. "You're being paid to tell us what's happened. This presidency, such as it is—or was, I should say—isn't totally over." She laughed. I knew she would. She actually laughed at herself making fun of the administration's futility, at my predicament. I could not let her take that any further.

I pulled the president's schedule from my pocket. When the pressure was on, I always went for a script, a crutch to hold my voice steady and my face stern.

"At 10:00 A.M., photo with the Executive Residence staff in the State Dining Room.

"10:15 A.M., Vice President and Mrs. Quayle join them.

"10:17 A.M., greet President-elect and Mrs. Clinton and Vice President-elect and Mrs. Gore."

Now for the color. "The president took a last walk around the grounds early this morning with Mrs. Bush. When they got down by the fence, a tourist yelled, 'We love you George!' That made him feel real good."

Helen took it down, but it didn't make her any happier. This was an item that made the president look good, which by definition does not please hardened reporters. But I knew Helen had a soft spot for old people, no doubt because she was seventy-three herself. This next item would be my best shot, perhaps only shot, at turning her attitude.

"He also went to visit the telephone operators over in the Old Executive Office Building," I said. The operators are legends, working long hours at old-style switchboards, with hand plugs that look like a wall of snakes, connecting the president with parties around the world, sick children and heads of state alike. Conference calls only take a second. The gentility of their "Hello" is never altered. They know the staff, where you vacation, who your doctor is, if the wife is hostile, if you answer your pager, your love affairs, your reliability, your maturity, and how much you love the president. They know. And the press knows they know. Helen has called them a thousand times in the dead of night, begging to be put through to the press secretary. They almost always say no, especially if there is a duty officer assigned to the day. Sometimes they would call me and ask if I wanted to talk with Helen. But they would never sandbag me, never put me on the phone unknowingly with a reporter, never admit I was available if I didn't want to be. They are treasures. Even the press know it.

Helen began to soften. "What did he say?" she asked.

"He told them thanks, how much he appreciated their efforts, their dedication and commitment to the presidency. He joked about calling other presidents in the middle of the night, or waking up congressmen because he forgot the time change." Helen liked that.

"That's nice," she said, and smiled—not broadly, or even noticeably. But to those who had studied her every feature for years, it was there, in the voice, the weakness she had worked so hard to cover. Perhaps only one muscle relaxed at the thought of a president bending over a switchboard of women, but it was enough. I had won. My heart leaped. I had won! But I could not show it. There could be no jubilation. I could not even let the others in the room know. It would have to be a silent victory. Only Helen would know. But she would respect me forever for not gloating, for not showing the others, and someday that would pay off. I always thought long-term.

Now I was feeling more confident, even warm toward the press, so I decided to spring the one piece of hard news worthy of a story. It just needed a couple of good quotes. It was the kind of story no reporter could resist, the kind that had emotional punch, perhaps anger, or sympathy, or humor.

"I took down the yellow ribbon this morning," I said. "It has been on the West Wing diplomatic entrance door for several years, since Ronald Reagan's secretary, Kathy Osborne, put it up in sympathy with the American hostages being held in Lebanon."

The ribbon had become such a part of the landscape that few people ever asked about it or even noticed it. It darkened with the weather, grew dirty with the atmosphere and the grit kicked up by the limousines, and then mysteriously became like new again. The years passed until one morning I opened the door and it occurred to me: "Who is replacing this ribbon?" It turned out that Frank Murray, correspondent for the *Washington Times*, had periodically replaced the ribbon, wanting to keep it secret to avoid any peer ridicule from the press corps. Any overt show of patriotism or sympathy for the government was condemned as "soft" by the press corps.

This morning, the last of the Bush administration, Frank was at his usual station, in the second row of the work area, near the aisle, patiently waiting to ask his questions. When I mentioned the ribbon, he looked up sheepishly, giving me a slight smile of recognition. He was waiting to see if I would identify him. I knew he had protected his own identity for years, but he had an ego. He liked recognition, fought for bylines in his paper, constantly complained about the *Post* getting credit for stories he had broken, and considered himself an investigative reporter. If this was the time to take down the ribbon, and confess that it was my decision, then it was also time to identify Frank Murray. The press might even praise him.

"It turns out that our own Frank Murray has replaced the ribbon often over the years to keep it clean," I said. "Thank you, Frank."

Frank edged forward. He decided to elevate the discussion, to legitimize his own role by dignifying the story. "Why did you take it down, Marlin?"

"I just felt it was time to officially signal the end of an era. The American hostages have all been released. Hostage taking has generally ended. The administration is leaving office. I believe President

Bush deserves some credit for creating the conditions that led to their release."

"Didn't you try to take it down earlier?" asked Larry McQuillan of Reuters. "Then you had to put it back up due to political pressure."

My face flushed, stomach muscles tightened, and nerves stretched. This must be what burnout feels like. I knew it was happening. I knew Larry's remark was not that provocative. But it galled me that he would accuse us of keeping the ribbon up for political reasons.

"Why does he question every motive?" I thought. "Even if he believes it, why not let it pass on this, our last day? Goddamn it, I know that's not true. But I know I can't convince him. I don't want to argue today. I cannot control myself. My anger is clouding my words. I must get out of the room before I say something foolish." I turned, but couldn't leave. People surrounded me.

"No, Larry," I said, "it was taken down by accident once, so we put it back up."

"No, Marlin, you had to put it back up. Why is it politically acceptable to take it down now?"

"That's it," I said, giving him my most hateful look. How could this guy challenge my statement? The ribbon had been taken down innocently months before. Larry was trying to make my courageous act of taking it down today look like political cowardice, as if I could do it only on the last day of the administration. My honor was challenged. How could he do this on our last day? My victory with Helen was turning into a defeat with Larry. I was looking petty and impetuous.

"I must get out before destroying myself," I thought. "My God, I am burned out. I would have sloughed this off easily just a few months ago. Now I'm having to run, to hide, to follow Fitzwater's third rule: You *can* run and hide. I must get out of the briefing room."

I turned on my heels, gently pushed aside three reporters, shouting over my shoulder "See you at the Capitol" as I rapidly left for my office.

Larry McQuillan is a bedrock journalist, typical of the working reporters for the wire services and daily newspapers. He makes the Newspaper Guild scale in annual salary, commutes from the suburbs, has two or three kids, wears corduroy pants and comfortable shoes, with a tie that only coincidentally matches the stripes in his shirt. But since his tie is always undone, sleeves rolled to elbows, and shirt wrinkled by hours of writing, few people notice the tie. Larry is part of the dynamics of the briefing room, where thirty to seventy people constantly move around like amoebas under a microscope. The room is strewn with standing, sitting, talking bodies that clutter the place alongside paper cups, discarded sweaters, battered cameras, stepladders for photographers, quarter-inch electrical wire for every manner of television camera, and torn newspapers from most of America's big cities. It fills with this collage every day, and the White House janitors clear it every night. In between, journalists like Larry McQuillan trudge from the telephones to their seats in the briefing room, to the press secretary's office, and back to their desks in a ritual repeated several times a day.

On this last day, Larry gave me that final lesson in press relations that can never be repeated often enough: Reporters are always reporters. Only secondarily are they your friends. It's a twenty-four-hour-a-day occupation and you should never expect them to be anything else. Larry had come to see me privately about two months before election day. I was already tired of the campaign, feeling low and unloved, put upon by a press corps that chased me day and night with repetitive questions. So I was a little short-tempered when Larry said he wanted to do a story about me and the good job I was doing. "No kidding?" I thought. "I don't believe this. What's the catch?"

Larry's background was similar to my own. From Stratford, Connecticut, the son of working-class parents, he worked for the school newspaper at St. Bonaventure College, was later a reporter in Bridgeport, Connecticut, then joined United Press International in Buffalo, Rochester, and finally Albany, New York. He knew the smell of the printing presses, had heard the splat, splat, splat as the neatly folded papers hit the concrete floor, belonged to the Newspaper Guild, wrote on old Olympia typewriters on top of metal desks, and had known the finest collection of drunks and reprobates ever to tread a shopworn newsroom floor. He knew how to read a police blotter, how to get a hospital nurse to discuss her patients, and how to tune in a police scanner to be first at the scene of a fire. He was real people.

Since coming to Washington in 1976, Larry had covered the White House. He worked at several newspapers while covering Presidents Ford, Carter, Reagan, Bush, and now Clinton. As he started to interview me, he also mentioned that he had worked for the government for a brief period, serving as a press officer for the Council on Wage and Price Stability during the Ford administration. He had walked in my shoes. He had had to answer reporters' questions about Alfred Kahn and a "Whip Inflation Now" campaign that was as silly and inconsequential as the buttons that carried the message.

I liked Larry, and his proposal for a story about me was a lifeboat of emotional support. "What a great guy," I thought, "thinking of me during this difficult period." I agreed to the interview, and it was a good experience. Larry was working at Reuters, the London wire service that had nearly run UPI out of business and was challenging the Associated Press for supremacy in America. His story about me was very flattering, tracing my background in Kansas, stressing my good sense and unfailing humor. Larry's article was a treasure. When it came across the wire machine I read it eagerly and, seeing that it was favorable, clutched it in both hands as I read it twice more. It was a tonic. I vowed never to forget the kindness of Larry McQuillan.

But my emotions got the best of me on this last day in office. I violated all the rules that I regularly preached to President Bush about mixing journalism and friendship. Reporters seldom, if ever, act on the basis of friendship. It offends their sense of principle. For years I would never thank or congratulate reporters on a story for fear they would think that I thought they were unprofessional enough to write on the basis of friendship. President Bush, on the other hand, could not resist thinking that friendships counted. They did in politics. Good deeds meant good deeds. They did in Congress, and he was first and foremost a congressman, molded by his two terms in the U.S. House of Representatives in ways that could never be altered. He gave speeches like a congressman, thanking everyone in the room, including the high school band and the ladies who served potato salad. He directed the White House like a congressman, even rehiring his first administrative assistant from 1966, telling her not to give out too many autographed pens because they cost taxpayers money. And he wanted to treat journalists as he had treated Jimmy Allison, who had been editor of the *Midland Reporter-Telegram* in Texas before quitting to become the first Bush campaign manager in 1966, and then his first legislative assistant.

"Treat them like professionals," I advised him, "and they will be your friends. But treat them like friends and they will betray you every time."

Yet President Bush, to the very last day of his administration, could not understand how the press could be so bad to him when he had been so good to them. He held 280 press conferences, at least twenty minutes long and open to questions on any subject, and had been generally more accessible than any president in modern history. He had them over to the White House for drinks, to his Kennebunkport home for hot dogs, and to the Oval Office for chats. And while they never responded to friendship, the president's yardstick for judging the press never changed; it was "I like him or her, or I don't." I urged him time and again to mitigate that feeling to say "I don't like him but he's fair" or "I do like her, but she can be critical."

Yet on this important last day of the Bush presidency, I also succumbed to the intoxicating draw of friendship and personal relations. I couldn't believe my friend Larry McQuillan, who had written so glowingly of me, would ruin my last day—would challenge my integrity and steal the glory I felt in removing the yellow ribbon. Yet he did. Later he said it was just instinctive. He heard something he didn't believe, so he challenged it. He was just a reporter being a reporter. It had nothing to do with friendship.

It was 10:15 A.M. on January 20, 1993, and the Clintons were due in two minutes. They would be walking up the front driveway from Pennsylvania Avenue. They had chosen to walk from Blair House, just across the street. I took one last look around my office, now barren of the artifacts of White House life, put on my gray Stetson, chosen because I was going to Texas for two weeks, and walked out to the driveway.

The two motorcades were lined up in front, one for the president and one for the president-elect. Even though both men would ride together, the motorcades would be joined to accommodate the vice presidents and both staffs. The driveway was full of limos and staff people strolling aimlessly. It was a strange collection of the departing veterans with no purpose left, and the awed and excited strangers, also in that limbo period without purpose or direction. Our White House press pool was in a van forward of the front steps, the Clinton pool was in another van just down the drive. They were like two foreign countries.

Dee Dee Myers, thirty-one, a stylish California blonde, had been named press secretary by President-elect Clinton but was relegated to a secondary role with George Stephanopoulos serving as presidential spokesman. She spotted me and walked between two Secret Service vehicles, waving as she came. I liked her. She had served in the Dukakis campaign of 1988, the Dianne Feinstein campaign for senator in California in 1992, and finally in the Clinton campaign. She knew the ropes and the press, and was probably being used as a token woman in the new White House. The minute she approached, the press started to run toward us. I could see the photographers jump out of their van to snap pictures, so I moved to an open area to facilitate the shots, hoping for a nice photo of the two staffs mingling in obvious civility. I wished her well and offered to help in any way possible. But I was a little self-conscious, so I said good-bye quickly and walked to my final motorcade ride. I slumped in the backseat and generally felt sorry for myself. It was over. My legs began to relax. Clinton was twenty minutes late, an affront to President Bush that I resented. But no matter. It was his show anyway. We had lost the election and, with it, all rights to be angry, or disappointed, or anything else. The awful finality of it. So we waited.

After the presidents visited a short time, they emerged smiling on the front steps of the White House, and gave the historic pictures that showed the peaceful change of power as dramatically as any other. There is no moment more symbolic than when the victor walks into the White House, not yet sworn in as president, but still knowing that it is his. It is the moment of the coup, the moment when the third-world general stabs the incumbent, or when the first bomb explodes and the incumbent jumps out a back window, or when the sitting dictator tells his wife that they must run for their lives. It is far more civilized in American democracy, but this is the moment, when the president-elect walks into the White House without credentials and throws out the incumbent. To be a part of it induces the greatest sadness, yet the greatest pride. The pain is physical, in the heart and chest, in the eyes and the mouth. Yet the pride of being part of democracy's march keeps it all in focus, in perspective. It is no wonder that democracy is so hard to teach in a developing nation—it requires enduring so much pain.

Finally, the motorcades were filled and we started the slow crawl to the Capitol. And then the sadness vanished. Spread out before us, on all sides, crowding the sidewalks and the yards and the malls and every square inch of Washington was America. The best of America, its people, dressed in every conceivable garb, even in the dead of winter. A few tears blurred my vision. It was like viewing a van Gogh painting six inches from the canvas, a multitude of brush strokes without form or structure. But dry the tears and you could see the faces, all smiling. Warm, wonderful signs of hope for President Clinton and love for President Bush were everywhere. No hate. A few abortion protests. To be in that motorcade, with nose pressed to window, was to be inspired by the goodness of the American family—of kids with runny noses, of women in fur coats and new hairstyles, of men who knew pride and patriotism and wore it on their sleeves. My emotions were having a tough time stabilizing.

When the motorcade made its final turn off Pennsylvania Avenue and onto the broad parking area behind the Capitol, I suffered another attack of "the lasts." The last motorcade. The last walk through the Capitol with the president. The last few minutes of presidential life. The lead cars came to a stop, the presidents emerged, waited for their wives, then walked up the red-carpeted steps to the swearing-in. I was about to climb out of the backseat of the Dodge van, designated as "support," for the supporting staff that rode in it. I crawled over and around the back of the front seat, making that swivel motion I had duplicated a thousand times in every small hamlet in America and in almost every foreign capital—fearing that split moment of embarrassment when the side door slides open and your fanny is sticking perilously out the door, one foot reaches for the street, and if there is any missed connection you end up on your tail in front of an onrushing crowd of staff and journalists from trailing vehicles. For some reason, translators are the most prone to suffer this fate. It had happened to several around the world, and usually to the pure delight of all concerned, owing entirely to the arrogance that seems to affect translators.

I hesitated, sensing it was time to savor my last moments as press secretary, settled back in the seat while everyone else rushed from the vehicle, and turned to stare out the window at the vast crowd stretched out below the Capitol. Then it happened. The end came. It was so sudden, so routine, that I barely noticed. The lions left.

They rushed past "support" as a full pride. First, the correspondents, carrying their three-by-seven-inch notebooks, suit jackets flying, tape recorders dangling by small black cords, women with seldom-worn high heels, their eyes searching frantically for the new escorts, the Clinton advance staff that would take them to stakeout positions or the swearing-in seats. You could see the uncertainty in their eyes, and I was secretly pleased. Then came the "photo dogs," cameras of every kind dangling from their necks or the pockets of their safari jackets. Their tan khaki uniforms were always the same. Finally came the television sound and camera men, tethered by a six-foot sound cable, running in a line while somehow knowing the exact distance that must be maintained to keep them from jerking each other recklessly to the ground. They talked, like a NASCAR racing team, telling each other where to go, which step to watch, and which turn to avoid.

And then they were gone. I watched them recede in a cluster up the Capitol steps, bunching up just outside the door, then surging forward, their heads bobbing and bodies swaying, their jangle of equipment disappearing into the inner sanctums of another world. I had such pride in those lions. And now they were gone. My time with them had passed.

CHAPTER TWO

The Howie Place

There is a place about ten miles south of Abilene, Kansas, where the earth, freshly plowed, is so dark and rich it looks like a blackboard freshly wiped with a wet rag. It is my home. The people there talk of politics as if it were the wind, a tornado, a flood, or some other natural disaster that is completely beyond comprehension.

It is a place on a hill overlooking Holland Creek, just a half mile away, with a set of farm buildings that bear my fingerprints on every stanchion, stall, and roost. It is the Howie place, laid out in a triangle with a small two-story frame house on the pinnacle of the rise, a red barn with stalls for a dozen milk cows, a shed for perhaps fifty pigs or sheep, and a hayloft even today full of bales of alfalfa that give the place an ageless aroma like the smell of a family lawn mower. Fifty yards away in the remaining corner of the layout is the granary, with middle entry opening for the tractors and trucks to pull in and unload the wheat and corn in bins along each wall. They are money bins. For as the winter progresses, or new shoes and a baseball glove are needed, Dad will shovel a truckload of grain into an aging pickup truck and haul it to the elevator near town. Somehow I never made that connection as a youth, the direct connection between a shovel of wheat and a dollar bill. It was just grain to me, to be played in, or thrown at my brother in great handfuls, or to be augered from a truck and endlessly scooped so it filled every corner of the bin and the maximum could be stored.

"Pick that up," my dad would say calmly when I dropped a scoop of wheat on the ground, "and don't get any dirt in it." I marvel today at his calm demeanor in this situation, and in all such misdemeanors of farm life, when I realize that it was dollars I dropped so carelessly to earth.

A lean-to shed was built on the side of our granary that was the family blacksmith shop. Dad spent long hours of mystery there, wearing a black spaceman's helmet and eye shield to protect him from the blue flame of the welder. He would touch it to plowshares, and garden hoes, and corn knives, and the big rough pieces of metal would stick together, with the line of weld forming a scar on the surface that seldom broke. Sometimes our old tractor would lose a metal attachment and Dad would say the weld broke, a depressing admission of failure. And if it was another reason, he would proudly say, "At least the weld didn't break."

My brother, Gary, two years younger, and I watched the glow of the welder for hours, marveling at its mystical ability to glue metals together, and listening for the sizzle when the weld was dipped in water to cool and harden. I always wanted to weld, even at age ten, to bring pieces of iron to a soft, red glow, and then hammer them into unnatural shapes on the huge anvil that stood in the middle of the shed. The sculptures formed in my mind, but Dad said no, it was too dangerous.

Between the house and the granary was a small chicken house, perhaps fifteen by thirty feet, that held the mainstay of our diet, a hundred chicks raised each year to cooking size, with a row of drawers with open backs that allowed the hens to roost and lay eggs. Each day Mom would pull out the drawers and empty them for breakfast.

Many years later, on *Air Force One*, the press pool asked me about the farm. For me, it resulted in one of the most interesting pool reports ever to come off the plane, and certainly a surprise to the hundreds of city-hardened reporters who scoured the report for news of the president's activities.

I explained to the press that, of the farm's various treats for a youth, my favorite was "dressing" chickens. The first responsibility was the kill, a process of chasing the chicken around the yard, diving for its legs without getting a peck on the hand, and holding it upside down as protection against that aggressive beak. The site preparation had been done several years before when a large tree stump was cut flat across the top and two sixteen-penny nails driven about a third of the way into the center of the stump. Stuck in the edge, as if lodged there by Daniel Boone on some ancient hunt, was a two-foot-long machete whose wooden handle had gone white with the snows of time and whose metal blade was covered with the rust that signaled that this instrument of death was never to leave its post for other uses.

Once you have the chicken, its neck between the nails, hold its feet straight out behind it and prepare to sever the head with one sure-handed swing of the machete. Strangely, once the chicken's head is between the nails, it seldom moves, a sense of resignation setting in that can be disconcerting. It's best to hurry past that moment when the destruction seems more than a mechanical movement. The trick is in your command of the blade and the follow-through. The greatest nightmare is to effect a partial cut that might require a second swing, when the legs are kicking and blood is spurting. The other great fear is of misaiming the machete and hitting the nails. Never hit the nails. The impact reverberates up and down your arm in most painful fashion.

Once the head is chopped, the most crucial moment comes. You must throw the chicken away from your body in one fluid motion, something like throwing a frisbee, so that the death dance of the chicken can be played out, a desperate reflex by the muscles that causes it to flop all over the ground, headless and bleeding.

My grandmother eschewed this high-technology process and opted instead to simply grab the chicken by the head, swing the body in a wide circle, then suddenly reverse direction in midair so that the head twisted off in her hand while the body flew on to continue its dance of death. I tried it once, but couldn't stand the feel of the head in my hand. The machete was better.

The press were appalled at this story, but as a boy of ten I found it as routine as any other farm chore. Besides, the sooner we ate all the chickens, the sooner we could clean out the henhouse for roller skating. I had discovered with great celebration that the henhouse had a concrete floor. What a treat. No farm had concrete—not patios, nor sidewalks, nor porches, nor any other slab of artificial surface harder than wood. Dirt floors, hardened by the rains and tromping of people and animals, were quite sufficient for barns, granaries, sheds, and most chicken houses. So my brother and I asked Dad if we could clean it out for roller skating. He was disbelieving, partly at the thought of using the house for such a frivolous purpose, and partly at the prospect of two small boys actually shoveling about a ton of chicken shit. But we did it. When my brother would get tired, I would paint for him once again a picture of how we would be the envy of the neighborhood. And we were. The old steel-wheeled, lock-on skates would hold up longer than the soles of our shoes. Our acrobatic skating under three-foot-high chicken roosts and jumping over large cracks in the concrete made us the heroes I envisioned.

Today these buildings still stand, indeed are still being used. And the ghosts of the Fitzwater boys live on. It is a generational thing. We were part of the Howie place, first purchased by old Hugh Howie, then rented by us, then inhabited by three more Howie generations. In July 1993, the newest inhabitant, Alan Howie, stood in the kitchen with his six-year-old son and told me how proud they were of my accomplishments. As he turned to politics, and started talking about the government's new tax bill, he shook his head as if encountering a tragedy of immense proportions, as if contemplating the recent flooding that had covered acre after acre of wheat and hay. "We can take a couple of bad flood years," he said, "but we can't take these taxes." Indeed, politics is a pestilence.

The old farmhouse looks better today than it did in 1951 when we first moved there. It was our third farm. "Sharecropper" has become a dirty word for its application to the poor, often immigrant, workers who pick fruits and vegetables and live in squalid little shacks on the dusty fringes of seasonal-crop farms, mostly in Florida, California, and Texas. But in Kansas in the '40s and '50s, a lot of farms were maintained by renters who paid with a share of the crop, usually one-third to the owner and two-thirds to the renter. The owners needed tenant workers, and the best way to provide housing was to build a new house for yourself and rent the old one to the tenants. In any case, the result was a lot of tenant farmers living at subsistence levels, farming with used equipment held together with baling wire and spit, eating butchered cattle and hogs out of their own barns, and planting enough vegetables to put Irish potato farmers to shame. We always had potatoes in huge backyard plots, planted by the entire family. Best of all, the new potatoes came from the last year's crop. You simply cut up the old potatoes into sections with one eye per section, stuffed them into the ground in long furrows dug with a hand plow, then covered them over with a spade. In Kansas soil, it's impossible not to make potatoes grow. And it didn't cost a dime for new seed.

Wheat was another matter. It was the cash crop, but you had to borrow money to buy the seed to plant the crop. After the Depression, all farmers hated borrowing money because it so often meant losing the farm. Bankers were to be feared more than a plague of locusts or grasshoppers, although they too could wipe you out. Even today, with pesticides that can kill a giraffe in ten seconds, farmers

still fear grasshoppers and certain other insects and speak of their hatred in passionate terms. Wheat is always susceptible to everything
destructive, but specifically to insects, rain, hail, tornadoes, and
drought. God made them all, and He is a formidable adversary. Yet
every year we put our lives in His hands, trusted in His benevolence,
and excused Him when lightning would capriciously kill a cow or
burn down the barn.

When harvest did come, when the fields were full and the waves
of yellow chaff floated and swayed in the hot summer sun, when the
air was so dry that your nose burned, and the kernels of wheat were
fat and hard, you knew that God was good. You were safe for another
year. You could sit under a shade tree on an August afternoon and
see a Thanksgiving table loaded with turkey and surrounded by a
thankful family, Christmas with plenty of gifts, and money for the
unexpected winter disaster, because the insurance policy for those
amenities of life was in the bin. At those moments there could be no
greater fulfillment.

Of course, there might not be enough in the bin for much im-
provement in your general condition, or fixing the roof, or installing
running water or indoor plumbing.

"Can I go out on the porch?" I asked Alan Howie on my last visit
to the farm in 1993.

"Sure," he said, with some embarrassment. "It's not in good condition. I plan to tear it off the house and expand the kitchen." Alan,
or perhaps his father, Alfred, who had also lived in the house, had
paneled the living room and dining room and replaced all the
kitchen cabinets, appliances, and electrical outlets in the main
house. But the porch was unchanged. Windows with screens allowed
a full view of the bottom land south of the house. Large cracks in the
concrete floor could still let snakes through from the ground. Dirt
was still caked in the crevices of the wall siding. Even the cistern
with hand pump was still in place.

We never had running water, just the runoff from the roof after
each rain that was guided down old spouts to the cistern. I often
dreamed as a child about bugs getting in the water as it traveled
down the roof, and I never trusted that cistern to keep the snakes
out. So when the hot months came every year and the water supply
diminished, I secretly approved because it meant we would haul
water in ten-gallon milk cans from the water plant at Sand Springs,
about ten miles away. I knew it was safe.

That porch also possessed one other absolutely overwhelming, overriding, swamping, and consuming aspect: the porch pot. It was a porcelain-covered tin pot that served as an indoor toilet during the winter. The outhouse was thirty yards away, and when the temperature dropped below zero, or the snow drifted and heaped itself in mountains in front of the doors, there was no alternative to the porch pot. I hated it. First, there was no privacy. Second, it smelled to high heaven. And finally, the flies. They filled the porch, and buzzed so loud that I could hear them from bed. They were unrelenting. But we had an answer: DDT. Dad bought it in jugs and poured it into a hand sprayer that hung on a nail just inside the porch door. We were taught the ritual: Spray when you go out and spray when you come in. There was so much DDT on that porch that a blue cloud hung in the air, and the odor permeated all surroundings. We came to rely on it, even to trust it, indeed to equate its odor with safety and good health. I somehow felt that DDT was man's greatest purification agent, a chemical so good that it made homes safe for children and protected against ants, flies, bacteria, and, if you sprayed enough of it, even the smell of the pot itself. I loved it. Thirty years later, working at the Environmental Protection Agency in Washington, I discovered it causes cancer.

I didn't mention any of this to Alan as we stood on the porch. I just looked around until I could smell the DDT and then I knew I was home.

We walked outside and my eyes were drawn to the barn. It is still red, undoubtedly repainted at some point, but still carrying the marks in my mind of the most fascinating discoveries of growing up. On the front side, over the door to the pigpen, there are marks in the paint, surely not forty years old, and yet hauntingly similar to the scars of a thousand gentle basketball nudges as I arched another great shot off the wall and through the rim. The rim was a steel band removed from one of the wooden barrels that housed every kind of farm supply, from nails to apples. It was nailed exactly ten feet high, or at least as high as Dad could reach. The ground was slanted, so that every shot was from a different level, and rocks in the soil meant that every bounce came up at a different angle. Quick hands and a quick eye, they said later. In one high school game against neighboring Junction City, we were five points behind with forty-seven seconds left. I stole the ball three times and scored on three successive shots. Quick hands and a quick eye, they said, borne of the imperfections in my private barn gym. Also born on those rocks, or at least discovered, was an intense competitive spirit. I virtually forced my younger brother to play, yet I never let him win. I still hate to lose.

Also in that barn were the first sexual stirrings, and the ugly lessons of deceit. No child can play in a hayloft without feeling an exhilaration. The hay is stacked in bales about three feet long, easily handled by an adult, and adequately managed by a ten-year-old. To have your own hayloft is to own Disneyland. I would stand in the middle of the hay and dream and plan of things to be built, houses and castles, forts and wagons, tunnels and hiding places so dark and so high that they could never be discovered, and if they were, the opening would be too small for Mom or Dad to ever follow. It was the kind of secret place every boy wants, or it could be shared with other children for a game of hide and seek, and it could be changed every day like Lego blocks. Every day we built a new playground.

One day, in the fifth or sixth grade, another boy pulled me aside at recess, looked over his shoulder for any teachers in the area, swore me to secrecy, and pulled a torn magazine page from his jeans pocket. It had been smudged and often handled. He unfolded it slowly, clearly indicating this was a forbidden treasure. It was a picture of a woman in a swimming suit, posed Greta Garbo style, but with a substantial bosom and cleavage showing. We just looked at it. Another boy rushed up. "Let me see," he said. We knew no other exclamations, hardly knew what we were looking at, and felt more excitement about the forbidden nature of the subject than any sexual arousal. But the spark was lit. There was something here. Some vague stirring that had to be pursued.

A few weeks later the opportunity presented itself. Mom and Dad and Gary and I went to Salina, a slightly larger town twenty miles away, to shop. Salina was a treat. It had Nicener's, the biggest, most exciting dime store I had ever seen, with a candied-apple machine that gave the aisles a carnival smell, the first escalators in our part of Kansas and the object of more attention than a Ferris wheel, and the first foot X-ray machine where you could look at your toes right through your shoes. Science couldn't go much farther than that.

Right next door was a magazine store. I spotted it when we went into Nicener's, and a dark sense told me the pictures were there. So while Mom and Dad were shopping, and Gary was looking at his toes, I slipped down a back aisle, out the door, and took those ten steps down the block to the forbidden fruit. The store was dark, musty, lined with magazines of every description, and tended by one old man behind a counter who eyed me very suspiciously. Fortunately, there was one magazine rack, just past the *Car and Driver* area and the *Popular Mechanics* display, where I could duck and be out of sight of the counter. I moved to it, looked about, frantically up and down the rack, and there it was. On the cover was a pinup, and one flip of the pages revealed several more. This was it. Now, how do I get it? I had to get back to Nicener's soon, so the decision was instant. I walked to the counter, laid down the magazine, and put a quarter on top of it. The old man looked at me warily, touched his scraggly beard, rubbed his bloodshot eyes, and asked, "Do you think you're old enough for this?" I instinctively knew that he had asked the right question, the one that allowed me to tell the truth, be confident, and still accomplish the task. He didn't ask if I *was* old enough, only if I *thought* I was. In later years I would often search frantically for the more narrow press question that I could seize upon to answer.

"Yes," I told him. He took the quarter. I took the magazine and walked quickly out the door. On the sidewalk, I tucked it in the front of my pants where it couldn't possibly be seen. I went straight to our car, a 1947 Dodge, and climbed into the backseat. I figured Mom and Dad had to be looking for me. They would know I wasn't in the store. So it would be logical that I had gone to the car.

It worked. They were angry but they believed me. I sat in rigid silence all the way home, partly because I was scared and partly because the magazine was cutting into my leg just below my shorts. So when everyone got out of the car at home, I was slow, the last to exit. As the others went into the house, I went to the barn, to my secret place, to the hayloft where I could sit for hours in warmth and comfort, staring at the pictures, and wondering about the new sensations.

While I was talking to Alan Howie, his son Evan, age six, ran excitedly to his father, pulled his shirt until he leaned over, and whispered that he had just called Granddad to tell him Marlin Fitzwater was home. "The word is spreading," Alan said. "All kinds of people will be here soon."

Alan's father, Alfred Howie, does not look like a granddad. For one thing, he is only a few years older than I, rode the bus with me in the '50s, married his high school sweetheart, and followed our family as tenants on the Howie place. His father, Art, had just died. His grandfather, Hugh, was the original owner who rented us the place. I had known five generations of Howies, and three of them stood before me this day. Alan and Alfred are both tall and lean in

blue jeans and plaid cowboy shirts with the fake pearl buttons that
snap on, boots worn with the remnants of mud, dung, and a thousand kicks against dogs, cows, and tractors. All five Howie generations lived, loved, and died within three miles of the spot where we
stood, which was smack in the middle of the baseball diamond of
grass that lay between the house, barn, and granary.

My dad would come home from the fields about seven or eight
o'clock on a warm summer night, wash up, change into clean overalls and a fresh blue Sears and Roebuck cotton shirt, then come out
and hit us flies for an hour before dark. It was the best time, to see
Dad at play, laughing, hitting great looping flies to center field and
telling us after each hit, "You have to run faster than that" or "Start
as soon as I hit it." Then he would mock himself, this most humble
of men, with a facetious brag, "This is the way we used to hit 'em at
Westfall. Why, those fielders never saw them coming." The corner
of his mouth raised ever so slightly, but the sparkle in his eyes lit up
like diamonds. The good humor was full and on display. My dad was
liked. He smiled easily and often, yet because he didn't speak unless
it was important, people took him seriously. I always remembered
that.

Standing there, shifting from one foot to another, I asked Alan
and Alfred about the recent flood. In July 1993, the Mississippi went
wild, breaking levees, destroying homes and towns, creating a thousand tragic stories that America watched on television for weeks on
end. But largely hidden, some 700 miles away, rambled the little
tributary known as Holland Creek, not officially so you could read it
on any sign, but official enough that everybody said Holland Creek
and it must have been on some map someplace. It crossed the road
just a half mile from the Howie place, and the receding waters this
July day had left the hayfield dark and dirty, the wheat plastered to
the earth like straw on a thatched roof, with huge gashes where combine tires had tried but failed to rescue a few bushels. It reminded me
of 1951.

I mentioned that this flood looked almost as bad as '51. "I remember the water coming up through the cornfield," I said, "but we
never thought it would come up the lane. Then it reached the hedge
tree with the big green apples I used to throw at Gary while we
waited for the bus. Then it came up toward the house, not really
close, but we were the highest house around, and we knew that if it's
that close to us, others were sweeping mud." I had grown animated
just talking about it.

Alfred laughed. "Do you remember all that?"

"Sure," I said, "and afterward Dad caught a fifty-pound catfish with his bare hands. Of course, it was just laying in the mud where the water had left it. He brought it back and hung it on that barn door and dressed it, and cut off the head and stuck it on that fence post right over there. Slowly it deteriorated until nothing was left but the skull, and it was hanging on that post until the day we left, maybe even after that."

William Least Heat Moon writes in *PrairyErth*, his wonderful epic about Kansas and its people: "They recognize but do not say how the river whets a fine edge on their lives, and I never heard any of them speak love for the river, or hate." My own recollection of the '51 flood gives testament to that fact. I recalled the one year we lived in the little Howie place, another of Hugh's places about three miles away. It was a small house, with coal heating and no indoor plumbing, located just across the road from old Hugh's place, and about 500 yards from Holland Creek. It was two years before the '51 flood, and old Holland Creek warmed up by throwing her waters right up to our doorstep. I remember watching it edge up, like the huge boulder in *Raiders of the Lost Ark* that just kept rolling toward Indiana Jones. Surely it wouldn't reach the house—but it did. Surely it wouldn't come up the steps—but it did. Surely it wouldn't come into the house—but we watched it creep on up as Mom started putting everything on bricks or pickle jars to steal a few extra inches. It was like a bad movie, where the curl of the water oozes through the floor. The waters assumed a hard fluorescent surface, as if some plastic coating were holding the water as it grew larger and would not break, and then it did. The crochet rugs became soaked. We put on our boots and lifted the furniture onto the pickle jars, and still the water came. It was dark and smelled like dirt, as if on the way into the house the creek had picked up the prairie and offered it a free ride, so the water still smelled dry and hot. Then it crested, about two inches above the floor, just under the lip of the jars, and we felt we had won. But the real work was just starting.

Even worse than getting water in is getting it out. As the river recedes, the water starts back. It is as if some unseen hand on a distant shore has lassoed the water and is pulling it away, sometimes fast and sometimes slow. It's crucial that you stay with it. Mom is in charge. When the water starts out, everyone grabs a broom and starts sweeping the water, because the water carries the mud, and if you don't sweep it out with the tide, it cakes in every corner and hardens in every thread of fabric. It seals the windows, and leaves dirt in buttonholes so hard that the shirts must be thrown away. So you ride the water, and you cannot get off. "Keep sweeping," Mom will say, till she sees that your arms ache and your feet are swollen. You keep sweeping because although no eight-year-old understands the theory behind "riding" the water, you do understand that there is no alternative. There is no place to sit, and besides, you are working side by side with Mom and Dad. They are depending on you to help save the house, to get the mud out, to sweep continuously until the water is gone, and then the aches are filled with pride. You do not hate the river. You do not love it. It is there to be fought, and the winners are those who fight the longest and hardest, because in the end the river always wins. Pretty much like dealing with the press.

Tornadoes are far more ominous for a boy. They are unfathomable, yet the subject of endless stories of tragedy and Ripley phenomena that are no doubt based in fact but fictionalized in their local application. I have no doubt that somewhere a tornado drove a piece of straw six inches into a tree, something about the pressure equalizing and creating a "straw of steel." But I doubt that it happened in our neighbor Tim Gruen's backyard, as the other kids said.

When we lived on the little Howie place, a cow was struck by lightning and killed, but I doubt that another neighbor's herd, Milton Nagely's, was picked up near the barn by a tornado and dropped in the pasture a quarter mile away with nary a scratch on them. At least I could never confirm it. And, according to school yard lore, several neighbors had their cars picked up and moved from road to field. Curiously, in these stories, the tornado seemed to have motherly qualities that picked things up violently but set them down gently and tenderly in some distant quarter. Such is the fiction of nature. Nevertheless, some credence had to be given these accounts because my father gave tornado drills and front seat car lectures the minute the sky turned dark.

"If we're driving," Dad would say, "I'll stop the car. Get out and get in the ditch. It will pass right over you. Don't raise your head until it passes."

"How will we know when it passes?" I asked.

"What if there's water in the ditch? We'll get all muddy?" Gary asked.

"You'll be fine," Dad said, "just get below the surface of the land."

I used to have nightmares about jumping in that ditch and finding snakes, or trying to crawl up the ditch to a culvert, which was a tin flow-through pipe, usually big enough for a body to crawl into, that was used to let water flow under a driveway. That would be the safest place. But in my dream, I never quite got to it before the wind picked me up and flung me into a tree, under equalized pressure that turned me into a "steel Marlin," and then I would wake up.

Several times, we saw the tornado coming over the far horizon. Dad would call us into the house: "Get in the basement, kids. Mom is already there."

We would go down the rickety stairs to the dirt-floor basement, cross the floor where Dad had once killed a black snake, and Mom would be under a large table in the southeast corner. Tornadoes always came from the southeast, some immutable law of God. He just never operated from the north. So, according to theory, the house, when it raised off its foundation, would move away from the southeast corner first, drop a few planks and foundation fragments on the table, and move on. Then we could get out using our ax, flashlight, hammer, jar of water, pickled beets, and assorted jams stored under the table.

Finally Dad would shout, "Here she comes." He would come stumbling down the steps, race across the basement, and crawl in. A huge noise would be just behind him, like a train on the downhill side, picking up steam and running easy, a hundred boxcars pushing it to oblivion, and it was right outside our house. The house would shake, little flakes of dirt would drop from the walls, the jam jars would tumble on their shelves like Humpty's men, and Gary would start to cry. But then it passed. We would wait, holding our breath, and Dad would go upstairs, look out the door, and give the "all clear" sign. We always lost a lot of trees, but never any buildings. I never found a straw stuck in a tree, but I did think my dad was very brave. In 1990, I attended my high school's thirtieth class reunion. Mom and Dad were retired and living in town. I left their home for the reunion dinner when the town siren went off signaling a tornado. The rain and wind were hard, so I circled the block and returned to the house. I ran up to the porch, jumped the three-step entrance, and banged on the door. No answer. I tried the knob, it turned, and I rushed in screaming for Dad. "Down here," a voice said, so I headed for the cellar, bounded down the steps, and moved for the southeast corner. Dad held the flashlight, leading me on hands and knees safely under the table with the ax, the jar of water, and the pickled beets. "Just think, Dad," I said, "how many people can say they've been on hands and knees, under a table in their basement, with the press secretary to the president of the United States?"

"That's better," Dad said, "than saying my son wasn't smart enough to get under the table during a tornado."

Unfortunately, neither father nor son was smart enough to get out of the sun, or at least to wear a hat during those endless hours of farm labor. Riding the tractor at age eleven was almost a treat. But the old Ford Ferguson with two-bottom plow soon became monotonous, as the engine droned for hours and I moved up one row and down the other, trying to stay awake to make the turns, burning my nose to a crisp in the Kansas sun. The ears and nose would burn first and peel first, but it was almost a badge of honor, a symbol of summer labor, and the only color that would tell my classmates of my summer pursuits. I simply could not tan. So we just got red, my dad and I, cutting sunflowers with machetes in the cornfield, or circling the harvest field with combine and truck, or pulling the hay out of the baler and throwing it onto the wagon. We worked together and burned together. Years later, we got skin cancer at about the same time. On television, during my press briefings, it showed red and blotchy on my face. I took to hats, as the doctor ordered. It got so I would not go out without one. I loved those hats, with the big brims and long bills, warm in winter and cool in summer. They became a personal symbol, a part of my countenance at Camp David or Kennebunkport. Sometimes on television they looked ostentatious or, as they say in Kansas, "show-off." But people came to understand. The word got out that I had skin cancer, and few people accused me of showing off. This pestilence, the sun, I could not beat. The water would recede. The tornadoes would pass. But the sun left its cancerous mark on my life forever in a 1971 nose operation to remove a basal cell carcinoma that left my nose with a graft from behind my right ear. It was a nine-hour operation by a plastic surgeon, who would remove a little nose, test it for cancer, and if any was left on the edge of the tissue he would cut some more. He went back for more tissue and more Novocain nine times. Twenty years later, when President Ronald Reagan had a similar skin cancer on his nose, removed with a "rhomboid flap" procedure, I explained the process to America with great confidence in my subject, and the memory of nine Novocain shots still stinging in my mind.

Farm life in the '50s was not guided by concern for pesticides, or skin cancer, or other scientific discoveries. It was basic, and it taught values. When Wilson Huffman, my Pee Wee League baseball coach, broke his arm the week before his hay was due to be cut, it was automatically assumed that the team, and its fathers, would help put up his hay. On the given day, at least twenty families gathered on the Huffman farm with at least five balers and a like number of hay wagons, and in a day's time did a week's work. It was hot and sweaty summer work, where by noon our overalls were a darker blue in giant splotches where the sweat had soaked through even the red country handkerchiefs that hung in our vest pockets. They wiped brow and neck alike with one fluid motion, starting on the forehead, moving down the face, under the ear, and around to the back of the neck. Also part of the uniform were Red Man boots, raw leather, in various states of wear, most rough and scratched with creases that had gone black with dirt while the toes had hardened from tromping through mud and manure. The men and boys worked together on hay wagons, pulling the bales out of the back of the machine. The tractor pulled the baler and the wagon, so the three contraptions formed a piece of field art with every angle showing, like some Calder exhibit being pulled across the skyline, with wheels, and wire, and exhaust pipes, and levers, and Rube Goldberg's many moving pieces. When it was time for lunch, the whole caboodle of equipment was brought to a halt, grinding and screeching until no single part was left moving. The tractor was shut down and people piled off, clambering into a pickup truck and heading for the house.

On this day at Wilson Huffman's, the women had prepared a whopper of a lunch, with chicken fried and crispy and piled high in glass bowls brought from home, potato salad as yellow as mustard and colored with green chunks of pickle and onion, and baked beans steaming hot in big blue metal bowls with lids that could be raised just enough to take a ladle full without letting the beans cool, as if they would in ninety-five-degree heat. At the end of the long tables, usually plywood on sawhorses, sat three-gallon containers of iced tea, dripping with condensation, cold to the touch of hand and tongue, and available mostly to the kids. On the ground in washtubs were soda pop and beer. All the men took beer, pushed the caps off on the edge of the table, and launched into a big swig with some sort of exaggerated vocal expression of relief. My father walked over to where Gary and I were sitting, kicked another bale around with his foot, and sat down to open his orange soda pop.

"Why don't you drink beer, Dad?" I asked.

"I just don't," he said. "I don't believe in it. It's OK if the others do. I'll stick to good old Nehi orange." That's all he needed to say, because that's how they teach values on the farm, or at least how my father did it. He didn't drink. He knew what he believed. He lived that way, and he let us know that you should live the way you believe. I went back to Abilene in 1988 to deliver the high school commencement address and I told this story to emphasize the importance of values, of knowing what you believe in. I spoke that day of Gorbachev, the end of the cold war, and the Moscow summit that I would be attending the next week. But my best story was about Dad and his orange pop. As I was telling it, I looked for Dad in the audience, and he was looking at me with such pride and love that I thought my chest would burst, and he was crying.

My dad, Max Malcolm Fitzwater, was amazingly secure with himself. His private code and good sense ruled his life, even in recreation. Once a year the farmers of Dickinson County declared a coyote hunt. Coyotes were the dread of all families, ugly mangy critters that lived in the fields and hedge lines and roamed the barnyards at night, killing chickens and lambs and calves, or anything small enough to be defenseless. Stories of coyotes killing small children abounded like tornado fiction, but I never actually knew a case. Even so, they spread fear. The county put a bounty on their heads, $2 an ear, which gave them a Wild West outlaw mystique, and it was with a posse-like patriotism that farmers went to the annual coyote hunt.

We gathered at Rural Center School, a newly consolidated school near our farm that brought to an end the little red school houses that had educated our parents. It was Saturday morning, the pickup trucks coming into the parking lot in a steady stream, with about every fourth vehicle being a one-ton wheat truck with large bed that could hold a hundred bushels or about forty men on coyote hunt day. The men milled around the yard, polishing and fondling their shotguns, checking the shells to make sure they had enough, and talking about the coyote problems they had during the winter. Inside, the organizers from the Rotary and Lions Clubs were mapping out the sections to be covered. Flatbed trucks would fan out around four sections of land, each section being a mile long, and in Kansas laid out as squarely and precisely as a checkered tablecloth. One man or boy would drop off the back of the truck as it slowed every thirty to forty yards, and wait in a line along the road until a given time, prescribed to allow for the line to be formed the full sixteen miles around the four sections. Then a signal would be given and passed along, domino-like, to begin the hunt.

It was up to each family to use good judgment in determining the

age limit for their children, usually thought to be about thirteen, because each man had to walk alone. There was one woman who
walked the line that year, but she was gossiped about, known generally as "a strutter" and a show-off. Some of the men were reluctant
to walk beside her. They said it was a "trust" thing. They said they
wanted guns beside them that would fire without hesitation, and
buddies who would not flinch from duty. Women weren't welcome,
and kids weren't totally welcome either, but it was a source of great
pride to walk beside my dad, even if he was thirty yards away. It was
close enough, especially when there was a little dew on the ground
to carry voices, to talk with Dad in a low voice so as not to scare the
animals. As we started across the fields, my first obscure feelings of
power were manifested by adrenaline as I could see the line of men
on both sides of me begin to move. It was like a machine, marching
before an unseen hand, guided to a destiny of death and destruction.

Suddenly a rabbit broke out of the underbrush in front of me,
darted about ten yards, then stopped to survey the approaching
threat. He sat up, as jacks do, with ears straight and long, stretching
for every murmur of threat, his eyes directly on me, questioning my
intentions. My eyes locked on his and froze. I knew he would bolt in
a second, with a movement so quick and swift I would never see it,
and the white backs of his legs would show his course under a bobbing tail. I raised my single-shot .410-gauge shotgun, a Sears special,
saw only the side of the jack as he turned to run, and pulled the trigger. Only a small kick in my shoulder, but I missed. Then on my left,
from someone I didn't even know, came a volley of shots, three in a
row, and the rabbit was down. The grass was high, but I could see the
bottom of his foot, presumably not his lucky one, kicking in the air,
then he lay still, waiting only to be picked up by the farmer and
stuffed in the carrying pouch that was slung over his shoulder.
"Sorry, Dad," I said quietly, and kept walking. "Don't worry. It took
him three shots," Dad said after several steps.

As the sixteen-mile square began to get smaller, the rumble of
gunshots was constant. The rabbits now could hear us coming and
were jumping up more than 100 yards ahead of us. Few men could
shoot that distance, but then I realized the inevitability of it all. No
matter which way the rabbits turned, they faced a line of men and
certain death. What evil had rabbits perpetrated on our life to deserve this? Destroying gardens, I guessed. They ate the lettuce and
cabbage.

We never saw any coyotes, but the word came down the line:

"Charlie Sexton got one. That oldest Emig boy shot two. Don't seem to be as many this year."

After three or four hours, when our legs were beginning to cramp from the strain of climbing through weeds and vines and prickly underbrush, tiny specks began to appear on the horizon, first one, then another, until it looked like someone had drawn a dotted line across the bottom of the sky, and you could tell they were men with guns. Still out of sight were the rabbits, thousands of them running at full pace with whatever energy they had left, darting in every direction, some even panicking and turning back toward the lines, running full-face into a fury of gunshots, leaving only the strongest to make it to that deadly center of the hunt, when rabbits would actually run into each other, jump high into the air when shot, and dozens of men would shoot continuously until every sign of life was gone. It was the mad flurry of shots that made me turn away in horror. Dad drew me back with about a quarter mile to go.

"It gets dangerous here," he said. "Let's start to ease back. Just stay here with me." He shortened his step. I shortened mine. The men on both sides of us began moving ahead, but because the square was tightening, the men were getting closer together, and no one noticed that we were dropping out of the hunt.

When Dad and I fell back and came together, he said, "Here's where somebody gets killed. These guys are shooting right at each other. All they see is rabbits."

The flatbeds were waiting on the road near where the hunt came together. Everybody climbed in for the ride back to Rural Center. They started emptying rabbits onto the bed of the truck, until fur covered our feet and blood was running down the metal bands that bonded the bed of the truck. Then I heard a loud thud and looked over the cab of the truck onto the hood. It was a coyote, large gash in his shoulder, teeth bared and lips curled back so it looked like he was still eating, his eyes glazed, hair matted by water and blood and cockleburs from the underbrush of many miles, spindly legs with protruding knee joints that had been scraped and healed, and scraped and healed, probably every month of its life. He didn't seem much of an adversary for our army, but he was ugly, dirty, and evocative of ridicule and fear. I was glad he was dead. We drove back to the school with the coyote draped across the hood, a sort of victory parade for the womenfolk, who were waiting with another covered-dish lunch in the school gym.

"I'm not too hungry," my dad said. "Let's go on home." We never went to another coyote hunt.

We moved off the Howie place in 1955. We were asked to leave, actually, so young Alfred and his new bride could move in. There were no hard feelings about it. If you're a renter, that's just the way it is. So we moved to the Funk place, a much larger redbrick house with barn and granary about five miles closer to Abilene. The farmland around the buildings was being rented by someone else; we had only the house. We farmed other rented property on the two-thirds, one-third basis. After two years, we moved to town, but Dad continued to farm rented property. I helped out whenever I could, weekends, summers, and certainly during the harvest.

The worst time for farming, in my limited view at age fifteen, was just after the harvest. The great euphoria of the harvest is over, the earth lies shorn like a lamb, marked by the stubble of the unshaven, and alive in only two colors: black and brown. The wheat and oats, cut near the ground, and the corn, either cut or shocked or still standing, is all brown, toasted under a scorching 100-degree summer sun. There is no movement by natural things in Kansas in August. Humans and insects, dogs and locusts, all move with the gait of the aged as they bear the weight of the heat, anvil-like upon their shoulders. I have walked the sands of Somalia, Egypt, and Saudi Arabia, and I cannot say the Kansas heat has been bettered. For the sheer weight of it, the sun fits like a bulletproof vest, heavy and uncomfortable, driving the water from your pores and leaving cotton shirts feeling like T-shirts after a swim, hanging long and sticking to your arms and stomach.

The smell of dirt is always in the air. It rises from every activity, every footstep, the movement of tractors, trucks, plows, dogs, and fleas, going straight up in a plume that seldom meets a breeze to sway it, hanging in the air with stubborn stillness, as Coleridge wrote, like a painted ship upon a painted sea. The ultimate incongruity is that, traveling behind the greatest dust-raiser in the world, a tractor and plow, are sea gulls. They hover and dive, flinging themselves at the black clods turned over by the plowshares, worn as smooth and shiny as polished silver, and cutting the earth in long strips behind the tractor. We had two tractors, a Minneapolis Moline with three-bottom plow that Dad drove, and a Ford Ferguson with two-bottom plow that I drove. Riding the tractor was knowing the eye of a hurricane, the drone of the engine that starts as a constant roar, then softens to a whine when your ears become accustomed. Toward evening, when the mind weakens with fatigue, the sound becomes a singsong dirge, rising and falling in time with the giant tractor tires, sometimes in perfect tune with a silent voice that sounds like Elvis but is really your own. You are alone at this point. The tractor bumps with every turn of the furrow, the front wheels have no support and they wobble as if stumbling over rocks and dirt, and no matter how much you pad the seat, after a few hours your bottom hurts, your stomach aches from the jarring irregularity of the bouncing, and your mind numbs as you totally relax all muscles to help them absorb the shocks. You ride with one arm outstretched, reaching for the fender to help stabilize your body, and always over your shoulder float the sea gulls. No farmer knows where they come from or why they are there. No one knows, least that I ever heard. For me, they were of another world, reminding me of another place, unknown and beautiful with sparkling blue water and no clouds of dirt.

I would dream of this place as the roar of the day settled in. Sometimes I would wake up just before the end of the row was reached, yanking the wheel hard to the left, stepping on the left brake to freeze it while the right wheel continued to turn, thus forcing the tractor to turn on a dime, much as a Boeing 747 turns at the end of a runway.

One day I was driving the Moline, pulling a three-rack springtooth, an ugly appurtenance comprised of thirty or forty curved ribbons of steel, welded to a single iron bar, that claw into the earth like a steel hand, breaking up the plowed earth in a further manicuring of the land. The rows were long that day and several times I almost woke up too late to make the turns. At midafternoon, after the bologna sandwiches and potato chips were gone, and dirt was caked on my face, when all the discomforts of the tractor had blended into another world of clouds and dreams, I hit the wire. The end of the field was marked by weeds allowed to grow unmolested in the space it took to turn the tractor, and the weeds stopped at a barbed wire fence. No longer useful for retaining cattle or sheep, the barbed wire draped and drooped itself along the edge of the wheat field, separating it from a crop of corn that now lay ruptured from the picker's jaws. As I woke up, I yanked the wheel from instinct, not even knowing my location, not knowing that the front wheels were in the wire and the barbs were locking themselves into the radiator fins in the front of the engine. I slammed my left foot onto the brake with the same motion, and as the huge machine started its spin, I realized I was too late, but I stayed with it. The wire started ripping and tearing, coming loose from the old wooden posts, spewing nails to a rusty grave in the dirt, and winding itself around the engine of the machine. Then just as the tractor came parallel with the remainder of the fence, the teeth of the springtooth caught another section of wire, which threaded itself into the matrix of machine and implement until they were bound like Gulliver by the Lilliputians. The pull on the engine was as if the tractor was tied to Mount Everest. It was overwhelmed, yet the front reared up like a horse making one desperate buck to free its unwanted rider, then died and settled to earth. I rode it to the moment of death, my hands glued to the steering wheel, my legs shaking with weakness, and then it was still. One moment it was a roaring, tugging, bucking monster. Now, it was so still that the quiet of the sun could be felt on the backs of my hands. I climbed down off the tractor and started walking, aimlessly at first, then with purpose, then in a circle as I searched for an opening in the far-off trees that signaled the house and my car. It was a long walk, almost as long as those few yards from my West Wing White House office to the last motorcade on inauguration day 1993, yet I made it to the car and started the slow drive to town to tell my dad about his tractor.

I walked into the house and he didn't say a word. Somehow he knew that I was in trouble. "I'm sorry, Dad," I said, "my farming days are over." And they were. I never rode a tractor again.

CHAPTER THREE

The Winds of Ike

Dwight David Eisenhower sat at my desk in history class. I swear it's true because there was a "DE" carved on the bottom of the seat, left-hand corner, right beside my own sculpture of "MF loves SH." It's a documented fact that Ike went to high school in the building where I went to seventh and eighth grade, played football there, walked the same hallways and front steps that I did, and left at least a whiff of ambition for all who followed. At minimum, he gave us a stereoscope picture of the outside world, a view of Europe, the big war, the presidency, and family honor. Every student at Abilene Junior High School, indeed every citizen of the town, was invited by destiny and fate to slide the hand-held pictures of Ike back and forth until they focused on his achievements.

My grandmother Seaton, on my mother's side, gave me an old stereoscope from her attic, with hundreds of slides of soldiers building the Panama Canal, many of the men bandaged from accidents, many in hospitals from malaria, and thousands digging with shovels to build this grand canal. I spent hours viewing it again and again, wondering what their lives were like, how did they get those jobs, and what if after all that digging they never saw the water flow into the locks? Ike's life in Abilene did the same for me, focusing me on the grand possibilities of life, the idea that a West Point career starts with a simple letter to someone, that a general is just a colonel who got promoted, and that even a boy from Abilene could take that first step. It was in the wind, never spoken about, and probably unrecognized at the time. But after our little high school class of 1960 graduated, at least six ended up in Washington and many others became successful corporate or community leaders.

After my junior year in high school, when farming was but a memory, and long languid nights in the city park playing basketball were coming to a close, and rich kids with college-educated parents were beginning to wear K-State T-shirts, I got a summer job at McKee Gardens that paid sixty-eight cents an hour. We were a crew: Steve Grubb, John Anguiano, Kent Ziegler, Kenny Klufa, Jim Simmons, and Quentin McKee himself, half owner and head laborer. Quentin was tall, always tanned even in Kansas winters, muscled without ever lifting a weight, with dark bushy hair and a drop-dead-beautiful wife who stayed indoors most of the time producing beautiful blonde daughters. We planted zoysia grass in new homes being built for Air Force officers at Shilling Air Force Base near Salina. In the late 1950s the B-52s were arriving daily. With them came complements of troops, new demands for housing, and new contracts for McKee Gardens to grade the lawns, plant the grass and shrubs, and generally beautify the grounds. Our job was to arrive at the sod farms near Abilene early in the morning, cut the sod into one-foot squares, load them onto a flatbed truck, drive to Salina about twenty miles away, and plant small plugs of grass pulled from the edge of a square like taffy from a jar. Steve would dig small gashes in the soil every twelve inches, John would walk behind him dropping plugs of sod, I would crawl behind John covering the plugs with whatever dirt I could scrape up with a fast swipe of the hand, Jim would follow with water, and Kenny, who was a year older, would supervise. Quentin was usually deep in negotiations with the lady of the house, selling additional plantings, discussing fees, or gossiping. He had a singsong voice, rising at the end of a phrase. "Come on, boys," he would sing, "you're slowing down."

I looked up from my crawl, knees aching from the hard earth and the small clods grinding into my blue jeans. "Oh yeah? Come spend a few hours on your knees and we'll see who is slow." But Quentin just walked on, never bothering to argue or fight. He was smart enough to know that his point was made, the work pace continued, and nothing could be gained from arguing. Years later I adopted some of Quentin's technique with the press. They would throw out taunts during briefings, and I would ignore them. When I would state an unpopular view on a controversial issue and the press would laugh as if incredulous, I would simply move on, my bald head doing its best imitation of Quentin throwing back his mane, looking straight ahead, and ignoring the irrelevant kibitz from the high school heathen at his feet.

My introduction to the Eisenhower Museum was in the flower beds, bright yellow with tulips given every year by a grateful Holland for Ike's leadership of the liberation of Europe, planted religiously by the crew from McKee Gardens—always, it seemed, on our knees. We crawled back and forth through the beds digging small holes for the tulip bulbs, thousands of them to be taken from their air freight boxes and pushed into the loam of Kansas. Quentin was passing among us one day when he spotted a large tattered hole in my shirt, always worn outside my jeans to increase air flow, with long sleeves to protect against the sun. It was obviously an old shirt, of little use for anything but day labor, but nevertheless a favorite.

"Marlin," Quentin said, "it looks like you have a hole in your shirt. Let's see that," and he reached for my back.

I dodged and twisted. "No. I need this shirt. Come on, Quentin, leave me alone!"

"Marlin," he said, laughing, "let's see this. You may need a new shirt." He fell on me and we started to wrestle, but I was outweighed by 100 pounds and not nearly as strong. He got his finger, then his full grasping hand into the tear of the shirt, and with one grunting, gasping effort tore the shirt from my back.

"Get off! Get off!" I cried, and started rolling, wiggling, until I was free. I scrambled up, got my balance, and cried large angry tears. "You son of a bitch!" I shouted. Quentin just stood and laughed. He wasn't mean. He wasn't hurtful. He just didn't care. While I hated him during these occasional episodes, it didn't last. I just couldn't carry a grudge. Perhaps if he hadn't torn my shirt off, I would never have gone into the museum to call Mom for a replacement. For that I am grateful, because in the museum was a fresh, stainless world of make-believe. It was a world of dreams fulfilled by a local man, of names like Morocco and Istanbul, of jewels and sabers from kings and queens, of documents weighty with meaning and import, of dresses and dinners and motorcades and, most of all, of *the picture.* The picture that is as clear in my mind today as then is the picture that tied me to that hot, dusty Kansas day of sweat and tears no matter where I went in the world. I thought of it while working in the Oval Office, once in the Vatican with Pope Paul, and hundreds of other times. It was the picture that said to me in the summer of 1959, "Anybody can make it to the top." In the 1980s it reminded me that I had made it, all the way from Abilene, to the parquet oval floor where Ike scraped the dirt off his golf shoes, to the Pentagon war room where Ike reviewed the military plans, to the presidential limo where we both propped our feet on the jump seats, to the very family quarters where Ike and I had a glass of sherry and marveled at our good fortune. It was a picture of Ike sitting on the steps of a small cottage in Colorado with James Hagerty, his press secretary.

It was huge, perhaps six or eight feet high and three or four feet wide, with both men dressed in mountain casual trousers, open-neck shirts, and functional shoes. They were smiling, had obviously shared a joke or a story or probably some verbal jab at the press, and had dropped to the steps to enjoy the moment and relax in an aspen shade. That's really something, I thought. Inside me there was a strange yearning sensation, with no form or intention, no idea of purpose or means, no motive or even conjecture, just a curiosity about the man with the president, a curiosity about how to get there, impossible as it must be.

In the world of journalism, there is a stratum of working writers who did not go to Harvard, did not take philosophy and Far Eastern art, did not go to Oxford, and did not start as copyboys for *Harper's* or *The New Yorker*. But they did start loving journalism in high school, worked on the school paper, loved the smell of ink and the sound of presses, and always say—every one of them—that they owe it all to their high school journalism teacher. Mine was Mrs. Dorothy Elliott.

Women like Dorothy Elliott are the bedrock of societies, the Russian babushkas who run the trains, the African women who carry pails of water from the river, the Indian mothers who nurse a child and weave a rug with simultaneous dexterity. Mrs. Elliott raised her family, taught school in a variety of small Kansas towns, believed people were honest, loved kids and teaching, and, most of all, revered journalism. She taught it straight—accuracy, accuracy, accuracy. Answer the five W's and an H, and when you've covered all the whats and the how, people can figure out for themselves what the motives were. She respected her audience in that regard. She didn't need a lot of essays and scenarios to tell her how to think. She taught her students to respect journalism, protect it, and never abuse it. "You build a great newspaper one day at a time," she said, "and it only takes one day of mistakes to destroy it."

I had joined the high school *Booster* primarily because its ad salesmen could leave school in the middle of the day, visit with local merchants, and stop at Callahan's Drug Store for a cherry phosphate on the way back to class. Even after seeing the Eisenhower-Hagerty picture, I never guessed I would love journalism so much. It was a

cause to believe in, rich with tradition from colonial pamphleteers
to the straight-talking *Emporia Gazette* editor William Allen White.
It was a history to belong to, an intellectual channel, indeed a profession—my God, I realized, I could have a profession. And wonder
of wonders, it fulfilled another new personality trait, the growing desire for public recognition. What's more, I discovered that when you
write your thoughts, your views, and publish them, people don't tell
you to shut up or mind your manners. They accept, even defend, almost any idea you have. Discovering journalism was my road map
out of Kansas. It gave me a liberating exhilaration. I was free. I had
direction. I didn't have to take auto mechanics class. No vocational
technical colleges. I had a reason for learning. I never had so much
fun as during that glorious senior year, playing basketball and scor-
ing eighteen points in the regional finals against Herrington, playing
the part of Mr. Dussel, the old uncle in *The Diary of Anne Frank*, and
even singing in the chorus. Journalism did it, and that love carried
me through ten years of White House challenges that questioned my
loyalty, my good sense, and my character.

My freshman year at Kansas State University featured living in a
one-bedroom basement apartment where the ironing board folded
onto the sink, the bed folded onto the kitchen table, and the dark
knotty-pine walls folded a deep gloom into my daily existence. I
thought I would never survive the basement. It was miserable,
crowded, moldy, and suffered from an overdose of linoleum. But it
cost only $50 a month, split between me and Richard Morehouse,
and I negotiated the entire freshman year for $750. In living with me,
Richard had the singular disadvantage of being a real student, a pre-
veterinary major who worked extremely hard, spent night after
night at the Formica kitchen table, only to have to move his books
and papers at about 10 P.M. every night when I demanded rights to
my fold-out bed. Even today when I fold out a couch, I expect to see
old underwear left in the fold, or a cricket squashed between the axis
of the frame, as if captured in middash along a steel pipe. Richard
simply found my life incomprehensible. My objectives were real, ca-
reer-oriented, serious, and purposeful. But they were pursued
through a meandering path of selling ads for the school paper, writing a bi-weekly column for small newspapers in the state, a loose attitude toward attending class, and front-loading my journalism
courses to the first year in case I had to drop out—which I did.

Of the $750, a third was borrowed from the bank on a one-year
loan. When summer came, it was payback time. So Richard and I

ended that first year on separate tracks, me into the kitchen of Delta Tau Delta fraternity where I worked for board and room, and Richard onto the straight and narrow academic ladder to the top. He made it, and is a practicing veterinarian in Phoenix. I made it too, actually, but not before spending the grandest summer in Lindsborg, Kansas, population 3,340, and home of the Swedes, the name of the local college's sports teams and the most accurate description possible of the town's inhabitants.

Small Kansas towns appear on the prairie like gopher villages that pop up suddenly, are wildly populated and active during their infancy, then fade over the years into contented clusters of retired farmers and merchants. But each retains a distinct physical outline. You see them sparkling from a distance when their collective lights glow in the night, but they grow darker the closer you get, when only an occasional streetlight or a neon A&W Root Beer sign lights the way.

A&W swept through Kansas in the late 1950s bringing fast food, frosted mugs, and social acceptance to a sort of rural cafe society. Families would end a day of harvest by piling in the car for a trip to the A&W. The hostesses wore short skirts, and they hooked trays onto your car window to hold the coldest, tastiest ice cream floats ever made. In addition, they talked with you. Beautiful young women of well-to-do families took orders from farmers who hadn't talked to anyone outside their neighborhood for years. People waved to friends who just pulled into a spot three cars down. High school kids sat on the trunks of their cars. The move from covered-dish dinners to fast food in the parking lot seemed like a social revolution. But it was just another gopher mound that emerged for a time and then faded into community hieroglyphics. Today the old A&W stands can still be found and identified by their covered parking stalls and small building that probably is now a gas station or a plumbing storage unit.

The one landmark that does not fade is the grain elevator. It is still the angel of the prairie. It stands high and erect, marking the hub of every community, signaling the collective prosperity and co-operation of all who spot its pinnacle red light, shining to warn off airplanes. As a child, the grain elevator appeared to me like the Empire State Building, something worthy of a King Kong climb, or certainly tall enough to have an airplane crash into the shaft, sticking like a fly on the window. I often had that dream, struggling to get out of the cockpit and waking up just as the tail section slid to the earth.

In 1961, driving a white 1950 Ford sedan with bucket seats taken from a panel truck, the kind used for milk deliveries, and a stick gearshift cut directly into the transmission that was topped by a lawn mower piston, I headed for Lindsborg and a new career at the *Lindsborg News-Record.* So far my strategy for life was working well. My journalism courses and experience on the college paper were enough for me to land a job as editor. I had to promise that I would not go back to college, but that seemed honest. It would take at least a year to pay back the college loan, and more time to make enough money to try another year of school. The advertisement in *Editor and Publisher* said it was a permanent, full-time job and that's what I wanted. In one year at college I had given myself an occupation. I was an editor. I would write editorials and tell people right from wrong. I would cover city hall and help build the town. Hell, I would even join the chamber of commerce and the country club. Maybe even wear a plaid sports coat like Henry Jameson, the editor of the *Abilene Reflector-Chronicle.*

I had worked for the *Chronicle* the previous summer, selling ads from a Ping-Pong table set up in the back storage room. Giant rolls of newsprint and barrels of ink lined the walls. The smell of the presses, a wonderful mixture of ink, oil, grease, and cleaning solvent, permeated my soul. "He has ink in his blood," I had read somewhere. I figured you couldn't be born with it and that this must be the way to get it. It was. I loved the smell of the paper, its freshness coming off the press, thousands of copies splatting against the concrete floor in quick succession, each to be delivered directly to the living rooms of my family, my friends, everyone in town. They would be reading my ads, admiring the layouts for Pinkham's Women's Wear that I had designed and sold to the Pinkham sisters.

Dorothy Pinkham had seldom advertised in the *Chronicle,* so I decided to try a new sales approach. Besides, I loved the smell of her store, the fresh new clothes, the mannequins wearing panties and bras and lingerie of a kind I assumed real people never wore. They don't, by the way. I have bought many negligees over the years for the wonderful women in my life, and they never wear them. I think I knew that, even at eighteen, but I did sell Dorothy Pinkham on running some ads. I spent hours searching through the advertising layout books, piecing together pictures of blouses and suits with glaring announcements of "10% OFF," and convincing Dorothy that the customers would come in droves. They didn't, of course. There aren't any droves in Abilene, just the same hardworking population that buys clothes for work, weddings, church, and getting the kids back to school. After two months, Dorothy reported that she could detect no increase in sales, and she had spent hundreds of dollars in advertising. I felt enormous guilt, lay awake nights worrying about her business, and resolved never to take people's money if I couldn't produce benefits.

Henry Jameson, however, saw my Pinkham's success as indicative of a remarkable talent and a rare opportunity. One day he invited me into his private office, the only one in the building, offered me a seat, leaned forward with his jowls drooping over the collar of his crisply starched shirt, and asked if I would be interested in staying on at the *Chronicle*. Henry was a natty dresser, complete with black and white wing tip shoes, suspenders, a summer straw hat, and a distinctively deliberate gait that made him a recognizable figure in the community. Sitting before him, I was awed. This was what I wanted to be. His "Ramblings" column ran front page two or three times a week and was widely read and quoted. He drove a new car, played golf, and had actually traveled to Washington, D.C. It was legend that he knew Walter Cronkite, and to hear Henry tell it, Walter would give up his CBS news anchor job in a minute to be editor of the *Abilene Reflector-Chronicle*.

"Marlin," he said, "I know your mom and dad are proud of you. You've done a very good job for us this summer. Everyone seems to like you. I talked to the rest of the staff."

Then he remembered that he should have started by at least asking what I thought of my situation.

"What do you want to do?" he asked. "Are you going to college? Would you like to stay in the newspaper business? Or do you know?"

"Well, sir," I stammered, "I'm not sure. I've enrolled at State but I don't know if I can afford it."

Henry leaped on that, his eyes widened at the opening. "Marlin, would you like to stay here at the *Chronicle?*" To Henry's credit, he loved the paper. It was his life and his identity. There could be no higher calling. He was giving me the ultimate gift, to be a part of the *Chronicle* family.

"Thank you, sir," I said, "but I had really hoped to go to college." I expected a lot from journalism and the first step was college. There was something vaguely troubling about going right to the newspaper, establishing a career at age eighteen, and not having a very clear idea of life beyond that. College was the key. Education was the way to success. College was new people and new places. Suddenly, this generous offer started to look like a setback. When measured against my dreams and ambition, it looked like old Henry might have been underestimating me.

"Well, Marlin," he continued, "college may be right for some. But it takes four years and you might end up right here. Take Bobby, over there." Bobby was slumped over his Linotype machine, typing madly, dropping the letter keys neatly into a line of type that would absorb the molten lead and later print the images on the paper. Linotypes were direct descendants of the earliest wooden letters carved to carry ink to the page. The California job case, a tray with thirty or more boxes for different letters of the alphabet, allowed the printer to set headlines by hand, place them on top of the columns of metal verbiage produced by the Linotypes, and produce the page. Bobby was very good at it.

"Bobby spent several years trying college, then came back to us, and is very happy in his job. He's doing real well," Henry said.

Wait a minute, I thought, this conversation has taken a bad turn. I was growing angry. I could feel the flush in my face, an early-warning system I would later grow to appreciate and use effectively. Even at eighteen, I knew it was a mistake to respond in anger. Suddenly a new picture emerged. Henry was using me. Comparing me to Bobby. Henry was looking for cheap help. His ambition for me was not nearly high enough, not by a long shot. I didn't want Bobby's job, I wanted Henry's job, and even that didn't seem like too big a jump.

"Thanks," I said, "I'll think it over." But I went to college instead. After that first year, however, I found myself driving to Lindsborg to drop out of college and work on a small paper, wondering if I should have taken Henry Jameson's offer in the first place.

Driving into Lindsborg in the summer of 1962 I could see the town's outline—the mounds of trees that formed a canopy over the town, the co-op elevator rising from its midst, the A&W Root Beer stand with kids not much younger than I sitting on their cars, and the trains that carried wheat from the elevator to the flour mills back East. The streets were brick, which was rare even in the '60s, and they were wide, three or four cars in width, with spreading elm trees on either side. Today it would be a postcard scene. It was a Monday, but seemed like a Sunday, with people strolling slowly along the sidewalks undistracted by any flurry of commerce, talking quietly to each other, waving and slowly opening their car doors as if checking to make certain no greeting had been missed.

I pulled into a parking spot in front of the *Lindsborg News-Record*, its name stenciled in large black gothic letters on top of the picture windows and the door. The term "picture window" developed for me when our neighbors on the farm cut a hole in the wall of their home and installed a huge plate glass window three times the normal size. We marveled at this tribute to modern architecture and our whole family went over for a visit to look out the window and exclaim that the world looked like a picture. My mother called it that, a picture window.

I parked my Ford car with the airplane steering wheel—the top third had been cut out so that during open road driving you could grasp both sides of the wheel and pretend to be piloting one of those new DC-3s. I noticed the staid black and brown Oldsmobiles and Pontiacs on either side. It struck me that I might have a generational problem, being editor at age nineteen, driving a souped-up car, wearing a green poplin suit and Bass Weejuns with pennies tucked in the tongue. I thought I would probably have to remove those pennies.

I introduced myself to Mr. Henry Weltner, publisher, a slightly built man in his sixties who talked in clipped syllables and moved his body quickly, like an overbred terrier, as he asked about my trip from Abilene. He was friendly, showed me about the place, and pointed out my typewriter and desk, a standard light mahogany desk with side arm for the Smith-Corona, situated in full view of the front window and just inside the door. It looked like I might be the receptionist as well. As one resident after another dropped by to see the new boy, I would lean over the counter that separated my work space from the door and chat about the weather and the harvest, ask about the family and boy at university, and pleasantly pass the day. In the White House briefing room, I would try to spend a few minutes each day in aimless discussion with the press, sitting in one of the staff chairs near my podium, often smoking a cigar, and chatting quietly with photographers and reporters just passing the day. Someone would invariably ask a serious question and I would have to leave before a press conference developed, but for those few minutes it was just like leaning over the counter at Lindsborg.

As a newspaper, the *News-Record* looked like *The New York Times* of the 1800s, with gray, single-column headlines that were only marginally larger than the story copy below them, no pictures, and stories that actually ended "... and a good time was had by all." It was like a dream. A real paper of my own, so basic and so bad that I could only improve it. A publisher who didn't know the first thing about journalism but was willing to trust me. He was a printer by trade, and had worked at the *News-Record* until a relative died and left him considerable wealth. He did what all men dream of doing: He bought the paper so he could fire his boss. He never spoke of this transaction, but I always imagined him walking into his predecessor's office, dressed in a suit and tie never before worn on any day but Sunday, opening his checkbook and buying the place. In any case the legend gave him an aura of independence and spirit that I admired. I hoped he might appreciate that spirit in me.

The paper was a weekly. My first edition made no changes. I was learning the ropes—how much copy was needed and the personality of the staff, which consisted of an advertising manager, a society editor, a backshop foreman, and three or four printers. To regular readers, the only observable change might have been to notice that in Lindsborg that week there was no mention that "everyone had a good time."

By the second week I was ready to recommend changes. The office after 5 P.M. was deserted, with only the glorious smells of ink and paper and the clicking of a grandfather clock to disturb the solitude. At night I designed a new paper. I drew up several dummy editions of a paper with multicolumn 36-point headlines, two- and three-column pictures, and some copy set two columns wide to add visual variety. The headlines and pictures came from the *Topeka Capital-Journal*, the state's largest daily. I cut out all the stories, picked a variety of headlines and pictures, and pasted it all together.

Then I went to the backshop, the private domain of the printers, strictly off-limits to all us "white-collar snobs" in the front office, and searched through the cobwebs for old California job cases. They were stacked in a corner of the room, used only for advertisements that blared the latest "SALE" slogans. As I discovered one font after another, gothic to roman to modern, my dream was becoming a reality. These letters, from A to Z in several styles, meant it could be done. They would have to be hand set, placed one letter at a time in a tray, then wedged into the pages. But it could be done. I grabbed a tray and tried to set various headlines myself. There was no ink to roll across them, so I placed a piece of paper on the letters and tapped them with a mallet normally used to wedge the lead type into form. The imprint was clear. Some letters were upside-down. Some had broken corners. But I was convinced it could be done, with no extra cost and a little extra effort. We wouldn't have to set more than twenty-five headlines to completely revamp the paper.

Then I called the nearest daily newspaper with pictures, the *MacPherson Sentinel,* and asked if they would provide photogravures. The photogravure machine looked like a wood lathe, with a photograph placed at one end and a clear plastic plate wrapped around the other. An electronic scanner passed over the picture and made the dot formations in the plastic that would allow the picture to print. It was an expensive machine, but the *Sentinel* agreed to engrave my photos if I would drive them to MacPherson, only twenty miles away.

On Tuesday of week two, I took the plan to Mr. Weltner. He was shocked. He just sat looking at my dummies. He murmured. He mumbled. I just let him look. Then I saw a twinkle, a gleam of understanding that this might be something, a new paper, something he could take credit for, something to make people understand that he was a real publisher, and that I was someone who could improve his product. But he shook his head. It was just too much. A nineteen-year-old kid with freckles and crew cut completely revamping his paper was just too much.

"We can do it pretty cheap," I ventured. "The headlines are in back. I can set them myself at night. The *Sentinel* has agreed to do the pictures. Let's just try some of it."

"Let me think about it," he said.

Two days later, he casually walked to my desk, tossed the dummies on the counter, and said, "Let's give it a try. But not too much. No eight-column headlines. No pictures. I can't take that much of a jolt."

The first new edition had one three-column headline and several two-columns, and no pictures. But in week three, we introduced the first photograph and by the end of the summer we had an eight-column headline over a feature story at the bottom of the front page. I was so proud. But it also became clear that I wanted to go back to college. Life in Lindsborg was great, but I was just too young to think in terms of a lifetime career. I was still dreaming of the city, of distant lands. So I summoned my courage one day and told Mr. Weltner that I was going back to college. I would borrow more money, having paid off the old loan, and I would get another job at school if necessary. He was disappointed, but he knew it was coming, and was maybe even relieved.

Coincidentally, within weeks he sold the paper for a handsome profit to a chain of Kansas newspapers, which gave me much satisfaction. I had given Henry Weltner a new product, a salable commodity, a newspaper with rising subscribers and a future. Circulation had increased by almost 300 in three months. Henry Weltner's gamble on me had paid off. Today, the *News-Record* still serves its readers well. In 1993, I drove through Lindsborg and visited with the current editor, Marty Hardy. The print shop and Linotypes have long since been replaced by offset cameras and computers. But the sign out front is the same. Most important for me, the *News-Record* today looks exactly like those cut-and-paste dummies from the summer of '62.

A phenomenal string of luck with jobs made the rest of college a breeze. I returned to Kansas State and set about the task of financing. My fraternity, Delta Tau Delta, let me serve meals and wash dishes in return for food. The college newspaper, the *Collegian*, paid about $35 a month to sell advertising to local merchants. The *Topeka Capital-Journal* paid twenty-five cents a column inch for stories published about K-State activities. The paper had a page each day devoted to "state news," and by picking up university news releases I could make a few calls, rewrite the stories, and get in the paper two or three times a week. Piecing all of these together gave me an income of nearly $100 a month, perfectly adequate to stay.

As a *Collegian* ad salesman, I would visit half a dozen accounts a week to pick up copy for ads and try to sell new space. My biggest account was Stevenson's Men's Clothing Store, particularly its shoe department, managed by a cantankerous veteran of the business, Doc Larsen. Doc was demanding and always in a hurry. I would stand politely in the corner of his store, or sometimes wait in the back room where shoe boxes were stacked to the ceiling, until he could get a break from his customers. Then he would motion me to the basement. Once again, we would work at large plywood tables set up on sawhorses, decide which shoes he wanted to feature that week, what kind of sales appeal to make, sift through large volumes of display ads that carried corresponding mats used to mold the lead, and then lay out the ad.

Doc was in his forties, bald, smoked incessantly, and was always stepping into the back alley between shoe sales for a quick cigarette. One day he had a heart attack. The bypass operation that followed scared him out of smoking but did little for his disposition. It always seemed to me, however, that behind the frown and a face that often flushed with anger was a faint smile. There was something of an act in his screams.

"You were supposed to bring my ads yesterday!" he would

scream. "Why didn't I see the galley proofs last week? If you're going to handle my account, you've got to do it right!"

But even as I trembled, I could see a hint in his eyes that this was not serious anger. He was in the middle of such a harangue when Leon Sanders, general manager of the *Manhattan Mercury* in 1963, came down the steps to join us at the ad table. Sandy and Doc had been friends for years. They talked about Stevenson's shoe ad for the *Mercury*.

"I need a new salesman," Sandy said.

"Here's one, right here," Doc replied. "He's the best there is. Sells me an ad every week. Marlin, do you want the job or not?"

I was staggered. Where did this generosity come from? What job? I'm in college. What do I say?

"Sure," I said, "if I can still go to school."

Doc wanted to wrap up the transaction right there. "Sandy can work that out. You can work part-time. You can sell ads for the *Collegian* too."

"Wait a minute," Sandy said. "That might be a problem. But let's talk about it. Come by my office tomorrow." Sandy was anxious to get back in charge of the conversation and get the negotiations on his own turf.

"Great," I said. "I'll come by about ten o'clock tomorrow." I left immediately, not believing my good fortune or the sudden and total endorsement by Doc Larsen. The next morning Sandy offered me the job, $80 a week, working from 8 until 12 in the morning, six days a week. I would carry thirteen hours a semester by attending class only in the afternoons, which would probably extend college by one year, but that was a small price to pay for a job that ensured my education. Suddenly, I went from the poorest kid in college to one of the richest. I kept the Topeka writing job, started writing a column for the *Abilene Reflector-Chronicle* on college issues, bought a Buick convertible, gave up the dishwashing job, and settled in at the *Mercury*.

On January 15, 1965, at about 11:30 at night, I was studying in my four-by-six cubicle at the Delt house when someone rushed into my room. "The auditorium is on fire!" he said. The old auditorium had been a monument to limestone and higher education for decades. It had housed K-State's earliest theater. I heard Dr. Edward Teller speak there and sang in fraternity chorus competition there. It was beloved, as buildings go, so the fire was a real shocker to most students.

I jumped up from my desk, laying aside the photographs of Botticelli's *Golden Doors*, a part of the easiest course on campus. The entire class consisted of viewing slides of great paintings. It never changed. Our fraternity files had copies of every slide ever presented. I went to class three times all semester, and memorized all the slides in two or three study sessions at night. One of them would have to be delayed due to fire.

I rushed over to the auditorium, located across campus, to find flames gushing from every window, three stories high. The interior was all wood, but the old limestone was thick and strong. It would not betray its foundation. Instead it burned like a kiln, shooting flames out the top and all the windows, looking like one of those 1950s porcelain bowls that sat on top of TV sets, with a small bulb inside and holes in the sides to emit a modest light. The purpose of the bowls was to save our eyes from the newfangled television that seemed sharpest in the dark. But even in the dark of night, the auditorium was so bright and fierce in its flames that students and neighbors would venture close, then back off, or shade their eyes from the heat.

Surprisingly, there weren't many people around, and no reporters. I talked to the police chief, the fire marshal, and several teachers. This was my first big story. I ran next door to an open building and called the state desk in Topeka.

"The auditorium is on fire! I'm here. I don't see any other reporters. Do you want me to write something?" I urged.

The night-desk editor seemed asleep, less than enthusiastic, as he tried to decide if anyone in Topeka cared about the story. "Sure, give us something," he said, "but we may just use the wire story."

"Great!" I exclaimed. I had a mandate. I ran back to the fire, which had not lost its intensity, and started searching for cost estimates. Who might know how much it cost to build this thing? Or the cost of replacement. One fellow ventured $1 million to replace it. He was a nobody, from the history department I think, but at least a source in the loosest sense of the word. I might quote him as an observer, or "one professor." I had the story. It was mine. I tucked it in my notebook, feeling like I had just robbed the bank of Boston. Now I just wanted that fire to die out, not because it might save some last artifact of ancient university life, but so late-arriving reporters would not see and describe those incredibly destructive flames.

Kedzie Hall, the journalism building, was a soul sister in antiquity to the auditorium. It was only 100 yards away. At that time of night, the newsroom was usually dark, but that night two students were furiously typing their fire stories. They were no competition. I sat down at the first typewriter available, threaded in a sheet of brownish recycled paper, and banged it out, as we used to say in front-page jargon. Then I called the *Capital-Journal* and dictated to the deskman. He asked what classes were still taught in the gym. I didn't know. Damn it. I hated not knowing. This sleepyhead in Topeka, probably drunk, barely awake, and obviously oblivious to the magnitude of my achievement, had blurted out one question and I couldn't answer it. I hung up. But even this small setback could not diminish my enthusiasm for the story, the chase of the facts, the competitive hunt, the accomplishment of the write, and finally the expectation of a byline. I walked outside, took a deep breath to slow the adrenaline, and headed home. The air seemed especially crisp. I loved this feeling; it was the same as after a basketball game in which every ounce of concentration had been focused on a simple task, followed by a rush of physical and mental activity as I drove for the goal, followed by the drain of fervor as the buzzer sounded. The game was over. Exhaustion, accomplishment, fear, anxiety, challenge, stimulation: they all blended into the finest emotional soup. It was more than intoxicating.

The next morning I got up at 6 A.M., an hour earlier than normal, dressed for work in khakis and tie, an ensemble adequate for five days out of six, and drove to the nearest corner newspaper dispenser. I fumbled with my dime, opened the front window of the machine, and the smell of fresh ink rushed out. I pulled the top paper off the pile, and my heart leaped. There it was. A large picture of the auditorium with fire leaping from every opening. Under that, the story: "by Marlin Fitzwater." All right. OK. There it is. I turned back to the machine, put in another dime to trip the locks, opened the door, and looked around. No one was in sight. I took all ten of the papers. I should have left a dollar but I didn't have one. Besides, I worked for this paper, I wrote the story, and just this once I was taking all the papers. I threw them in the front seat beside me, too precious to risk in the backseat, and drove to work.

At the *Mercury*, my advertising boss, Jim Findly, and the general manager, Leon Sanders, were poring over the Topeka paper. The *Mercury* was an afternoon paper. Jim was starting to compliment me on the story when the editor, Bill Colvin, stomped at full trot through the door, heading for the general manager's office.

"Goddamn it, Sandy!" he shouted. "Would you look at this! We get scooped by our own staff!" He never looked in my direction.

"Don't worry, Bill," Sandy said. "We get the afternoon story. This doesn't hurt us."

"The hell it doesn't!" Colvin said, his face flushed, his crew cut shimmering still from his morning shower, and his stomach shaking well over his belt. "This kid works for us! Now his name is on the front page of our biggest competitor, over the biggest story to hit this town in years. Shouldn't he have at least called us?"

I stood silently. I wanted to offer to write his story too, but thought that might seem presumptuous. Then I wondered how bad a newsroom could be if it couldn't produce a great story for the P.M. editions.

Sandy calmed Colvin down with reassurances of support and several pats on the shoulder. Actually, Bill was a good editor who cared about his paper. It always impressed me that editors were so passionate about their products.

In 1992, I returned to Abilene for an Eisenhower Library anniversary celebration, to join former President Ronald Reagan in commemorating the Eisenhower years. As President Reagan and I walked side by side down the library sidewalk, an old and familiar face appeared along the rope line, thrust his arm through the crowd, and called my name.

"I'm Bill Colvin," he said, "I'm proud of you and I just drove over to Abilene to shake your hand." It had been almost twenty-seven years since Bill Colvin had last shouted at me, and I almost cried.

When college ended in 1965, I was actually tired of newspapering. Four years on the *Mercury* and *Capital-Journal,* the column, and summers in journalism left me wondering about another fifty years in the profession, at least another fifty in a small town. I interviewed with *The Wall Street Journal* in New York. They referred me to Chicago, where the bureau chief suggested they might have something on the *National Observer,* another Dow Jones newspaper. But it wasn't in writing. They wanted me in advertising. After several interviews, it was clear they didn't really want me there either.

So I did the only thing a country boy would think of doing in 1965, I threw everything I owned in one suitcase, withdrew my savings of $300 in cash, and drove to Washington, D.C.

CHAPTER FOUR

Civil Servant

Youth is so resilient. It never dawned on me that I couldn't get a job in journalism in Washington. I arrived in August 1965 to find work and to marry a girl from Virginia who had gone to Kansas State University, Linda Kraus. Linda and I had dated most of our senior year. She received a teaching contract in McLean, Virginia, upon graduation. We decided to get married, so it seemed reasonable for me to go East to find a job.

Once in Washington, I set about the task of writing a résumé and calling for interviews. We had a small one-bedroom apartment in Arlington, just across the Potomac River from Washington, with a couple of lounge chairs under orange slipcovers, a couch, and a new dinette set. I had never thought much about Formica before, but after staring at my old Royal typewriter perched on the Formica top of the dinette for three months, it became a new symbol of poverty and frustration.

First, I interviewed with the daily newspapers, *The Washington Post*, *The Washington Star*, and *The Wall Street Journal*, never seeming to get past the personnel department. I never even got into the newsroom. The *Post* gave me a battery of tests, multiple choice about world affairs and English, which I never heard the results of, receiving only a form letter saying they had nothing available. Results at the other papers were the same, so I retreated to the wire services and out-of-town bureaus.

UPI's bureau chief in 1965, and for twenty-five years thereafter, was Grant Dillman, a small, bespectacled man of serious demeanor, who advised me to go back to Kansas and get experience. But I thought I had experience. This was a very depressing juncture, to be rejected so totally and to be told I had no future in Washington.

I gave it one last try: the newsletters. The largest publisher of these, then and now, is the Bureau of National Affairs. It publishes a newsletter on every issue in government from *Environment Reporter* to all sorts of health publications. They have hundreds of reporters turning out copy by the ream on regulations, rules, and blueprints of every dimension. For some reason, the one person I talked to worked for *Labor Reporter*, and he told me all their reporters had law degrees. "Maybe if you go to law school," he suggested.

This was very disheartening. Finally, I consulted my father-in-law, a thirty-year veteran of the government, employed at the Office of Management and Budget, part of the White House complex, and a true believer in the government pension as a primary motivator. He always thought journalism was a relatively dishonorable profession, no doubt due to his proximity over the years to the White House press corps, which never took his budgets seriously. He said President Johnson had just gotten Congress to pass a poverty program for the hollows called the Appalachian Regional Commission. He said it was totally flawed in its concept of building roads in the mountains so people could leave the mines, but it had a lot of money and was the kind of public-works boondoggle that politicians love. It was new and hiring, he said, but unfortunately the law called for the commission to go out of business in 1972, presumably the date by which poverty would be eliminated.

I walked into their offices at 1666 Connecticut Avenue and asked to see the director of public affairs, Mr. Raymond L. Courage. Ray Courage gave me the best interview I ever had for a job, the most straightforward, and it ended with an assignment. He asked if I would go home and write an article about the commission, based on a copy of the act that established it and a *New York Times* article published when the law passed. I thought this was eminently reasonable, although never again in my life was I asked to actually produce a work product at an interview, nor did I ever have the courage to ask anyone else to do it. I spent two days staring at the Formica and trying to figure out "Act 1, Section 2, Part B," and "whereas and wherefore." I could not fathom it. So I decided to simply read everything I was given, not worry about truly understanding it, then lean back and think about it, and write whatever I thought. Maybe he would just judge my writing ability. In any case, I took it back two days later and he hired me on the spot. My career in government was launched in the social army of LBJ. I believed in his war on poverty, primarily because in Kansas they teach that presidents are right and honorable and deserving of our support. I was proud to be working for him. I never forgot that feeling, that although I was at the bottom of the civil service totem pole, a GS-7 bureaucrat making $5,400 a year, I felt I was working for the president. Presidents should not forget that. The ones who hadn't spent much time in Washington before their election—Jimmy Carter, Ronald Reagan, Bill Clinton— always seemed afraid of the bureaucracy, and talked about civil servants undermining their administrations. My experience was just the opposite. Civil servants at every level want to please the president, or at least the president's representatives who work above them; they identify with the president even if they don't agree with his party; and the ones who do undermine their bosses would do so whomever they worked for. My advice in this regard to new presidents is: Send your transition teams into each department with this message—"All political appointees will be asked to leave. All civil servants will be asked to stay. We want you." Everyone wants to be asked.

My name first appeared in *The Washington Post* as a spokesman for the Appalachian Regional Commission in 1965. It was exciting to see, and to feel the power of the perception that I spoke for the entire commission, most of whom had never met me. The "spokesman" concept interested me: one person who reconciled views through words, and used words to convey group action. This is when I first learned that a spokesman derives his power from the press as well as from his boss. Media deadlines, for example, were my best friends. With deadlines, I could impose limits and decisions on colleagues, often saying, "You have to decide by the *Time*'s five P.M. deadline." If no decision was made, I could assume the power to portray the decision, or at least the process, myself—what an ego trip. This was even better than reporting.

In the course of thirty years, my name must have appeared in *The Washington Post* almost as frequently as presidents'. Twice during my White House years, I was the named source in every story on the front page of the paper.

In 1966 official Washington was becoming consumed by the war in Southeast Asia. Protest marches were taking over the streets, college campuses, and the evening news. Individually, everyone that I knew expected to be drafted and to serve. To evade the draft was simply too cowardly to contemplate.

In late 1966, only months after I had started at the Appalachian Commission, my number seemed certain to come up soon in the draft and there was little time to decide which service to join. I liked the idea of choice, even if all the options were bad. There was no military tradition in our family because most were farmers and therefore exempt during World War II and Korea. I did have uncles in the Army who brought coconut piggy banks home from Guam, but I was too young to discern any particular pride of uniform that might influence my later life. Rather, the question was: Which branch would allow me to retain the most of what I had—a wife, a job, a home in Washington. At the time, I was not aware of any special stigma about the National Guard, Air Force, or Army. The Guard was six years of meetings, with six months of basic training and two weeks a year of active duty. It seemed suitably onerous, even if I was never called to active duty.

When Senator Dan Quayle was selected by George Bush as his vice presidential running mate in 1988, the press hammered Quayle for having joined the National Guard during the Vietnam War. Four years later, the press gave a pass to Bill Clinton, who dodged the draft entirely and marched in war protests in England against the U.S. government. That change of attitude may have been the liberal press bias, or just changing public attitudes, which have made several left- and right-hand turns since the Vietnam War ended. But in 1966, joining the National Guard was a perfectly acceptable option for military service.

I found an opening in the Air National Guard, 113th Tactical Fighter Wing, at Andrews Air Force Base, just outside of Washington, as a munitions maintenance enlisted man—that is, the mule of the Air Force. I was put on a "load crew" with George Padgett, Charles Surmacewicz, Michael Desimone, and Art Howard. Our job was the one shown on television in almost every newscast about airplanes taking off from aircraft carriers, or leaving a base, or just starting a mission. There are always three guys lifting a Sidewinder or Snake-Eye missile in their arms and hoisting it up under the wing of the aircraft. Sometimes the picture shows an enlisted man driving an MJ-1, which is a low-to-the-ground garden tractor with frontloader arms about ten feet long, lifting a 750-pound bomb up under the wing of the aircraft. The guy on the MJ-1 was me. The pictures tend to play up the dangerous side of the job, loading live fifty-millimeter guns, fusing bombs and rockets, screwing in the napalm canisters that explode the tanks of fire, and, lastly, meeting the planes upon their return at the end of the runway to disarm them before they can accidentally blow up a hangar or base housing. This part was dangerous. First of all, the Air National Guard weekend pilots are mostly your friendly airline pilots during the week. Going from a Boeing 707 to an F-100 fighter jet, even thirty years ago, was like going from a Mack truck to a Harley-Davidson. It was a chance to escape the rules, forget the FAA, nose that little baby straight up, and pretend you're a real pilot. Target practice was a real treat. Nobody could hit the targets. A lot of National Guard pilots were lucky to hit the ocean, let alone a deserted island bombing target. In fact, most pilots didn't even hit the ocean. They left their guns jammed and bombs hung up on the wings of the aircraft and circled for home. A lot of farmers around Andrews Air Force Base thought those pilots were pretty friendly for flying over their fields and waving their wings. In fact, they were trying to shake off the twenty-five-pound target bombs before landing, if only to avoid the embarrassment of having an enlisted man laugh at them as they taxied up the runway.

Thursday afternoon, January 25, 1968, someone brought me an Associated Press wire story announcing that LBJ had called up 10,000 Air National Guardsmen to go get the Navy's USS *Pueblo*, captured by North Korea in the Sea of Japan and accused of spying. We were to report for active duty within twenty-four hours. The next day, wearing green khakis with one stripe (few in the military can remember ever having just one stripe), I reported for duty at Andrews Air Force Base. We were herded into the open hangar of the 113th for a talk by the wing commander. Located just across the runways at Andrews AFB sat *Air Force One*. My world of extremes was seldom more stark than when standing in that hangar as an airman third class, staring across at *Air Force One*; or twenty years later standing in *Air Force One* with a diplomatic rank of four-star general and looking across at the open 113th hangar. They were different worlds. In spite of hundreds of trips on *Air Force One* and *Two* between 1983 and 1993, I never went back across the field to visit the 113th.

The commander's call on that first day of active duty was a big part of the reason. The commander was Major General Willard W. Millikan, a fighter pilot and a civilian lobbyist for one of the aircraft companies.

"Men," he said, "the president has honored us with this call-up.

He believes we are the unit to carry out this important mission: to save the men of the *Pueblo*."

"Wait a minute," I said quietly to Art Howard, a George Washington University graduate trying to fathom the transition from Washington Gas and Light Company executive to arms monkey. "These old F-100's won't even fly to Korea. Our pilots can't hit Turkey. I don't believe this. I bet we all go to Vietnam."

"You're right, Fitz," he said. "This is just a cover. Johnson is building up in 'Nam with fifteen thousand new people."

The general continued, "I don't know exactly what is going to happen next. We could be split up and put in with regular units, or we could stay together. I know you men would rather stay together, and I know it would impress the Pentagon if you all told them how you feel." He paused, then came to the point he was aiming at: "How many of you want to be split up?"

No one raised his hand. Several boos rippled across the hangar. Art saw it coming.

"This is a setup," he said, laughing at how we were being used. "Who would vote to be split up?"

Sure enough, when the question was asked if we wanted to stay together, everyone shouted yes and raised their hands.

"Wait," I said to Art, "what about option three? How many don't want to go at all?"

"He got what he wanted," Art said. "He can tell the Pentagon his men are fighters. They want to go together. And he gets to go as our leader. Put this guy in with the regulars and he'll be lucky to mop floors."

Outside the hangar a camera crew from a local Washington TV station was conducting interviews. Someone thrust a microphone in my face and I gave the first of several thousand sound bites over the next three decades. I said something to the effect that we were really called up for Vietnam.

Suffice to say, we spent two years on active duty with the Air Force, and most of our unit went to Vietnam. I was stationed at Homestead and McDill Air Force Bases in Florida and Myrtle Beach Air Force Base in South Carolina. The men of the *Pueblo* were released by North Korea and went home months before we did.

Leaving active duty with the Air Force in 1970, I went to work at the Department of Transportation, then under Republican control and the administration of Richard Nixon. Writing speeches for the secretary, John A. Volpe of Massachusetts, was fascinating, and proved to be good training for the Reagan years. Everything Volpe did was scripted. Every remark. Every letter to friends. Every speech. We gave him cradle-to-grave instructions, not because he needed them but because he had been a three-term governor of Massachusetts, meeting three or four groups a day, attending three or four ceremonial events, with an unscheduled speech or two thrown in. Executives with this kind of schedule have to trust their staffs to do their homework and the preparation. There simply isn't time to do otherwise.

Volpe was a pol. Transportation just happened to be his assignment by President Nixon. Volpe once gave me eight themes that he wanted in every speech. They were patriotism and pride in country, support for the president, religious beliefs, the role of family, the need for discipline in life and work, praise for his wife, humor, and the need for a strong work ethic.

The secretary paused after number eight. "What about transportation?" I asked.

"That too," he said, without ever smiling.

It became clear that I probably wouldn't reach the top of the Volpe speechwriting heap, however, because I wasn't Catholic. Dick Shea was. He was Harvard Irish from Massachusetts and could write a perfect meld of Catholic/Republican/family values that Volpe loved. For my money, Shea still holds the world record for number of references to the pope in a single speech.

Volpe had gone to Rome to visit the pope when his staff accepted a speech for the night of his return in Johnstown, Pennsylvania, to the Knights of Malta. Shea wrote the speech, mentioning His Holiness twenty-six times in fourteen pages, creating an entire conversation about the need for world peace and a better transportation system. When Volpe's plane touched down at National Airport, an aide rushed aboard with the speech. They took off for Johnstown and the secretary delivered it without changing a word. His Holiness would have been proud.

I had good luck with new federal agencies. Appalachia was established in 1965, Transportation in 1967, and the Environmental Protection Agency in 1970. I went to EPA as a press officer in July 1972. The environment was a hot issue with incredible power given to the bureaucrats charged with cleaning up America. The EPA was founded on a rather simple principle: Pollution of the air, water, and land could be stopped by just yelling "Stop!" The new laws EPA was to administer gave the agency power to set all kinds of cleanup standards, demand that industries and businesses meet them, then levy huge fines and an occasional prison term if they didn't. The bill for all this didn't matter. In the first few years, the agency was alive with success. Steel mills quit polluting. Gary, Pittsburgh, Birmingham, and other cities became cleaner. Strip mines closed. Raw sewage couldn't be dumped in the water. America was visibly cleaner.

But in the mid-1970s, the job got tougher. The first 95 percent of the cleanup was the cheap part. The last 5 percent cost ten times as much. After we took care of sewage, we found heavy metals and chemicals of every kind, and they were much more expensive to clean up. Power plants eliminated 95 percent of their sulfur oxide emissions, but we discovered that the last 5 percent caused acid rain. All of these bills were coming due in the late 1970s when the nation also discovered hazardous waste. Toxic chemicals were in the ground and, most frightening of all, in basements and on the shoes of children. The location was Love Canal, of all places, near Niagara Falls, New York.

In the summer of 1978, word began spreading through the EPA that Niagara was about to be known for more than the falls. By August EPA and the state of New York were ready to act: They declared a health emergency, evacuated residents living near a former chemical waste disposal site called Love Canal, and started buying the homes of 239 residents at a cost of $10 million. This was exciting. Most bureaucrats work for years and never see a brick move as a result of their efforts. They write regulations that no one can understand, six lawyers interpret them, fifteen chemical engineers implement them, and presto, one day power plant smokestacks emit 85 percent less. A lot of industries had to turn cartwheels and spend millions of dollars, of course, to make this happen. But the government workers seldom see or feel that part. Love Canal was real: Basements smelled like gasoline, children's shoes actually melted, birth defects were too numerous to account for, workers seemed tired all the time, and scientists were so afraid of their findings that they told people to pack their bags and get the hell out of town.

In the 1890s, excavation was begun on a canal near Niagara Falls to provide power and water for a model industrial city envisioned by entrepreneur William T. Love. The plans died, but the canal gradually filled with water and looked like a perfect place to dump chemical wastes. The Hooker Chemical Company assumed ownership in the 1940s, and by 1952 had buried approximately 20,000 tons of toxic chemical wastes in the canal. Hooker sold the site to the Niagara Falls board of education in 1953 for $1. The school board, no doubt thinking it had pulled a fast one on the boys at Hooker, immediately built an elementary school on this highly prized land. Twenty years later they must have felt quite foolish when a $1 freebie turned into a multimillion-dollar health hazard. In December 1979, the U.S. Justice Department on behalf of EPA filed a $124 million suit against Hooker Chemical. The board of education should have been put in a wooden barrel and floated over the falls, but they weren't.

I had worked up to being EPA press director in 1980 when Love Canal was on the verge of breaking into the national news big time.

The Love Canal had been an important story, but largely a local one, until the state evacuated residents living closest to the canal. By May 1980, the dimensions of this crisis were beginning to be understood nationally, people were frightened of the chemicals in the soil that were leaching outward, acute health problems were developing, and general fears were rising. The news bomb was waiting to explode when the government completed a study of thirty-six Love Canal residents and found that eleven of them suffered chromosomal damage, which was feared to cause birth defects and possibly other problems.

I felt we had to make this information public, and quick. To later be accused of hiding or delaying such information could destroy the reputation of EPA as a public-health agency. I called my oldest friend from Abilene, Trudy Bryan, who was an assistant to Barbara Blum, deputy EPA administrator, to lay out my case for an activist press policy at Love Canal. Heretofore, the state of New York had done most of the work and received most of the publicity. But chromosomes would change all that. Trudy had grown up on a farm just three miles from me near Abilene. We rode the bus to grade school together, and after college we both migrated to Washington. I had introduced her to Barbara Blum as a speechwriter and she soon grew into an adviser on all sorts of issues.

"Here's the deal, Trudy," I said. "We have a health effects study that says the chemicals at Love Canal have altered people's chromosomes. That raises the possibility of birth defects and all kinds of other health problems. When this gets out, people are going to go crazy. The courts will have it. Mothers will be scared to death. We can't let this situation develop in a way in which EPA is to blame for not telling pregnant women about birth defects."

She instantly agreed. "We need to advise women what this means, to reassure them."

"Right," I said. "Plus, if we're not careful, if we don't stay in front of this story, people will transfer blame for all this from Hooker Chemical Company to the government."

"Do we announce this in a press conference?" she asked.

"We have to," I said, "and we need to have people in Niagara Falls, doctors to explain this to mothers, people to go door to door. No more town meetings where people can shout and raise hysteria levels. We need one-on-one communications with every resident in Love Canal."

"You mean actually give government a face?" she said. "Bureaucrats leave Washington and go deal with the problem?"

"We have to or we'll be murdered on this," I argued. "Let's establish some basic public relations principles. First, we're open and honest about all information, health tests, sewer tests, whatever. Second, we communicate directly to the people—flyers door to door, conversations, so it's not just filtered through the press. Third, we treat all groups equally, the renters and the homeowners, the apartment house people and the old folks' home. Fourth, we hire locals when we can. And last, we move EPA on-site. Let's have a Washington EPA official with direct ties to the administrator's office living in Love Canal, in one of the houses as close to the inner ring of contamination as we can safely get."

"Who do we get to do it?" she asked. "Who wants to go live in a chemical waste dump?"

"Simple," I said, "we hire someone, someone who knows up front what they are getting into. There are a couple of other problems. Nobody knows for sure what it means to have chromosome damage, and what these people want is not more health tests. They want the government to buy their homes. Fat chance. Can you imagine that precedent? So we have to calm fears up there as well."

Trudy presented our plan to Barbara Blum and she agreed, a little nervous at first from the thought of increasing the spotlight on EPA, but understanding the reality that the light was already on. The only real question was: Would we get burned by it?

On May 17, 1980, we released the results of the chromosome study and it played big in the press, on most of the evening news shows across the country. This kicked in all the normal reactions: activist protests in Niagara Falls that not enough was being done for the residents, a furious debate over the validity of the study itself, and calls for the government to buy the contaminated homes. President Carter, on May 21, 1980, offered temporary relocation to approximately 800 families, and ordered his EPA to do further testing. Now we had a real horse to ride, a story to stay on top of. It was a classic case of how public-interest, academic, citizen, and political groups come together, without planning it or even knowing it, and create a mammoth political force that eventually sweeps through the courts, through Congress and the White House. In this case, the Justice Department took after Hooker with a vengeance. The Superfund law was only months away. And President Carter would end up buying nearly every home in Love Canal.

"Trudy," I said in calling to assess the press coverage after the relocation announcement, "we have to go to Love Canal, let people know that EPA's leadership is represented there."

"We'll start a riot," she said. "What about the citizen groups?"

"Let's not tell anybody we're coming," I suggested.

"Now, Marlin," Trudy said, "don't forget your roots here, boy. You're going to be open and honest about this. Remember Abilene." Trudy was always lecturing me on my roots, admonishing me not to get "high falutin'," as they say on the farm, and not to forget the workingman's perspective. I reminded her that I wasn't that successful as a GS-15 civil servant, or that old at thirty-seven, to forget my beginnings. But she lectured me anyway and said we should go, quietly announce our presence, and meet as many people as possible.

Immediately after the chromosome press conference, word began filtering back that mothers and pregnant women were scared, as well they should have been. So Trudy and I took two women doctors to Love Canal for two or three days and set up office hours. One of the doctors was Vilma R. Hunt, deputy assistant administrator for health research, not a practicing medical doctor but a scientist who understood chromosomes and what these studies meant. Even more important, she was central casting's answer to our problem: a woman of scientific integrity and a strong will to hold her own if protests developed, a sympathetic countenance behind horn-rimmed glasses and a floral print dress that instilled confidence in women, with a basic human concern for the welfare of Love Canal mothers.

I told her to give a lot of thought to two basic questions: "Is my baby safe?" and "What should I do now?" The rest would be easy after that. We set up shop with Dr. Vilma Hunt in a small two-room house just yards from the inner ring of Love Canal contamination. Her office included a government-issue metal desk with secretary chair, a more comfortable pre-scan wooden chair with maroon cushions for the visitors, and a picture of President Carter on the wall. For two days the women came, in every shape and size, and Trudy and I met them at the door. We welcomed them on behalf of EPA and told them we had no papers to fill out or names to take or notes to make. We were not going to be bureaucratic. I kept thinking what it would be like if my own mother were in this situation. She would be scared, intimidated, and wanting reassurance. These were working-class women just like my mother, and I was determined that on this day, at least, they would not be scared or intimidated, and hopefully reassured.

Love Canal also taught me how good intentions can go bad. Fourteen years after the events described above, *The Washington Times* editorialized on March 28, 1994, that a federal judge had just ruled that Occidental Chemical Company, which now owns Hooker, would not have to pay punitive damages for chemical wastes Hooker buried there nearly fifty years ago. The Clinton administration was trying to rewrite the Superfund law, passed in 1980, which had spent $14 billion to clean up only 217 of 1,289 hazardous waste sites. *The New York Times* editorialized in February 1994 that Superfund had failed on nearly every count. Of every dollar spent, nearly two-thirds went to lawyers.

The final irony of my EPA years was that the woman who gave me my biggest break in the agency also gave me the biggest break in getting out: Ann Dore McLaughlin. Ann became director of public affairs at EPA in the Nixon administration, just after I had joined the press office staff. Nixon had created the new agency by combining a raft of old water, air, and health agencies, mostly from the Department of Health, Education, and Welfare. The employees were primarily Democrats collected through the Kennedy-Johnson years, and young firebrand liberals who had migrated from Earth Day in 1970 through another year or two of college and into EPA. The attitude toward Nixon was cool at best, tempered only by the personal popularity of administrators Bill Ruckelshaus and his successor, Russell Train. The arrival of Ann Dore was not celebrated. She had come out of the Nixon reelection campaign, was thirty-three, beautiful, brilliant, and knew her own mind. The old-boy network at EPA was struggling with all this. In the end they just couldn't hide their feelings, and the top two career press officers found themselves in other assignments.

Ann was reportedly looking for a Republican political type to serve as press director. But as the days passed it seemed that she was caught in a sort of catch-22: The job of press director was designated for a career civil servant, and few of them were certifiable Republicans. So I decided to give it a shot. I was only a GS-14, making $26,938 a year. The director was a GS-15, and I had just been promoted to the 14 slot. Also, I was only thirty, in a civil servant society where people spent twenty-five years working up to be a GS-15 at about age fifty. So I decided to propose a deal.

I walked into her office trembling. She often wore black suits and dresses to highlight her dark hair and flashing dark eyes, had just the right jewelry, knew people in high places, was whispered to have a close relationship with White House speechwriter John McLaughlin (whom she later married), suffered fools badly, demanded high quality work, and always had ten more ideas and questions than anyone could answer. She was Junior League, Catholic girls school, proper, powerful, and probably a dozen other attributes that scared the daylights out of a Kansas farm boy. So I decided to make it quick. I was ushered into her office, took a seat in front of her desk, and said, "I would like you to consider me as press director. I think I can do it and I would like a chance."

She smiled. But I don't think she had ever thought about this possibility—in fact, had probably never thought about me.

"How long have you been here?" she asked.

"Only a couple of years," I said, "and I know I'm young. I would like to make a proposal."

"What is it?" she said, starting to wonder if this was going to be a problem.

"I would like to try the job for three months," I said. "I could be assigned to it on an acting basis. If you want to get someone else after that, fine, I'll go back to being a press officer. But if I get the job, I get the GS-15 that goes with it."

"I'll think about it," she said. "Do you think you could do the job?"

"Yes, ma'am," I said. "I know the business. I know the press. I know the people here. But I realize that I'm young, so I'll understand if you say no at the end of three months."

It worked. By the time she left EPA in 1974, we had become good friends. She later became a member of the Reagan cabinet, first as undersecretary of interior and then as secretary of labor. Today she serves on the board of directors of several of America's largest corporations.

Ann also hired Leslye Arsht, a young political appointee from the Nixon campaign, to run a student environmental program. Leslie was probably the first person I ever met with a truly strategic mind, able to analyze situations in terms of future repercussions. She also could read people, their motives, their reactions. She could lay out a strategic plan, look me in the eye, tell me my own limitations, and then advise me how to overcome them in order to carry out the plan. Years later when I was named press secretary to President Reagan, my first call was to Leslye Arsht, begging her to be my deputy.

The transition between administrations is terrible for civil servants. Everyone is afraid of losing their job, or losing the boss they love, or losing the program they worked four years on. It's not hostility. It's the uncertainty. And after Ronald Reagan commented during his campaign that trees cause pollution, the EPA bureaucracy was scared to death. We expected to get a shopping center developer for administrator.

Ironically, Reagan's first press secretary, Jim Brady, was reprimanded and kicked off the campaign press plane for joking about Reagan blaming trees for pollution. "Look at those killer trees," he said as their plane passed somewhere over the Great Smoky Mountains. I later kidded Jim that the only people who truly appreciated his humor were at EPA, because his comment was the first indication of anything less than total disdain for the environment by the Reagan team. Indeed, Brady was kicked off the press plane for two days because of his comments.

As fate would have it, in January 1981 Ann Dore McLaughlin called. She had been hired as a consultant to the new secretary of the Treasury, Donald T. Regan, who was leaving his position as chairman of the Merrill Lynch brokerage firm in New York to come to Washington. He wanted people to teach him how Washington worked. Ann asked if I would help, particularly if I would help write his first speeches.

No one had been appointed EPA administrator. The agency was in irons. So I volunteered to help Ann, took two weeks of annual leave at EPA, and headed to Treasury. Two other momentous events happened about the same time. My marriage was falling apart in

1980. We had separated in the summer for a few months, went to a marriage counselor, and then parted for good during the Christmas holiday. Our children, Bradley Charles and Courtney Lynn, were nine and six respectively.

Who knows what a midlife crisis means? But I must have been in it. I was at the top of my profession in the civil service, near the top of the pay scale, but only thirty-eight years old. That meant spending another twenty-four years on a career plateau before retirement. Every time I thought of this, plus my disintegrating marriage, plus a demotion by the new administration, my mind whirled back to those Kansas wheat fields and the clouds drifting toward other worlds. It was time for a change.

I went to Treasury for two weeks, learned everything I could about supply-side economics, became reenergized by the new subject matter and the stimulating people coming into the administration, and got a job offer to be Ann McLaughlin's deputy. I went back to EPA, called a staff meeting to announce my resignation, and two hours later left the agency for good. There was no one to resign to, except the personnel office. Within hours I was a political appointee of the Reagan administration, and on my way to to the White House.

Dave Gergen is majestically tall. His body moves slowly and swoops down on you, like a swan. He suddenly appears behind you at dinner parties and his body seems to wrap around your chair. In the summer of 1983, he climbed out of a black White House Mercury in front of LaMaree, a French restaurant just a few blocks from my third-floor office in the Treasury Department, held the car door for Joanna Bistany, a member of the White House communications staff, and walked purposefully away from the curb. I was nervous, even scared, as I looked down the row of single tables along the wall, to see his six-foot-four frame blot out the gold letters on the window. As a seventeen-year bureaucrat, now serving as deputy assistant secretary of the Treasury, to me Dave Gergen was a political legend, a survivor of the Nixon White House and now a trusted member of the Reagan inner circle. We had never met.

He had called me earlier in the summer, out of the blue, to compliment me on newspaper quotes defending the president's 10 percent across-the-board tax cuts. Since I was totally unknown to the Reagan staff, they must have been asking, "Who is this guy who's defending supply-side economics?" Little did they know that prior to 1981 I had had no economics training, no background in finance, and little knowledge of tax incentives. But like an empty blackboard, my mind was ready to be written on.

I spent endless hours with Norman Ture, godfather of supply-side economics and undersecretary for tax policy; Beryl Sprinkel, world-recognized monetarist and undersecretary for monetary policy; Paul Craig Roberts, another supply-side guru and Treasury assistant secretary; and Steve Entin, an economist and prolific writer who turned out page after page of philosophy about tax incentives. I found these guys fascinating. I never really understood or believed the Laffer Curve business whereby cutting taxes would eventually cut the deficit due to increased tax revenues. Even Laffer later said his curve wouldn't work quite that way. But for me, a young man who had never made more than $65,000 a year, and whose father had never made more than $12,000, the mysteries of taxation had never preoccupied my thinking. Now I was beginning to look at money in a new light.

I asked Donald T. Regan, secretary of the Treasury, before his first press conference if he had a passbook savings account. The theory behind supply-side tax cuts was that lower marginal rates would increase savings and investment. My own form of savings was the lowly passbook account, usually paying around 3 to 5 percent interest, and the favorite teaching tool of high school accounting instructors. Indeed, most people on fixed incomes in this country, particularly the old and the young, still save money in mattresses or passbooks.

Secretary Regan looked at me as if I were crazy. "Of course I have a savings account," he said.

"Is it passbook?" I asked.

"No, it's a money market account."

"That's not the same," I said. "Most reporters have passbooks and that's why they think our program is only for the rich."

"Do you have a passbook?" he asked.

"Of course," I said, "all of us poor boys do."

"Will the press ask?" he said.

"You bet," I said, "and I suggest you hit it head-on by saying that you have a personal savings account in the form of a money market account, instead of a passbook, because it pays more interest."

The press did ask the question and my stock went up immeasurably. I began to speak out more on the savings incentives for low-income earners, and many of these comments had come to Gergen's

attention. When he called, he said the president had decided that
Larry Speakes, who became White House spokesman following the
shooting of James Brady, needed an assistant for domestic policy.
Would I be interested?

As Gergen pushed the restaurant door open, and held it with outstretched arm high above Bistany's head, I had a premonition that
my life was about to take a drastic turn. He walked directly to my
table, introduced Joanna, and flashed his trademark smile of sincer-
ity.

"How have you been?" he asked perfunctorily.

"Fine," I said, genuinely overwhelmed by his presence.

"I was just telling Joanna," he said, "about your background and
your defense of tax policy."

"Thank you," I said, "I'm just a bureaucrat."

"Let's see," he said, "you were at the Environmental Protection
Agency for several years, were you not? Then you came to Treasury
with the Reagan administration."

That seemed like an excellent way to put it. "Yes," I said. "Ann
McLaughlin brought me in to help Don Regan with speeches and
press, and it all seemed to work out."

"Let me tell you our situation," he said. "Larry Speakes needs
help. John Herrington, who's in our personnel office, did a study of
the press office, and he concluded that Larry needs some domestic
policy support. I'm looking at a number of candidates, but I just
wanted to talk with you about it."

I didn't know beans about White House organization, but I got
the clear impression that Dave Gergen was in charge of hiring for
this position. It made sense, since he was director of communications. The lunch lasted about an hour and ended with Gergen saying
I would hear from him later. I floated back to Treasury, proud that
the White House was interested in me, awed by Dave Gergen, and
definitely impressed by the government chauffeur who held the door
as Gergen and Bistany climbed back into their car.

Two or three weeks later, Larry Speakes called and asked if I
would be interested in working at the White House. Some inner
alarm system said not to mention the Gergen lunch. Speakes invited
me to the White House for a personal interview.

Although the press secretary's office was my own for six years,
my most vivid memories of it occurred under other occupants. The
first was a 1978 visit with the head of the EPA, Douglas Costle, just
before he briefed the press. I was EPA's director of public affairs. Jody

Powell, President Carter's press secretary, stood behind the enormous circular desk, made out of three sections, all with slightly different shades of wood or stain, and curved to form a half horseshoe. As Jody and Doug talked, I stood and listened, not even thinking to sit. I wanted to hear every word from the president's press secretary, the man who epitomized all the power and prestige that my career field could offer. I never expected to be in this office again, let alone know Jody, and I tried to memorize the surroundings: the clocks showing different time zones, the couch under the bookcases where every luminary from the last twenty years must have sat, the small round conference table with four chairs positioned under the clocks, and pictures of President Carter. Jody asked me to sit, but I just stood there, numb, until Costle finished his conversation and we all walked down to the briefing room. "Call the briefing," Jody had said.

My second strongest memory is the interview with Larry Speakes. It was just after lunch and Larry had been jogging. His hair was wet from a shower, his face red from the exertion of a long run around the Ellipse and Mall, and a tall glass of ice sat on his desk, which he munched on like popcorn. He invited me to pull a chair over from the small conference table, which I placed at the curve of his desk, then reached out and touched the desk, just in case I was never invited back. Amazingly, the office looked exactly like it did under Jody, except for the large mantle picture of slaves picking cotton in a Mississippi field that some local artist had given Larry, who grew up in Mississippi.

"Thanks for coming over," Larry said. "I remember you from the Ford administration. I was here in the lower press office and you were at EPA. I used to call you for answers on the environment."

I searched my mind to remember if I had been responsive, although I must have or I wouldn't have been there that day. "I hope I was helpful," I said.

Larry laughed and began to tell me about the Herrington study, which concluded he needed two new deputies, for domestic and foreign policy. It seems Herrington actually took an office in the press suite for a few days. What a break for Larry. It's impossible for any outsider to spend one day in the press office without knowing the pressure of deadlines, the abuse by reporters, the constant ring of telephones, the demands for accuracy and responsiveness, and the furious pace of press inquiries. It's also impossible not to feel the intensity of the briefing, the demand for information, and fear of failure if the briefer is not prepared. John Herrington took one whiff of all this and came to the right conclusion, help—and I was it.

I still had not mentioned the Gergen phone call and luncheon. Curiously, neither had Larry. So I asked how the press office related to the communications office. Larry was careful. He said "Tall," meaning Gergen, was responsible for planning, but had little to do with the press.

"You would work for me," Larry emphasized. I left the White House in a trance—I might actually be offered a job—working for the president. I had never met Ronald Reagan. But I had worked for seventeen years for every president since Lyndon Johnson, and I respected the presidency, no matter who held the office. I had subdued all political activity to serve as a career civil servant, but I was a Republican and ready to change my life. I was fully prepared to offer my total loyalty to Ronald Reagan. But there was this nagging perception that both Gergen and Speakes were trying to vie for control of my services. I decided it was their problem, not mine, and returned to the Treasury to wait.

In mid-August, Larry Speakes called to ask if I would come to the White House again to discuss the job. I arrived, a little anxious because Larry gave no indication of the nature of the interview.

"Jim Baker is the chief of staff," Larry said, "and he would like to interview you."

"Fine," I said. "I've never met him."

I walked into the chief of staff's corner office that hot summer day never guessing that I would work for seven chiefs in ten years, and see more personal anguish and turmoil in this room than anywhere else. Three chiefs would shed the tears of good-bye in this office, Supreme Court nominees would plead and appeal for more time, wars were planned, and petty arguments were held by the fistful over egos out of control. But that day it was quiet. I was overwhelmed by the heavy dark wooden desk brought to the office by H. R. Haldeman under President Nixon. It stood along the wall, just to the left of the entry door, and rose almost to the ceiling, with cabinetry that hung over the writing space like some medieval torture machine that might swivel down at any moment to trap the arms of an intruder. It made one worry about whether or not the back was attached to the wall, perhaps a diversion that gave an edge to the original chief in conversation with Watergate conspirators. The desk so overwhelmed the room, and all those around it, that James Baker seemed remarkably fragile and soft.

"Larry and Dave have told me about you," he began. "Please sit down."

"Thank you," I said.

"They told you about the job. I can't explain what it's like to work in the White House, but loyalty to the president is very important," he said. "This is a very political place. I assume that doesn't cause you any problem."

In view of my civil service background, that seemed like a very normal question. In fact, I expected even more direct questioning on my years in government. But Baker seemed quite comfortable with that, no doubt happy to get someone with a clean political slate and no ax to grind.

"There is one thing," he said. "Larry and Dave are a little competitive, and I know you've talked to both of them. But I want you to know that you work for Larry. I'm hiring you on behalf of the president, but you take direction from Larry."

"Yes, sir," I said. "I hope I can serve the president and all of you well."

Baker smiled.

Larry was waiting outside to escort me to the door. He told me he would call later about a starting date and other matters. Once again, I went back to Treasury to wait.

It was routine to receive a copy of the president's Saturday radio address for clearance, especially if it dealt with economic matters, and almost all of Ronald Reagan's did. They were circulated to cabinet officers by Richard Darman, the cabinet secretary, who melded the staff comments and criticisms into a final text for the president to read at Camp David on Saturday morning. The following week, the five-minute address was about interest rates and monetary policy.

As the Treasury secretary's speechwriter, I received a copy. I noticed the content would have an impact on the Federal Reserve Board, so I routinely recommended to Deputy Secretary of the Treasury Tim McNamar that he send the copy over to Federal Reserve chairman Paul Volcker for his comments, which he did. But Volcker, always defensive of his independence, and also aware of his status about six steps above me or the deputy secretary of the Treasury, immediately called Richard Darman in the White House to complain about the radio address.

To all those who know, or have ever heard about, Richard Darman, the above paragraph will strike fear and terror. He screams and throws paper when he is not happy. And he's not happy when he's not in total control. By the time Dick Darman had suffered the embarrassment of being chastised by Paul Volcker, and had forced a plea bargain from Tim McNamar to the effect that "Fitzwater made me do it," his rage was reaching inferno dimensions. He had been upbraided by a peer (Volcker), disobeyed by a subordinate (McNamar), and embarrassed by a nobody (Fitzwater). Had I been in his presence, I'm sure he would have thrown a handful of paper clips at me, screamed until his face was red and a few strands of forelock fell over his forehead, hitched up his pants and stomped out of the room. But since he had never met me, and Treasury was a block away, his challenge was to duplicate those conditions over the telephone.

"Are you Marlin Fitzwater?" he asked.

"Yes, sir," I said.

"Did you send the president's Saturday radio address to Paul Volcker?"

"Yes, sir, through Mr. McNamar."

"Who told you to do that?" he asked.

"No one," I said. "It just made sense to me that the chairman of the Fed might have some useful comments."

"First of all," he said, "it doesn't make sense. If I want the Fed chairman to review something, I'll send it to him. Second, I have written two memos telling people in the departments that the president's speeches are never to be passed along. McNamar shouldn't have shown it to you, let alone Volcker."

It occurred to me that substance was not always going to be the main issue at the White House.

"Yes, sir," I said meekly.

"I understand you may be coming to work over here," he said.

"Yes, sir," I replied. "In a couple of weeks."

"We'll see about that," he said calmly, and hung up.

Strangely, I never heard another word about the matter. But I never forgot the potential penalty for crossing Richard Darman. I started work at the White House on September 1, 1983, in a tiny office once occupied by Diane Sawyer, the current ABC television news star, just twenty steps from the Oval Office. It was such a dream that I never asked about salary till my second day on the job. It was $57,000, a $7,000 pay cut from Treasury. Best sacrifice I ever made.

By late 1986, I had spent two years as deputy press secretary to the president, and had moved on to become press secretary to Vice President Bush. During one of the vice president's many congressional campaign trips, I asked Ken Walsh of *U.S. News & World Report* to walk with me along the Mississippi River in Davenport, Iowa. This was another trip to Iowa to help raise money in the off-year elections. Only two or three reporters traveled with the vice president, and nights in small towns were usually spent at the bar or the "best restaurant in town" where the biggest newspaper in the group paid the bill. The TV networks would have paid because they are richer, but TV networks don't often travel with vice presidents. This night, however, there was no offer to buy dinner, so I suggested a cigar walk. It was dusk along the Mississippi, and pretty in spite of the old factories along the bank, the broken planks in the deserted piers, and the near-derelict warehouses that had held the hopes of Iowa immigrants nearly fifty years before.

"They say Larry Speakes is leaving the White House," Ken said.

"I don't believe it. He will never leave," I said.

"No. He's leaving. And you're in line to be press secretary to the president."

"No. Never happen," I said.

It did, of course, in January 1987, and like my original hiring, it happened in a most mysterious way.

In early 1985, after President Reagan's reelection to a second term, Vice President Bush began to prepare for his own run for the presidency. A first step was to hire a new staff that had campaign and presidential experience. Craig Fuller, who had been President Reagan's cabinet secretary for four years, was named chief of staff, and he recommended me to the vice president. It was a very simple and straightforward move. Vice President Bush invited me to his office, just a few steps from my own, outlined his plans for the next four years, said he intended to run in 1988, and asked if I would like to join him.

"I believe in what President Reagan is doing," the vice president said, "and I support all his decisions. I offer him advice in private, which of course you know, but I never differ with him in public. Also, I don't believe in leaks or backgrounders by all these unnamed officials, and I don't want you to do any of these things either."

"I understand," I said.

"If we would all talk on the record," he said, "everyone would be better off."

I packed a few files from my small office and a few days later moved quietly across the street to the vice president's offices in the

Old Executive Office Building. The next two years with Bush as vice president were the most fun, delightful, and peaceful of my career. My press strategy was to introduce the vice president to as many reporters as possible during this period so that by 1988 he would know the press corps. During the next two years, he gave nearly seventy-five interviews. Unfortunately, almost every one of them was bad. The reporters begged him to criticize President Reagan or tell them the inside story of the decision-making process, or "who shot John?" as the vice president would say, but he would never oblige. The stories always came out that Bush was loyal to a fault. But I still felt that the relationships would pay off in the future.

By the time Larry Speakes resigned from the White House in 1987, I had developed an enormous loyalty to the Bush family. The vice president and Mrs. Bush had a knack for making the staff feel wanted and appreciated. He was master of the small gesture that made a big difference: the arm around your shoulder after you had made a mistake, the signed photograph when you needed to feel important, the private dinner when you felt left out, and, most remarkably, the ability to recognize the everyday problems of staff frictions and competitions. He could always patch things up and took the time to do it. So I felt some guilt for even thinking about leaving the vice president just as he was beginning to build a campaign team for 1988.

Dennis Thomas, deputy chief of staff, called one afternoon to ask if I was interested in being President Reagan's press secretary. Thomas was compiling a list. I figured the real candidate already had been selected, but good staff work always requires a long backup list. I said yes, it would be a great honor.

A few days later, Tom Dawson, executive assistant to Regan, called and asked if I could "meet with the chief" that afternoon to talk about the press secretary job. Dawson is the only person in my ten years in the White House who ever called the chief "chief."

"Could you meet the chief at three o'clock today in room 274 of the Old Executive Office Building?" It was a newly restored and very elegant office once belonging to the secretary of the Navy during World War II. He asked if I could slip down there without being noticed. It escaped me why I should not want to be noticed. Dawson spoke in a whisper. He had worked for Regan at Treasury when I was there. He was tall and lanky, with rubber legs that sort of floated when he walked, and thick black hair combed to the side that had to be pushed from his forehead every three or four steps. Perhaps because of his height, he stooped when he talked, thus adding to the conspiratorial air that permeated his conversations. So when he whispered into the phone, "Can you meet in room 274?" I thought little of it.

At exactly 3 P.M. I turned the knob on the fifteen-foot wooden door to this special room. It was locked. I stood outside, wondering if I should be seen in the wide marble hallways of the old building, but deciding there could be a thousand reasons for my being there and I should not worry. After about five minutes, I began to feel like half of the old Rowan and Martin comedy team that would appear under a streetlight on *Laugh-In*, and one would say, "I've got the yo-yo," and the other would say, "I've got the string." I felt mostly like the yo-yo.

Then I could see a long, loping gait at the distant end of the hallway. Like an airplane landing at the end of the runway, he was blurry and small but becoming taller and more detailed with each step until he was the definitive Tom Dawson.

"The chief will be here in a minute," he said. "Door locked? I've got the key."

He opened the huge double doors and invited me in. Almost before I could turn around, he said he had to go, and turned and left, locking the door behind him.

The room was beautiful, but entirely empty save for one small bench along the far wall. At either end of the forty-foot room were six-foot mirrors, framed in ornate gilt-edged wood reminiscent of eighteenth-century paintings by the old masters. They reflected the green and gold brocade wall paper and two large crystal chandeliers that dominated the room. I pinched myself to be sure I wasn't wearing a waistcoat.

This was slightly ludicrous. I paced the parquet floor from one end of the room to the other, wanting ever so desperately to shout out a funeral oration or some such monologue that might bounce off these perfect walls like music in a shower. I did say a few words to test the echo, and sure enough, there was one. I waited.

The door finally opened, exposing only the long arm of Mr. Dawson, which quickly withdrew to admit the presence of Chief Donald T. Regan. He favored light plaid business suits that seemed to enhance his ruddy Irish complexion, with French-cuff shirts and collars with heavy starch, highly polished black shoes and stylish ties that indicated he kept up with the trends, which he did. Swept-back gray hair was the final touch. He was a Wall Street businessman through and through, and could have modeled for any fashion magazine, with high cheekbones, a long, angular nose, and darting, mischievous eyes. Always the eyes. They gave away every emotion—red when angry, small when pensive, mad when mad. And sparkling when mischievous, which was often, about intellectual matters such as a well-turned phrase, a good pun, a riddle solved, or a joke retold with exaggeration and animation. He was elegant and strong, a man who had become chairman of the board of the world's largest brokerage, and secretary of the Treasury. A former Marine, he creased his clothes and his life accordingly, and was a man of honesty and loyalty. He gave it and expected it. He was the most honest and direct man I ever knew in the White House, except for Ronald Reagan. Together they were a smashing pair, like Ronald Colman and Dana Andrews on the movie screen, standing in the Oval Office, telling stories, planning summits with Gorbachev, both of them handsomely starched in an Old World dignity with Old World values. But despite the proper appearances, the ground was beginning to crumble under their relationship.

I stood along the far wall and moved a step or two toward the door as Regan entered. He walked straight to me, looking me in the eye as he crossed the room, and the smile started. It began as a smirk at the corner of his mouth, then pulled his entire face to one side as the mirth of the moment hit his eyes, and they gleamed like a boy about to drop a water balloon on his best friend. With real excitement, he reached out his hand and said, "Do you want it or not?"

I was unprepared. I expected a little foreplay, some discussion of the situation, the candidates. But that would not be Don Regan's style. I should have known.

"You mean the press secretary?" I said, still not quite believing this was happening.

"Yes," he said.

"Well, yes," I said. "But I would like to discuss a couple of matters."

"Sure," he said. "Fire away."

I had already talked to Vice President Bush about taking the job. He encouraged me from the first moment, with no hesitation. I loved him for that. I always remembered when Henry Jameson, the Abilene editor, had failed to recognize my ambitions. George Bush never made that mistake with anyone. In this case, he told me to be sure to raise the "access" question with President Reagan. I suspect he knew that Don Regan ran a tight ship and the door to the Oval Office was heavily guarded, so I took his advice.

"I want to raise three issues," I said. Regan's face began to change, to get that look that asked just exactly when it was that I became so demanding, so I softened the preface.

"These aren't too much," I said. He relaxed. "I just need some assurance of access to the president. I realize I work through you, but it's important for me and the press to know I can go to the president if I have to. Also, I would like Jim Brady to keep his press secretary title, and I would like to be titled 'assistant to the president for press relations.' "

I knew the president would want Brady to keep his title anyway. This would allow me to abolish the Speakes designation of "principal deputy press secretary" that he had inherited after the Brady/Reagan assassination attempt. Larry hated it. Even though he had gotten the job as a result of Brady's misfortune, the title was denigrating, since Larry was in fact and practice the press secretary. I didn't like it either, so I asked for the more formal title knowing the press would probably just call me "presidential spokesman."

"The president is still recovering from his surgery," Regan said, "but I'll talk to him as soon as I can."

Several days passed and I heard nothing. I thought maybe Regan had changed his mind. He was a proud man and I thought he might have backed off my candidacy because I asked to talk to the president. Then his secretary called and asked if I could meet the chief in the Oval Office. I rushed across the street, tried to calm my nerves as I walked up the back stairs, and hurried past the press office hoping not to be seen.

The president's secretary, Kathy Osborne, ushered me into the Oval. The vice president was already there, seated near the wall. Regan was on the president's right. They all stood as I walked in. I inched toward these three powerful men, easily the most important men in my life, with tongue tied.

The vice president spoke up. "Mr. President," he said, "I'm here to give Marlin back to you."

"Well," the president said, smiling, "I'm happy to get him back. Marlin, I understand you've agreed to be my press secretary."

"Yes, sir," I said, "I'm greatly honored."

Regan stepped forward. "Mr. President, Marlin wants to ask you a few questions."

I felt embarrassed, like the little boy who threatens to tell off his father but cringes when faced with the opportunity. "Sir," I said, "I just wanted to ask if I could talk directly with you when problems come up?"

"Yes," he said, "that's fine."

"And I would like for Jim Brady to keep his title. Maybe I could be 'assistant for press relations.' "

"Yes," he said, "that's fine."

"That's all I had," I said, visibly relieved.

"Well, it's all set then, Marlin," the president said. "You'll work out the details with Don?"

"Yes, sir," I said, standing and turning to leave. "I promise to do my best, Mr. President."

"I know you will," he said, and I rushed out the door.

I stood in the Oval reception area and said nothing. Kathy Osborne just smiled. I was so proud. This was it, the pinnacle of my career. It had happened, and history would always record it so. Even if I was fired tomorrow, the footnote would always be there: "For a few brief moments on January 12, 1987, Marlin Fitzwater was press secretary to the president." I was determined to make it at least two years. My first briefing was February 2, 1987.

It was much later that I discovered the reason for all the secrecy in my hiring. The differences between Mrs. Reagan and Don Regan had almost reached the boiling point. They had argued over the president's scheduling and his appearances. Regan was frustrated by the role of Mrs. Reagan's astrologer in selecting the timing of meetings and press conferences. Their phone conversations became abrupt, punctuated by long silences. When the press secretary position became vacant, both had a candidate. Reportedly, Mrs. Reagan wanted Sheila Tate, who had been her own press secretary in the first term. Don Regan wanted Ann McLaughlin, who had been his press adviser at Treasury. Regan had some other candidates as well, but whoever it was, Mrs. Reagan objected. I was the compromise candidate. Regan knew that I had worked with President and Mrs. Reagan before, as deputy press secretary, so he figured she would accept me. Even so, he wanted the appointment approved by the president before the first lady found out about it.

I'm glad that I didn't know most of this at the time. Within just a few weeks, Don Regan and most of the White House staff he had hired were forced out.

CHAPTER FIVE

The Press Corps

Every morning they read *The Washington Post* that hits their front door, listen to National Public Radio while they shower, and when their appetites are fully whetted by the news of the day, they creep out of the underbrush of Washington neighborhoods and come to the White House briefing room. They are the lions of the press. They enter through the Secret Service gate on Pennsylvania Avenue, submit their cameras for search, show their passes for the 500th time, snarl at the uniformed police manning the identification computers, and finally trudge up the long and winding driveway to work. As they pass the naked camera tripods set up along the drive, they know they are voluntarily entering a cage as real as any zoo ever constructed. At the gate they are questioned, challenged, stalled, and harassed by guards who know and hate them. The guards watch television and see the constant criticism of their president. The guards are loyal, and they retaliate with the only power they have: the badge and the threat of access denial. From this point on, the reporters' lives are totally controlled. Their movements within the White House are monitored and managed, the president's schedule determines their lunchtime and their leaving time, and the president's agenda controls their thoughts and ideas. Presidential minions just out of college will tell them to "wait here," "move there," and by the 11 A.M. briefing time, widely called "the feeding time," they are pissed. It's no wonder.

As one reporter joins another for the walk up the drive, the conversation is often the same.

"That goddamn guard," one says, "he knows me. He held me

there because my name didn't come up on the computer. It's just harassment. Why do we have to take this?"

"Because no one cares," the other says. "They probably even
enjoy it. Marlin might care, but no one will do anything about it."

They are right, of course. No one does care. The press corps is an
unwanted appendage, like a cocklebur that attaches to your pants
leg. For the White House staff, it's a problem to be managed, a block
of people to be moved around like a checker—brought into the Oval
Office at the top of each meeting, ushered into the Rose Garden to
witness a bill signing, and wedged into a maze of hallways that can't
be freely entered. This is not the Harvard Business School work-
place. This is the power center of the democratic universe where the
president of the United States rules with total power and authority.
The more that power is challenged by sources outside the White
House, the more it is exercised within the White House. In March
1987, the outside challenges could be counted in truckloads—from
Iran-Contra prosecutors, from congressional committees, from the
Tower Board looking into the "arms for hostages question," from
Democrats hungry to run for president in 1988, and from a press
corps that smelled the blood of an injured president. Tempers were
short. The leashes were drawn tight. The president conducted public events the way groundhogs test the day, by sticking out his nose
for a short period of time, uttering a few well-crafted words, then
quickly ducking back into the Oval Office. Sensitivity or concern for
the press was nil. They were not wanted.

It is Friday, March 13, 1987. I have been press secretary for just
six weeks, yet a routine is developing. My old green Mercedes, faded
and rusted in every spot imaginable, arrives at the southwest gate located between the White House and the Old Executive Office Building. The Pennsylvania Avenue gate is for the foot soldiers, the
southwest gate is for the executives and their cars—at least that's
the way it works out. Security is geared for cars, with concrete stations forming a maze that prevents high-speed approaches—highly
unlikely in a 1980 diesel-powered Mercedes, but possible in a rental
van driven by Saddam Hussein. Tourists stand on the sidewalk near
the gates and stare at the cars, along with the occasional stakeout
television camera hoping to catch a guilt-ridden public official as he
drives his foreign-made car to work. I figure the rust spots make up
for the guilt, and perhaps even demonstrate that foreign is no more
able to resist salt than domestic. I proudly sit at the gate while

guards check the computer for my pass and onlookers check their memories for my face. Then, slowly, the big black iron gate hydraulically withdraws on a ground rail, allowing entry. It is always a heady moment.

On most Washington mornings, at 6:30 A.M. or 7 A.M., fog persists. It helps create a White House dream world in which the gates close behind you and the only enemies are back-stabbing colleagues and a handful of nations with nuclear arms. Just outside are the great unwashed, that mass of normal Americans who will never see the inside of this eighteen acres. It is safe in the physical sense, or at least it felt like it until an airplane tried to land in President Clinton's bedroom and a lone gunman sprayed bullets across the front of the mansion.

My parking spot was number 24, right in front of the steps leading up to the diplomatic driveway and the "front" door of the West Wing. "Old Green" was visible from the press stakeout microphones just outside the briefing room. A quick glance would alert the entire press corps to my presence at an unusual time, like weekends or midnight. I would climb those steps every morning, salute the guard in his little house beside the steps, look down the driveway to see if any reporters were coming in, then proceed to the Marine guard stationed by the West Wing door.

This is another great treat of the presidency. Every morning for ten years, a handsome, tall highly polished Marine in full dress red and blue uniform, with gold braids gleaming, would snap to attention at my approach, click his heels, say "Good morning, sir," then reach for the brass door handle and pull it open. In the winter, an electric foot plate was provided for the guard, with a short cord that plugged into an outside wall socket. The effect was to make him appear to be an electric toy, voice-actuated, and wooden as a tree. But no matter, it was such an uplifting way to begin the day, always swelling my ego, reminding me that I was important, and even suggesting that this guard was eager to have me on the job.

Inside was Carl Jones, six feet five, 280 pounds, African-American, a veteran of seven administrations and twenty-five years of greeting guests. From terrorist dictators to Mother Teresa, he took their coats, welcomed them to the house, and showed them to the Oval Office, always in good spirits but never obsequious. He had a fourteen-inch TV set stashed in the coat closet, and could stand in the doorway watching the morning news, take my coat, welcome me to the day, and never miss a beat. Sometimes he would warn me, "Lot of reporters around here today," which he said on March 13.

"Oh Christ," I thought. "What have I missed? Got a paper, Carl?" He motioned me to the coffee table. The stories seemed harmless on the *Post*'s front page. Something about new verification procedures for the Soviet arms-control treaty. No emotion there. Certainly wouldn't cause reporters to come in early to try to ambush me going into the White House, or even cause Carl to notice.

Must be *The New York Times*, I thought, which was buried beneath *The Wall Street Journal* and *The Washington Times*. I dug it out, glanced on both sides of the fold, and my heart stopped. The headline was "Reagan Counsel Recounts Chaos Over Iran Affair." My day was made. Peter Wallison, who had just resigned as the president's counsel, must be defending himself. The first paragraph confirmed it: "President Reagan's chief legal adviser today depicted scenes of chaos in the White House in recent months and said he had been prevented from looking into the Iran affair for several weeks after its disclosure last November." The story said Wallison gave the interview to Gerald Boyd of the *Times*'s Washington bureau.

"This is great," I thought. "I haven't even reached my office yet. It's seven o'clock in the morning. My ten A.M. briefing will be war. There is nothing the press likes better than internal squabbling, one staffer blaming another, even a hint that he might be blaming the president, and most of all, this provides them with an opportunity to break my rock-solid policy of not discussing Iran-Contra from the White House."

When I first came to the new job on February 2, 1987, the Iran-Contra investigation was just getting into full swing. The Tower Board, including former Senator John Tower, General Brent Scowcroft, and former secretary of state Edmund Muskie had been appointed by President Reagan to look into the sale of arms to Iran and make policy recommendations. The Congress was about to hold hearings. And an independent counsel, Lawrence E. Walsh of Oklahoma City, had been appointed to investigate any criminal activity related to the affair. It took me only one day in the White House to realize that no one there knew the story of Iran-Contra, had any idea what had happened, or knew how to deal with the aftermath. All of the real participants had left or been fired. Oliver North, John Poindexter, and Bud McFarlane had all departed the National Security Council. I saw the outside investigations as a blessing. After all, the independent counsel law was passed on the theory that a White

House could not investigate itself. So why try, in any way, shape, or form? My policy would be: "This matter is being fully investigated by three outside bodies and not by the White House. We will leave all answers to them."

This strategy worked rather well. After President Reagan turned the whole matter over to the independent counsel, and after a complete turnover of the White House staff, the investigation—even the congressional hearings—caused little stir within the White House. It was a problem to solve in terms of providing documents to the investigators, and that was assigned to lawyers in the counsel's office who were not involved in policy matters. Thus the whole investigation was not threatening to the new staff in any personal way. Except for the president, none of us were involved. We didn't even watch the hearings, except the day Admiral John Poindexter testified that he had not told the president about diverting Iranian arms money to the Contras in Nicaragua.

Whitewater has been so destructive of the Clinton presidency because the White House sticks to it like flypaper. First they took two months to turn it over to an independent counsel. Then Harold Ickes was brought in to "manage" the affair out of the chief of staff's office. Then Mrs. Clinton kept demanding to know what was going on. Staff contacts were made with Treasury officials, all of which resulted in grand jury subpoenas, testimony, and more personal anguish and lawyers for those trying to run the country. The White House never could sever itself from the debilitating effects of the investigation.

In the winter of 1987, if I pretended to know even one fact in my briefings about Iran-Contra, the press would tie me in knots. Now Wallison had put me in a box. Worse, Helen would be waiting and she would be livid.

It's only about twenty yards from the West Lobby to the Oval Office, and halfway down that hallway was the door to my press secretary's suite. Outside it were two straight-back chairs beside a small table holding an Alexander Proctor sculpture of the *Buckaroo*, a cowboy on his bronco, on loan from the New York Metropolitan Museum of Art. I sat down to collect my thoughts. The next few minutes would be the most dangerous of the day, even worse than the briefing itself. I stared at my door, knowing that just beyond it, just inches away, Helen Thomas and two or three other wire service reporters were waiting. Helen was always there, usually sitting on the credenza just inside the hallway door. I had to get past her to the safety of my own office, and I knew the price of admission.

The wires just wanted a few lines, one or two sentences from the press secretary, for their P.M. stories. Generally, the deadline for wire stories that would reach their afternoon newspaper subscribers was 10 A.M. In addition, every morning the wire reporters were expected to write a "setup" story that outlined the president's day. That story would also dictate my own. Over the years, afternoon newspapers had diminished, beaten out by television and the evening news. It was hard to read a paper and watch TV at the same time, so most Americans gave up their papers. But the setup story took on new importance because it influenced the television coverage. Thousands of television editors would come to work that morning, check the wire services, and know that the White House was in disarray because of Wallison's comments on Iran-Contra. As I sat beside the Proctor sculpture, faintly wishing I was a "buckaroo" on some lonesome prairie, I gave myself the pep talk that took me through more than 2,000 such mornings. It was one word: "Charge."

I had watched professional golf for years, even though I seldom played, and had always admired Arnold Palmer's charge more than anything else. The pressure would grow silently and ominously for Arnie through seventy-two holes. Then at the end, about the sixteenth or seventeenth hole, when the crowd was wild, other players were dropping like flies, and it absolutely counted the most, Arnie would charge. I could feel it for him. It was a tightness in my chest and stomach, and in my mind the word "charge" would blast as if from a loudspeaker. I knew Arnie felt the same, just knew it, but his exterior was always calm and open. That's how I faced these moments with the press.

"Charge!" I said to myself, slowly opened the door, so as not to hurt anyone standing inside, and pushed it open against the credenza.

"Why couldn't Wallison get the facts?" Helen said, cutting straight to the point. "Is the White House in chaos?"

There you had it, why Helen is the best. In two short, no-nonsense questions, she had framed her objectives. The first question would prod me to advance the story, give her something new that would generate news. The second would get me to confirm the story so she could change the source from Wallison to me—that is, "Fitzwater said the White House was in chaos." I was determined not to allow the latter. Actually, I couldn't answer either question. I had not talked with Wallison, had no firsthand knowledge of the circumstances he was discussing, indeed was a total blank. But if I said nothing and claimed ignorance, she would write that I refused to comment, or stonewalled, or was upset, or all of the above. So I had to go to the "feed the lions" strategy, to give her a sentence on the subject so she could update the story and use my name, but nothing that advanced the story.

"Helen," I said, "I don't have any information on this. But let me say this: We are pleased that the independent counsel and the Congress are investigating this matter. We are not investigating ourselves. We will leave it to them to sort out."

Helen knew the game. She sat on the corner of the credenza, dangling black slacks over the edge into bright red patent-leather boots, the kind that only cover the ankles. With a solid black sweater, she had assembled a costume for the day that matched her mood, dark and ominous. As I spoke, she stared directly at me, writing feverishly in her reporter's notebook, in long, sweeping letters that amounted to only two or three words per line. She never looked at her writing. I was always mesmerized by her blind ability to write during interviews, and the quotes were indeed accurate.

"So what about Wallison?" she said.

"I'll check it out," I said, and turned to escape into my office. As the door closed, Roman Popadiuk came in behind me. He had been standing quietly in the back corner of the outer office, listening to the exchange with Helen. Roman worked for my foreign policy deputy, Dan Howard, was quiet and reserved, and had worked in the White House situation room before joining the press office staff. He was very smart. He was thin, with Eastern European features. And his eyes worked. You could actually witness information being assimilated through his eyes, as if his pupils were magnets that picked up words or actions and transmitted them by conveyer belt to the brain. I grew to rely on him completely, to the point of feeling insecure without him. Later he would become my deputy, always on call for work, and always responsive, even with three children under the age of three, and his wife, Judy, expecting their fourth. In 1991 he became America's first ambassador to the newly independent nation of Ukraine. But in 1987, I had only known him a week, and he was a Foreign Service officer with no press experience.

"What do you think, Roman?" I asked. "Is this a problem?"

"Nah," he said. "Wallison is a bit player. The press won't care about this."

At this point in his press education, Roman had a blind spot. He really didn't know what the press would do or be interested in. "Wrong, Roman," I said. "They love this. Internal feuding. Chaos. Legal counsel turned away. Another stone wall in the making. They will kill me at my briefing."

"Nah," Roman said. "They won't."

"I'm right on this, Roman. You don't know the press. Now get me everything you can on Wallison. What did he want this information for? What's he doing? When did he start? I'll take care of the nasty stuff, like why he's accusing his own president of covering up and how much longer he's going to work here."

"What will you say when the press asks if the president agrees with Wallison, or if he's going to fire him?"

"There is only one right answer to that question, Roman, and don't you ever forget it. The president has full confidence in everyone in the administration, right up until the day he fires them," I said. "If you don't say that, if you ever imply the president is down on someone, that person is dead. No one will return his calls. His power is gone. And you'll end up having to apologize to someone, probably the president. My rule is this: Never criticize anyone in the name of the president unless the president tells you to, and even then, don't do it. Two days later both of you will be apologizing to someone."

"OK," Roman said, thinking I was a bit melodramatic. "What will you say?" Howard Baker had just replaced Don Regan as chief of staff, Wallison had officially resigned but was still on the job, and other members of Regan's team were leaving daily. (More on the departure of Don Regan in Chapter 8.)

"I stall," I said. "Wallison is history. He has already resigned. His chief of staff, Don Regan, is gone. Howard Baker is bringing in a new counsel. I'll just say I have to check it out. Once Wallison's gone, we chart a new plan. Once he's gone, the press won't much care anyway. No power, no press."

"Listen, Marlin," Roman began shyly, "I don't know you very well, but you seem like a nice guy."

I thought it interesting that he was willing to be judgmental and tell me to my face. That meant he had independent support. Probably couldn't be fired by me. Probably didn't care.

"I worked in the situation room all through Iran-Contra," Roman said. "I don't know everything that happened, but I know these guys North and Poindexter and McFarlane were working all kinds of angles on Nicaragua. The NSC never tells anybody what's going on. And now, they are all running for cover, boy are they running for cover. I'll tell you one thing, you are never going to know what happened, you are never going to know the truth, and if you say anything on this it will probably be wrong."

"Come on, Roman!" I exclaimed. "What about the Wallison chronology?"

"That's a joke," he said. "Wallison will never know what happened."

I looked out the window that stretched from the floor to the eighteen-foot ceiling, at the quiet beauty of the north front grounds of the White House. People were moving along Pennsylvania Avenue, pointing cameras at me, and urging their children closer to the fence. An occasional pigeon landed on the drive, pecked for lunch crumbs, and flew off. It was a late winter morning, with the first hints of spring being artificially installed by the U.S. Park Service. Bright red and yellow tulips were being placed in the flower beds, fully grown and ready to sparkle for their president until it was time for the next season of color to spring up. I thought to remind myself to ask for some of those tulip bulbs in June when they are dug up and discarded in favor of the pansies and begonias.

"It's hard to believe this is happening," I said. "The world looks so peaceful. Nobody out there is lying to each other. Christ, I know you're right, Roman. We need to figure out about three lines to use on this thing and never deviate till it's over, even if that's a year or so. Let's write them down."

I swung around in my chair, away from the five clocks telling time in Moscow, Paris, London, Washington, and Abilene, pulled a yellow legal pad from my credenza, and wrote the lines I had already used with Helen. I couldn't get the picture out of my mind of Helen as a benevolent garden troll, at least as I had imagined it from my mother's reading of the Mother Goose fairy tales. Mom always described the troll who lived under the garden bridge as some half person, half animal who jumped out to capture innocent children, much the way Helen captured me every morning. But it also occurred to me this morning that the wire services performed a very useful purpose, as an early-warning system. I was now preparing answers I would have to give at the briefing, and Helen had given me a three-hour head start.

I wrote: First, the arms sales to Iran are being investigated by three independent bodies. We are not investigating ourselves. The independent counsel law was designed to prevent that.

Second, we are not going to comment on any revelation, or new information, or announcement that comes out of these investigations. We will comment only when the full investigations are completed.

Third, President Reagan brought this matter to the public's attention as soon as he discovered it. He asked for an independent counsel and the White House will fully cooperate with the investigations.

"Roman, do you think we should add a line that says the president had no knowledge of the diversion of funds from the arms sale to the Contras?" I asked.

"I don't know, Marlin," he said. "What if Poindexter testifies under oath that he told the president?"

"The president already has said he didn't know," I continued. "I assume he didn't. If anybody testifies otherwise, the president is dead meat anyway. This is the one solid conclusion that keeps the president out of this mess. I believe it's true because I know Poindexter and North. They are both 'need to know' freaks. And I believe they would rationalize that the president is better off not knowing. They certainly think everybody else is better off not knowing.

"This mess is so screwed up, and so complicated, no one will ever know what happened. It's important to get this one fact out, the president didn't know, and keep repeating it ad nauseam," I said.

"Who are you going to clear this with?" Roman asked.

"I don't know," I said. "Howard Baker just got here. A. B. Culvahouse, the new general counsel, hasn't arrived. I know the president will approve. It's not a formal statement or position, and it's in my name. I think I just go with it. It's eight A.M., time for senior staff, I'll see if anyone raises the story."

I got up from my desk, took my jacket off the back of one of the formal chairs grouped around a blue couch by my desk, and opened the door. Helen was still there. "What's Wallison say, Marlin?"

"Haven't talked to him yet, Helen." I walked past her, out the second door and into the hallway, past the *Buckaroo*, three quick steps to the Roosevelt Room, an oval-shaped conference room in the middle of the West Wing. It is the working meeting room for groups throughout the day. I always sat on the same side of the long table, about eight chairs from the end seat, which was always occupied by the chief of staff. We went through the president's schedule for the day—all routine. It was clear that Senator Baker had had a previous meeting in his office, attended by his personal staff just brought into the White House and Will Ball, assistant to the president for legislative affairs, one of the few holdovers from the Regan staff. I was not included, but experience told me that would come. Certainly, I could not ask to attend. That would be presumptuous. No, my plan was to do my job, brief every day, and use the press leverage to show my usefulness. It would soon be clear that if the new team wanted to get into the papers, I was the best conduit. It would also be clear that I was not promoting myself. I had been through this ritual before and I knew what to do. I had to prove myself all over again, that I could deal with the press, that I would say the right thing in public, that I reported press inquiries honestly, accurately, and quickly to the chief of staff, and lastly, that I cared about the president and about Howard Baker.

I had one other advantage. I knew that Senator Baker had asked President Reagan to bring Tom Griscom to the White House as press secretary. Tom had been his press secretary in the Senate, and was now opening a public relations firm in Washington with Jody Powell, former president Jimmy Carter's press secretary. President Reagan said no, Marlin was his press secretary. President Reagan bought my loyalty forever with that commitment, and I vowed to live up to his trust in a way that never threatened Howard Baker. I was lucky, because Senator Baker was a great chief of staff, one who probably saved the presidency during the Iran-Contra period, and Tom Griscom was the best communications director the White House ever had. In addition, both men were more than honest and generous with me. After I had been on the job about six weeks, Griscom leaned over to me during a staff meeting one morning and said I should be going to Senator Baker's private staff meeting at 7:30 A.M. The next morning I became part of the team.

On this Friday the thirteenth, however, the regular staff meeting was uneventful; Wallison was not there and was never mentioned. It ended quickly and I returned to my office to hold my own staff meeting. Helen was still waiting. "What did Wallison say?" she asked.

"He wasn't there," I replied and hurried past her.

Helen sort of slid off the credenza, and began her deliberate walk down the hall away from my office, through the press briefing room, still dark in the early morning, and into the work area where the UPI booth was located. The table in her five-by-five booth was low to accommodate computers, and Helen's swivel secretarial chair was screwed down as far as it could go. She had used it for so long that the seat was concave where the padding sank into the springs. When you peered through the glass window in the booth, Helen looked like a lump of coal, always dressed in black to highlight her dark hair and Lebanese features, slumped over her computer, with her ever-present notepad on the desk corner. Sometimes I walked up to the window and watched as she turned the pages of the notepad, seldom containing more than five or six scrawled words per page, and translated them into sentences on the green glowing screen. She turned those chicken scratch words into full quotes, accurate to the smallest pronoun and transcribed with every verb and adjective in place, the product of decades of note taking and mental discipline. Anyone finding her notebook with every page filled could never put together a complete sentence. She has her own secret code of note taking that even she cannot explain. "I just remember," she says.

My staff began collecting in my office at 8:30 A.M. The "lower press office kids," I called them, young and attractive, from the best schools, mostly products of successful families and a history of volunteering for Republican candidates. But all were enormously hardworking, from eight in the morning till eight at night, often till midnight, and on the road two or three days a week. Their social life was scarce, usually measured by the constant awareness that their actions might reflect on the president. They worked in a small office with seven desks along the walls, adjoining the press briefing room. Reporters were in their faces all day, some from boredom, some inquiring about schedules, press releases, pools, and speeches. And the reporters, like customers, are always right. There is no talking back. Discipline is the key and tolerance is essential. If corporate employers saw these kids in action they would be hired away in a minute.

In any situation where people face a common threat, if only to their sanity, there must be a release mechanism for their emotions. I made my office that mechanism. On my first day on the job, I laid down this dictum: "We never discuss outside my office what goes on inside these walls. We meet every morning at eight-thirty and every afternoon at five-thirty. During these meetings you can do or say anything you want. During your day, you will come to hate reporters, hate me, hate the president, hate the person at the next desk. But get over it. No antagonism is allowed to last past the end of the

day. And here in this room is where we laugh, play, and hate together. Then we go out and do a professional job."

Since I had been hired to replace Larry Speakes, who resigned
after serving nearly six years as presidential spokesman, most of my
staff had been hired by him. After only six weeks, they were still sizing me up.

Normally, there was one story each day that dominated the news
and my briefing. My goal was to find some way to "advance" that
story, to make it new, to give it a White House dimension, to add
color, to give it urgency, all with the aim of influencing the story so
it reflected the president's viewpoint.

My second goal was to know five basic facts about five other stories that would be of interest to the press. If I could do this, I would
be smarter than they.

On this morning, I was lucky. Helen had tipped me to the story
of the day. It would be the follow-up on Wallison. Since he had given
his interview only to *The New York Times*, every other news outlet
had to match the story. The secret to my getting ahead of the story
was to tactically advance it with new facts, a most difficult task
when my strategy was to say nothing substantive about Iran-Contra.
I decided to go with my new policy on White House comments, read
the statements as if written by God or at least the chief of staff, and
then hope they dominated the Wallison story.

Gerald Warren, a deputy press secretary in the Nixon White
House, told me once to always research the top story myself. But I
needed my staff for the other five. I opened the staff meeting with
the president's schedule, which was routine all day. One pool to be
escorted to a ceremony. Nothing on the president's schedule would
overwhelm the Wallison story. I was left to fight this one alone.

"Keep your ears open down there today," I told my staff. "Listen
for the anger. Is anyone really pissed at this Wallison thing, or do
they dismiss his comments as CYA [cover your ass]? Also, let me
know if this is the television network story of the day. If it is, I have
to be stern as hell, to treat this really serious. If they are dismissing
it, I will try to get in and out of it quick, not build up the story. Also,
try and find out what Lou Cannon or David Hoffman of *The Washington Post* think. They may be so mad that the *Times* got the story,
they will ignore it just to devalue the *Times*'s scoop. If that's the
case, I really want to lie low."

We had only two hours for all this to happen, but in that time
every reporter in the building would pass through the lower press of-

fice. Half of them would call in to check the president's schedule. If my people were alert, I would have those answers by eleven o'clock.

I started getting ready for the briefing one hour in advance, with all three deputies and one lower press office representative with me. We began by going through the issues.

"Roman," I asked, "what have you got on the foreign side?"

"Sam Nunn says we're trying to reinterpret the ABM treaty so we can test Star Wars."

"Are we?"

"Probably," he said, "but we're saying no."

"Christ, Roman, I don't know anything about the ABM treaty, and I always get twisted around on our position. One wrong word and I make policy. What do I say?"

"I'll write it up," he said. "You stick to it. Read it. No matter what they ask, just reread it."

"Roman," I protested, "that makes me sound so stupid. Can't we get an arms expert down here to explain it to me?"

"Sure, but you still won't understand it," he said, laughing, not at my inability to learn, but at the missile man's inability to explain anything in plain English.

"Get him," I said. "I would rather humiliate myself in front of an arms control colonel than seventy reporters. What else have you got?"

"Israel still doesn't want to investigate the Jonathan Pollard spy case, at least according to the *Post*. Pollard spied on us for Israel. He's already been convicted here and is in jail. Now Israel is trying to decide what to do."

"What the hell do I say about that?" I demanded, as if Roman was responsible for U.S. reporters asking irrelevant questions.

"Someone's going to ask," he said.

"Of course. 'Tell me why our best friend, Israel, to whom we give three billion dollars a year, would spy on us and why don't we care,' " I said, instantly recognizing the logic of why this would come up.

"Can't I brush this off?" I asked. "Just say that we have convicted Pollard. He's in the slammer. Israel is an old friend. But we have expressed our disappointment publicly about their action. We have, haven't we?"

"Yes. I'll get you Secretary Shultz's statement to Congress this week," Roman answered.

"Good, pull out three paragraphs that I can read with the proper indignation. That way I can register emotional anger, but the words are Shultz's. Also the nets won't use it if I say exactly the same thing. Remember, my goal is to please them, not to make news."

"Right," Roman said, "but it's high-risk. If you say one extra word, they will say you ratcheted up the rhetoric against Israel."

"I'll be careful. Anything else? No? What have we got for domestic policy? Iran-Contra is taken care of."

"Duberstein as chief of staff," said Laura Melillo. Kenneth Duberstein, who had earlier worked in the Reagan legislative affairs office, was being brought back as deputy chief of staff under Howard Baker.

"What about it?" I asked.

"I don't know," she said, laughing. "I just saw it in the clips."

"Think. How can the press twist this?" I said.

"How about this?" she said. "They ask if Duberstein is going to run things here so Senator Baker can find time to run for president in 1988? Or is Duberstein here to handle Mrs. Reagan?"

"Very good, Laura. You're learning," I said. "Now what's the answer?" Before she could respond, I answered myself, "No to the Baker run for president. Even if it's true, he won't say it or admit it. No to the second because nobody handles Mrs. Reagan."

"Poor choice of words," Roman said.

"Anything on the economy?" I asked. "Who has an inflation statement?"

I loved these economic statements because the press hated them. They were statistically based, and real news that the press could not ignore. The government's economic indicators are reported around the world every month, and the White House reaction is always sought. I knew that if I could craft one colorful sentence, at least more colorful than the stock index, it would get into print. So I never missed an opportunity to jump on good news, and in 1987 the economy was booming.

Rusty Brashear or B. Jay Cooper, my domestic policy deputies at the time, would hand me a statement that read, "February figures for industrial production and the producer price index show a growing American economy that continues to produce more goods, all without the pain of the crippling inflation that the president encountered when he first took office." Guaranteed to run on all the wire services today and in every paper in America tomorrow. The press would groan when I read this. But it would be at least one small victory for the day.

"All right, I'm ready," I said. I collected my notes, especially my statement on Wallison, shoved them into a black briefing book, and stood up to get a breath. I couldn't seem to get the right briefing book system. The first week I just used loose sheets of paper, but they kept sliding off the podium, so I ordered a new podium that could hold volumes of papers. It had big rolled sides that fit my clenched fist like a baseball bat, and when tensions were high I grasped those sides and hung on as if clinging to the rail of a battleship. But the podium wasn't enough.

I went to the State Department to see how they gathered policy statements on every country in the world and placed them in clear plastic folders in a black briefing book that the press spokesman seemingly could scan in a matter of seconds. There must have been a dozen people working on this book, reviewing each policy position, editing it into harmless prose, signing their initials at the bottom, and passing it along until it reached the deputy secretary of state. Sometimes I called State and asked for a position before their briefing book had gone to the "DepSec"—that's the way they talk over there—and they always refused to give it to me. I always pictured the "DepSec" sitting in his enormous antique-and-Persian-rug office on the seventh floor of State, waiting for his briefing book to come, and singing to the tune of a popular wine commercial, "No policy before its time."

I clearly couldn't use this technique. Not enough time or people. Also, I didn't want a review process that squeezed all the juice out of the statement. Once, when I had run out of things to say in a briefing, I admitted it at the podium. Bruce Drake, a quick-witted reporter for the New York *Daily News,* spoke up: "Why don't you read us the highlights of the State Department guidance?" The place roared. State Department blandness was legendary.

I put my jacket on and fought the butterflies and the fear. Always the fear, from the first day in 1987 to January 20, 1993, there was always fear. Unfortunately, fear leads to an overwhelming desire to use the bathroom.

"Call the briefing," I said to Liz Murphy Kloak, a young assistant. They were always the last words spoken before heading for the podium, my signal that the prebrief was over. If I hadn't learned it now I never would, at least not in this news cycle. When my staff heard the word "call," they began to run. Liz stepped outside and told my secretary to call the briefing. She immediately swung around in her chair, pressed three special buttons on the phone, and announced on the loudspeaker system that Mr. Fitzwater's briefing was about to begin. Liz headed for the lower press office to alert the staff, get the podium secured, the klieg lights on, the microphones and amplifiers in place, and clean up any old newspapers left strewn about the podium. She also checked to see that no one had placed obscene pictures or derogatory comments on the stage. All of this had to occur in the two minutes it would take me to stop by the bathroom next to the Oval Office.

It was a one-holer. Can you imagine? In the West Wing of the White House, the only bathroom for guests and staff near the Oval Office is a one-holer. Worse, it's so small that when you open the door, you have to turn sideways to squeeze between the door and the sink to get to the throne. And if you forget to slide the 1896 Thomas Jefferson all-brass door lock into place, someone is bound to walk in on you, most likely the vice president or at least a cabinet officer. This could be very disconcerting, especially when I was en route to the briefing room.

As I reached the briefing room, the television lights flashed on. The standing-room-only crowd was positioned around the back and side aisles, reporters were holding their tape recorders, and the White House Communications Agency Army enlisted man was ready with electronic boxes that would beam my briefing into the Foreign Press Center across town, to the State and Defense Departments, to other White House staff, and finally to the Oval Office, to an audience of one that loomed behind me like the Wizard of Oz. "Go get 'em, Max Marlin," Laura said as I rushed past her into the briefing room, and took my first reading on the group before me.

The press was relatively calm. The $2 million front row was in place. Kindly and dignified Ralph Harris of Reuters, his British accent and manners making him a continual delight to work with, sat on the far left. Next to him, Sam Donaldson of ABC News, perennial shouter at presidents and general all-round champion show-off, seen by the general public as rude, but in fact a rather nice guy and probably the most objective and hardworking journalist in television. He knew his medium, and could boil a complicated story down to thirty seconds with ease. He chewed up producers because he was demanding, often waited till the last minute to put his script together, and yelled at people. Yet there was an honesty about his reporting that raised him above the masses, an ability to ask tough questions of everybody. During the 1992 campaign, I recommended Sam for every campaign debate panel, not because he would be easy on President Bush, but because he would be tough on both candidates. I could always count on Sam for a fair fight, even though he jokes at cocktail parties about kicking people when they're down.

Next to him sat Helen Thomas. Close to seventy at this point and a fixture at UPI for nearly forty years, she could sense a White House story three days before it was conceived. She set off a lot of smoke in the briefing room, and challenged me not to turn it into fire. That means she often asked questions designed to raise my hackles and get an angry response. If I succumbed, she got the story. If I said nothing, she lost nothing. It was all part of the psychological warfare. Few reporters in the White House can create news the way Helen Thomas does. There is no other reporter like her.

Next to her, and directly in front of me, sat Lesley Stahl of CBS News. Lesley fought her way to the top in a man's world by taking no guff from anyone and keeping her on-camera beauty well into her forties. Ambition is her guiding light. She is tough, unyielding, and, unfortunately for flacks and press secretaries, seldom swayed by the power of an argument. What counts is her initial position, usually dictated by her New York producers, or her sense of the little guy versus the institution. She makes several million a year in total income yet always takes the reporting stance that money corrupts. You can argue a story with her until you are blue in the face but she will never change her angle. This makes her difficult for press secretaries, but absolutely perfect for the *60 Minutes* show where she now appears. They have the same attitude.

Next to her, Terry Hunt, White House bureau chief of the Associated Press, whose round face and gentle complexion often lead people to underestimate his age and the pepper in his reporting. No spokesman lasts long in the White House without being burned by Terry. It is a strange phenomenon, in which about twice a year he reports a conversation overheard in the men's room or a quote that was said in jest, so the White House staff is always afraid of him. If you can overlook those two occasions a year, he is an excellent reporter.

Next to him sat two people in one chair, or so it seemed, Chris Wallace and Andrea Mitchell of NBC News, who shadowed each other through the day with Shakespearean staging. I viewed them both as dark characters in a play, perhaps *Who's Afraid of Virginia Woolf?*, slightly humorous in their personal competition, driven in their quest for prominence and network adoration, and Machiavellian in the lengths they would go to gain advantage over one another. Their personal relationship was even written into their contract:

Chris was number one and Andrea number two. But if Chris was sick or out of town, then Andrea was number one. And God help us on those days, because Andrea would get on the evening news one way or another. It could be gentle if we helped her with good information and a high-level official for a sound bite, or painful if we ignored her or refused to help. It wasn't blackmail, really, just a fact of life. They were like kids that you have to watch constantly to keep out of trouble.

Chris Wallace had a special burden to bear because his father is a famous CBS newsman. Further, Chris was raised in the finest penthouses and private schools with appropriate Martha's Vineyard summers. Thus, when Chris Wallace accompanied Ronald Reagan into the barracks of U.S. troops at the demilitarized zone between North and South Korea, he looked at the row after row of bunk bed and exclaimed, "Gee, this is just like on TV." Television was his reality.

Normally, Chris was in the front-row chair, being number one. But often, Andrea would stake out a seat in the second row by identifying someone who was sick or late. It always seemed her face was near the front when the briefing began. It was unwritten, unspoken, and never told to me, but I always felt it would have been a violation of their contract for me to call on Andrea first. I never tested the fates enough to try.

The overhead camera lights were on that day for a local television station doing a profile story on Helen Thomas. Normally, I didn't allow "sound and cameras," which meant no TV coverage, so that if I made a mistake during the briefing the networks couldn't show it every night for a week, as they often did high-level slips of the tongue. Connie Lawn of Radio New Zealand once asked for my reaction to a decision by the Danish parliament not to allow U.S. warships in Danish harbors unless we acknowledged the presence of nuclear weapons on board. As a matter of U.S. policy, we never acknowledged the presence of nuclear weapons on board, period. I knew the policy but not the flap. I simply missed the story.

"I missed this," I said, hoping to deflect the question with honesty and humor. "To me Danish means breakfast." The press laughed then moaned, like any group hearing a bad joke or one they knew would get me in trouble. The AP headline in London said "Fitzwater Says Danish Means Breakfast." By midafternoon, the headline had been changed to read "Fitzwater Eats Danes for Breakfast." I issued a public apology to Denmark, the Danish ambassador in Washington, Secretary of State George Shultz, and anybody else who asked. Thank God it wasn't on film.

"No sound" was a self-protection, waived for five minutes at the top of this briefing to accommodate Helen. Since I had gone this far to curry favor with her, I sealed the bargain by opening with a tribute.

"The sound and cameras today are in honor of Helen Thomas, who has been with the White House press corps for 342 years." Everyone laughed. "Helen starts my day every day by saying, 'What's cooking?' "

I figured that would be a good sound bite. Helen picked up on it immediately.

"Well, what *is* cooking?" she asked. "(Laughter.)" The word "laughter" in parentheses was printed in all transcripts of my briefings. This notation of audience reaction was crucial in a briefing setting where kibitzing was normal, but no matter how funny the comment, it often was not so funny in print. Thus comments made in jest were often read a few hours later by the prime minister of another country as derogatory. The transcript helped.

I moved quickly from Helen to a mistake on our daily presidential schedule.

"We mistakenly put on the schedule last night that the president was having a National Security Council meeting this morning at eleven A.M. It's a general information meeting and not a decision meeting." This last phrase was designed to downplay the meeting, but the press was not to be thrown off.

"What's the information about?" they asked.

"I can't divulge the subject, but it's a general kind of update meeting," I said.

"You mean you regret that it was put on the schedule?" they said.

"Yes," I replied meekly. They had me. They knew better than I that we never acknowledged NSC meetings, let alone announce them. I would have to explain this one to the president's national security adviser, Frank Carlucci, and quick, before the first reporter could call him, which they would do immediately after the briefing.

"Are you going to the meeting?" they asked.

"Yes," I replied.

"So it can't be important," came the retort. They never missed an opportunity to slip in the knife. It was also a test. They wanted to see if I became defensive or testy under ridicule.

"Oh, what a cheap shot," I said, smiling. "On camera, with sound, and you pull that on me? (Laughter.) Have you no shame?" The humor worked. They moved on.

I went through the president's schedule for the day and read the statement on inflation. That was my transition to serious matters. The press dutifully took it down, then turned to the business at hand. My heart began racing. The preliminaries had gone well, a little humor, a good economic story, no one seemed really angry.

"Did Wallison tell the president that Poindexter told him that he had no role—as the Iran affair broke? That he had no role in investigating it? I mean, was the president aware that there was this standoff?" Leave it to Sam to get things rolling. His famous television voice was rising and falling in each sentence, punctuating the incredulity of his question, making it clear that he could not believe the president's naïveté or Poindexter's collusion. Reporter questions are seldom uttered in full sentences. One question tends to bounce off another. Even Sam was hard to follow.

"I saw the story in the *Times* this morning where Peter says that—talks about his relationship with Poindexter," I said. "I have no reason to doubt that, but I don't have any independent knowledge of what his relationship with Poindexter was." I mentioned the *Times* to signal that I had no independent knowledge and did not intend to make news on this matter.

"Well, it isn't just that," Sam said. "We want to know if the president was told that Poindexter was stonewalling on giving information?" The press always wants to take the information to the president, put it in his mouth, and then figure the consequences. Indeed, all that really matters to them is the president.

"I don't think the president was told at the time," I ventured, "but I don't know about subsequent conversations." I had no idea, of course, but decided to take a chance on the first phrase in order to give credibility to the second. If Wallison had told the president, he would have said so in the interview.

"We were told every day here at briefings that Peter Wallison was working on a chronology for the president, that's why you couldn't answer questions. Excuse me, your predecessor."

Now Sam was getting worked up. He was about to enter a sensitive area of questioning about my predecessor, Larry Speakes, who had left the White House with a lot of antagonism between himself and the press. I had to get out of it quick.

"Well, unfortunately, Peter is out of town today . . ."

"Yes, I bet," Sam said, smiling.

Then Chris Wallace picked up the trail, holding a copy of the *Times*, as he often did, and trying to ascertain some ambiguity between my comments and Wallison's. "But when did—yes—Wallison also says that referring to the president then—the Iran initiative—he says the president does not agree with the Tower Board that he shouldn't have done it and he still believes the policy is valid. Is that an accurate reflection of the president's views?"

Accurate? I couldn't even tell what Chris was saying, let alone Wallison.

"Do these people think I go to the president every morning and get him to reflect on stories?" I thought. "Do they think we just sit around and chew the fat each morning on what's in the news?" Whenever the press got around to the "What does the president think?" questions, I knew it was time to lay down some rules and get serious.

"The president's position was stated in his March fourth speech at some length. It has not changed. And I refer you to that speech," I said, inferring that I was not going to speculate.

"So Peter is wrong about the president having no regrets?" Chris said.

The president's speech on March 4, 1987, his first following the Tower Board report released on February 26, accepted the board's conclusions and expressed his regret about the arms-for-hostages action. Now Chris thought he could get me to acknowledge some kind of change in the president's position, thereby ratcheting up the story for his evening news piece.

We argued back and forth for several minutes, just repeating questions and answers. I got so involved in the questioning, and trying to follow the twisted logic they were presenting, that I forgot to present my new policy. I did get it in piecemeal, saying the White House was not investigating itself, the president did not know of the diversion of funds, and we welcomed the independent counsel investigation. But it was a poor performance and I knew I would not capture the offensive in tonight's stories. At least I hadn't gotten into trouble by offering any new evidence that could be presented to the Congress or used to embarrass me.

Then Helen took a wild guess, or maybe it was her sixth sense, or maybe someone told her, and she asked if the president was going to amend his acceptance of the Tower Board report in his Saturday radio address. The cat was out of the bag. I had to be careful not to say anything that would later be contradicted. Indeed, Secretary of Defense Caspar Weinberger was begging the president to exonerate him in the Saturday address. The Tower Board said that although Weinberger did not support the policy of arms for hostages, he did not stop it or try hard enough to stop it. Among the president's legal and personal advisers, from new chief of staff Howard Baker and his legal counsel, A. B. Culvahouse, to Ambassador David Abshire, who had been brought in to help the president understand the complexities involved, the consensus was that the president had to accept the entire Tower report. He could not pick and choose among the conclusions, or the American people would never believe the report or the president. Now Weinberger was pushing to have the president say he accepted everything in the report, except the part about Weinberger.

"There will be some mention of Secretary Shultz and Secretary Weinberger in the address," I said, "but that's all I can say."

This prompted a chorus of questions. Once I let them know that Shultz also wanted absolution, the pressure was even greater. They knew that Secretary of State George Shultz threatened to quit every time someone in the administration questioned his authority. At the drop of a hat he would march into the chief of staff's office, snorting like Ferdinand the Bull, to announce he would quit if he couldn't have his way.

"In other words, Weinberger is really putting pressure on the president?" someone asked.

"Has Secretary Shultz weighed in on this question?"

"Does the president accept it in full or not?"

"The president's position is quite clear in his speech and it will be clear tomorrow in his Saturday radio address," I said. "I have nothing to add."

They started again, like cannon fire.

"Well, how can it be clear in two ways?"

"How can you tell that it's clear tomorrow if you haven't seen it?"

"Because everything the president says is clear," I said, hoping for levity.

"He's the Wizard of Oz," someone joked.

"Do you enjoy your job?" Helen asked sheepishly.

What they didn't know: My job was precariously balanced at that moment between the competing forces of presidential loyalty, a cabinet officer's pique, and staff authority. The press had been asking for days about the president's acceptance of the Tower Board conclusions. This was the vehicle for President Reagan to use in admitting he had, however inadvertently, traded arms to Iran for hostages in Lebanon. The press always demands its pound of flesh. In my judgment, this admission by the president added up to at least fourteen ounces of that demand. But I reasoned, and everyone else in the White House agreed, that the president's acceptance of the Tower Board report must be total.

So when the press started pressing me on specific aspects of the Tower Board report, I gave the same boilerplate answer to every question. Again, my purpose was to not weaken the president's acceptance of the report.

"Does he accept the need for NSC reorganization?" Answer: He accepts the entire report.

"Does he agree that a civilian should head the NSC?" Answer: He accepts the entire report.

"Does he agree that Shultz and Weinberger could have done more to stop the transaction?" Answer: He accepts the entire report.

Oops. One too many boilerplate answers to suit Cap Weinberger. He was outraged. He proclaimed his innocence in phone calls to Chief of Staff Baker and others. Finally, he visited Howard Baker's office to demand that Press Secretary Fitzwater retract his statement, or that the president make a statement. He also suggested that I was not up to the job and should be replaced before further damage could be done. This recommendation was made to Howard Baker, a man who had been on the job only two weeks himself and who had tried to hire his own press secretary in the first place.

But Howard Baker agreed with me, and he realized it was his job to protect the president, not cabinet officers. Privately, I was disgusted that someone who claimed to be Ronald Reagan's oldest and dearest friend, as Weinberger did, seemed so willing to do this to the president in order to purify himself. It struck me as damn selfish.

Nevertheless, I was more than a little frightened by Weinberger's continuing anger toward me. I stopped Howard Baker in the hall: "Have you talked to Cap?"

"I have," Howard said matter-of-factly. Sometimes, when Baker was angry, or felt he was being needlessly and foolishly cornered, his comments got very short.

"What's he want?" I asked.

"He wants a presidential retraction and he wants you," Howard said.

"He wants me fired?" I asked.

"Yes he does," Howard said, "but I don't think we'll do it." His Tennessee accent was most pronounced, and tended to accentuate the last syllables spoken, so that "do it" became "doit." But long years in Washington had no doubt taught the senator to separate the words and accentuate the difference, so that the last word of the sentence, no matter how small the pronoun, seemed to have special meaning and emphasis. In this case "I don't think we'll do it" became a clarion call of support that bonded my loyalty to Senator Baker forever. Although I knew this Weinberger feud could not be allowed to fester.

I rushed back to my office and dictated a note to Weinberger saying: "I just want to let you know personally how much I regret the stories involving my comments on your advice to the president concerning Iran." It said more, but the essential grovel was there. It was Fitzwater's second rule applied: "Grovel if you have to."

But Weinberger was determined. He demanded a meeting with the president, got it, and convinced the president to "say something" in his Saturday radio address. The actual language was: "In the case of the Iranian arms sale matter, both Secretary Shultz and Secretary Weinberger advised me strongly not to pursue the initiative. I weighed their advice, but decided in the end that the initiative was worth the risk—and went forward. As we now know, it turned out they were right and I was wrong."

I could not believe it. How could these people hold the president up to more ridicule just to protect their own reputations?

Ten days after the radio address, I received a note from Cap that read in part, "I share your assessment that we are both here to serve the president to the best of our abilities, and I hope that we are able to establish a good working relationship in the future."

How ironic that, six years later, Caspar Weinberger would need a lot more help from President Bush than he was being asked to give President Reagan. I was in the Oval Office with President Bush as he stuffed his briefcase in preparation for a last weekend at Camp David in December 1992. Cap Weinberger was about to go to trial for withholding documents in the Iran-Contra matter as charged by Independent Counsel Lawrence Walsh. The president looked up, snapped the locks on his briefcase shut, and asked me for the third time that week, "I have to decide the pardons this weekend, Marlin," he said. "What do you think?"

I said the same thing I had said the other two times, "I think you should pardon them all, Mr. President," I said. "Certainly Weinberger, and probably the others too. The Weinberger indictment shows how vindictive Walsh has become, and everybody in America recognizes it. They know it's ludicrous to indict someone who was against the arms sale in the first place. The press will raise hell if you pardon anybody." As I walked back to my office, I pondered my special place in heaven for defending Cap Weinberger. I also made a mental note that one of President Bush's last official acts, the pardons, sacrificed some of his own reputation to save that of Secretary Weinberger. Cap had not been nearly as generous to Ronald Reagan.

My press briefing on this Friday, March 13, 1987, droned on. I made a second attempt to get my new Iran-Contra statement out, but in halfhearted form: "The Iran situation continues to be investigated by the independent counsel. There will be hearings and further investigations by the House and Senate select committees. All indications are that these will go on for several months. The president wants to get the facts out to the American people; he wants all the investigations to continue as rapidly as possible; and to be as thoroughly investigated as possible."

At least I wasn't defensive. I was still standing. The briefing had lasted only thirty-nine minutes, relatively short by daily standards.

When Helen said "Thank you," as she did by tradition as the "dean" of the White House press corps, it was with reluctance. She always acted like she hated to give up that control, to let me go. She knew that no press secretary had ever walked away from a briefing without being excused and survived. It was the tightest unwritten rule: "The Press Secretary Stays Until He Is Dismissed by the Press." It is their iron grip on your life. It is why there is no premium on snappy answers, or concise statements, or even great presentation. The premium is on patience and survivability, because they will hold you at the podium until everyone has tried breaking you.

There is a Wild West quality to it. You feel like the gunslinger at first, armed with presidential words and deeds, dressed a little better than most correspondents, in the spotlight, and full of confidence in the rightness of your cause. But each reporter has a hold on you, an invisible string tied to your belt buckle that pulls and tugs with each question, as if you were tied to the ground near anthills, and they torture you with repetitive questions. When they see that your mouth is dry, and you have squandered every ounce of knowledge, and you have probably made at least one embarrassing slip that will elicit ridicule from White House colleagues and a frown from the president, then Helen turns in her seat, twists until she can see over her shoulder, and decides if the lions have any fight left. If not, you are thanked and dismissed.

I moved quickly off the podium and retraced my steps up the hall, past the lower press office, past the Oval, and toward my door. Behind me I could hear the footsteps, like a herd of horses, fast and hard as if galloping, and reporters calling my name. "Marlin, what about Weinberger? Marlin, when's the press conference?"

I rushed into my office, allowed Roman to enter right behind me, then firmly closed the door. I walked over to my desk, totally drained, legs weak with strain, my suit soaked from the sweat of fear and tension, and dropped into my chair. Roman said nothing. He could see I was an empty vessel.

"Roman," I asked, "why do these people rush up here behind me to ask the same questions we have just argued about for forty minutes?"

"They think you'll give them something more," he said, "say in private what you wouldn't say on the podium."

"That's crazy," I said. "If I did that just once, they would never again believe what I said on the podium. I would have to give two briefings every day. I won't do this."

Roman said nothing. He just sat and let the anger flow out of me. How could either of us have believed that we would do this more than 850 more times over the next six years. We were both wondering how we could do it even one more time—tomorrow. I was so exhausted that I totally forgot about the anguish over Peter Wallison that had loomed so large just one hour previously. Indeed, Wallison left the White House that weekend to join a prestigious Washington law practice, and the press corps never asked about him again.

This was my first experience in the eye of a Washington scandal frenzy, in which the spotlight searches every day for a new victim, a full media cycle of newspaper articles, evening news broadcasts, and weekend talk shows will be dedicated to any face that falls in its glare. Then, in about five days, it moves on. This is a reflexive, not a contemplative process. Wallison was a nonplayer in Iran-Contra, but he raised his head above the fog with one newspaper interview, and the media pounced on him like a leopard on sheep.

The independent counsel law is the perfect catalyst for this process. It is a legal process outside the law. It establishes a group of prosecutors to go after people even before it's shown that a crime has been committed. It joins the press, feeds the press, in a public prosecution that destroys individual reputations and finances well before crimes are ever established. It criminalizes public policy by allowing investigations to destroy political opponents, and creates media frenzies that drive people from office. The list is long of public officials destroyed by independent counsels long before their innocence is established. It is a Washington dance of death in which politicians, the press, and most of official Washington become mesmerized by the scandal they have created, and cannot stop their feeding until the victim is devoured. The ultimate irony of all this is that the independent counsels haven't been nearly as successful as the Department of Justice in investigating government misconduct.

CHAPTER SIX

Showdown in the East Room

I hate sweat. We all sweat, especially under pressure, especially under television lights that raise the room temperature to over ninety degrees. At President Reagan's first press conference following the release of the Tower Board report, the East Room of the White House was white hot with media intensity. The president had given one prepared speech on the report in which he took responsibility for the arms sales to Iran and acknowledged that it amounted to trading arms for hostages. This was not illegal, of course, but it was a violation of his often-stated policy against it. Now the press wanted their shot, to see if he could take the pressure, to see if the old Gipper could enter their den and face them down as he had so many times before.

The press thought they had him this time. The issues in Iran-Contra were complex and the sequences of "who talked to who, and when?" were impossible to follow. In one of the most complex and strongest political alliances in history, the press, the relevant congressional committees, the independent counsel, and the president's political opponents had managed to weave a web of apparent conspiracy in which people actually believed that it was illegal for government officials, especially the president, to have known about their own policies. In Watergate, a simple and obvious crime had been committed when the White House plumbers broke into Democratic National Committee headquarters to steal campaign information. At that time, the questions centered on White House efforts to cover up the crime. As Senator Howard Baker, of the Watergate Investigating Committee, put it about President Nixon, "What did he know and when did he know it?" In Iran-Contra, the

power sources of Washington had managed to resurrect this same
scenario, but without the crime. Yet after seven years and nearly $40
million, the independent counsel and his team of lawyers never even
attempted to prove that it was illegal to sell arms to Iran, or provide
arms to the Nicaraguan Contras. But they did manage to make people believe it was illegal to know about it. Thus Senator Baker's famous axiom became a measure of criminality even though no crime
had been committed. Ironically, it now fell to the same Senator
Baker, as Ronald Reagan's third chief of staff, to prove that all this
didn't matter in terms of a functioning presidency. The president's
speech on March 4 accepting the Tower Board report was the first
step.

The president's press conference on March 19, 1987, was the second step. The press had built up expectations to the point where people thought Ronald Wilson Reagan might actually wilt under the
intense pressure of Sam Donaldson, turn in his six-guns, and stumble off the stage in total humiliation, with Dan Rather intoning in
the background about how the great and righteous media arm of
democracy had once again saved the country—what a cockamamy
idea! I did think it possible, however, that a bad performance by the
president could leave his presidency in a sadly weakened state, with
the press continuing to describe his remaining two years as "lame
duck" and mortally ineffective.

As in any gunfight, it's hard to win when the other guy is wearing a bulletproof vest. In any case, the press can never be destroyed.
They determine their own condition. Winning means convincing
the press to let you live. So the trick was to get headlines that said
the president gave a good performance, shot straight, and was still
tall in the saddle. One of the most crucial tasks was to not make the
press look bad. The president could not be too good. He certainly
could not lose his temper and lash out at any individual reporter.
They would never forgive him for that. Fortunately, that was not
Ronald Reagan's style.

A New Yorker magazine article in 1992 chronicled the reopening
of an enlarged Guggenheim Museum that was widely heralded in the
popular press. The author, a Mr. Adam Gopnik, found the opening
was attended almost entirely by art world professionals and not the
general public. He wrote, "The message that had been sent, however
subliminally, by all the hype in the press was: This one's for us. The
pros had elbowed the public aside."

So it was with this press conference. This one was for the media.

It was an anointment of their growing post-Watergate power, affir-
mation of their right to determine criminal conduct, the ultimate in
political correctness. The president was being brought before the
press.

I was sweating. Only the day before, after a presidential meeting
with congressional leaders, Senator Alan Simpson, Republican of
Wyoming, walked from the front door of the White House West
Wing, strode over to the waiting stakeout cameras, and laid into the
press about their treatment of the president. "You're asking him
things because you know he's off balance and you'd like to stick it
in his gazoo," he shouted, as he raised his hands in front of his face,
cupped his fingers into claws, and twisted his face to represent a
snarling animal. The picture appeared on the front page of nearly
every newspaper in the country. The press laughed, because Senator
Simpson had been a darling of the press, always witty and slyly humorous, a favorite in the Washington after-dinner circles where the
elite meet to reaffirm their power by poking fun at their own foibles.
But the trick of humor in Washington is that it has to be about subjects everybody agrees are humorous, and in settings where humor
is expected. This occasion did not qualify. Plus, the senator committed the most heinous crime—holding the press up to public
ridicule, for which there is no forgiveness.

Almost everyone in the White House loved this episode. For me,
it spawned fear and trembling. Success draws mimics. While I recommended that everyone support Senator Simpson, we could not
mimic his performance or use it against the press. This incident was
fresh in every reporter's mind as they gathered for this press conference, another factor that gave tension to the evening. Now the press
corps knew it had been targeted as the enemy. It also knew that the
Simpson gazoo was widely applauded around the country. It
spawned angry articles and letters to editors. It established a yardstick for measuring the press's performance, and they resented it,
deeply. I hoped for some way to relieve the tension. It did not help
the president to have the press trying to destroy him in order to destroy Simpson. So I tried humor.

I walked to the microphone at three minutes before eight o'clock
and laid out the standard ground rules for the press conference. It
would be thirty minutes long. Terry Hunt of AP would have the first
question. Then I added, "I have one announcement tonight. Senator
Alan Simpson is my new deputy press secretary." They laughed,
somewhat tentatively, but they laughed. By joking about the matter

I had hoped to show that we didn't share his anger. It seemed to work, although I still expected someone to ask the president if he shared the senator's view of the press. They simply cannot take criticism.

I turned and walked off the podium, down the red carpet, between the heavy oak doors and past the Marine guards, then turned left quickly into the Blue Room. The camera monitors were set up for viewing and the president had been watching my performance. "We just saw you," he said like a father, with such wonderment and innocence that I wondered how he had avoided cynicism all these years. I never heard him ever say a cynical word about anything.

It was one minute till the television producer would signal the president to walk out of the Blue Room, retrace my steps to the podium, and begin. He had done it thirty-nine times as president. He had done it a thousand times as an actor. He was the best walker in the business. He strode with purpose, straight and erect, well tailored and ready for any script. You could not look at Ronald Reagan without feeling good about America. But I was sweating.

I walked into the East Room through the back door, edged along the side of the room, and picked a location just behind the television boom mike. Basically, my job was done. But I was ready, a quick four steps from the president if some crazy reporter tried to physically approach him, as a Lyndon LaRouche reporter had once done, or as Helen and Sam would undoubtedly try at the end.

The press ascribes high intellectual anxiety, or alarming emotional weakness, to even one drop of sweat that mysteriously seeps from one pore on your upper lip. They are right, of course. So you fight it, wanting to push it back into your skin, but knowing that even the swiftest brush with your index finger will be noticed and recorded by cameras and reporters. Maybe the trick is to relax. I let my arms drop to my side. But then I couldn't take notes. Relaxation was not going to happen. So I went for the all-out brazen approach that said "Hell yes I sweat, and now is the time to do it." I ran the full length of my arm across my face, hoping my all-cotton pinstripe suit would be sweat-absorbing and relieve me of the need to repeat the action for the remainder of the press conference. But only two questions had been asked and we had twenty-six minutes to go. My mind froze as the characters continued to play out this drama—scripted, rehearsed, and produced with tedious detail. My only fear was that someone would forget their lines. The East Room press conference had become a dance, sometimes of joy, sometimes of anger, but always with partners who knew their role and knew the script, not in the Hal March *$64,000 Question* sense of a rigged game, but in the sense of intensely tutored professionals who know the game, know the issues of interest, know which questions have to be asked, and know the cameras bind them together according to a rigid set of performance rules. These preparations started nearly a week before.

Preparation for a Reagan press conference started by casting a wide net. At least a week before the target date, a memo was sent to all cabinet agencies asking for questions and answers that covered any controversies that might arise. The NSC coordinated those from State and Defense, because they were usually the most crucial. The White House press corps always asks about foreign policy, although this time it was certain that Iran-Contra would dominate. Fifty or so pages would be distilled to about twenty and those would go to Camp David with the president for weekend study.

The president liked written briefings. In his professional career as an actor, he followed the scripts. It soon became apparent that the president memorized a lot of his briefings. If he read a fact from a source he respected, it stayed with him. So there was always some danger in sending him pro and con arguments, or philosophical discussions, or any figure that had not been confirmed. The good news was that once he retained an answer, he could recite it almost verbatim. This trait put a very high premium on staff work, and aides would argue and fight endlessly about one word in a sentence because they knew every word would be stated. In later years, we found this phenomenon to have just the opposite effect on President Bush. He resisted using any word that someone else gave him, mostly out of a stubborn resistance to the idea that he was being programmed or "handled." Thus his general disregard for written speeches, texts, or any document that could be interpreted as putting words in his mouth.

In the week before this press conference, all manner of briefing documents had been sent in to the Oval Office. My staff had prepared a list of forty-three Iran-Contra questions that covered every question the press had asked me. This was the most reliable system. The press is a creature of intellectual habit. Guessing their press conference questions is easy. Simply look at what they had asked the day before. It always amazed me that they would expect the president to answer differently than I had. In most cases, he had given me the answers in the first place.

The president's Camp David reading the weekend of March 14 and 15 included twenty pages of single-spaced talking points on Iran-Contra, foreign and domestic policy issues, and the economy. David Abshire, a former Foreign Service officer, ambassador, and friend of Mrs. Reagan, had been hired to help the president sort through Iran-Contra issues. He sent another twenty-five pages to Camp David summarizing the Tower Board report. David spent several hours that week reviewing the report with the president in the Oval Office, returning time and again in their discussions to the central question of whether or not the policy was one of trading arms for hostages. At one point, David came to my office, his head down in frustration. "The president just will never believe it was arms for hostages," he said. "That wasn't what was in his mind when he did it, and it never will be." David was right, of course. President Reagan never came to believe he traded arms for hostages. But he did understand that it happened and that one could reach an honest conclusion that a trade took place. He also understood that it had to be publicly acknowledged. As I looked at the detailed material to be sent to the president for this press conference, it seemed hopeless to expect a stellar performance. I never could get all those dates straight, and I knew that David Hoffman's computer would be waiting to trip the president up.

David Hoffman was *The Washington Post*'s number-two reporter covering the White House, behind the venerable Lou Cannon, who had covered Reagan as governor of California. Cannon wrote books about Reagan, knew every member of his personal and professional family, and knew the brain waves of President Reagan so well that he could recite the genesis for every new policy, usually in some Western movie or actors' labor dispute thirty years before. He was from the old school of journalism, when reporters worked their sources in bars and office picnics, and hitched car rides to political rallies. He took notes and fumbled with these newfangled tape recorders, always spilled soup on his tie, usually dressed as if going to church on a *Mayberry RFD* sitcom, had a mustache that advertised lunch, with an open, affable charm that made sources open up to him. It always seemed as if he wanted to write good things about the president and was truly sorry that he had to say the president was a slow-witted bum. Lou had an infuriating habit of writing a laudatory column about the president's leadership style, only to follow it with a scathing column attacking the president's ability to walk and chew gum at the same time. As thunder follows lightning, the second column always came. I always gave wide distribution to

Lou's first column, so the White House staff would have a good feeling about him when the second arrived. I liked Lou very much. To this day I really believe he didn't enjoy writing those second columns, but rather submitted to peer pressure.

David Hoffman was to be feared. He was a new generation of intensity, always serious with a deeply submerged anger that would mushroom out of him, not in a loud voice but in a sullen glance that would signal his disdain. He worked by very exacting standards, was amused by those who had not mastered the high technology of computerized reporting, and almost disgusted with those in government or the press who performed with less than total commitment.

David Hoffman brought the laptop computer to political reporting. There may have been others before him who had the machine, but none who used it as effectively, as an integrated information weapon to be aimed at any subject. His computer had bounced around every political bump in America in the 1984 campaign, resting on David's knees about midway back on the bus, because it's a smoother ride there, and recording every speech and utterance made. He conducted a one-man crusade to wipe out political deceit, to catch the politician making different statements in different locations on the same issue and hang them high on the *Post*'s yardarm for all to condemn. He used a cellular telephone to call Washington or conduct interviews from the press bus. His tape recorder was strapped to him like woolen mittens. You wouldn't find him at a bar or napping in the lounge. He was always at work, with time off only for a fine meal at the best restaurant with the best wines. It was his personal payoff, and even then he usually took a source to dinner with him. I liked and respected David for his professional commitment, and because he turned his back on the shallowness of Washington, the social incestuousness of reporters on the make. He was honest. Yet I always approached him with the caution of a cat, wary of the possibility that he might lash out at any time. Indeed, in my daily briefings I tried to never compare present events to historical happenings as they related to the president because David would know the history better than I, and if my dates were wrong, or my interpretation different from his, he would call me on it. And he would invariably be right.

It was not a fair match to put President Reagan against David Hoffman on Iran-Contra. David knew all the dates, all the sequences, all the incriminating statements, all the congressional testimony, and what he didn't know was resting comfortably on his lap, just an "enter" button away. As it turned out, David didn't come to the press conference. Lou Cannon represented the *Post* and David covered from the television set in the *Post* newsroom.

I had readily agreed with David Abshire that the president should not even try to answer Iran-Contra questions about times, dates, and statements. Rather, he should make the same general statements about policy and responsibility that he had given the American people in his speech, and refer all specific questions to the many investigations under way.

All presidential staff members lament the fact, of course, that presidents don't do what their brilliant advisers tell them to do. President Reagan was the greatest receiver of advice. He seldom argued. He just nodded his head affirmatively, as if in profound gratitude for staff wisdom, then ignored your comments. That's why everyone wanted to go to the president's rehearsals, to find out what he had retained and what he was actually going to say. It was the moment of truth. In addition, they were always fun. One could almost hear Ed Sullivan introducing him, then the Gipper would walk in and begin his act.

The "prebrief," as it was called, was the press conference rehearsal, a larger-than-life production, always playing in my mind under a twelve-foot marquee like *Quo Vadis*. The two-day, two-hours-a-day session was held in the Family Theater of the White House. Everyone wanted to go, and tight discipline had to be maintained. The chief of staff picked every participant and listed them by memo. Those not selected would often appeal that they had vital information, or their protocol status demanded a presence, or they represented a special constituency. But briefing the president under these conditions was an art form, a painting that could easily be ruined by a casual brush stroke.

This prebrief was crucial. It had to establish that the president was ready on Iran-Contra. It was also the first by the new chief of staff, Howard Baker, and his team. My deputies for domestic and foreign policy served as questioners, and we produced the questions to approximate the style and language of reporters. The questions themselves had been cleared by the senior staff. President Reagan liked these sessions because the audience was friendly, he was behind the podium where he loved to be, and he could improvise humorous one-liners—that is, say what he really wanted to say without consequence. For him, it was a performance. The danger, of course, was that sometimes he would say at the press conference what he had joked at the prebrief. So I took a quick opportunity to warn the staff, before the president's arrival, of the consequences. Because the stakes were so high, I decided to go one step further.

"Please remember," I said, "that the president sees this as a rehearsal. He uses this forum to practice his lines. It's not a briefing to educate the president. He either knows it or he doesn't. If he doesn't, we'll send him briefing materials later. So don't argue with his answers if they are essentially on-target."

I had been through horrible prebriefings in the past with David Stockman, who objected to the way the president said everything. He would endlessly try to explain how Social Security affected the deficit, so that minutes later no one in the room could understand the equation. Martin Feldstein, the chairman of the President's Council of Economic Advisers, would invariably suggest a theoretical answer that was either incomprehensible or didn't reflect administration policy. The president would listen patiently, then repeat his answer the same way as before.

The most successful approach was to, in effect, rewrite the script. The president had a unique talent for saying an answer the way he liked and, if satisfied with it, pushing some inner button that committed it to memory. He would give it that way the rest of his life. His explanation for Iran-Contra was in that category. He wrote it out himself in longhand, a seven-minute explanation of the arms sale. He gave it in the prebrief, in the press conference, and at every opportunity afforded him during the rest of his presidency. Later on, when reporters stumbled into asking the Iran-Contra question and the president would begin his recitation, they would audibly groan and simply lay down their notebooks until it was over.

This session was mostly serious, because the press had made the stakes so high. We hit him with every nasty, accusatory question we could think of. I knew from my own podium experience that every question is easy if you've heard it before. Panic is in the surprise. So we swallowed hard, told ourselves it was for the good of the presidency, and tried to embarrass the president by every means possible: about Mike Deaver's indictment, Ollie North's treachery, John Poindexter's secretiveness, Don Regan's ego, and endless questions about dates and times of various statements. Finally the president had been serious too long.

"The Iran-Contra affair, and all the things you did not know about, have undermined your credibility with the American people and world leaders," we said. "How are you going to go about rebuilding the Reagan presidency when this is all over?"

A smile appeared at the corner of his mouth, his head cocked, the eyes came to life, and he looked at the floor to establish a sense of timing, then delivered the line: "Who the hell wants to rebuild when I'm quitting in two years anyway." We all laughed. A big part of President Reagan's humor was in the exaggeration and absurdity of his statements. Everyone in America heard him tell stories. But those who heard his quips knew his unique ability to see the ironies of life, and he exposed them with exaggeration.

Howard Baker turned to A. B. Culvahouse and commented, "I hope he doesn't say that tomorrow night." A.B. laughed, but we all had the same fear. The president was weak on his Iran-Contra answers. It was not a case of not knowing the millions of facts in this continuing drama, because no one knew the facts. No one could keep all those dates straight about arms shipments and phone calls from Ollie North to some Middle Eastern con man. But the growing scandal, and probably the Tower Board report, had weakened the president's confidence about himself. He wasn't sure what he knew. This was tragic, because Reagan's great strength as a president was that he knew himself and what he believed.

President Reagan was a product of his small-town Midwestern upbringing in Dixon, Illinois. He loved to tell stories of his alcoholic father, who had trouble holding a job but was "still a good man." Another favorite story related to the one black player on Reagan's college football team and the way the team fought discrimination. Always the moral of the stories was the same: Good people would do the right thing. Above all, Ronald Reagan believed he was a good person.

This belief was at the core of his political principles—that conservatism was good for America, and America was a good, hardworking, ethical nation that should be a role model to the world. Iran-Contra shook those beliefs in Ronald Reagan for the simple reason that it made people doubt his word.

One night the president and I went to dinner at the home of R. Emmett Tyrrell Jr., editor of *American Spectator* magazine, in the Virginia suburbs of Washington. It was about a forty-minute drive from the White House. On the way home, sitting in the back of the presidential limousine, enclosed by the darkness of the night and the silence of the limo, the president just stared at the lights of Washington along the George Washington Parkway as if in a trance. Suddenly, but almost forlornly, he said, "I just don't understand why they don't believe me."

"You mean about the arms sales?" I asked.

"I wasn't trying to trade arms," he said. And when we pulled into the White House driveway, he was still talking, almost pleading, explaining again about the moderates in Iran.

The tragedy was that if Ronald Reagan lost confidence in his own goodness, he might lose confidence in his presidency. Clearly, that was a possibility. It also seemed to me that Ronald Reagan knew he had been betrayed by his staff, and that also shook his foundations. Basically, he trusted people. In his years as governor, candidate, and president, at least eight different staffs had served his needs. People he hardly knew wrote his speeches, prepared his schedules, arranged his meetings. It was nearly impossible for him to believe that men he trusted, like Robert McFarlane and John Poindexter, could let him down. It was another challenge to his goodness.

Howard Baker recognized this problem and knew it had to be corrected, not in the Family Theater, but in the Oval Office with just a few people. "Set up a private briefing tomorrow, Marlin," he said. "In the Oval with just Frank [Carlucci], A. B. Culvahouse, Ken [Duberstein], Tommy [Griscom], you and me." Howard Baker was the best at this. He began that day to restore the president's confidence, and in doing so he stabilized the presidency. The next day we patiently went through essentially the same questions as the day before. The president sat at his desk, hands folded in front of him, and carefully considered each answer, then raised his head and delivered the lines. If no one objected, you could almost see him push the memory key. The answers were locked in. He was ready. And Howard Baker had taken every opportunity to reinforce the president's belief in himself.

Now that the press conference was actually under way, it seemed like light years since Howard Baker and I stepped into the small family elevator on the basement floor of the White House to meet the president in his second-floor living quarters. It had been only seven minutes ago. It was so quiet. The little elevator, walnut-paneled but badly scuffed from heavy use, opened just inches from the main hall of the family quarters. The family living room was immediately to the right, the president's bedroom straight ahead, and to the left were the other less-frequented Lincoln bedroom and sitting rooms. I was never prepared for that first step off the elevator, to find myself standing smack-dab in the middle of their private lives, usually unannounced, at least to the first lady. But it was the vastness of the rooms and the silence that made it so ominous. It was jolting to see them in such private surroundings.

"Anything new, Marlin?" the president asked.

Usually I brought some wire stories on late-breaking news. "No, Mr. President," I said. "Tonight there is only one subject."

"Well, OK, let's go," he said.

Now he was taking a question from Helen. The show was on.

"Mr. President," Helen Thomas said, "there have been reports that you were told, directly or indirectly, at least twice, that the Contras were benefiting from the Iran arms sales. Is that true or were you deceived and lied to by Admiral Poindexter and Colonel North? And I'd like to follow up."

The president said that he told the American people and the Congress all he knew as soon as he discovered the diversion of arms sales profits to the Contras. Helen's follow-up was equally aggressive: "Mr. President, is it possible that two military officers who are trained to obey orders grabbed power, made major foreign policy moves, didn't tell you when you were briefed every day on intelligence? Or did they think they were doing your bidding?"

The president said he too wanted to find out what happened. The follow-up questions are always easy because your mind is already working the subject. Some years ago the press got it into their head that follow-up questions allowed them to be tough, to ask that penetrating second question that would render the president utterly helpless. I'm sure they dream about the president, faced with one of their sizzling follow-ups, turning into a mound of quivering Jell-O. In fact, the result is just the opposite. The follow-up question allows the president time to more fully consider his first answer, and then leave the issue with just the right words. It also means that the president in thirty minutes will receive about twenty-six questions on thirteen subjects. If follow-ups were eliminated, he would have to cover twenty to twenty-five different subjects, a much harder task. I always feared that reporters would discover this and return to the "one question" format, but by the time some reporters made the connection it was too late. Television had taken over. With the cameras trained on the questioner, and reporters standing before the world with one fleeting chance at fame, none wanted to give up the "follow-up" question. It meant more air time, the new lifeblood of journalism. The longer and more accusatory the question, the more chance it would have to be repeated on the evening news. Not only that, it takes nearly twenty seconds for the television producers to identify the questioner and put his or her name on the screen below the picture. That is crucial. So everybody wants to ask a follow-up.

Television is an opiate for journalists. It gives them fame, power in the eyes of their peers, recognition by their families, lecture fees from the Storm Door and Sash Associations of the world, and ego gratification. By the time Sam Donaldson of ABC News stood to ask his question at the March 19 press conference, it was clear who the stars of this show were going to be.

Sam was the best at exploiting presidential weakness. He knew Ronald Reagan wouldn't remember yesterday's office schedule, let alone some obscure Iran-Contra phone call. The president simply had a terrible memory, especially for names. He didn't even try anymore, leaving it to aides to write down the names to recite. It wasn't the Alzheimer's disease that would strike him in later life. He simply never had a good memory.

"Sir," Sam began, "Robert McFarlane, who was then your national security adviser, says that in August of 1985, he called you on the telephone and asked if you wanted to give the green light to Israel to send arms to Iran and have them replenished from U.S. stocks, and then you said you did. And he said that he reminded you in that conversation that your secretaries of state and defense were against it and you said you understood that, but you explained to him the reasons why you wanted to authorize it. Do you have no memory of that, whatsoever?"

The president said he remembered the authorization, he just didn't remember when. The follow-up went about the same way. So much for the details.

Ronald Reagan was winning the same way he won almost all press encounters. He let the press talk past him. He addressed the issue that people understood. Of the 50 million people watching that night, nearly all of them could remember that they had had to replace the battery in their car, but they couldn't for the life of them remember when—neither could the president.

By the next question, from Bill Plante of CBS News, the Gipper was ready to give his full rendition of Iran-Contra, from start to finish, how it happened and what he thought of it. It was in the memory bank and always would be.

As the press conference ended, the front row of reporters surged forward like the Dallas Cowboys' offensive line. We had coached him on how to handle this situation. The president must accept

Helen Thomas's "Thank you," turn on his heels, and walk decisively away. It sounds so simple. Yet when the press surged, shouting, "Mr. President! Mr. President!" Ronald Reagan, as always, turned back to face the questions and was immediately surrounded. Pandemonium broke loose. The cameras, still trained on him to record the departure, zoomed in for a close-up of the president's face. If they lost sound, maybe they could read his lips. The radio correspondents rushed forward holding their tape recorders to pick up any bit of response, and still photographers were shouting "Down in front!" I tried to get as close as possible to record what was said, and to help the president out if the pushing became too severe. The Secret Service agents quickly moved to the president's side, but they were careful not to touch or push a reporter, especially on nationwide TV. The press asked something about the vice president. The president delivered a phrase as he walked sideways. I heard nothing but allowed myself to be carried out the door with him by the flow of the crowd.

As we got through the double doors leading from the East Room into the hallway, we left the thick red carpet, hit the hardwood floors, and stumbled toward the relative calm of the Green Room a few feet away. For reporters, hitting the hardwood was like hitting the warning track in baseball; it was a warning signal to stop before your brains get smashed against the outfield fence or the palm of a Secret Service agent. The crowd of reporters drew back into the East Room, and I joined the president for a few quick words of encouragement.

"It went well, Mr. President," I said. "You did a great job." He quietly said thanks, talked briefly to Howard Baker, and headed back upstairs to receive the only review that counted, from Nancy.

The press conference went on for the full thirty minutes, but it was over after the third question. The president stood tall and strong, and gave not an inch. The reporters' dreams would not be fulfilled that night. But Ronald Reagan did give them one important prize—the show. He let them put on an East Room extravaganza with themselves as the stars. They built up the suspense and the size of the audience. They performed all the key roles. And afterward they proclaimed it a great success.

Sam Donaldson said, "Ronald Reagan is back from the standpoint of style, if that is what you are looking for. He was number one tonight. Fifty years in Hollywood came right through . . ."

Bill Plante said, "He had been pretty carefully rehearsed, as you probably noticed."

Chris Wallace said, "I think his performance was first-rate. The president was clearly ready for this news conference."

Robert Strauss, Washington lawyer and Texas godfather to all Democrats, told Ted Koppel that the president had done quite well on style and general impression.

But in the end it all came down to sweat, and Dan Rather, CBS anchorman, was on the case. He said the president was "well rehearsed, heavily perspiring, seemed to be in charge and in command . . ." Later he asked his White House correspondent, "The president seemed to be perspiring, any particular significance to that?" Dan Rather has had a thing about perspiration ever since Richard Nixon. He covered the Nixon White House and Watergate, never quite getting over the role of perspiration in witness after witness as they testified about Watergate crimes. Thank God I didn't have to take his sweat test after this press conference.

The next day's *Washington Post,* arbiter of establishment journalism, ran a banner headline in its "Style" section: "Showdown in the East Room: Reagan at the Ready." Tom Shales, their television critic, wrote: "If it was a fight, Ronald Reagan won it. He seemed clear-eyed, assertive, emphatic and confident from the very outset of last night's televised press conference."

After the president left and the press were leaving the East Room, I walked through the back doors of the red and blue reception rooms, crossed the main hallway in front of the State Dining Room, slipped into the president's private elevator, and pushed the basement button. There are about forty yards of open colonnade between the main mansion and the West Wing that passes beside the Rose Garden. Were it not for this brief outdoor exposure, presidents might never leave the White House. As I walked along the colonnade, I looked to the stars and gave a silent prayer of thanks. For the president, and for the process of governing, Iran-Contra was virtually over.

The public trial was over, and that was the main thrust of Iran-Contra anyway. The congressional committee hearings were yet to conclude. The independent counsel investigation, which would last seven years, had yet to begin. Individual trials and appeals would continue for months, with the independent counsel even trying, perhaps successfully, to influence the presidential election of 1992. But for Ronald Reagan, it was over that night. He knew there was nothing criminal about his policy decisions. He had come to terms with the mistakes. All that mattered was to give the media its pound of flesh, give them their show, cry "uncle," let the investigations proceed, and move on. There was some anxiety about whether any of the congressional testimony would try to implicate the president, or whether the committee might start posturing about impeachment. But tonight's performance showed the president's political enemies that he would not be slain easily and their derision began to subside.

I walked into my office, where most of my staff was waiting, and closed the door. "Great job, boss," someone said. "The Gipper did it again." In the White House, your self-identity is inextricably tied to the president. As press secretary, you feel his pain and jump with his glee. And your staff feels the same way. It's perfectly natural for everyone in the room to think that if the president did well, we all did well, and vice versa. Football players know it. Military squads know it. It's the fraternalism and commitment that make the White House so special. We had won.

The next day in my briefing, Julie Johnson of *Time* magazine asked, "You said earlier that White House aides found the president to be strong and decisive and in command. Is it also the view of aides here that too much has been made of how he should or should not have performed before the cameras last night, and too much attention has been placed on whether or not he just didn't make any gaffes and got through the thirty minutes without trouble?" I declined to comment, of course. This was exactly the "test of appearances" that the press had set up, and to denigrate that test would be to diminish the victory.

Before the press conference, on March 9, the *Farmer-Stockman of the Midwest*, a weekly regional newspaper published in Belleville, Kansas, by Merle M. Miller, one of the most distinguished publishers in the Midwest, surveyed 1,817 readers in thirty-nine states. They responded 1,461 to 346 that the news media had been vindictive to President Reagan over the Iran issue. God bless those farm folks. The trick now would be to demonstrate that the president could govern at the same time the Iran-Contra sideshow was going on.

Our answer was the Economic Bill of Rights, a public relations masterpiece. The acronym was EBOR, which, if said fast enough, sounded like Eeyore, the donkey of *Winnie-the-Pooh* fame. I always said it fast enough. Initially, EBOR sounded like the most empty, nutty idea I had ever heard. It had no action item associated with it. It didn't do anything, promised nothing, gave nothing away. It didn't even require a study or commission. It was pure PR, but the longer it lasted, the more it became obvious that we had discovered genius.

I was afraid to have Tommy Griscom go to the president's speeches on EBOR for fear the press would see the extraordinary smile on his face.

The Economic Bill of Rights became the vehicle through which America would once again see Ronald Reagan at his vintage best, and it would help remind voters why they chose him to be their president not once, but twice. It would also demonstrate to the media that the president was still very much engaged and busy, that he still expected to accomplish legislative objectives in his last eighteen months in office, and that he was undaunted by the daily revelations of the Iran-Contra hearings taking place on Capitol Hill.

EBOR was Griscom's brainchild. Like any "better tasting," "fresher smelling," "deeper cleaning," or "longer lasting" product found on the shelves of the local grocery store, EBOR was, quite simply, a perfect example of successful repackaging. It was a "new and improved" version of economic principles fundamental to the Republican way of thinking. Written in the style of the original Bill of Rights, it began with the premise that every American was guaranteed certain freedoms: the freedom to work, the freedom to enjoy the fruits of one's labor, the freedom to own and control one's property, and the freedom to participate in a free market.

To secure these freedoms, it proposed a "truth in spending" plan. The plan required Congress to say how much a government program would cost and how it would be financed. It also called for a "super-majority," that is, at least a three-fifths majority vote by Congress for passage of any tax increase.

Substantively, EBOR was a powerful political weapon. When coupled with the president's ceaseless calls for a balanced-budget amendment and the line-item veto, EBOR enabled the Republicans to continue to command the high ground over the Democrats on the tax issue. EBOR became the president's weapon of choice in his arsenal of rhetoric used against the "tax-and-spend" Congress during the budget fights that summer, and it worked. The $1 trillion budget the Democrats put forth, which proposed a tax increase of $19.3 billion deemed necessary to reduce the deficit, was vetoed by the president in the fall of 1987, with nary a whisper of protest from the American people. And the themes of the Economic Bill of Rights lived on after that. They formed the bedrock of George Bush's economic platform during the 1988 campaign.

Stylistically, the fanfare that accompanied the introduction of

EBOR was reminiscent of a George M. Cohan production. Jim Hooley, President Reagan's head of advance, created a "Star-Spangled Salute to America" event, held at the Jefferson Memorial on July 3. The timing and symbolism were pure poetry. The date was the eve of the celebration of the Bicentennial of the Constitution. From a press standpoint, it allowed us to take advantage of the holiday news lull. Creating our own story was especially important that weekend because Ollie North was scheduled to testify before Congress on Iran-Contra the following Monday.

The U.S. Chamber of Commerce, long a friend of Republican administrations, hosted the event and filled the grounds of the memorial with close to 10,000 people. When President and Mrs. Reagan took the stage at 10 A.M., the day was dazzlingly sunny, hot and humid, typical for Washington in July, although none of the 10,000 smiling and expectant faces in the crowd seemed to mind. The pool reporter that day, Al Sullivan of the U.S. Information Agency, commented that the event had all the trappings of a campaign stop: thousands of red, white, and blue balloons, a daylight fireworks display, and several patriotic guests booing the arrival and departure of Sam Donaldson. Ronald Reagan was at his greatest espousing American and conservative principles. For several months, the president traveled around the country, proudly extolling the virtues of EBOR, always received by wildly cheering crowds. Iran-Contra was left far behind.

In 1994 EBOR was resurrected by President Bill Clinton in the form of the "Middle Class Bill of Rights." The themes behind EBOR were terrific back in 1987, and they proved to be an extraordinary success for Ronald Reagan. We knew EBOR was a great idea back then, but none of us would have guessed that it would be brought back to life seven years later—by a Democratic president trying to imitate Ronald Reagan in tone and substance and trying to stabilize his own presidency. President Clinton's confidence in himself had been severely shaken by the Republican sweep of Congress in 1994. Clinton used his bill of rights theme for the same reason Reagan did: to reassure himself of his own beliefs.

In another irony, it should be noted that the Contract with America, fashioned by House Republicans to nationalize the 1994 campaign, contained most of the elements of the Reagan Economic Bill of Rights: balanced-budget amendment, line-item veto, and all the economic freedoms. What started as a public relations scheme to get our administration back on track became a blueprint for politics in the 1990s—by both parties.

As the Iran-Contra hearings and independent counsel investigation dealing with the old National Security Council staff were going on, one of the new leaders who came to everyone's attention in the White House was Deputy National Security Adviser Colin Powell. By the time President and Mrs. Reagan made their annual New Year's trip to visit the Walter Annenberg family in Palm Springs, California, General Powell and I had become good friends. Unlike previous national security advisers, Colin had made himself an active participant in the communications planning process, even attending meetings on domestic policy activities. He was popular, especially compared to Secretary of State George Shultz, who ignored the president's staff and was sometimes referred to as "Mr. Potatohead," partly as a rather sophomoric response to his imperious nature, and partly because the secretary tended to denigrate the White House's political involvement in foreign policy. Colin suffered no such slights. As an African-American, he was especially interested in civil rights matters and policies related to housing and the inner-city poor. He was supportive of administration policies but clearly wished some of our officials were a little more sensitive to affirmative action and equal rights. I shared his views and sometimes we sympathized with each other when a fringe political position would emerge.

General Powell and I were the only two staff members accompanying the president to Palm Springs in 1987, and neither of us had been invited to the Annenbergs'. So we made plans to attend the press's New Year's Eve party at the Gene Autry Hotel, where we were staying. The television networks, having the most money and the most people working, always threw a party. In addition, New Year's Eve was Cal Marlin's birthday. Cal was a CBS cameraman who had been filming presidents for decades and each year shared his birthday with the New Year's revelers. This year the press presented Cal with birthday cakes in the form of a key and a bible, just as Oliver North and Bud McFarlane had done months before in meeting with Iranian arms merchants.

When Colin and I arrived at the celebration and saw the cakes, we immediately realized it was a test. The press wanted to see if we were afraid of the Iran-Contra symbolism, if we would be photographed eating a piece of the key, and if we were willing to share their humor. It was a "good guy" test. Colin and I glanced at each other. I put on a New Year's hat, picked up a kazoo noisemaker, and cut myself a piece of cake. Colin was slightly more dignified, but he took a piece of cake and posed with me for pictures. The word went forth among the press corps that Colin Powell was a good guy as well as a great general.

CHAPTER SEVEN

Old Enemies, Not Old Friends

Cold war fears shaped much of American life in the '60s, '70s, and '80s, but only in the White House, and perhaps the Pentagon, was it such a pervasive force that personal activities were designed according to the time it would take a nuclear missile to fly from Russia to the United States. The rule was: The president should never be more than two minutes from a telephone. Even the White House press corps designed its daily life around the possibility that the president might push the nuclear button at any moment. The rule was: A press pool is always with the president. A "situation room" was built in the basement of the West Wing. It was little more than a soundproof, teak-paneled conference room surrounded by secretarial desks with computers, teletypes, and video-conferencing telephones, but it had mythical proportions in the movies, and in the minds of White House officials who would rush to the "sit room" at the first hint of world turmoil.

A "hot line" was developed that actually wasn't hot at all, and usually took hours to connect via teletype. But Americans wanted to know that their president could call off a war as fast as he could start one. A military aide stayed at the president's side at all times with "the football," a briefcase carrying the nuclear codes in case the president wanted to push the button.

It would almost never happen that way, of course. None of these precautions was likely to be used. The president would want to talk with a jillion people before starting nuclear war. I often thought, while standing around a Long Island swimming pool with a bunch of fat-cat campaign contributors wearing satin slippers with monogrammed toes, that pulling the president away from this setting to retaliate against a nuclear attack would make the Keystone Cops look organized.

Years later, after the cold war was over, President Bush and Russian president Boris Yeltsin signed a long-range-missile reduction agreement in the Kremlin, and the military aide left "the football" in a motorcade van. He said the football "just didn't seem to be relevant anymore" so he didn't even take it into the Kremlin. Later Secretary of Defense Cheney wanted to ground the B-52 bombers with nuclear devices that were kept in the air on a twenty-four-hour basis, and we debated the issue for weeks, as fearful as caged animals that people would be afraid of this new bomberless world. As it happened, only a few veterans groups even took notice. And the underground bomb shelter for presidential command during a nuclear war sits forlornly in a West Virginia mountain, unused, unnecessary, and unwanted.

These fears were perhaps greatest when Ronald Reagan came to power in 1980. A brief history of U.S.-Soviet military defenses over the ensuing decade shows the role of Reagan's "peace through strength" approach, particularly his strategic defense initiative (SDI), in the collapse of the Soviet empire. In the late 1970s, the Soviet Union had at least as many nuclear bombs as the United States and they were concentrating on a buildup of conventional forces, tanks, in the Warsaw Pact. When the United States decided not to build the neutron bomb, which theoretically would kill tank drivers without having to pierce the tanks, the Soviets were feeling rather secure in their decisions.

But when Ronald Reagan came to Washington calling the Soviet Union "the evil empire," the Soviet military got the shudders. As more and more former Soviet leaders emerge today from obscurity, they recount how every Reagan speech resulted in more Soviet defense spending. By some accounts, one-third to one-half of the Soviet gross national product was going for defense.

When President Reagan, and Vice President Bush, convinced the European allies in the early 1980s to put Pershing II and cruise missiles in Central Europe, the Soviets knew their tanks and short-range missiles were not enough. They countered with long-range missiles capable of carrying nuclear warheads directly to the United States.

Then, on March 23, 1983, President Reagan unveiled his SDI dream, a "Star Wars" system that would put missiles in space capable of shooting down all incoming missiles. The American media ridiculed SDI and Reagan's "fanciful notions." Even today the liberal establishment in America resents having to give Reagan credit for the strategic effect this idea had on the Soviets, who bought it hook, line, and sinker. Their economy was already sagging and they soon saw themselves with no deterrence to SDI if it was used offensively, and no money to keep up in such an audacious arms race. Ironically, in 1995 many conservative congressional leaders wanted to revive SDI, apparently not realizing that it was primarily the Reagan bluff that made it so successful. The technology itself never materialized, at least as Reagan envisioned it.

Bernard Ingham, the wonderfully gruff and masterful press secretary to Prime Minister Thatcher for more than a decade, writes that Mrs. Thatcher "never expected this defensive system would be able to neutralize every nuclear weapon," and she thought Reagan's idea that SDI could lead to a nuclear-free world was "fundamentally misguided." Nevertheless, when Mrs. Thatcher first met Gorbachev on a rainy Sunday in December 1984 at Chequers, he told her his primary aim with President Reagan was to get him to abandon SDI. She said it would not happen and she was right.

In the summit meetings between Reagan and Gorbachev during their terms of office, the ultimate objective of every meeting and arms-control negotiation was to get America to back away from SDI. As former Soviet leaders now admit, there was skepticism in Moscow about SDI, but Field Marshal Akhromeyev was convinced it was real, and Gorbachev concluded that the Soviet Union could not win this arms race, if only because they couldn't afford it. In Geneva, negotiators for Gorbachev and Reagan soon began the treaty discussions leading to nuclear-arms reductions, and the Soviets were suddenly willing to bargain.

The result was that by 1987, in the last two years of the Reagan presidency, the handwriting was on the wall that significant changes were occurring in Moscow. The anticipation was in the unknown. Gorbachev was an exciting new figure whom Americans could identify with, at least in appearance. It seemed the whole world was electric with hope and excitement about changing East-West relations. Thus when Gorbachev made his first visit to Washington, more reporters from around the world converged on Washington than at any time in history. Probably more than will ever attend a summit meeting again.

This chapter describes much of the hoopla and hysteria of the Washington and Moscow summits. It was a moment in time when the focus of the world was singular, and in fact the end result was as smashing as the promise: The cold war ended. Another fascinating angle is now emerging from that period concerning the role of the Strategic Defense Initiative, "Star Wars," in convincing the Soviets to give up the arms race. This chapter contains much of the actual conversations between Gorbachev and Reagan on this subject.

I believe the news media largely missed the SDI story for two reasons: first, because the Soviet Union was so insular that few people truly understood their fear of SDI and what it meant to their view of the arms race; and second, because the U.S. media always thought Star Wars was a quack idea. They didn't believe it would work, so why should the Soviets.

In retrospect, we can see the remarkable portrait of an American president who changed the world through the sheer force of an idea, one that few people believed in but in which he believed so strongly that other nations had to take it seriously. How often has that happened in our history? Wilson and the League of Nations. Kennedy and going to the moon. Not often.

It's also interesting that the Soviet Union virtually ignored the American media in making its own judgment about the feasibility of offensive weapons in space. They believed it would happen. Yet as the Reagan-Gorbachev summits unfolded, little attention was paid to the Star Wars implications. Even today, many people wonder if Reagan's Star Wars impact on the Soviets was calculated or lucky. But they should know that at the first summit in Geneva, Reagan took Gorbachev aside and told him: "You will never win an all-out arms race with us because we will outspend you." Gorbachev never forgot those words.

On December 7, 1987, the lobby of the J. W. Marriott Hotel in Washington was packed with television technicians trying to keep their tripods from getting caught in the revolving doors, Indian and Pakistani journalists in brown suits and expensive wing-tip shoes sitting on lobby couches and smoking homegrown cigarettes, Afghan reporters dressed in guerrilla fashions, and nearly 7,000 other journalists milling about and packing the escalators. A strobe light would come on and some midlevel Pentagon official would stop to give a three-sentence interview to a reporter he had never met and never would again. Along one wall two young men in sport jackets were seated at a green-felt-covered table selling T-shirts that read "REAGAN-GORBACHEV SUMMIT, DEC. 7–10, 1987," underneath the picture of a missile that was being crushed into plowshares. They were $10 each and selling fast.

I saw the mob in the lobby and instinctively headed for a side door. The rule here was the same as in any urban street situation: Never make eye contact with anyone you don't want to deal with. Reporters were shouting at me, but I never looked back. I ducked into a conference room, totally lost, headed for a back door that thankfully was unlocked, and finally emerged in a hallway behind the kitchen. I went through the kitchen, past the wilted lettuce salads, the giant garbage cans full of discarded food, and the baskets of bread, finally emerging in a hallway near some executive offices.

"May I borrow your phone, ma'am?" I said to the receptionist in the first open door.

"Oh, Mr. Fitzwater!" she exclaimed. "Of course. Here. I'll dial it."

"No, I can do it."

As I started to ring my office on the lower level of the hotel, the woman turned to a coworker. "He just walked in," she said. "He's from the White House. This whole madhouse is for him."

"Mark," I said, after reaching my assistant, Mark Weinberg, "I'm lost. I'm in the executive offices behind the kitchen."

"Where is that?" he asked.

"I don't know. Room 12," I said, stretching my neck and peering over the door. "Come get me, and figure out a way for us to get to the pressroom without going through the lobby. It's crazy out here."

I knew Mark Weinberg would not fail me. Indeed, he would probably bring the manager of the hotel and six house detectives with him. They would be here within two minutes. He would lead me back to an alley, down a fire escape, through a back door, and directly into my office. I knew it would happen that way, and it did, except he didn't have the six detectives. Mark was assistant press secretary in charge of logistics and press management. He had single-handedly picked the Marriott Hotel for this summit, arranged for its setup to handle the largest political press briefing in history, and organized hundreds of U.S. Information Agency employees and others to credential the most elite press corps in the world. He did all his work between Monday morning and 4 P.M. on Friday afternoon because that's when he went to Camp David with President and Mrs. Reagan. And he always went to Camp David. After eight years he had not missed more than a handful of weekends. The Reagans trusted him completely. There was nothing he would not do for them, perhaps not politely, but certainly with efficiency. He was tough, and tart, and sometimes harsh to colleagues who had to live with his demands. He was also very good.

He guarded the press ferociously, like a sheepdog that watches its flock and nips their heels and chases strays, but if they are attacked by any predator, it turns on the attacker with a vengeance. Mark was that way with Secret Service agents, local police, presidential staff, and anyone else who threatened the press, which was just about everybody.

Once, a Secret Service agent ordered the press charter aircraft to taxi to some distant location before letting the press disembark, just so space could be made for *Air Force One*, which was ten minutes from landing. But the whole purpose of the press being there was to see the president land and disembark. Mark jumped into the doorway of the cockpit, ordered the pilots to keep the plane right where it was, and then turned to the agent in the door of the plane. "We are not moving this plane until these people are off. I want you to tell your supervisor to present himself to me on this spot, now." His face was red and his neck veins straining. The agent starting talking into the microphone near his cuff links. He paused for the supervisor's response, gave a meek OK, and left the plane. *Air Force One* would park elsewhere. Nobody, but nobody, fooled with Mark Weinberg.

He led me into my temporary office in the hotel. I said hello to Connie Gerrard, my secretary, who had served every press secretary since Bill Moyers in the Lyndon Johnson administration, and circled the room to give a word of encouragement to each member of the staff. They had worked long hours for the past several days, 7 A.M. till nearly midnight, and they would do it for several more days. The war was coming. These people would do a thousand battles for me in the next few days, with abusive press, with Xerox machines that failed, electricity failures, schedules that changed, and tempers that flared. But they would never desert me, and this was a last chance to say thanks before heading into my own tunnel of concentration.

Dan Howard, Roman, and I went into my office and closed the door. It was nearly noon and time for the first joint briefing by the American and Soviet press secretaries. There had never been a summit meeting between the two superpowers where the countries were friendly enough to even consider such a thing. With the "glasnost" and "perestroika" policies of General Secretary Gorbachev, this was still an arms-control summit where the two countries would take the first step in history to actually reduce nuclear weapons.

"Roman," I said one day in November, "what if I asked Gennadi Gerasimov, Gorbachev's press secretary, to join me in the summit briefings?"

"Side by side?" he asked.

"Sure. I guess." I hadn't thought this through, but it was a good sign that Roman didn't exclaim that I might be crazy.

"Look," I began, "we're signing the first nuclear weapons reduction treaty in history. Gorby is pushing reforms and a new openness in the USSR. I know Gerasimov is a pro who speaks English fluently. He has a great wit and the U.S. press likes him. Neither of us will want to embarrass ourselves or our presidents. What better symbol of cooperation than to have us brief together."

"It's high-risk," Roman said. "He doesn't brief like you do. What if he just spouts propaganda?"

"We'll talk ahead of time," I said. "I'm sure he'll agree. How do I do it?"

"Just write him a letter," Roman said. "We'll send it by diplomatic pouch. Then we'll have the National Security Council staff raise it with the Soviet advance team."

"Great. Let's do it," I said.

Gerasimov accepted immediately. He had been on many U.S. television shows, including *Face the Nation* and the other Sunday talk shows. In many ways, he had more TV exposure than I. In the seventies, he had been stationed in New York with the Novosti Press Agency and knew American customs and language, even joking with me from his podium halfway around the world. I knew his résumé from CIA material, which included a stint as a consultant for Yuri Andropov in the Central Committee apparatus, and three years as the editor in chief of *Moscow News*. It was far less clear what kind of relationship he had with Gorbachev—possibly none. He was actually press secretary to Foreign Minister Eduard Shevardnadze, but assigned to General Secretary Gorbachev. Nevertheless, he showed no reluctance to speak for Gorbachev, although I noticed it was always cast in policy terms. He said what Gorbachev believed, but seldom spoke of what Gorbachev said privately or in special meetings. Whatever the relationship, it was clear he had no hesitancy about briefing with me.

In preparation for this meeting, the White House had spent weeks nurturing a public image of encouragement for Gorbachev and his reforms, yet wariness of the Soviets' military intentions. Then, on December 2, just five days before the summit, the administration had to release a congressionally mandated report on Soviet violations of existing arms-control treaties.

It was quite harsh in certain aspects, especially the charge that the USSR's Krasnoyarsk radar installation violated the Antiballistic Missile (ABM) Treaty. In my press briefing the day the report was released, the press was all over me about the tone of the report, about appearing tough one day and accommodating the next. Finally I said, "This is not a summit or a session to be taken lightly between old friends. This is a summit between old enemies."

You could hear the "gotcha" buttons going off all over the room. Those are the shuffling, sneezing, and stifled laughs that occur when you have made a mistake that the press knows they can exploit, that can be shortened to one brief headline that will hold the president up to ridicule, or that can be thrown back in the press secretary's face when the need arises. I was aghast with myself. We had spent days, weeks, and thousands of words in briefings by every general who had ever touched a missile, trying to cultivate a positive public relationship with the Soviets. Now my slip of the tongue would be used to anger Gorbachev.

Sure enough, the AP wrote, "White House spokesman Marlin Fitzwater said today that President Reagan's tough rhetoric towards the Soviet Union reflects his belief that his upcoming meeting with Soviet leader Mikhail S. Gorbachev is 'a summit between old enemies, not friends.'" Notice the AP's liberty of immediately putting my words in the president's mouth. It took nine paragraphs before the AP printed the actual quote in my name.

I knew what would happen next. This was standard procedure. My briefing was transcribed and transmitted immediately by the Federal News Service through a tape recorder in the Foreign Press Center. Stenographers at the service typed as I spoke, producing a full text within minutes after I finished. The full text was then fed on private ticker machines to thousands of government and corporate outlets in Washington, including congressional press centers and every embassy in the city. Within minutes of the briefing, several members of the Washington press corps called the Soviet embassy for a response to Fitzwater's characterization of the summit as being between old enemies—anything to start a fight. The Soviet ambassador immediately sent a cable to Moscow with a verbatim transcript of the offending phrase. The Foreign Ministry sent a copy to the general secretary's office, where his chief of staff and top advisers debated whether to show it to Gorbachev. In this case, they did. And the general secretary of the USSR tucked it away for just the right occasion to fire back.

Gennadi and his deputy, Vadim Perfiliev, walked into my office in the Marriott just before noon on December 7. We shook hands all around and exchanged pleasantries. Gennadi knew the summit's physical layout better than I did. He had been in Washington for a week, giving interviews, setting up briefings for their arms-control experts, and eating at the best restaurants. He appeared confident.

I had written an opening statement introducing Gennadi, welcoming the Soviets, and presenting greetings from President Reagan. I also outlined the schedule of events for the week and gave some overall comments about the peace process. Gennadi read it passively, handed it back, and said OK.

"Do you have a statement?" I asked.

"No," he said. "I just say a few words, then we take questions."

"That sounds fine," I said, noticing for the first time that my suit was more wrinkled and probably cheaper than his. His shirt was plain white, firmly starched with plain collars, and his suit was black with a diplomatic pinstripe. His face was sharply defined, looking remarkably like Alexander Dubček, the hero of Czechoslovak independence long ago ousted by Soviet tanks. The resemblance was so striking I always made the connection, and tended to imbue Gennadi with democratic longings he may not have had.

"I guess we're ready," I said. "Call the briefing." We walked together on a prearranged course around the outside of the huge ballroom, entering just behind the stage. As we circled to the edge of the stage and began to climb the four steps up, the magnitude of the event hit me. Lights were popping in every direction. Normally, the strobe lights on modern cameras make little noise. But this crowd was filled with many reporters from poor third-world and East European countries where the cameras were sometimes ancient. Flashbulbs left a patchwork of dots in front of my eyes, and it was easier to see the back of the ballroom than the front. Chairs were lined wall to wall, some thirty yards to my left and right. To see the end of a row, Gennadi and I had to turn our bodies almost fully sideways. The television camera lights were in full glare. It was show time, and until 4:40 P.M., when Gorbachev arrived at Andrews Air Force Base outside of Washington, we were the only show in town. Satellite space had been reserved by television networks around the world. Entire buildings in Washington were transformed into television studios, editing rooms, conference rooms, and interview sites, all for the express purpose, at least today, of analyzing and viewing the comments by Marlin Fitzwater and Gennadi Gerasimov. In many ways it was the absolute peak of hopefulness and hysteria about U.S.-Soviet relations, certainly for the seventy years prior to that moment, and perhaps since. Just six months later, by the time of President Reagan's trip to Moscow, the analysts were speculating about the limits of perestroika. But on this day in December 1987, all eyes were innocently trained on a better future.

It was like a carnival, with reporters smiling and laughing, photographers strolling in front of the podium, couriers waiting in the back of the ballroom with their bicycle helmets on, and USIA employees standing along the walls, just watching the show. As we reached the podium, someone in the audience said, "Fifty dollars on Gerasimov."

Sam Donaldson, sitting just to our right in the front row, picked up the challenge, "My money is on Marlin to tear him apart."

Oh no, I thought, this is not the atmosphere I want to instill. I wanted to show cooperation, so I quickly started reading the opening statement. I finished and Gennadi stepped forward for a few words, basically just a welcoming sentence, but he ended with a quip:

"Now I think we must have a division of labor," he said. "You answer all questions which are put in English and I will answer all questions put in Russian." (Laughter.)

"I'll answer the easy ones. You answer the hard ones," I responded.

"Oh, no," he said, "I have never costarred with Errol Flynn." (Laughter.)

"This is going to be a real treat," I said, recognizing that Gennadi was geared up to match my humor and compete quip for quip. His Flynn reference referred to President Reagan's comment to high school students in Jacksonville, Florida, the previous week when asked about Gorbachev's popularity. "No, I don't resent his popularity or anything else," Reagan said. "Good Lord, I costarred with Errol Flynn once."

After a question about schedules, Barry Schweid, the Associated Press's State Department senior correspondent, asked the first substantive question. Schweid was tough and sometimes irascible. But he knew foreign policy, the tender spots between countries, the issues that were thorny, and the areas of government thinking that were soft. Star Wars was such an issue. It touched all the nerves.

Ronald Reagan was a romantic. As an actor, he made movies out of life. As president, he tried to make life like the movies. And sometimes he did. It always struck me as politically ironic that it was Robert Kennedy, paraphrasing George Bernard Shaw, who spoke the famous line: "I dream things that never were and ask 'Why not?' " That's what Ronald Reagan did, and early in his presidency he saw in his imagination a giant missile shield in the sky that would catch any incoming missile from anywhere in the world, and he asked, "Why not?" Then he set out with Reaganesque determination to make it happen.

The United States spent about $8 billion between 1984 and 1987 to develop a strategic defense system that would protect the United States. It was a wonder to watch the president tell about it. The subject would come up in Oval Office discussions. The president would stand up behind his desk, his eyes would light with that sparkle normally reserved only for riding horses and chopping wood, his hands would spread before him as if holding down a helium-filled globe, a little crook would develop at the edge of his mouth, and he would say, "Wouldn't it be something if we had this shield, right there in the outer atmosphere, and it could catch any missile coming in? Then we could get rid of all our bombs." He would pause at the prospect, at the sheer miracle of a nuclear-free world, at the freedom from fear of nuclear destruction, and he would add, "I don't see why we couldn't give it to other countries." Everyone in the room would be quiet. The president would return to his desk and the discussion at hand.

I heard these comments many times. There was such a sincere innocence about them. There were thousands of reasons, of course, why Star Wars could never work technically, or why it couldn't be fail-proof, or why some other country might turn it to offensive purposes, or why it simply cost too much. Ronald Reagan had heard them and dismissed them. It was this dogged determination that scared the Russians to death. This was never more evident than at the Reykjavik summit in October 1986. The Soviets offered, in effect, to eliminate their entire nuclear arsenal in exchange for an end to Star Wars. And then the most frightening thing of all happened: Ronald Reagan refused. The Soviets had never seen that kind of determination before, at least not since they had tried to put missiles in Cuba.

Schweid asked us both to give a status report on Star Wars. I summed up our position: "The president's position on the Strategic

Defense Initiative is clear. He has said that he intends to research, develop, and deploy such a system. That position is well known to the Soviets." It felt funny saying something so challenging with Gennadi standing beside me, but I figured we might as well test this new briefing system early.

Gennadi dodged. He gave an answer within the context of allowable SDI testing in the ABM Treaty. No headlines there. The briefings were going to work. We made it through the other questions without mishap. But there was one unexpected ramification related to image. I had not done a lot of television, and really had not considered the impact of my appearance on the image of the United States. I cared about saying the right thing, being accurate, and knowing the issues, but never worried much about appearances.

After the briefing, the London Daily Telegraph's Washington correspondent, Hugh Davies, wrote, "As Mr. Gorbachev flew across the Atlantic yesterday, his spokesman, Mr. Gennadi Gerasimov, his face caked with television makeup, and Mr. Marlin Fitzwater, President Reagan's man, appeared before the world's press to set the summit scene. The contrast in styles was ironic. The Russian is tall and elegant in the manner of Cary Grant. The American, squat, ruddy-cheeked and balding, has the look of a jolly Russian peasant."

We ended the briefing and headed for the edge of the stage. The press were getting up from their computers, moving toward the front of the room and starting to gather in my path. Suddenly, a camera rushed through the crowd and a beautiful blonde woman thrust a microphone toward me. "Marlin, this is Entertainment Tonight. What's it like briefing with a Russian?"

I was flabbergasted. "Entertainment Tonight?" I exclaimed. "You're kidding."

"No," she said. "Will you give us an interview?"

"Not now," I said evasively, and rushed out the door. My God, Entertainment Tonight! What kind of sideshow had we created? We're talking nuclear-arms control here.

Dan Howard and I left immediately after the briefing for the White House. "My God, Dan, do you suppose I've made a mistake with these briefings? This isn't going to turn into a damn beauty contest, is it? Is that fair to the president?"

Dan looked at me as if I were crazy.

The next morning, at exactly 9:56 A.M., Mrs. Reagan walked off the family elevator in the basement of the White House, quickly crossed the hallway filled with Secret Service agents who were waiting to pick up their assignments, and stepped into the Diplomatic Reception Room to wait for her husband. Secret Service agents have a way of "coming to attention" military-style without any external show of movement. Their arms and hands remain in casual postures, but their eyes and mouths are locked, cocked, and ready for firing; their insides are tight, ready to react to any situation, whether it be an intruder or a presidential request for water. Everyone in the "Dip Room," as the staff refer to it, was equally tense, and even if in conversation with a companion, they had one ear cocked to pick up any murmur from the first lady, who had just arrived. But there was no time for that. Almost immediately, President Reagan entered the room.

He walked directly to Nancy, as always. They did not like to work separately on these occasions. They preferred to work as a team. The president and Mrs. Reagan were always in their own world, always attached by an invisible string, always aware of each other's presence, even if both were working a handshake line or visiting at a reception. Today was their favorite kind of event, working together like two performers in the same play. The president walked to her, leaned over, and kissed her on the lips. Then he leaned back, turned a half turn and held his arms back so Manuelo the butler could slip his black cashmere topcoat on, with white scarf to set it off. Mrs. Reagan stepped around to the front of him, gave him another kiss, then wiped the lipstick from his lips with a tissue wadded in her hand.

This was the big game and she knew it. Her eyes never strayed from his, the actress in her was coming to the fore. She was oblivious to all around her, and the room was filling rapidly. Then she took his scarf in both hands and pulled his face close to hers, nose to nose, for a private pep talk. It was too quiet to hear, even for those straining next to her, but it clearly was a phrase he had heard before. His face was illuminated as he took her hand and they started for the door to greet the Gorbachevs. They stopped at the outside door, waiting to see the flags on the general secretary's limousine before going out to greet them at the car. The Marine Band, which heralds every White House visit of a head of state, began to play. The president squeezed her hand one last time and they went outside.

Just as Gorbachev stepped out of his Soviet-made ZIL, the long black limousines that look like a cross between a hearse and a 1947

Studebaker, the White House ushers started one of their vacuum cleaners in the Dip Room.

I ran over to the machine. "Are you guys crazy? Turn that damn machine off! They're coming right back in." This exquisite moment started a six-year feud between me and the ushers, based on my conviction that they cared more for the carpet than for the president, and would gladly sacrifice the latter for the former. They left with downcast eyes, worried no doubt that one last scrap of dirt might remain forever lost on the Dip Room carpet.

President Reagan and General Secretary Gorbachev gave welcoming remarks to a waiting crowd of thousands on the South Grounds, the largest number I had ever seen for a state visit arrival ceremony. Everybody in America wanted to be there: the rich capitalists who wanted this new breeze of Russian change to caress their cheeks, the socialites who sought the glamour of rubbing elbows with the first Russian in seventy years to smile and mean it, the powerful senators and congressmen who knew that something historic was happening. This was a most incredible event. Old men who had feared communism were smiling at this reformer Gorbachev with the Western striped ties, the European suits, and the polished shoes. Academics who had written for decades of the babushkas who raised the Russian families came to marvel at the Soviet first lady with a great figure and a hint of glamour. It was a national happening, like men going to the moon, where every television set in the land was recording motorcade movements, focusing on empty hotel doors, with feature stories on the Gorbachevs' clothes, menus, habits, and family life. It was one of those sparkling moments in history when everyone feels, if only for a day or two, that the world is moving in the right direction. Ronald Reagan could not compete with that, but he did not have to, and saw no reason to. He was in a supporting role, as he had been throughout his movie career, and he knew how to do it well. When the two leaders and their wives moved back into the White House, still wearing their coats, it was as part of a choreographed pageant as grand as a Busby Berkeley production.

In the Diplomatic Reception Room, the president remarked on Washington's cold December weather. Gorbachev said, "Washington is the same latitude as the southernmost city in Russia," a very nice way of saying he was used to the cold.

Then the unveiling. Both world leaders turned to their wives and helped to take off their coats. It was as if both men were bringing out the fine china. As both women shook their shoulders to rearrange the pads, and pulled on their sleeves to set every crease in its proper place, they both stole a glance at each other's dress. They were both immaculate except for one glaring, earth-shattering, bone-chilling, and gasping realization: Mrs. Gorbachev's hose were down around her ankles, not all the way, but far enough to fold and to make her look for all the world like a Russian peasant woman just in from the fields. Mrs. Reagan caught it, just a flicker of recognition in her eyes, but she moved on so quickly that no embarrassment could develop. She took the first lady of the Soviet Union by the arm and led her directly across the hall to the elevator, up to the State Floor, and into the Green Room for coffee. I cannot say when the hosiery adjustment was made, but I do know that Mrs. Gorbachev never again was less than perfect in her wardrobe.

That morning President Reagan and General Secretary Gorbachev began their first working meeting, a private one-on-one session in the Oval Office with only interpreters and note takers present. This is a summit definition of private, partly because of the language difference and partly because no utterance can be left to unrecorded misinterpretation. The other institutional part of every meeting is the "photo opportunity," a term first used by President Nixon's press secretary, Ron Ziegler. The press pool, consisting of cameras and correspondents from the three major networks, still photographers from the largest newspapers, magazines, and wire services, and one newspaper writer to file a written report for all other journalists. The pool was ushered into the Oval to take the first pictures of the superpower leaders in the Oval Office.

I hate pools. They are necessary because of space limitations, but every reporter left out is angry. And if the pool reporter, selected by rotation, is not up to the task due to incompetence, sickness, a hangover, or any one of a hundred other maladies, the written report may be less than helpful. Worse, if the pool reporter wants to become a part of the story, he or she may ask some irrelevant or challenging question that embarrasses the president. Or worse yet, some pool reporters see their report as a chance to show off their questionable taste in humor. Often pool reporters record events with a degree of color they would not, indeed could not, use in their own publications. At one point, I had to make a rule that we would not reproduce pool reports that used swear words, reported profanity, or could not be printed in *The New York Times.*

That day's pool writer was Owen Ullmann of Knight-Ridder newspapers, whom I had known for years when he was an AP reporter in Detroit. He would do a professional job, especially with 7,000 other reporters looking over his shoulder, but he didn't shy from the embarrassing question. At the very end of the picture taking, after Reagan and Gorbachev had both commented on the hopeful outcome of the meetings, Owen stepped forward, knowing he had only an instant, and shouted, "Old friends or old enemies?" My heart jumped, and my legs weakened.

The president responded, "Well, I think you can judge for yourself." The Gipper had saved me again. But I looked up to see Gorbachev staring straight at me. He said nothing, and the press rushed from the Oval to get these first pictures on the wires.

Sitting in front of a crackling fire, the two men began talking of their hopes for the meeting, the reforms that Gorbachev had enunciated in his policies of glasnost and perestroika, and the parameters for their talks. In the years that have elapsed since these 1987 talks, it has become hard to remember the cold war tensions between the United States and the Soviet Union, the personal nature of our fears about each other, and the tensions inherent in believing that both sides might want to, or be forced to, destroy each other. But at the time, there was a very strong feeling of personal responsibility that to anger Gorbachev over any issue might trigger far-reaching hostilities. It was impossible to set aside the personal anxiety of knowing that all the members of the Soviet delegation were in some way planning to hurt the United States.

We had CIA briefings about being bugged somehow during the meetings, about delegation members leaving listening devices in our offices, about listening radars being trained on our windows from high-rise buildings blocks away, about all our telephone conversations being intercepted by a foreign government, and probably by our own intelligence services. Every night during the summit, our offices were swept for eavesdropping devices.

While the Oval meeting occurred, the two leaders' staffs loitered in the small lobby outside the Cabinet Room and in the Cabinet Room itself. The language barrier kept small talk to a minimum, but there was some chatter and nervous smiles as we politely sized each other up. I sought out Gennadi in the lobby, and asked if he would be sitting in on the expanded meeting that afternoon.

He said no. "I'm not on delegation."

"How will you know what happened?" I asked.

"I will meet with Shevardnadze. I will make notes," he said.

It was clear that he was not a routine attendee. It was also clear that I did not want to take myself out of the meetings, and then try to go through a press briefing. First of all, if I depended on our foreign policy team to fill me in, there would be nothing to say. Secretary of State George Shultz, who distrusted White House staff, would give me one line about cooperation and expect me to dance with that for an hour. Frank Carlucci, the president's secretary of defense, would give me an overall tone of the meeting, but no quotes and few details. I had to be in the meeting. So I figured the best recourse was to invite Gennadi in.

"I usually sit along the wall on the far side of the room," I told him. "You can sit beside me if you want."

"I will see," he said.

"I usually just hang around the back, then take a seat where no one notices me," I said, trying to make him comfortable.

"I will see," he said again.

I had determined early in my tenure as press secretary that I had to be in presidential meetings, especially National Security Council and other foreign policy discussions. It was the only way to pick up the nuances of foreign policy—what the president was thinking, the differences between cabinet secretaries, and the rationale for our actions. I needed all that information to stay out of trouble with the press, to know what not to say, and, most importantly, to shape my comments in ways that would account for policy changes and new developments and be reflective of the president. Foreign policy is a process. It seldom is a final decision to be wrapped in ribbon and put in a press release. It always changes. There are no final decisions in foreign policy, only the ones that best reflect current situations. I was determined to demonstrate to the president, the cabinet secretaries, and other staff members that I understood that process and could be trusted to sort out the right information for public dissemination.

My basic decision had been that I would go to any meeting on the president's schedule if I needed it to do my job. I would never wait for an invitation. If I was ever asked to leave, then I would consider resignation. Fortunately, in six years with two presidents I was never asked to leave a meeting.

Of course, this was my first superpower summit, so my attendance in this setting had not been established. At 12:15 P.M., the private meeting ended and Gorbachev left for lunch at his embassy. I joined Senator Howard Baker, the president's chief of staff, and Jim Kuhn, the president's executive assistant, in the Oval Office when the president returned from walking Gorbachev to his car.

I met the president at the door of the Oval that opens onto the colonnade. He stopped before entering and said, "We had a real go-round." But he was excited, entered the Oval, and told us, "Almost all of the conversation was on human rights."

"He asked about our limits on people coming into the U.S.," the president said, "I told him there is a big difference between people wanting in and people wanting out."

The president walked over to his desk. "He complained about the Jews wanting to go to Israel. I said, 'Why not give them religious freedom so they don't want to leave the USSR?'"

"What did Gorbachev say?" I asked.

"He didn't say anything," the president said.

The president had raised the Jewish emigration issue in the meeting, saying he was "saddened" and "worried" about the pace of human rights advances, and Soviet backsliding on the promise to allow Jewish immigration to Israel. Then the president had done the one thing that always drove the Soviets nuts: He handed Gorbachev a list of people who had suffered human rights abuses and demanded that their cases be reviewed.

As the afternoon session was about to begin in the Cabinet Room, I once again invited Gennadi to join me.

"I told them you are always in meetings," Gennadi said. "It's OK."

Both leaders swept into the Cabinet Room, smiling, shaking hands all around, and taking their seats on opposite sides of the table. The White House is remarkable among world centers of power for being small and simple in design and space. It also is slightly behind the times in terms of communications technology. There is no built-in translation equipment, or ceiling-installed microphones, or wall-mounted cameras. In meetings such as these, the White House Communications Agency and the State Department set up portable headsets and translating equipment at the end of the cabinet table, just in front of the fireplace. A translator for each side sits within a few feet of the principals, and speaks into a mouthpiece that carries his voice to the participants' headsets. Wires are strung all over the floor. The equipment has two or three cables running out the door to electrical switches. Almost every such meeting begins with someone tripping over a cord, or sitting on his headset, or being unable to turn the blooming thing on. Then, once you get your headset on, you hear three voices: the principal's voice, the interpreter's voice in the headset, and the interpreter's actual voice. The result is that everyone is always straining to filter out the unnecessary voices. As all of these events occurred, Gennadi and I settled into adjoining seats along the wall.

The president deferred to Gorbachev, as the guest, to begin the discussion.

Gorbachev began by taking out of his suit pocket a small five-by-seven spiral notebook, lined like the ones we used in grade school, with a shiny green cover. He opened it to the first page and laid it on the table beside his formal notes. His tongue moved around in his mouth, obviously savoring the moment. He had big plans for changing the Soviet Union. He was in America, their superpower enemy for nearly seventy years, and he was shaping events. He was bursting with pride, and he was ready to perform, like a symphony conductor about to move his baton and command the roar of his orchestra. Gorbachev had his facts, his ideas for Soviet reform, and his little green notebook. He was ready to roar.

Gorbachev started through his agenda with great enthusiasm. He spoke of the need for arms control, of reducing world tension, of the historic value of the Intermediate-Range Nuclear Forces (INF) Treaty that had just been signed in the East Room, of the need to reduce the long-range missiles in the Strategic Arms Reduction Talks (START), of ending the growth of chemical weapons, and of the need for progress in reducing conventional weapons. His writing was obvious in his little green book. As each page turned, it revealed a quite legible cursive style in blue ink that in places was smudged, as if bearing down in spots had left periods with excess ink. One could imagine him working late at night in the Kremlin to prepare himself, determined that the Americans would marvel at his knowledge.

Then he started on perestroika and the aspirations of his people. He was expansive, his hands circling in front of him as if caressing a grapefruit, then stopping in midair and turning palms up, as if begging for understanding, then one hand would come down on the side of the other, karate style. Then he would move his elbows to the table, lean toward President Reagan, and move his hands to form a tabernacle in front of his face. Between sentences his thumbs would twiddle, almost as in the old childhood game where Mom taught us to intertwine fingers and say, "Here's the church and here's the steeple, open the door and here's the people." The general secretary of the Soviet Union was showing off.

In the plenary session, the president was clearly impressed with Gorbachev's knowledge and the forcefulness of his presentation. He felt overwhelmed.

As Gorbachev began again to tell about the problems of his economy, the president interrupted with a story of the differences between America and Russia.

"An American scholar, on his way to the airport before flying to the Soviet Union, got in a conversation with his cabdriver, a young man who said that he was still finishing his education. The scholar asked, 'When you finish your schooling, what do you want to do?' The young man answered, 'I haven't decided yet.' After arriving at the airport in Moscow, the scholar again hailed a cab. His cabdriver, again, was a young man, who happened to mention he was still getting his education. The scholar, who spoke Russian, asked, 'When you finish your education, what do you want to be?' The young man answered, 'They haven't told me yet.' That's the difference between our systems," the president said.

Gorbachev frowned the same way he always did when President Reagan said his attitude toward the Soviet Union was "*dovorey no provorey*—trust but verify." Gorbachev seemed to understand the Reagan sense of humor, and while he registered some offense through a smirk or a frown, he never became truly upset. In this case, again, Gorbachev quickly moved on.

Secretary Shultz always seemed concerned about the script going astray. He jumped in to make several points about the need for progress in conventional-arms reductions. "We must finish the mandate from the Vienna talks," he said, "then get on with the asymmetries that allow us to go on to a lower level of armaments."

Shultz loved using this diplomatic talk about asymmetries and blank references to the Vienna talks, which half the room was scratching its head to recall. But Gorbachev was ready. "What about chemical weapons?" Gorbachev said. "The treaty of 1925 banned the use of chemical weapons." Shultz responded that production had proliferated and the 1925 ban on the use of chemical weapons was not working. In other words, if you won't use them, why build them?

It was a nice recovery by Shultz, but the whole conversation disturbed the president. When he heard Gorbachev reciting the details of a 1925 treaty, he knew he could not stay in the conversation. As he did so often, without embarrassment or hesitation, he simply launched into a philosophical defense of America and its intentions.

"There have been four wars in my lifetime," the president said, "and we've never taken an inch in any of them."

"People in Moscow ask if I'm afraid of you," Gorbachev said. "They ask if I will genuflect to you."

President Reagan dipped his head to the side, a sort of "aw shucks" recognition of any praise coming his way, smiled and said, "With regard to your genuflecting, if you ever try, I'll stomp on your foot." It was vintage Reagan humor, not the long story told to him by a friend, or the Irish charm at imitating a character, but the one-line response that found its humor in the slightly outrageous, the picture it painted of incongruity, in this case of one superpower leader stomping on the foot of another.

After the meeting President Reagan and Secretary Shultz escorted Gorbachev to his limousine parked just behind the Oval Office, at the "C-9 Station," as the Secret Service called it. I waited in the Oval with Howard Baker and Colin Powell, the president's new national security adviser, for the president's return. He walked back in, downcast and shaking his head. He was disappointed by his own performance, and overwhelmed by Gorbachev's.

"I better go home and do my homework," he said. "Mikhail has all those details."

"No," Senator Baker said, "you go home and relax. All you have to remember is that no matter what he says, you're the president of the United States." The president smiled, his head perked up, and a small twinkle developed in his eye. "I guess you're right," he said proudly. "See you tonight." And he left for home and the state dinner to follow.

All was glory for Gorbachev. The press loved him. Gennadi and I were able to give several joint briefings without mishap. And I was looking forward to the reception and state dinner on December 9 that Gorbachev was holding at the Soviet embassy. Not many Americans had been in the embassy. For one thing, to go there meant you automatically became part of the FBI, CIA, and National Security Agency collection of famous faces photographed in even close proximity to the place. Second, there was the fear that KGB torture experts might mistake you for a villain and rip certain desirable limbs off before the true facts could even be considered. It was a forbidding place.

The foyer was packed. A long line was formed out the front gate as guests waited to be frisked, or passed through metal detectors, or have their invitations scanned. Secret Service stood to one side, KGB to the other. They eyed each other like stray dogs. Their detail leaders stood together at the top of the stairs, no doubt as a visible sign to the troops that on this occasion they were all on the same side.

Suddenly, some lady screamed that she had been pushed, a fairly normal occurrence with the KGB, who treated pushing as a rather polite way of saying "excuse me." KGB agents pushed through the crowd to survey the problem, which frightened others in the line, and prompted normally stoic bankers and bureaucrats to mutter about atrocious behavior. Suddenly, two hands picked me up under the arms, lifted me off the floor, turned a quarter turn, and deposited me along the wall. I looked about helplessly as the KGB person put his hand on my chest and grunted something about my mother having been related to a Cossack chicken. I looked up the wide marble winding staircase. Standing there, watching with some humor, I thought, was Boris Malakhov, an embassy press officer who had visited me at the White House in preparation for the summit. I caught his eye and shrugged my shoulders, and he hurried down the staircase, gesturing and motioning, presumably to let me go. It was an act of heroism I vowed to repay. Boris took me by the arm to the top of the stairs, and inserted me back into the receiving line just a few feet from the Gorbachevs and the Reagans.

Although Gorbachev and I had shaken hands several times in the course of the summit, we had never actually talked. I had no way of knowing whether he had watched any of my briefings. So I was a little nervous at the prospect of the greeting.

As my turn came, Gorbachev's interpreter, Pavel Palazchenko, a slight, bald-headed fellow, leaned in to the general secretary and said, "This is Marlin Fitzwater. He's the one who said we are old enemies." I was standing right in front of Gorbachev, holding his outstretched hand, and looking him straight in the eyes as Pavel's words, "old enemies," registered. Gorbachev's eyes instantly hardened, as if a switch had been turned, his hand pulled away, and his body muscles visibly flinched. He raised his right hand, squeezing it into a fist almost at the level of my face, and said, "If you had said that in my country, I would scold you."

His closed fist in front of my face scared me. I froze. Then, from somewhere, a low Kansas voice came out of me nervously, "Sometimes I get scolded in my country." But Gorbachev gave no sign of recognition. He lowered his hand, and turned to the next person in line. I stumbled away. It seemed to me the only time during the entire summit that he wavered from his obvious purpose of showing a new kind of Russian leader.

On December 10, Mr. Gorbachev had breakfast with Vice President Bush before coming to the White House. The president's staff was nervously pacing the Cabinet Room, anxious because Gorbachev was late. No one knew why. The fear was that Foreign Minister Shevardnadze and Secretary Shultz had run into some snag over the final communiqué language on the ABM Treaty, again the debate was over Star Wars testing. It was becoming clear that these missiles in space held a special fear for the Soviets. But the Soviets always had to check with someone back in Moscow, even if it was Gorbachev making the decisions, so we thought this might be the cause of delay.

I knew the press would be monitoring Gorbachev's every move, so I flipped on CNN in the president's secretarial office, a small suite between the Cabinet Room and the Oval. Gorbachev's motorcade was center screen, moving slowly up Connecticut Avenue. Suddenly, in front of Duke Zeibert's restaurant, a legendary watering spot for the rich and powerful of Washington, the motorcade stopped and Gorbachev emerged. KGB agents circled the car and looked helpless. Gorbachev plunged into the crowd, shaking hands, speaking in Russian to a screaming crowd that couldn't care less what the language was.

I looked over my shoulder to see President Reagan emerge from the Oval to ask about the commotion. We stood and watched as Gorbachev gave the American people the same show he had given the president in the days before: the sight of a gregarious spirit, an open smile, a Russian who looked like an American, a friendly sort of chap who couldn't possibly want to dominate the world.

The story of the day was made. All the TV networks were consumed by motorcade film, most poignantly by the sight of the venerable Duke Zeibert, standing on the balcony of his power eatery, inviting Gorbachev to come for lunch, no doubt savoring the knowledge that he would spend the rest of the day accepting the congratulatory greetings of reporters, friends, schmoozers, and patrons. It was clear that Gorbachev's advance team had learned how to maximize coverage of an event, and they knew the value of symbolism.

The two leaders finally met again in the late morning, then had lunch before a scheduled 2:30 P.M. departure. The work of the summit was done in terms of the arms agreement, and most of that was done before the summit started. Only one issue remained, the final communiqué and the language on Star Wars.

Secretary Shultz, Secretary Carlucci, and Colin Powell ducked out of the working lunch to join their Soviet counterparts in trying to agree on the ABM Treaty language that would be in the final statement. The president seemed unconcerned.

After lunch, the leaders went to the Red Room, a ceremonial sitting room on the main floor of the White House, to wait for their wives and the short walk to Mr. Gorbachev's waiting ZIL. Gorbachev was nervous, fidgeting, and asking where George and Eduard were. Anatoly Dobrynin, for nearly twenty-five years the Soviet ambassador to the United States, was now a member of the Gorbachev foreign policy team, but without a specific function. He hovered close by. Dobrynin had served all the modern Soviet leaders, had negotiated with President Kennedy during the Cuban missile crisis, and had parried with every president since on some aspect of cold war relations. Yet he also was a spokesman for better ties with the West and had closely associated himself with Gorbachev's "new openness" policies.

"Anatoly," Gorbachev said, "where are they?"

"Working on communiqué," he said.

Senator Baker recognized their anguish. He also knew how Ronald Reagan kept to the schedule. He was never late. He was ready for this summit to be over. Baker called Shultz in the Cabinet Room. "George," he said, "I don't know how close you are, but the president is leaving at 2:30 P.M. If you want a communiqué, you had better be here before then."

Baker reported that the group was just finishing. Suddenly, President Reagan started telling Gorbachev about a 1,200-pound man who never got out of his bedroom. "It was in *People* magazine," the president said. "This is a real man. He went to the bathroom one day, and he fell in the doorway and got stuck. It frightened him so much to get stuck that he went on a diet."

Vice President Bush, Secretary of the Treasury James Baker, and Dobrynin, sitting on a couch across from the president, looked slightly incredulous, as if they were all fighting an internal battle of muscles so their incredulity wouldn't show.

"Is this real fact?" Gorbachev said, looking strangely at his interpreter.

"Yes," the president said. "Since his diet, his knee measurement shrank to one and one-third meters around. When the diet is complete, he wants to visit the grave of his mother."

Gorbachev couldn't figure out the meaning of this story, and he was getting a little frustrated. He asked Dobrynin about a men's room, quickly excused himself, and went into the hall. He began gesturing wildly to Dobrynin, no doubt asking what in the hell this 1,200-pound man was all about.

Finally, the entire group could wait no longer for Shultz and Shevardnadze, so they went downstairs to the Map Room, located just beside the diplomatic reception entrance. Just as the first ladies joined them, Secretary Shultz rushed in and asked if the president could briefly meet him in another room. Gorbachev stepped out also, joining Shevardnadze. The two groups huddled, looking for all the world like two high-school football teams, praying for one last play before the bell rings. Shultz was excited. "This is a big big advance on START," Shultz said, and he read the language. The president agreed, and in less than two minutes rejoined the Gorbachevs to say good-bye. President Reagan asked if Gorbachev agreed to the language. Gorbachev said yes, and the happy foursome, followed by their entourages, headed for the door.

In my press briefing that night, I neglected to mention the 1,200-pound man. But four years later, on the same day that Mikhail Gorbachev was officially removed from office as president of the Soviet Union, *The New York Times* reported that the 1,200-pound man had died. It didn't say if he had visited his mother's grave.

Six months later we made the reciprocal visit to Moscow. The dramatic moments of world euphoria had passed. Gorbachev needed real concessions from the Americans to keep his hard-liners in check, and the arms negotiations were difficult.

In the course of their talks, Secretary Shultz and Foreign Minister Shevardnadze had produced a position on all the issues at hand, and laid the basis for further negotiation on mutual reductions in long-range nuclear missiles.

Gorbachev quietly raised the document in his right hand, waving it gently like a treasured testament. "This is a solid document," he said. "We approve it on the level of principle. The principle that the art of politics is the art of doing what's possible. We have to learn to live in peace."

But then he placed the paper on the table, and slowly raised his closed fist in front of his face. His voice was even, and he stared straight at the president. "But we could strengthen this statement by adding a few phrases on living in peace."

Minor alarm bells started going off around the table. Secretary Shultz, General Powell, and Secretary Carlucci gave only the slightest signs of recognition, but they feared a reopening of the language that their teams had argued over the night before. Shultz never moved a muscle. When conversations became tense, Shultz became granite, every word measured. He waited as Gorbachev's eyes began to change.

Gorbachev moved forward to the edge of his chair. Sitting across the room, Gerasimov and I could see his feet move forward, then plant themselves wide apart like a fighter getting ready to throw a punch. He was rigid and his eyes sparkled. There was some inner gleam of intensity that rose through his body as he prepared to challenge, a small white light in the corner of each eye that appeared and receded with each rush of adrenaline. It was there in Washington, and this day it appeared again as his chin protruded to offer one last gambit.

"Why is 'peaceful coexistence' a bad term?" he demanded. "What are you against?"

His face was growing red. "What about you, Mr. President?" he continued. "What about you, George?" He paused for the direct challenge to register. He knew that "peace" and "coexistence" were valued words to President Reagan, uttered often in various political contexts, and used frequently at this table as the president spoke about the benefits to the world of America and the Soviet Union working together. But they meant something entirely different to Shultz and the others. They were code words in the world of diplomacy for a return to détente, an agreement to live and let live, a backing away from the Reagan era of realism in which the Soviets were being challenged on every front—militarily, economically, and ideologically. Gorbachev was pulling a "Hail Mary" pass, one last attempt to back America away from Star Wars, for them the ultimate offensive weapon.

"Here is a text for circulation," he said, as aides passed around the single sheet of paper. "What do you think?"

Our side was uneasy, twisting in their chairs as they read the few sentences. This language had been rejected in the working groups. Gorbachev knew it. He knew his only chance was to isolate the president and get him to approve the language at the table. He grew audacious.

Seeing the shaking of heads around the table, Gorbachev demanded, "Do you disagree with your own president?" He made eye contact around the room, with Howard Baker, then Shultz, Powell, and Carlucci, wondering if they would engage the issue. "Your president has already agreed," Gorbachev said, throwing a new element of uncertainty into the equation. In the very first meeting of the two leaders, on the afternoon of our arrival, Gorbachev had handed Reagan a brief note that he said he hoped could be in the final communiqué. It read: "Proceeding from their understanding of the realities that have taken shape in the world today, the two leaders believe that no problem in dispute can be resolved, nor should it be resolved, by military means. They regard peaceful coexistence as a universal principle of international relations. Equality of all states, noninterference in internal affairs, and freedom of sociopolitical choice must be recognized as the inalienable and mandatory standards of international relations." At first glance, which is about all it was given at the first meeting, it seemed innocuous. But in fact it was designed to head off further criticism of the USSR for its human rights violations, and at least slow down our military buildup. At least that's the way our diplomats saw it, assuming, as they sometimes naively do, that these statements will actually guide governmental actions. Secretary Shultz had argued in the working groups that the "peaceful coexistence" sentence meant the United States would not challenge the USSR's expansionist activities, such as invading Afghanistan.

The two leaders had been together privately many times during the visit. No one could know for sure what they might have agreed to. Plus, no one wanted to start a contentious debate at this late point in the meetings. So no one responded. There was only silence. Gorbachev moved on.

He settled back in his chair, pleased that he was on the offensive, and moved on to the regional issues that were so divisive.

"The hand of Moscow will be a constructive hand," he said, "in helping with regional issues." He said they would be helpful with a Mideast peace conference; he welcomed U.S. negotiations for peace in Angola; he couldn't give an ultimatum in Ethiopia; he was ready to discuss limiting arms supplies to Central America; he could help intensify the pressure on North Korea to cease aggression toward the South; and finally he suggested more ministerial meetings on these regional issues.

President Reagan summarized our position in these areas, always returning to the theme that only America and the Soviets could bring peace to these regions. He traced the history of recent changes in Central America.

"Your aid made the Sandinistas more powerful than all the countries in Central America. Your participation in Central America is the problem," he said. "If we are to be partners in peace, don't we have a right to say the people of Nicaragua must be set free?"

"I disagree with your assessment," Gorbachev said sternly. "Let's not come back to these assessments, or we will never get out of it." He said there were no Soviet advisers in Nicaragua, an assertion we knew to be wrong.

Gorbachev did not want to fight on these issues. They distracted from his central objective of trying to convince us of his peaceful intentions, and that we should drop SDI and other cold war pressures. The two men returned to the vanilla language of diplomacy, trying to end the meeting on a high note.

"We can cooperate," Gorbachev said. "We can cooperate" was a phrase that reminded me of when my mother said "Maybe later." It was always meant to delay, to put off, to paper over. "We can make contributions," he continued. "We must exchange information. The summit is a major political event."

"It's a great accomplishment that we can be friendly nations," President Reagan said. "But with that must go agreements on other people's rights in the world."

"The baton has been carried forward to new heights," Gorbachev said, "and I'm sure we have achieved much."

"We have been successful when they see that we are cooperating and will not set the world on fire," the president said.

Gorbachev was a virtuoso. Now he had us in a good mood, feeling expansive about the summit, embraced in warm and friendly discussion about cooperation and peace. He was ready for one last pounce.

He turned to Shultz. "George, are you ready on this language?"

"If we take out the word 'coexistence,'" Shultz said.

Colin Powell passed a brief note to the president, "It's a statement that would stop us from criticizing the USSR." There may have been other arguments that Colin could have made, but he knew this one would register quickly. Ronald Reagan would never let himself be muzzled.

"Let us talk about this among ourselves," Shultz offered. Gorbachev agreed. The two sides got up from the table, and we gathered in tight huddles on both sides of the room. It would have been a great picture: these two groups representing virtually all the tanks, divisions, and nuclear bombs of the world, meeting in Catherine the Great's Hall, divided by a thirty-foot blond mahogany table and several giant chandeliers, with a background of green brocade wallpaper and solid gold wall molding, huddled like two rugby teams about to have a scrum.

"I'm sorry if I screwed this up," the president said.

"No, Mr. President," Shultz said. "We thought we had this resolved. This language would return us to détente."

"I don't want that," the president said.

"Just say you want the language that's in the [full] statement," Shultz suggested. "That's what we negotiated."

The president looked over his shoulder and across the table. Gorbachev was watching us, waiting to see when we were ready. When he caught the president's eye, he motioned for him to meet him at the end of the table. President Reagan turned, and both men left their huddles and started walking toward the far end of the room. I couldn't believe it. Gorbachev was making another play, this time to get the president alone.

They met at the end of the table, with interpreters trailing.

Less than two feet apart, Reagan looked directly down at Gorbachev and said, "I want the language that's in the statement."

Gorbachev erupted. His arms flew up. He stepped even closer to the president, so he was looking up, almost at the ceiling, to make eye contact with the president. Their shoes were literally toe to toe. "What is it you object to?" Gorbachev shouted. "What did they tell you?"

The president never moved, but his jaw set. Ronald Reagan was seldom angry. Few had ever seen him angry. But many had seen him when his mind was made up, and they always noticed the jaw, hard and braced with the determination that came from a lifetime of political and personal challenges. Once again, the president said, "I want the language that's in the statement."

Gorbachev slumped. His body sagged, as if suddenly growing shorter. But it only lasted a second, then the adjustment was made, the defeat endured, and his head came up with a smile. He took President Reagan's hand, turning him toward the door, and motioned for them to go. Both men were smiling as they walked through their delegations and back down the long white hallways to St. George's Hall for another ceremony.

Seldom had the face of a summit meeting ever been so different from its soul. The press, and indeed the American people, were still basking in the glow of perestroika, the Washington visit of Gorbachev and his open personality, and the Soviet decision to withdraw from Afghanistan. The press corps was covering the substance of the historic arms-control treaty, but their real fascination was in seeing Reagan the cold warrior walk in Red Square. Their cameras were set up on tops of buildings and from every angle that would measure Reagan the man as he stared at Lenin's tomb. The cameras would be there when the Reagans visited the Eastern Orthodox church and admired its long-forbidden icons, when the president stood under the marble bust of Lenin to tell Moscow State University students about democracy, when the ambassador's residence would open its doors in welcome to Soviet dissidents who had spent years in jail or hiding. These were the faces of the summit that Tom Griscom, our director of communications, had brilliantly conceived to demonstrate U.S. interests. They were strong images that painted a clear picture of repression. If Gorbachev could show a new face to the American people, we would show a new face to the Soviet people—a profile of what freedom could mean, freedom of religion, of speech and academic thinking, of assembly and dissident thinking.

In the weeks before the summit, it had begun to dawn on the Soviet advance team that they had a problem. Vladimir Chernyshov, the Soviet chief of protocol, who was a dead ringer for the movie actor Cesar Romero, headed the advance delegation and soon reported back to Moscow that these crazy Americans were up to no good. He tried every tactic possible to dissuade Griscom from his plans for the president to make a number of public and symbolic appearances. Prohibition wouldn't work, because they knew that Reagan could get in his car and go anywhere in Moscow. Delay worked only until it was clear that the Americans were determined. What the Soviets didn't know, of course, was that Mrs. Reagan's mind was made up. There would be a dramatic response to Gorbachev's walk on Connecticut Avenue, and that's all there was to it.

On Sunday afternoon, after the first meeting of the summit, President and Mrs. Reagan decided they wanted to walk down the Arbat, a pedestrian mall. The Arbat is made up of four or five blocks of shops and street vendors, closed to traffic, where Russian merchants sell fur hats, lacquer boxes, and wooden stack dolls to tourists. It is always crowded with people, and the American embassy residence, Spaso House, is a short two blocks away. In Helsinki, Finland, the day before arriving in Moscow, the president and Mrs. Reagan called in the executive assistant, Jim Kuhn. Mrs. Reagan said they wanted to walk among the people: Find something.

By the time we arrived in Moscow, the advance staff had found the Arbat, but the Secret Service was opposed. It was too open for them, with too many people crowded between exposed buildings with too many open windows. They recommended a rather desolate lookout point outside the city near Moscow State University. The Secret Service always had trouble getting the point that presidents want to be seen with people, preferably without a couple of trench coats on either side of them.

On Sunday in Moscow, the Reagans found themselves at Spaso House with some spare time. The president had tested his bed. He had stared out the upstairs window where the radio waves read maximum on the CIA meters, which meant the Soviets were sending maximum force radio signals into the house trying to pick up voices and conversations. Now he was ready to take a walk. But the Secret Service was still balking. The advance staff was yelling at the Secret Service. The head of advance, Jim Hooley, and Ray Shaddick, director of the president's Secret Service detail, were red-faced from screaming at each other. And Ken Duberstein, the deputy chief of staff, took a discreet walk. Suddenly, Jim Kuhn got a call from Mrs. Reagan, who said, "We're ready."

Jim grabbed Hooley, advance man Rick Ahearn, Shaddick, and another Secret Service agent, Dick Griffin. "Let's go resolve this," Jim said. Jim had a very clear understanding of what it meant when Mrs. Reagan said "We're ready." So they all trooped upstairs and into the president's bedroom.

"We want to go," the president said.

"I'm told there are already thousands of people in the Arbat," Griffin said discouragingly.

Ahearn picked up his radio and called another advance man, Bobby Schmidt, who was surveying the Arbat at that moment. "How many people are around?" Ahearn asked.

"Not more than a handful," Schmidt replied.

Both Hooley and Shaddick made their cases, for and against. There was a moment of awkward silence before Kuhn asked, "Are you saying you can't protect the president on the Arbat?"

"Well, no, we're not saying that," Shaddick said.

"Then we're going," Mrs. Reagan said. "It's done."

I was standing at the bottom of the stairs when this group came rushing down. Hooley was barking orders and Shaddick was shaking his head even before they hit the bottom stair. Bodies were flying in all directions, drivers to cars, advance men to the Arbat, and Secret Service agents throughout the area. Every walkie-talkie was in use as people scattered to set up a perimeter in the Arbat, and do it without causing any commotion. Shaddick had the unpleasant task of notifying his counterpart in the KGB, who was pissed. No notice. No preparation. No warning. And I'm sure this guy's KGB life was meaningless if anything happened to the president.

Fifteen minutes later, the Reagans came down the stairs, as excited as any tourists in town, and climbed into their car for the two-block ride to the Arbat.

The best description of what happened comes from this pool report by Jerry Watson, the *Chicago Sun-Times* White House reporter, who died in 1993 of a brain tumor. For nearly ten years he covered the White House with objectivity and insight. He wrote:

> The most notable event of the President's first day in Moscow observed by your Air Force One/motorcade pool was the unscheduled walk about that took place from 6:10–6:20 P.M. It turned into a panicked scene of zealous Soviet security roughly pushing and shoving reporters and the public, with U.S. officials in some cases pushing back. At a couple of points, the President seemed to get pushed a bit forward and seemed taken aback by the mob scene. Mr. Reagan sometimes seemed alarmed. U.S. security was rough, too, until towards the end of the walk.
>
> At 6:10, the President's motorcade emerged from Spaso House and drove only about 250 feet down a side street that came onto the Arbat, Moscow's well-known pedestrian street/mall that is lined on either side with shops, cafes, etc. The street was already full of Sunday strollers. As the casually-dressed crowd of men, women and children realized who was there, they applauded and cheered and surged toward the Reagans. The President shook hands as he went along. About 75 feet down the relatively narrow mall, the President and First Lady climbed up into an open horse-drawn carriage (without the horse) and waved to the crowd. They shook the hand of a blond woman who is said to operate what amounts to a tiny amusement area for children.

The crowd cheered as the President and First Lady waved from
the carriage. Several women looked on from windows in a limestone apartment building above.

The crush became so great that your reporters sometimes
could not raise their arms or even get their footing. CBS cameraman Cal Marlin was considerably roughed up by the Soviets,
with intrepid Mark Weinberg fighting back in his behalf so the
whole scene would not be lost to the world of television. At some
points, a number of White House staffers—including Duberstein
and Fitzwater—were shut out from the inner ring around the
President by arm-locked Soviet security, who were yelling and
shouting throughout. "It was very scary at the beginning," said
one staffer who stood close to the President. "The President was
very close to the crowd."

At times, the security agents were frantically elbowing everybody in sight, punching people in the stomach, etc. Reporter
Peter Maer said he was punched and felt sick afterwards. Ira
Schwartz reportedly has a face injury. John Uts was reportedly
bear-hugged and choked by camera straps. Some had clothing
torn. Soviet security seemed far more numerous and rougher
than the Secret Service. The crowd continued to surge toward
Reagan and, as he was departing, were driven back very roughly.
Reporters and citizens were crushed up against walls in the relatively narrow Arbat pedestrian street, a vegetable stand half
knocked over, some folks nearly injured against a concrete trash
receptacle.

The Soviet security were obviously very concerned about the
President's security and reportedly had been given no more than
15 minutes warning about the stroll. Some reportedly apologized
to U.S. security afterwards, according to a U.S. staffer. Rumors
had flown all day long about some unscheduled event, presumed
to be a visit to a dissident's apartment. The walk about came as
a relative surprise and was known to your pool only 15 minutes
before it happened.

The pool report failed to note our hasty retreat back to Spaso House.
It had taken only five or ten minutes for the huge crowd to form, and
the Secret Service started moving the president and Mrs. Reagan out
soon after. But the crowd moved with them. The KGB was totally
unprepared for this type of confrontation. Soviet officials normally
didn't wade into public crowds, and Soviet crowds normally receded
quickly in the face of nightsticks and police strength. The KGB

agents assigned to protect the president tried to move their arm-linked fence as he moved. In the midst of this confusion, the White House press pool, with Helen Thomas in the lead, ran with the president in a galaxy of bodies moving down the street, some being knocked down as if in a rugby match with players being picked off and hurled aside as one gets closer to the ball.

As this clamoring group turned down the side street, only 100 yards from the embassy residence, two KGB agents grabbed Helen and started dragging her to the side of the street. Jim Kuhn motioned to the president that the security people had Helen. As the president turned and said "No! No!" Mrs. Reagan stepped back three or four steps and grabbed Helen by her coat. "She's with us!" Mrs. Reagan screamed, and the KGB released her. The first lady put her arms around Helen, led her to the president, and together they walked to the gates of Spaso House. This scene was so extraordinary that the entire crowd stopped and the confusion ended. We joked later about losing another chance to be rid of Helen, but in truth it was a touching moment and another tribute to the remarkable tenacity and durability of Helen Thomas—and Nancy Reagan. Even more remarkable, the stories and pictures were great, showing the president being overwhelmed by the affection of Soviet citizens.

The idea for President Reagan's walk in Red Square, for this ultimate photograph of the old cold warrior coming to terms with a new East-West relationship, smiling at the evil empire he had castigated so many years ago, was borne in the winds of time. It simply had to happen. It was shouted about by Sam Donaldson in the Rose Garden. It was talked about on the Sunday talk shows. It was amusement in the liberal drawing rooms of Georgetown. So as it often falls to diplomats to point out the obvious and give it meaning, it was George Shultz who suggested to the president one day in the Oval Office that he and Gorbachev should walk in Red Square. Curiously, President Reagan didn't want to talk about it, as if it might be signaling some sadness, perhaps the closing of a door in his life. But there was a sparkle in his eye whenever the subject was mentioned, and we knew he would be ready. It would be a fine performance, one of the greatest of his career.

When Gorbachev issued the verbal invitation to take a walk, everyone was excited. It was a beautiful, warm afternoon on the last day of May, with a full sun that glistened on the golden domes of Assumption Cathedral like full sun on a bed of Kansas snow. As people began to rise from their chairs, I rushed to the door of the meeting room, wanting to be the first out to ensure full press coverage of the walk.

In the anteroom, all was confusion. People were running everywhere. KGB on walkie-talkies, Secret Service talking into their sleeves, staff trying to get into the pictures. Then our advance agent, Rick Ahearn, rushed up to me, breathless. "I can't believe it, Marlin," he said, "the Soviets won't let our cameras in. We don't even have a pool camera."

"What?" I exclaimed. "That's impossible!" I looked up to see Gorbachev and Reagan heading out of the room. They probably would go down the long back stairs and hallway to St. George's Hall, then down another long stairs and out to the square. Unless they had a shorter route I didn't know about, we had a few minutes to change the arrangements.

"Where's Gennadi?" I screamed, moving back into the meeting room. He was talking with a staff person. I grabbed his arm. "Come over here, I need you quick," I said. We sat on two straight-back chairs in the anteroom.

"Gennadi," I began, "our advance man says they won't let U.S. television cameras into the square to walk with the president. You have to get our cameras in. This is the picture of a lifetime. This is the picture that says to all the world, 'We are friends.' That message is a major goal of the summit, but U.S. television has to see it."

He listened politely, waited till I finished, and said, "OK. I will take care of it."

I motioned to our advance man to go get the cameras. Gennadi would take care of it. He picked up a corner phone, called some unknown soul, spoke in Russian, and said it was taken care of. He was very calm, too calm, and I wondered if it was really going to happen. When he hung up, I took his arm and suggested we catch up with Gorbachev. Somehow, Gennadi was not nearly as eager as I was to be a part of this historic footnote.

When Gorbachev and Reagan reached the square, the entourage had been reduced to about a dozen people, with a tight rein of security around everyone. Howard Baker, Jim Hooley, and I stayed close to the president. Jim Kuhn was nearby.

We immediately came to a small group of people, all Russian by their appearance, some men in working-class suits, women in babushkas with long skirts and full figures, and a few children being held tightly by stern hands. Someone in the group asked about peace and Gorbachev launched into a long monologue on the peaceful intentions of the Soviet Union. The cameras were there, including the U.S. pool camera and several still photographers. Gorbachev was playing to them like an old pro. He smiled and waved. He put his hand on Reagan's shoulder. It was hard to believe the Soviets had not wanted U.S. cameras there.

Then Gorbachev moved Reagan gently to the next group of people, perhaps a walk of twenty or thirty yards. By now I was beginning to relax, even complaining that I didn't have a hat or suntan lotion. Oh well, I thought heroically, if I die of skin cancer I can say I got it with Ronald Reagan in Red Square. Then I noticed that one of the people in this second cluster looked familiar. He was a slight man with a thin mustache and protruding Adam's apple. He was familiar. He was my driver, and all the drivers were KGB.

As we moved to the third group, I was beginning to recognize others in the crowd: a female hallway guard from our hotel, a doorman, two or three more of the drivers who hung around the hotel lobby waiting for our delegation. My God, I thought, these people are all KGB. This whole thing is a setup.

Then a woman in the third group asked, "Why won't you join in our space program, Mr. President?" What? What had I heard? That had been talked about only minutes before in our Kremlin meeting. And how is it that this Russian peasant woman is so interested in space? Even the questions are fixed. All the while Gorbachev was rambling on about space and the need for cooperation.

At the fourth gathering, I grabbed Howard Baker to say, "Howard, this whole walk is staged. These people all speak English, work at the summit hotel, and are probably KGB. In addition, listen to these questions. They are all on summit topics. Each group of people is a different subject. Not only that, Gorbachev is lecturing the camera at every stop. And the whole world is watching."

"Just what do you propose to do about it?" Howard asked, in that incredulous voice reserved for the sick, insane, and feeble of character.

"Can I at least tell the president what's going on, so he can speak up more?"

"Sure," Howard said.

I gently pulled on the president's sleeve just as Gorbachev launched into another monologue on eliminating nuclear arms.

"Yes, Marlin," the president said politely, as if I might be interjecting something at a dinner party.

"Mr. President," I said, "you might want to say a few words at each stop about the major summit issues." That wasn't a very full description of the problem, but I figured it might alert him to at least respond more. The president was uttering only about one sentence at each stop, and then leaving the entire limelight to Gorbachev. The president said OK to me and turned back to face the small crowd.

But as we moved to the final three crowds of people, nothing changed. At every stop, some pseudo-shopkeeper would ask a policy question, and Gorbachev would lecture. We finished just in time for lunch. I was sunburned, and immediately went back to the press hotel to clean up. I was slightly depressed. Everything was set for this great picture session in Red Square and the Soviets had stolen the show.

I went around to the television network editing booths in the hotel, the surest way to get an early reading on the walk. The rooms were filled with editors and producers racing from telephone to splicer, barking out commands to delivery boys, and trying to make phone contacts with New York. The first room I went to was CBS. Bill Plante, their White House correspondent, was reviewing the tape, getting ready to cut a piece for the evening news.

"Look at this," Bill said, watching the Red Square footage. "Everywhere they go, Gorbachev bores us with a monologue, but look at the Gipper. He's still the old pro. He has one line for each group that we can use. He stole the show."

"Yes he did," I said sheepishly, realizing that once again the president knew exactly what he was doing. He had demonstrated another good axiom for dealing with the media: Give them only what they can use.

CHAPTER EIGHT

Rituals, Pain, and the Chiefs

W hen President Clinton's old Arkansas friend and deputy White House counsel, Vince Foster, committed suicide in 1993, he left a note complaining of the mean people in Washington, those who would "ruin people for sport," and of the paranoia and backbiting that he witnessed in the White House. It was a picture I recognized. It's a mystery of the human psyche why one man lives with it for ten years and another succumbs in less than a year. But the swirling waters of White House pressure catch everyone who works there to one degree or another. They are the most intense for the chief of staff to the president, who is indeed the most powerful man in America, short of the president, of course.

It's about power. Power attracts greed and deceit like honeysuckle on a summer afternoon. It smells so sweet and enticing, luring the strongest of men and women to seek it. They want the decision-making power, they want to control events and people's lives, they want to change the way the world works or at least some small part of it, and they want the accolades and the celebrity as the masses stroke their egos. But there is a price for these rewards, for they are guarded jealously by more curses than were buried in King Tut's tomb: a press that examines every corner of your life, colleagues who want the same power and will smudge just a piece of your reputation in order to steal just a piece of your power, political forces who see opposition as their duty, and an ego that will feed on the power and drive you to irrational acts. So often these forces lead to a terrible conflux of events that results in the chief of staff being forced out of office. Furthermore, the chief of staff, in the final analysis, is just another hired hand. All his power, and his tenure, are decided by the president. He has no other constituency.

In Vince Foster's case, he was subjected to public ridicule for the most innocent, yet most horrible, of Washington crimes: failure. He had shepherded the nominations, or almost nominations, of Zoë Baird and Kimba Wood to be attorney general of the United States. Zoë apparently didn't know her nanny was an illegal alien, and Kimba had a similar problem. President Clinton was embarrassed by the failure of these nominations, and the predictable recriminations ensued. Enemies of the Clinton administration, including conservatives and *The Wall Street Journal*, targeted Foster as the point of incompetence. Inside the White House, friends were starting to wonder about him. In Clinton circles, people asked about his relationship with Mrs. Clinton, which had included being law partners in Little Rock. Foster, obviously from his notes, was feeling depressed about his service to the president. The suicide that followed was the most tragic conclusion that can happen in this scenario.

But the more commonplace conclusion, firing or resignation, can be almost as tragic, and occurs far more frequently. In addition, this painful conclusion to some errant aspect of the power equation is almost always part of an amazing ritual. Like something out of African witchcraft, it is a dance in which the press begins publishing leaks that threaten the chief of staff. The chief fights back with interviews and counterleaks, then there are confrontations. Finally, like the deadly strike of a snake, there is one story of such consequence that the president acts to cut his losses, and a once-proud man is humbled into tears, rage, and frustration as he simply walks out the door, defeated. Those last moments are the saddest for the vacant look in the former chief's eyes. He was cornered by all the pressures of Washington, and caught up in a frenzy that can never be fully controlled.

Within four weeks after I became press secretary to President Reagan, Chief of Staff Donald T. Regan was forced out of the White House and most of his staff with him. He was the first of three chiefs of staff forced out in my presence against their will. It was always a sad occasion, as is the humbling of any man. Falling from the heights of White House chief of staff is a draining, debilitating experience, and most of the "mean" pressures of Washington come into play.

My first day as press secretary was February 2, 1987, and almost immediately the first stories started appearing that the president wanted Regan to leave. I took most of them as mischief from somebody Regan had offended and I routinely denied them from the podium. I felt close to Regan, having worked for him at Treasury for two years. In fact, Secretary Regan had asked me, before he came to the White House, for a memo of advice directed to him personally about how to be chief of staff.

The initial items in my memo were:

—Ronald Reagan is fast becoming a legend, perhaps approaching DeGaulle or Nasser in terms of identifying with his nation's people and their ideals. But the legend is bigger than the man. As Chief of Staff, you will have to protect and enhance the legend as well as the man. In doing so, you or your organization will spend more time than you ever dreamed in managing the President and his time. Those are tasks not every, otherwise successful, manager can handle. You will need people who can subvert their own egos; people who understand the historic role of the Presidency and people who are willing to define their jobs entirely in terms of how best to serve the President. There is a lot of "standing in the rain" that goes with being a Presidential aide.

—Don't underestimate the First Lady's role. If you have taken any of her calls, you probably already know the demands and the priorities she commands. Probably through someone on your own staff, you must find a way to manage her requirements.

—How you define your relationship with the President will define your job and those of your assistants. For example: If you have a visible policy role, the press will say you have taken over for this laissez faire President—the Prime Minister effect. If the President will not allow that, you may need a low key "on background" strategy for dealing with the media and the Congress. You may need a policy mechanism for direct attention to Cabinet Secretaries, etc. In summary, how much power you assume will determine whether you need policy makers or policy coordinators.

—Living up to expectations. The media, the government, and probably, the public expects you to take charge: to carry out the conservative agenda, to make Ronald Reagan a dynamic executive, to position the Administration for maximum influence on the 1988 election, to lead Republicans in Congress, and to pass the President's programs. Those expectations are a tribute to your reputation, your proven leadership, and your style. But you will not succeed in all of these things. So begin now to put expectations in line with reality. Speak of the complexities of the job, the sharing of responsibility with the Congress, and the need for public support.

—The difference between line and staff management. You are now two people: Regan and Reagan. Always speak in the editorial "we." On the Brinkley show you said, "I want an arms control . . ." You are now positioned as a "strong, tough new Chief of Staff." But it is a fine line between "strong" and "arrogant" when 100 members of the news media are examining your every word. There is no experience to prepare you for the public scrutiny you are about to receive. You must show you are managing for the President, not managing the President. This will be difficult because he may be willing to let you manage him.

Unfortunately, Don Regan stepped over the line on most of these points: ego subversion, appeasing the first lady, the prime minister effect, "I" versus "we," and the appearance of arrogance. All of this at a time when the search was on for Iran-Contra scapegoats, making his tenure perilous at best. The *Washington Post* stories were therefore not particularly surprising.

The morning the third such story appeared, I received my first call from Mrs. Reagan—dread. No one on the staff wanted to hear from the first lady because no one wanted to ever get in her sights. It had long since become a tenet of staff longevity that to offend Mrs. Reagan was suicidal. When I first went to Camp David in 1984 as deputy press secretary, Larry Speakes told me a successful weekend would be one in which Mrs. Reagan never learned my name.

"Hello, Mrs. Reagan," I said meekly.

"Hello, Marlin," she said.

"What can I do for you?" I said.

"Well, Marlin, you know those stories about Don Regan?" she said.

"Yes," I replied.

"Well, you should just stay out of them," she said.

"Yes, ma'am," I said.

"Good-bye, Marlin," she said.

The message was clear: Don't defend Don Regan. I hung up the phone, sat down in my chair, and let the anxiety flow away. What in the world would I do now? The stories were true. Mrs. Reagan was out to get him. She had decided that Regan should have somehow prevented Iran-Contra. She resented his occasional upstaging of the president, and perhaps she even resented his closeness to the president. Now I was in the middle. I was also in over my head and needed a little education on how these things worked. So I went to the best source in town, a *Washington Post* reporter. "Here's how it works," he said. "Mrs. Reagan tells Paul Laxalt, the president's oldest friend, that Regan is hurting Ronnie and has to go. Laxalt calls Stu Spencer, the California political consultant who has advised all the Reagan campaigns, and says Regan has to go. Spencer calls Lou Cannon of *The Washington Post*, his old friend from many California campaigns, and says Regan has to go. Cannon writes that close Reagan friends and associates feel Regan has to go."

I knew the rest. Once that story appears, the White House press start asking the president if Regan will be replaced. The president says he has full confidence in Regan. Regan, however, reads the story and knows damn well that it came from Mrs. Reagan. He knows the end is at hand and begins making plans to leave.

All this had occurred by the afternoon of February 27, when I walked over to the Old Executive Office Building to visit the vice president's press secretary, Steve Hart, and to smoke a cigar, still allowed at that time in certain offices. I had just settled into an overstuffed, 1950s, dark brown leather government-issue armchair, and lit a Baccarat Churchill cigar, handmade in Honduras, when the pager on my belt began vibrating to indicate I should call my office. Connie Gerrard, my secretary, screamed into the phone. "Get over to Regan's office! They're looking everywhere for you. Hurry!"

Connie was a cool customer. She had survived Vietnam, Watergate, Iran-Contra, and personal encounters with every modern president, even hiding behind an oak tree at Camp David in observance of the Nixon rule that he should never see a staff person at the Camp. She was not easily flustered, yet her voice that day was clearly alarmist. I ran from Steve's office, down the long marble hallway, down two flights of winding marble stairs, out a side driveway under the building, and across the executive driveway to the White House. I stopped briefly in the basement to catch my breath, then went up the back elevator that stopped just a few feet from the chief of staff's door. His secretary motioned me in.

I opened the door slowly. The inhabitants of the room froze in place. I took two steps and froze also, looking slowly at the three figures in the room. They were like bronze statues, carved in natural poses about the room, like an urban street gallery where someone had placed clothes over the metal sculptures. Standing behind desk:

Don Regan. Sitting at table: Dennis Thomas. Standing by window: Tom Dawson.

The chief of staff was crying. His face was red, his eyes swollen, in a wild combination of anger and sorrow. No one spoke. Slowly, he picked a single page of paper from his desk and held it out to me. I hesitated, then stepped forward and took it. I couldn't imagine what terrible thing had happened.

It read: "I hereby resign as chief of staff to the President of the United States. Respectfully yours, Donald T. Regan."

I looked up, bewildered. The words were so sparse. There was anger in every space and every letter.

"Issue it," he said finally.

"Has the president seen it?" I asked.

"Issue it!" he screamed.

"Yes, sir," I said, turning for the door. I hurried out, walked quickly down the hallway to my office, through the outer office, past Connie and into my office. I paused at the doorway to address Connie: "No calls except from the president or Regan's office." I closed the door, slid the brass lock in place, walked across the room, closed the long, sixteen-foot curtains in the windows that faced Pennsylvania Avenue, and went behind my desk to call the president.

The operator put me through to the family quarters.

"Hello, Mr. President, this is Marlin."

"Yes, Marlin," he said.

"Sir, Secretary Regan just gave me a resignation letter to issue," I said. "I'm just checking to see if you've seen it."

"No," he said.

"Let me read it to you," I said, and I read it without emotion.

There was a long pause. Then he said, with the sound of sincere regret in his voice, "Well, that's too bad." And I knew he honestly felt that way, felt it was too bad that a warm friendship was ending on such a difficult note. What I didn't know, of course, was whether he knew the whole episode had been engineered by Mrs. Reagan. It turned out that the president had already approached Howard Baker about becoming chief of staff. Regan knew it was coming, had even discussed his departure with the president, but was hoping to hold off resigning until after the Tower Board report had cleared him of any improprieties in the Iran-Contra investigation. But as soon as Baker said yes to the job, it was leaked to the press in order to lock the deal in place. Don Regan was sitting in his office when National

Security Adviser Frank Carlucci rushed in to say CNN was reporting Howard Baker as his replacement.

"I suggest, Mr. President," I said, "that we release a statement by you accepting the Regan resignation, and at the same time, announcing the appointment of Howard Baker. I'll be glad to draft those for you, sir."

"OK, Marlin," he said. "You should call this fellow Grissom and tell him." The president never quite got names right. But it was clear that he and Howard Baker had discussed the job, and other staff changes as well.

"You mean Griscom," I said, recognizing that the president was referring to Baker's longtime press secretary, Tom Griscom.

"Yes," he said.

"I'll call you back soon with the statement," I said.

I hung up and immediately dictated a one-paragraph statement accepting the resignation of Don Regan and appointing Howard Baker. It took about ten minutes to dictate and type. I called Griscom, told him what had happened, and read him the statement appointing Baker. He said he would call Baker to fill him in.

I then called the president.

"May I read you this statement?" I said.

"Go ahead, Marlin," he said.

"It is with deep regret that I accept the resignation of Chief of Staff Donald T. Regan . . ."

When I finished, there was a long silence as I waited for the president's response. Finally he said, "I only have one change. Take out the word 'deep.'"

We were duplicating the press release when Howard Baker called.

"I understand you have a lot of excitement over there," Baker said.

"Yes, sir," I replied. "Can I read you the statement announcing your appointment?"

After I read it, he asked if there was anything else he should know.

"It's my understanding, sir," I said, "that Don Regan has left the building. There's a lot of confusion here about what's happening. I will be releasing this statement within minutes. It might be good if you could come over this afternoon, just to show the world a little stability."

As I hung up, I couldn't help but contemplate the vision of a very proud, but angry and hurt, Don Regan walking out the back door of the White House alone. It always seems to end that way.

This was very painful to me, because Don Regan had given me my first political appointment, and because he was a good, honest, humorous man who had not been saved by any of the normal fire walls in a person's character. It was my first lesson in the destructive pressures of the White House and how difficult they are to stop. It's almost impossible to voluntarily walk away from power, even when the forces of the press, political enemies, circumstances, and those around you give every warning that it is time to go. I would face this situation on two more occasions, with two more chiefs of staff who struggled to stop the process. But they couldn't because power also insulates. And those of us below the chiefs could never quite find the courage to grab these guys by the lapel and say: "It's over, get out of here before you destroy yourself." They wouldn't have listened anyway.

In November 1988, my old boss, George Bush, won election as the forty-first president. I had enjoyed my two years on his staff, but I didn't expect to return. New presidents normally don't want holdovers from old presidents. I was preparing to start a job search from a position of relative strength: a Republican with high visibility and close relations with the new president. Washington firms of every stripe pay highly for that kind of background.

In addition, Bush had finished his campaign with a new press secretary, Sheila Tate. I figured the new president would like to appoint the first woman press secretary. Sheila had good press relationships, she had worked for Mrs. Reagan, and President Bush liked her. But one evening in November Craig Fuller, the vice president's chief of staff, called me at home to ask if I would be interested in staying on as press secretary.

Craig was smooth at this personnel business. He could slip a person out of one job and into another and nobody, including the incumbent, would understand what had happened. Indeed, all parties would end up thinking they got a good deal. In this case, Craig said Sheila felt she wanted to return to the private sector, to her job at the Hill and Knowlton public relations firm, where she had been making a six-figure salary.

Sheila also called me at home to ask if I would be interested in staying as press secretary if she decided to return to Hill and Knowlton. I said yes. This was classic Fuller. It was clear that the president had decided Sheila would not get the White House appointment, and Fuller was greasing the skids. The press corps had turned on Sheila during the campaign. They accused her of never being available to them for questioning, and of spending too much time in the cushioned embrace of the presidential entourage. I must say that one of the more natural reactions to being beat up by the press every day is to avoid them, except when you have specific information to deliver.

It's one of the cruelest tricks played on press secretaries—to hire them to fight the daily press battles, argue with reporters, make the rules for press behavior, and generally oversee the manor, then let the press judge their performance. In any case, when the campaign ended, the press did not recommend Sheila for the next promotion.

She was told, and allowed to set up her own departure. The call to me was simply to establish the idea that she made the decision herself and, further, to allow her to take some credit for my appointment. By the time she actually resigned to the vice president, all the groundwork had been done. She would be invited to White House parties, would be known as a Bush insider, would be making tons of money, and everyone would be happy. With the benefit of historic hindsight, it was Sheila's good fortune. She successfully helped to establish the Powell Tate public relations firm, makes a bundle, and has a fine reputation.

Nevertheless, when President-elect Bush asked me to come to his office on November 28, 1988, I went with great anticipation. We both read our lines well. He offered me the job. I was excited. His fifth official appointment had been made, behind Secretary of State James Baker, his personnel director Chase Untermeyer, General Counsel Boyden Gray, and Chief of Staff John Sununu.

"Do you have any questions?" he asked.

"Just the one you advised me to ask when I joined President Reagan," I said. "Will I have access to you, and to all meetings?"

He frowned a little, but quickly answered that he thought that would work out.

"Including National Security Council meetings?" I asked.

Now he really frowned. "Well, I don't know," he said. "Some of those may not be appropriate."

I knew this might be trouble for him. He had a penchant for secrecy. As an undergraduate at Yale he belonged to the secret fraternity Skull and Bones. As CIA director, of course, he learned the full discipline of secrecy. His personality was naturally prone to compartmentalization, which means secrecy. He asked people for advice

on their specialty—economics, foreign policy, press, etc.—but seldom held open discussions. This later proved to be a weakness, especially in considering the country's economic conditions. Even at
this first meeting to offer me the job, his compartmentalization was
troubling. It meant he would never think to invite me to a nonmedia
meeting. My own attitude was that every meeting of government
has a media component because at some point almost every action
by government has to be explained to the public.

I sensed a no might be coming, so I moved to stop it. "Let's wait
and see how it works out," I said, and he agreed.

One of the truly wonderful things about working for Ronald Reagan was that he kept few personal secrets, and he never manipulated
people. People kept things from him, but he seldom kept things to
himself or from others. I went to almost every meeting, including all
NSC meetings. Sometimes other staff would look at me as if I were
an intruder, but they seldom said anything. Everyone assumes
everyone else is invited by someone. And no one wants to ask the
president if he invited so-and-so. Fortunately, one of those people
who saw that I was in every Reagan meeting was George Bush.

The trick to pulling this sort of thing off, of course, is to restrain
yourself from saying anything in the meeting. That way the other
participants, the experts, are not threatened by your presence. I modeled this tactic after the vice president's own experiences with President Reagan. If I wanted to comment on the substance of a policy
that didn't relate to public attitudes or information, such as the content of civil rights legislation, I did it in the helicopter, or standing in a waiting room in some hotel, or in the president's study at
7:15 A.M. I never tried to overstep my bounds by undercutting a fellow staff member, and the president would not have stood for that
anyway.

The second task is to prove that you can handle inside information: no leaks. And the third challenge is to show the other participants that they can benefit by your presence: that you could be an
ally for their position. They know that a press secretary probably
spends more private time with a president than any other senior staff
member. I worked very hard on this process. I figured that if I could
get a few months under my belt with President Bush, I could win his
trust.

"When do you want to announce this?" he asked.

"I don't think it matters," I said. "I'm here. We could do it anytime, maybe in a week or two."

"Let's do it today," he said.

"Sure," I replied, realizing that my first piece of press advice had been rejected, and furthermore that he had been right. There was no use in letting my appointment leak out. We decided on 1 P.M. in the press briefing room. I left his office that morning with the same sense of pride and excitement as when President Reagan selected me. In a way, this was even greater. This was real history: the first press secretary to ever be appointed by two presidents. Pierre Salinger had been kept on by President Johnson for a few weeks after President Kennedy's death, but it was not a permanent situation. Indeed, Johnson went through five press secretaries.

John Sununu was a tough political operator. He made his reputation during the Bush campaign of 1988 against Michael Dukakis of Massachusetts. He and Dukakis were from neighboring states, both governors, and both representing strong ideological viewpoints. They clashed on many issues, and during the campaign Sununu would debate anyone, anywhere, anytime on the Dukakis record. He challenged the Duke in Massachusetts and elsewhere, to the point that Bush saw him as a hired gun who would go up against anybody.

After Bush narrowly lost the Iowa caucus to Senator Robert Dole of Kansas, his campaign was in danger of sliding into oblivion. For a sitting vice president to be upset in the first primary contest was humiliating. But Bush was a fighter, and he rallied the troops for the New Hampshire primary. When he arrived in New Hampshire, standing on the doorstep of history to greet him was John Sununu, ready to turn things around. He took the campaign staff by the nape of its neck and shook it up, pulling the vice president out of his limousine cocoon and putting him in the driver's seat of eighteen-wheelers and assorted other blue-collar modes of transportation. He persuaded Bush to challenge Dole on taxes in a state that treated taxes like head lice, and the vice president won. Sununu's reward was to replace Craig Fuller as chief of staff to the president, not just because Sununu had helped him win, but because Sununu was a demon fighter who would challenge any authority without regard to his own safety. He was a political fullback whose body would take all hits, a loyal lieutenant who was smart, conservative, and a natural entrée to the Republican right. Bush loved these qualities of blind devotion in his staff, every politician does. The governor was also closer to the president's age than Craig, and he had passed the "sheriff's" test. Bush often referred to House Speaker Sam Rayburn's quote about political wisdom coming from "running for sheriff." Sununu had been twice elected governor of New Hampshire.

Imagine an overweight Kermit the Frog walking head down with his hands in his pockets, along a narrow corridor in the back of the White House. He shuffles as he moves his webbed feet in slow motion, trying to keep them in line. That's John Sununu, only shorter. He is a nerd, and nurtures his reputation for brilliance. In college he was the one with a slide rule. In the White House he carried computer games around.

But there were flaws. His loyalty had a price: power. His intelligence had a blind spot: arrogance. After a few months as chief of staff it was clear that one day his enemies would reach up and devour him. He was adding enemies daily, such as congressmen he yelled at. He once arrived late for a briefing in the White House for members of Congress on the subject of new environmental rules to protect wetlands. A congressman had prepared a special briefing book on the subject and was rather proud to be making this presentation in the White House. He was talking when Sununu arrived. John walked directly over to the congressman, reached down and grabbed the corner of his open book, then slammed it closed with great flourish as his arm whipped around in exaggerated follow-through. The congressman was humiliated and would never forget it.

But congressmen don't have the power of the press, especially the power to write so persuasively that a pack forms. Sometimes it's the power of the argument, sometimes the political passion of the movement, sometimes the outrage of the offense, but when the White House press corps reaches a consensus about any individual, that person's station in life is as predictable as the social castes of India, and just as difficult to change. So it was with John Sununu. As he offended one person after another in Washington with his bellicose personality and belligerent meetings, his pack of defenders grew smaller. By the time he was discovered to have used presidential aircraft for private purposes such as ski trips and golf outings, his personal flanks were totally exposed.

In April 1991, both *The Washington Post* and *U.S. News & World Report* broke the story of the chief of staff's frequent flying. Initially, they reported that in December 1989 the governor and two other passengers had flown from Andrews Air Force Base to Salt Lake City and then on to Vail, Colorado, on an Air Force jet. The plane, a C-20 twelve-seat, corporate-style jet, returned to Andrews without any passengers and then, just three days later, flew back to

Vail to pick up the governor and his guests, at a cost to the government of more than $30,000. As the story unfolded, Pentagon records revealed that between April 1989 and April 1991 the governor had made seventy-seven trips on military aircraft, forty-nine of which were listed as official, meaning the government and, consequently, the U.S. taxpayers, had footed the bill, which was estimated to be over half a million dollars. It was the kind of abuse of power that makes people's blood boil.

The press loves this kind of "waste and abuse" story because it's visual, it's easy to understand, it's highly symbolic, and it offends the American people. The right way to deal with this problem is first to determine if you did anything illegal; if so, the lawyers take over. If not, there are some basic rules to follow: 1. Come clean. It's all going to come out anyway. Do it fast and all at one time. 2. Make restitution. The public will never forgive you as long as you keep the booty. 3. Most important, give the press their pound of flesh. It is an absolutely nonnegotiable demand for ending a public controversy. Usually it's just an apology or admission of guilt anyway.

Governor Sununu rejected all these courses of action. He made every possible mistake in dealing with this kind of personal crisis.

"I'm not going to give them a damn thing," he told me, his face growing red, and puffing a little as if it were some natural defense mechanism like bugs that change color to match the leaves. "It's none of their business. Every trip I made was authorized on behalf of the president."

The governor self-righteously tried to hide behind a 1987 White House directive that authorized the use of such aircraft for the chief of staff and the national security adviser in order to ensure that they could always be contacted and to protect them from the threat of hijacking. But even the original directive was just a self-serving perk. Reagan Secretary of State George Shultz got the president to approve this new policy so he could take a presidential plane to homecoming weekend at Stanford, and visit his nearby home in Palo Alto, California. The directive did instruct, however, that the officials "should evaluate the use of military air transportation on a basis of appearance of impropriety." The governor's argument soon backfired when the press reported that, in contrast, National Security Adviser Brent Scowcroft had used military aircraft only twenty-three times in the same period. The media wasn't the governor's only problem. For many White House staffers who had lived for three years with the governor's preaching and practices of austerity and penny-pinching, his argument held absolutely no water and his indignant insistence of innocence fell on deaf ears.

From that point on, we went through day after day of revelations in the press about another Sununu trip: golf courses visited, ski vacations with the family, visits to a Boston dentist, multiple-use travel in which he flew a small presidential jet to a meeting, then spent the weekend at his home in New Hampshire before returning to Washington.

By mid-June, the press was in high dudgeon. Bill Safire, the *New York Times* columnist and former Nixon speechwriter, wrote: "John Sununu should be dumped because he lacks a Presidential aide's most essential attribute: political judgment. Ethical breaches, if acknowledged, might be forgiven; but sustained obtuseness, bringing deserved ridicule on the administration, imperils the success of a Presidency."

Safire went on to say, "He is widely perceived to be a pompous ass . . . because he has repeatedly demonstrated arrogant asininity." Wow. How would you like to read that about yourself in the morning?

"They will never get me!" Sununu once screamed at me, as I asked about the latest press report that his wife had participated in securing a corporate aircraft for a private trip. "That is absolutely not true," he said. "She had no involvement whatsoever."

The press had taught me through many painful episodes to never totally discount their leaks, or rumors, or information tips. Never make a total denial. There was always an element of truth in their questions. So at my briefing the next day I hedged. When asked about Mrs. Sununu, I said, "John Sununu says she had no involvement." I felt sick that I couldn't give John a more emphatic defense, but I knew in my stomach he was not telling me the whole story. I think he felt he was being chivalrous.

The next day's *Washington Post*, of course, had all the details of Mrs. Sununu's involvement, verifiable by written records. My reputation with the press was fine because they knew I had publicly sourced my information, but I never trusted Sununu again. As his travel mess drew to a close, it was clear that he was alone in his own defense. What he did was not illegal, but it was a mistake to do it, and to try to convince the press that it was unimportant. He was cornered. With all defenses gone, neither staff nor political allies to argue his case, the calls for his resignation came from every corner, including the media.

Maureen Dowd of *The New York Times* is a gentle writer of such nuance and charm that her criticism seldom has the sting of pain. Rather, it causes you to laugh and hold your chest, self-mockingly, as you realize you have been skewered by a rubber knife. But she knows the soft spots where only a rubber knife will fit, such as in the psyche, just below the brain, where strange currents cause people to do stupid things. She writes of leaders without grace, women without charm, men whose motives are true and honest but sometimes misguided. She knows the face of integrity, and she knows when it is masked. John Sununu hid his behind a steel plate so thick and so obvious that everyone knew he was hiding the truth. Maureen Dowd understood the insecurities that drove him to wear the mask and she wrote about them. John Sununu hated her for it.

One morning in Florida, the Bush motorcade pulled into the cavern of the Miami convention center for a speech to Cuban-American supporters. Two forty-foot recreational vehicles were parked near the door as portable offices for the president and his staff. John Sununu had left the motorcade and entered one of the RVs to make his calls back to Washington when he was told of Maureen's latest article about his motives. He emerged from the RV where the staff was gathered. He walked over to me and, in the presence of everyone, asked if I had seen the article.

"Yes," I said.

"I will destroy her," he said, "if it takes me the rest of my life, I will destroy her. I don't know where or when, but I'll get her." He turned on his heels and went back into the RV. Our small group was stunned, afraid actually, by the depth of his venom.

In fairness to John, by 1995 he had been out of government for nearly three years and had made no move to destroy Maureen Dowd. He even became a media star on CNN. But it was in the midst of this hatred and fear following Sununu's improper use of government aircraft in 1991 that most members of the president's staff concluded the chief must go.

Although the "Air Sununu" scandal was subsiding in November 1991, the president's staff was facing the beginning of an election year with growing concern. No one seemed to be able to get along with Sununu, who had assumed dictatorial powers as chief of staff. His staff meetings were a farce in which no one said anything for fear of being publicly humiliated by Sununu or Dick Darman. He even refused several requests to let the various communications staffs meet to coordinate efforts, and he controlled all presidential sched-

uling. Nearly every member of Congress had been bloodied in a Sununu fight. And Bob Teeter, the Republican pollster who was sure to
be a key part of the president's reelection campaign, let it be known
he would not share power with John Sununu in the 1992 election.

Everybody seemed to have a Sununu story. Mine dated back to
May 22, 1991, when President Bush went to St. Paul, Minnesota,
to visit a "Saturn School," so named for its innovative approaches to
educational goals. On *Air Force One*, the president told me, "I want
to announce Colin Powell's reappointment as chairman of the Joint
Chiefs soon. I want people to know this Woodward book doesn't
mean anything. People want to drive a wedge between us. I don't
like that."

Bob Woodward of *The Washington Post* had written a book about
the Desert Storm war entitled *The Commanders,* in which the chairman of the Joint Chiefs of Staff had supposedly expressed reservations about military action.

"I don't know why he gave those interviews," the president said,
"but he called me as soon as the book came out, and I told him not
to worry."

Later, in St. Paul, Andy Card, the deputy chief of staff, took a call
in the president's holding room from Governor Sununu.

"Have you talked to the president yet about *The Commanders?*"
he asked.

"No," Andy said. "He's been with Lamar Alexander all the
time." Alexander was secretary of education and accompanying the
president on the trip.

"Don't forget," Sununu admonished Card.

"What's that all about?" I asked.

"The governor wants me to tell the president that the White
House staff—at the mid and lower levels—are really upset about the
revelations and leaks in the Woodward book."

"Why?"

"Because he wants to discredit Cheney and Powell," Andy said.

"Why?" I asked again.

"I don't know," Andy said, "but Sununu has called me about it
twice already today."

"Andy, my boy," I said, "don't you dare tell the president that
stuff." It amazed me that Sununu would put Andy in the position
of telling the president such a story. In the first place, Andy
wouldn't do it. Secondly, Andy would have to tell the president what
the governor was up to. He was the most honest person on the staff,

ABOVE: Growing up on "the Howie place" was like having a personal sports center: henhouse, roller-skating rink, basketball against the barn, and a hayloft playground. RIGHT: At home in Abilene, Kansas, with a new sport coat and a 1952 Chevy.

ABOVE: With my dad and his camper. His values were solid. RIGHT: Courtney and Bradley in the Rose Garden. Often with me on weekends, they answered the phones: "White House. Want to talk to my dad?"

TOP: An Environmental
Protection Agency press
conference in the 1970s,
when I still had hair.

MIDDLE: Chief of Staff Donald T. Regan, Vice President George Bush,
and President Reagan welcome me to the spokesman's job in January
1987. Iran-Contra was heating up. Regan was about to leave. BOTTOM:
The first of many "tick-tock" sessions with reporters during the Persian Gulf war, in the press secretary's office.

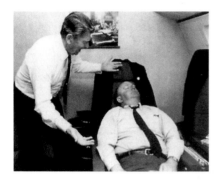

TOP: On *Air Force One*, President Reagan loved to catch me asleep. I gave him plenty of opportunities.

MIDDLE: President Reagan, Chief of Staff Howard Baker, Deputy National Security Adviser General Colin Powell. and me at the president's Santa Barbara, California, ranch house. It was a very private refuge for the president.
BOTTOM: The last hour of the Reagan presidency, January 20, 1989. The Gipper walked to the door, turned and saluted the office, and marched away.

TOP: President Bush couldn't wait for the new horseshoe pit to be finished. We tore the plastic off the clay pits before the backboards were painted, and tossed away. BOTTOM: Mikhail Gorbachev visited the horseshoe pit at Camp David, asked the photographer how it was done, then picked up one shoe and threw a ringer. He walked away with a perfect record.

TOP: The informality of President Bush's home in Kennebunkport, Maine, led to this personality portrait: CIA Director Robert Gates, always with paper and pencil; Secretary of State James A. Baker III, always with cowboy boots; and President Bush, always with a telephone tucked under his chin. BOTTOM: A staff meeting on *Air Force One*. The Boeing 747's spaciousness provides a relaxed setting, especially on intercontinental flights.

TOP: President Bush at the Gridiron Club as "Tarmac the Magnificent." He seemed to enjoy calling his press secretary "a snack-sneaking snowball." It was great fun.

MIDDLE: Somalia was hot and dangerous, but the troops were terrific. In January 1993, morale was high and America was saving lives. The heat was like Kansas in August.

BOTTOM: In this photo, Sarah McLendon of the McLendon News Service is eighty-four and still outraged by her government's insensitivity to our citizens. She has covered eleven presidents and never shies from asking the tough questions.

TOP: On my last day in office, the press corps surprises me with a champagne good-bye. The shelves were empty but my heart was full. The press are good people. BOTTOM: Hats. A photo by the late George Tames of *The New York Times*, a legendary photographer who covered the White House for decades.

had the most common sense, no axes to grind, good political instincts, and everyone respected him.

En route home, President Bush called Andy forward to his cabin on *Air Force One.* "What's Sununu up to these days?" the president asked. Somehow, the president always had inside information, always seemed to have the answer before he asked the question. "Has he got you up to any mischief?"

"Well, Mr. President," Andy stammered, "he wants me to tell you something that I can't verify."

"What?"

"He says a lot of mid-level White House people are complaining about the Woodward book, about the Department of Defense leaking everything and people there spending time with reporters," Andy said.

The president looked disappointed, slouched in his chair, folded his hands in his lap, and looked at the floor. "He's always trying to undercut Cheney," the president said. "I don't know why."

"I'll be damned!" I later exclaimed to Andy. "He knows. He knows. The president knows damn well how devious Sununu is. I can't figure out why he puts up with it."

By December, John Sununu's world had no defenders, and his once-timid detractors in the president's inner circle were beginning to find a voice. Their message was that Sununu must go—before the campaign of 1992.

In late November, the president called me to his study behind the Oval Office.

"Can Sununu get through this?" he asked. "Does he have to go?" The president did not want to fire Sununu. He liked him and his take-charge attitude. Furthermore, he had staked a good deal of his presidency on Sununu. The governor had prevented any real economic reform or activism during the recession of 1991 and 1992, and had successfully gotten the president to veto the one economic program the Congress passed because it had a tax on millionaires. Ironically, it was also Sununu who convinced the president that he could get away with breaking his "no new taxes" pledge by calling the 1990 tax increase "enhanced revenues"—more about that later. The president needed Sununu around to keep reminding him why those were great decisions, when in fact he didn't like any of them.

A few days later, as my staff was giving me a small birthday party, Margaret Tutwiler called from the State Department. She was assistant secretary for public affairs and Secretary Baker's closest adviser. We had become very close over the four years through daily phone calls about the press, coordinating our responses, and taking many of the same media bruises. She said she wanted an off-the-record conversation about White House staff.

"The president has called Secretary Baker," she said. "He wants to talk tomorrow [Saturday] about changes. What do you think of this? Get a big name like Volcker that will signal the country we mean business on the economy. Do you know any other names?"

"No," I said, privately feeling relieved that Baker was involved and we were going to recognize the economic problems and make changes.

"Then put Skinner in charge of the campaign," she continued. "Move Sununu to Transportation or an embassy. Then we need a chief of staff. Any ideas? Maybe change a lot of White House staff."

"You might think of Will Ball for chief of staff," I volunteered. "He comes from Senator Tower's staff. Was secretary of the Navy. Knows the Hill and would run the staff without running the campaign."

"Secretary Baker thought about Cheney," she said, "but I can't believe he'd leave Defense."

Baker, of course, didn't want to leave State. It was clear that the president was asking for help and Baker was looking for alternatives.

"Baker thinks we need a dramatic economic plan," Margaret said, "like we did on arms control."

"I agree. Why not shut down all the national parks or something to symbolically get money for a tax cut? Urge the Fed to drop interest rates. Something dramatic to get money into the economy."

"Well, think about it," she said.

It's about this point in the firing ritual, where people are actively looking for replacements, that the chief of staff begins to lose perspective. He knows the press is after him, his enemies are stoking the fires, his friends have gone underground to protect themselves, and the president has signaled that he's about to desert the cause. In this case, Sununu began searching for a grand solution that would raise his value.

On November 25, the governor brought me a seven-page speech to be given by the president on television the night before Thanksgiving. I read it hurriedly and became depressed. It was seven pages of repetition that had the president saying, "I know people are hurting. I'm thinking of you." It never said we were going to do anything about it. No action plan. No real description of the economic problem in the country.

I showed it to Dorrance Smith, a new communications adviser who had been producer of *Nightline* with Ted Koppel and had good news judgment.

"Hell," he said, "the nets won't even carry this. The Democrats will demand equal time, and worse, they'll be better." So we agreed to go tell the president.

"Why won't they carry this?" the president asked.

"Because it doesn't have any news," Dorrance said. "The nets will see it as political."

"Well, we're not getting the message out," the president said. "How do we do it?" He was angry. First, he felt helpless in dealing with the Sununu problem. Now he was being told we were helpless in getting on TV. We came up with the idea of having the president leave Camp David over the weekend, take the press pool with him, and go down to the little town of Thurmont, Maryland, to talk to people about their problems, their jobs, their fears, and their families. The purpose was to demonstrate a sincere effort by the president to understand people's problems, to be seen with tradesmen and farmers and ordinary, hardworking people.

Somehow the scenario got changed between the close of business Friday evening and the time of the Thurmont visit. Instead, the president drove to a sparkling, high-tech concrete shopping center in Frederick, Maryland, and visited a J. C. Penney store where he bought some socks. The symbolism of this adventure not only failed, it signaled everything wrong about our attitude on the economy: We didn't understand people's problems, we thought the economy just needed a few more consumers, and we were out of touch with the common man.

Whether Sununu could have, or would have, prevented this if he hadn't been so distracted is problematical. But the president wasn't getting much direction.

I made a note:

> The President is lost about what to do regarding the economy. He knows there is a problem. He listens to Darman, Porter, Boskin, Brady, and Sununu and asks questions about the tactics of our legislative program. These guys talk about Senator Byrd getting his CIA building in West Virginia, Rostenkowski getting tax shelters, but seldom about what's going on in the economy. No one

ever asks the most basic economic question: 'How do we get more money into the economy?' The President feels helpless and doesn't like it. He's not in the game, not competing. Worse, he may be afraid that Kemp and Gingrich are right [they had been urging the President to lay out an economic program and run on it, instead of relying on Senator Mitchell and the Congress to give him a program]. He doesn't look at me much in these meetings because he knows I can see the trouble in his eyes. Unfortunately, everyone sees it. And CNN reported tonight that his favorable rating dropped below 50 percent for the first time.

By Friday, November 29, 1991, the president had received complaints and recommendations about Sununu from nearly everyone he knew, including his family. More than six months had passed since the initial revelations about Sununu's travel. The president defended him throughout this period, always hoping that he would resolve the matter. If the president's popularity had remained high, the governor might have escaped entirely. But when things started going bad, without obvious explanation, even the first family began asking why Bush was letting this matter drag on for half a year. They liked Sununu and always defended him, but they knew the extent of his alienation with others. It was then that the president started raising it with Sununu, gently asking him in their morning meeting about his relations with the staff, joking about his congressional reputation, and finally telling John that he appeared to have lost the confidence of the staff. Sununu understood many of the president's motives, but he never understood the president's compartmentalization of friendships and how to deal with it. Sununu certainly never believed he would be judged by what his own staff thought. He treated staff as irrelevant because to him they were. But to George Bush, they were trusted friends, each with a specialty of value to him, and each deserving of downward as well as upward loyalty. Sununu had no idea how to lobby this group, except by superficial inquiries about health and welfare. It never dawned on him to give staff some of his power, to draw them into his circle and take their advice, to make their roles meaningful and, in doing so, make them allies. He did it the only way guaranteed to fail: by asking staff for help in saving his own skin without giving them any real reason to do so.

The president asked Andy Card about staff attitudes.

"I hear the natives are restless about Sununu," the president said. "Is it not working?"

"Well, Mr. President," Card said, "right now there is a feeling he's worrying more about his own situation than about yours."

Andy Card, ironically, was the closest aide in the White House to both the president and the chief of staff. He had worked for George Bush in 1979 in Massachusetts when he first ran for the presidency. Card had been a member of the Massachusetts legislature, and was dedicated to politics and Republicans. He was loyal beyond question to President Bush, and had been Sununu's loyal assistant during the 1988 campaign and transition. Both men trusted him. In fact, he was honest beyond any standard for presidential assistants. Andy virtually ran the mechanics of the White House for three years while Sununu directed legislation on the Hill and schemed to ingrain his right-wing agenda in federal agencies like the Environmental Protection Agency and others. Andy always defended Sununu to the staff, and when John decided his back was completely against the wall, he turned to Andy for help. He asked him to solicit staff members to call the president in support of his record. He suggested Roger Porter, assistant to the president for domestic policy, Ede Holiday, assistant for cabinet affairs, Boyden Gray, general counsel, and Dorrance Smith, assistant for media affairs and long a family friend of the president's. Andy asked each of them for help. Sununu himself had called Ron Kaufman, the president's political adviser, Senator Robert Dole, Congressman Robert Michel, Congressman Newt Gingrich, and Secretary of the Treasury Nicholas Brady. He was begging for his life.

The president went to Camp David for the Thanksgiving weekend, and invited Dorrance Smith to come up Saturday for tennis. Dorrance was an outstanding player who grew up in Houston with the Bushes, playing tennis with the president's sons and rummaging through the family refrigerator on Saturday afternoons. Dorrance told Andy he would raise the Sununu issue then.

During the match, the president was called off the court by his military aide to take a call from Ede Holiday. It was the first of the solicited calls.

Within hours, Ann Devroy of *The Washington Post* called Ede at her home to ask if she had called the president about Sununu.

Ede was in a panic. She wanted to cooperate with the press, especially Ann Devroy. Ede knew the value of good relations with the press, and she knew the pain of bad relations. Ann had her over a barrel with this leak, obviously from someone on the inside. She did not want to mislead Ann and incur her wrath later, nor did she want to admit what was happening.

"Can you be more specific?" she asked.

"Did you call the president to urge him to let Sununu keep his job?" Ann said.

"No," Ede said, seizing on the phrase "to keep his job." In fact, she had called the president simply to say "the staff supported" Sununu.

This is the reason, of course, why the press thinks people in government are less than truthful. It also shows why the press is so good. They not only know the questions, they know how to interpret the answers. In this case, Ann Devroy knew the truth the minute Ede Holiday said, "Can you be more specific?"

At 10:30 Sunday morning Andy called me at home to say the president would return to the White House at noon and planned to meet with the governor then. This was routine notification so I could notify the press. But the meeting with the governor was intriguing. I happened to know that James A. Baker III, secretary of state and the president's longtime confidant, had also spent Saturday at Camp David. It looked to me like Sununu was about to get the ax.

At eleven o'clock Sunday morning, Dorrance Smith called to see if I knew anything about Sununu. Dorrance said the governor had called him twice that morning, first begging him to call the president. Then he called Dorrance back to see if the call had been made. Dorrance told the governor he just didn't feel comfortable discussing something like that over the phone.

Sununu then called Andy Card to say that the president had full confidence in him, but the president thought the staff didn't. Sununu said the president wanted him to talk to the staff and "do what you think is right." That, of course, was an invitation to resign. But a chief of staff, in the midst of a fight for survival, never sees the signs. He even interprets "do what you think is right" as confidence in his judgment. It isn't.

Sununu then asked Andy to ask other assistants to the president to support his retention as chief of staff.

Later in the day, Andy spoke with the president, but the president seemed noticeably reserved over the phone, as if someone else might have been in the room. Andy, always looking after the interests of both the president and the governor, had decided not to inventory the staff, as Sununu had suggested. If the call leaked, Sununu would look like a beggar, and the president would look bad as well. That hadn't dawned on the governor. So the conversation related mostly to other White House business.

It turned out that someone else was in the room with the president when Andy called: the next chief of staff, Samuel Skinner.

Monday morning the president called Andy in his office and suggested a meeting with Dorrance, Andy, and Boyden. It's not easy for the president to have a meeting that excludes the chief of staff. The West Wing of the White House is small. Sununu was watching the Oval Office closely in case any of his enemies tried to slip in unnoticed to see the president. Andy had to wait until the afternoon to arrange the meeting.

Once in the Oval, all three made a case for Sununu's survival, although their body language was hesitant and nervous. These were the three that Governor Sununu thought were his strongest defenders. They did their best, but then the president asked the key question: "What do each of you say personally?"

All three reluctantly said it would be best if Sununu left the White House. The president shook his head sadly. President Bush had a warm personal relationship with John Sununu, and firings are never easy.

"Who will deliver the message?" the president asked, looking for a process that would let Sununu resign with dignity. The staff and the public had to see a process in which Sununu went to the president and, for the good of the presidency, resigned. The group discussed several possibilities: the vice president, the president, or the three staff members. The objective was to find a messenger who would convince Sununu to voluntarily resign amid praise and recognition by the president, thus avoiding the embarrassment of a firing. We often talk about the Japanese preoccupation with "saving face" in their negotiations and dealings, but Americans are just the same. If all parties cooperated, the president could praise Sununu, Sununu could claim he wanted to make way for someone else to direct the campaign while he became a private adviser to the president, and the press would dutifully report all this, even while speculating in their columns that in fact it was a firing. Thus it was agreed that the three staffers would give Sununu the word to leave so a face-saving method could be found.

The three left the Oval, a bit sheepish and a lot troubled. When they went into Sununu's office at the end of the day, he was sitting at his desk. He looked up and surveyed the faces, looking for signs of optimism, any positive signal about his own situation. The telltale smiles were not there. All three were cold sober, slightly hangdog in appearance, stopping in front of the chief's desk, then edging backward as if trying to fade into the woodwork.

Andy did the talking. He summarized the conversation with the president, trying to be true to the actual words spoken, to be honest in reporting the actual mood to this man whose future rested on the outcome, wanting to be positive in a way that would prevent unnecessary pain, but also needing to be direct enough that Sununu would know there was no escape. Finally, Andy said, "Governor, the president will accept your resignation."

The governor asked questions at various points, mostly to see if Andy's words were the president's. He blamed everyone: the staff, the press, the Congress, even Andy Card. But he knew the time had come.

At five o'clock that afternoon, Governor Sununu had his first formal meeting with the communications directors on the president's staff. At this point, he knew he would resign, but the meeting had been scheduled when he was looking for support. The governor was obviously distracted during the meeting. That became clear when he suggested that the president could show empathy with the common man by allowing the press to film people talking to the president at the White House Christmas party. We sat, stunned. Finally, someone said quietly, "Christmas in the White House is not a common affair."

The next morning, December 3, 1991, the president traveled to Florida and then to Meridian, Mississippi, to visit Peavey Electronics, a company that makes stereos, amplifiers, and the like. Every patron of rock concerts knows the company well, or at least has heard of it. As a small staff contingent gathered outside the Oval Office to see the president off, Andy Card slipped over next to me and whispered, "No matter what happens, just be professional." This was a very strange admonition, even for these circumstances. I was about to ask for an explanation when Sununu walked in. Andy abruptly turned and left. That was my answer. Either the resignation was coming today, or Sununu was going to create some disturbance, or quite possibly both.

The senior staff compartment on *Air Force One* had four chairs, three of them permanently assigned to the chief of staff, the national security adviser, and the press secretary. The first two because of their prestige, mine because the press secretary is the only person who makes every trip with the president. The fourth seat was for guests. As soon as we were airborne Governor Sununu left the compartment. A few minutes later, Rig Rogich, who headed the advance office, walked in to exclaim that the governor was doing his own xeroxing. "It's his resignation," I said. "He apparently wrote it last night and we're going to release it today. But I don't know any of this for certain, so be cool."

After making a brief, campaign-like stop in Florida, *Air Force One* lifted off later that morning for the continuing flight to Meridian. As soon as we were airborne, Sununu asked me to accompany him to see the president.

The president's office on *Air Force One* is quite spacious for an airplane, with a mahogany desk that wraps around one corner of the room, and the president's high-back leather chair "in the slot," reminding me of the copy desk on newspapers. There is one chair across from the desk, which Sununu immediately took, and a couch that covers the two walls opposite the desk.

"John has submitted his resignation," the president said, holding the letter that the governor had given him early in the flight. "It's very gracious and generous. I've written a response I'd like you to look at." He handed his letter across the desk, where I could just stretch off the couch to reach it. Sununu's eyes never left me for a second, and I never made an expression. Now I knew what Andy was talking about. The ritual had reached its crescendo. Sununu could go one of several ways—an emotional breakdown, outrage and outburst, or sullen anger—any of which could be directed at me, partially because I had been right in the middle of the "Air Sununu" episode that destroyed him, and partially because I was there, on the plane, in his compartment, and stuck with the situation for at least five or six hours.

The president's letter was two handwritten pages in green ink on yellow legal-sized paper. I immediately started reading. It was very gracious, as only a Bush letter would be, and praised the governor's contributions.

"Take a look," the president said. "Does it need any changes?"

Oh sure, like I would suggest a change during this supercharged situation.

"No," I said, "it looks fine."

"When do we put them out?" the president said.

"Well," I said, "you both could go to the filing center." The White House has a "filing center," usually a gymnasium or ballroom, at every presidential stop that is set up for the press with tele-

phones, typewriters, computer terminals, and editing rooms. They
are also available for surprise presidential announcements. I didn't
really want the president to take this course of action, and I knew
the president wouldn't either. But with Sununu staring at me, I
wanted to be sure he knew the option was offered.

"I was thinking we could just put out the letters," the president
said.

I looked at our printed schedule, which showed the president's
activities and movements in fifteen-minute segments all day long.
"We could put it out right after your speech at Peavey," I said. "That
way the wires will have carried our message of the day about the
economy, the big newspapers will have filed on your speech, then
we'll put out the letters just before takeoff. This is all the networks
will cover anyway, but at least we can salvage some newspaper coverage of the event."

I handed the letter back to the president, who handed it to a stew-
ard to have typed on presidential stationery. Sununu and I returned
to our cabin without saying a word or making an expression. I sat
down, motionless, and froze, waiting for the explosion that Sununu
was famous for. He was like a can of beer, which if shaken or dropped
or tossed around would surely blow up the minute it was opened.

The governor just sat silently, defying all expectations, until
tears started running down his face. His eyes became watery and red,
and his face started to sag, almost as if I could see the fluids moving
through his body, up to the face, causing the contortions. Finally, he
said, "I've never been through this before." Then there was a long silence. "My one regret," he said, "is that I could never break through
that Kansas crust."

"I'm very sorry," I said. "I always tried to say the right thing for
you and hoped you would know I was trying to give you my best advice."

Then he blamed the press. "They'll be celebrating, I suppose," he
said. "I didn't think they could get me."

Peavey Electronics was housed in a series of metal buildings containing assembly lines; manufacturing crates were stacked everywhere. A makeshift auditorium had been established in the middle
of the largest structure, with portable seating like you find in a
small-town baseball stadium and a few offices located behind the
seats. Nearby was a small yellow frame house, with front porch,
dormer windows upstairs, and the standard 1940s architectural layout of three rooms: living, dining, and kitchen. This was the press of-

fice. I rushed in as soon as we arrived and ordered the staff to start xeroxing the letters. I went to Lynn Sanford, a secretarial assistant who could take any press abuse with a smile and withstand almost any pressure when situations got tense. "Hold these letters until I come back for them," I told her. "Don't give one copy to anybody without my approval. Anything can happen in this situation. Sununu could still go nuts. The president could have second thoughts. Anything. I'll be back just before the president ends his speech."

When the time came, and there could be no turning back, I called Lynn in the office and told her to bring the letters to me at the back of the event site, a three-minute walk. Michael Busch, who ran the logistical staff for me, was bringing the fourteen-person press pool from the speech platform where they had been listening to the speech. As this group came running toward me, I looked up at the rear ends of about 2,000 people seated above me, at the crates and boxes stacked around the building, at the corrugated tin structure and the barren concrete floor. Somehow, the ritual always ends ignominiously, and this time would be no different.

I hand the pool the letters. They grab for them, shouting questions, demanding to know when it happened, where Sununu is, what the president thinks, and who will be his successor. The radio reporters run for a telephone. The television correspondents get on their two-way radios and signal the editing booth to tell New York that a big story is coming, and that they will get video at the airport of the president and Sununu departing Meridian. I tell Michael to help them coordinate, to make sure they get their tape from the plane to a local transmission point, usually a local TV station. At the same time, my staff in the yellow house press office is giving copies of the letters to the rest of the press corps, and faxing it to the White House for distribution there.

After the pool rushed away to file their stories, knowing they would have only a few minutes before the president departed, I hurried back to a small room where Governor Sununu was sitting with Dave Demarest, director of communications, and Phil Brady, the president's staff secretary. The governor was crying. I told him the letters had been released and he should think about what he wanted to say. It was the same face I had seen on Don Regan three years earlier.

"Are my eyes red?" he asked.

"Yes," I said, "but it's OK."

We all leave together and get into the motorcade. He has about fifteen minutes to compose his thoughts, although I don't know what he will do. Our car is about four vehicles behind the president when we arrive at *Air Force One*. The press pool has gathered under the wing of the plane, waiting to shout questions. The president goes into the plane without commenting. The governor and I move slowly toward the stairs, when someone in the press asks him to come talk to them. At this moment the press is respectful. They know it's a tough personal time. But they do their job. The governor turns to me and asks, "Should I go over?"

I know he wants to, and I say yes. I turn and ask the military aide to hold *Air Force One* for a few minutes, which he does. I mutter to no one in particular, "Sununu has a right to say his piece," and by then he is talking to the pool, gracious, sad, and generous to the president. He says all the right things.

On the plane, the president whispered to me in the hallway, "Be generous to John. This is a very good letter. He's doing it the right way. Really, very nice. Say so."

I did. Then the president said he wanted to go back to the pool on the plane and talk about Sununu. He praised the governor, defended his air-travel situation, wished him well, and said he would always be a dear friend. That gave the networks film of the president and provided an on-the-record statement for the newspapers, both of which had to be done before the ritual could finally be called over.

Another example of the ritual was much shorter, but it started earlier. Samuel Skinner was secretary of transportation, had worked in two of President Bush's campaigns, and was generally perceived to be an aggressive, smart, and hardworking Chicago lawyer who could get things done. True, he was a little too ambitious, lobbying for the chief of staff job through the president's daughter. Everyone knew that and put a small question mark beside their mental note of his arrival, but generally he was welcomed as the new chief who would lead us into the campaign.

Almost immediately, however, things began to go wrong. In his second week on the job, I recommended that Sam go to the White House briefing room to meet the press. Every chief has to do it sooner or later. I always figured sooner, because the press expected less. So I advised every new chief to develop one substantive idea—perhaps a staff appointment, or a reorganization, or a presidential plan—something they could talk about and appear thoughtful, substantive, and supportive of the president. There was plenty of experience to support this approach.

When John Sununu did his first briefing as chief of staff, with no subject in mind, he let the questioning lead him into a discussion of the soon-to-be-proposed bailout for failed savings and loan institutions. Sununu offered an idea that had not been accepted by the president, was widely perceived to be wrong, and was indeed later rejected. The press immediately dubbed Sununu a loose cannon. The age-old rule at the White House is that a staff person never usurps the prerogative of a president in announcing a major decision. If it is meant to be a trial balloon, it is always leaked without attribution so the president can later back away from the idea. On this occasion the stories were so bad, and the press so hostile, that Sununu never wanted to go back to the briefing room again. Worse, the press formed a bad first impression. They concluded that Sununu thought he was still governor, that he wasn't properly deferential to the president and the decision-making process, and that there was a touch of arrogance that would someday get him in trouble.

Howard Baker had asked to go to the briefing room in his second week on the job. I gave him my standard advice, but he said it wouldn't be necessary to plan anything specific to say because he had met with the press every day in the Senate when he was majority leader. He knew the press and had a good relationship with them. I argued that this was not the same press. The congressional press tend to associate themselves with the Congress. The White House press think of themselves as the loyal opposition. Howard did a good job, and the press liked him, but they asked a hundred questions he couldn't answer. They didn't show him much deference. The press conclusion was that Howard was a fish out of water with a lot to learn about the White House. But Howard learned fast. The first thing he said after the briefing was: "I'm never going back there again," and he didn't.

Sam Skinner took a similar view. He said he had dealt with the press at the Valdez oil spill in Alaska, so he knew hostile press. He could handle this first briefing without preparation. But after about the twentieth question that he couldn't answer, his frustration began to show. Worse, the press was quickly making up its mind about the new chief.

John Cochran, NBC News correspondent, was sitting on the end of the first row. I was sitting along the wall facing him, only a couple of feet away. He looked at me, pained. I grimaced like I didn't un-

derstand. He started jotting a note on the corner of his notebook, tore
it off and handed it to me. It read: "Looks like you got yourselves a
jerk." I felt the air swoosh out of me, deflating my hopes. I turned the
paper over and wrote "Give him a chance" and handed it back.
Cochran's conclusion was unfair to Sam. He had been a very successful and respected Chicago lawyer, an adviser to Governor Jim
Thompson in Illinois, and an aggressive member of the Bush cabinet.
But like most chiefs of staff before him, he didn't understand the ritual. He walked into the crosshairs of the semiautomatic that is
Washington like a baby deer raising its head in a forest.

The ritual of a chief being removed from office, if reduced to a
board game, would look like a target, with the chief in the center and
hundreds of arrows around the outside of the board pointed inward,
each representing a special constituency to the president: staff, wife,
oldest friend, Speaker of the House, leader of the party, biggest con-
tributor, and the White House press corps. Actually, this last arrow
is a little bigger than all the rest, because the press's influence
reaches all the other arrows. At the beginning of the game, they all
start moving toward the chief of staff, who, as you may have
guessed, is a surrogate for the president. The chief throws all kinds
of obstacles in their way—promotions, appointments, legislation, favors, presidential dinners, etc.—in the hope the arrows won't reach
him in four years. At the very end of the game, when all the arrows
are close, and the president has to step in to defend his chief so he
won't look like a cad, that's when the game enters "final ritual," in
which the president picks the person who gets to bell the chief. The
chief is reduced to tears and fears, and the winners are declared in
terms of who got the chief. Often it's the press. Almost always the
final frenzy is so intense, like the final scramble of jack rabbits in the
coyote hunts of my youth, that the chief of staff is crazy with anger
and humiliation.

In the strange and complex case of Sam Skinner, the game started
early. On December 4, 1991, the day after Sam was appointed chief,
President Bush called me to the Oval Office in the afternoon to meet
with his new 1992 presidential campaign team. He said the effort
would be a shared responsibility, with Bob Mosbacher, his longtime
Texas oil friend, as general chairman, Bob Teeter, his pollster in several previous campaigns, as chairman, Fred Malek, a rich former
Marriott Hotel executive and Nixon staff member, as campaign
manager, and Charlie Black, a political consultant and adviser to

conservative leaders like Kemp and Gingrich, as senior adviser. Skinner was not mentioned.

This group was typical of the Bush compartmentalization of people: Each was selected for a different specialty. Unfortunately, as so often happens when people are stereotyped, the players didn't agree with their compartments. Indeed, all wanted to run the entire show, or at least some piece far greater in size than the president imagined.

We planned to announce the new appointments the next day. I drafted a press release and sent copies to all participants. Bob Mosbacher called immediately to say that his name should be mentioned first in the list, that Teeter should be described as having day-to-day responsibilities, and Mosbacher himself should be described as "standing at the president's side in campaigns for the last twenty years."

Then Teeter called. He said my release was fine, until I told him of the Mosbacher changes. He objected, saying he should be listed first, and that the "day-to-day" language was wrong.

"We agreed over lunch," Teeter said, "and the president was firm, that I would have overall responsibility."

With this kind of major split developing, I called the president. I suggested we add Political Director Mary Matalin and Republican National Committee chairman Rich Bond to the announcement and the press conference, and then told the president about the press release problems. Mosbacher had already called the president, objecting to the press release. The president soon called me back to review the situation and he was clearly exasperated. I said I would try to work it out. The president sighed, "Gee, if it's this bad on the first day, what are we in for?" I went home thinking we could work all this out the next day.

At nine that night, Jim Baker called from the State Department. "Read me the press release," he said. "The president has asked me to work this out. It makes me wonder if we have the right group."

This lack of leadership and identification of responsibility never changed until eight months later when Baker came back to the White House in August 1992 to take over as chief of staff and unofficial director of the campaign. In the meantime, poor Sam Skinner floundered. He transformed the president's trip to Japan in early 1992 from foreign relations to "Jobs, jobs, jobs!" as he would scream at staff meetings. And while some notable achievements were made in Japanese trade, the trip was generally judged a failure. Expectations for a breakthrough with Japan on jobs were raised far beyond reality. Bob Teeter, who had long enjoyed Ford Motor Company as a client of his polling firm, and Bob Mosbacher, who had been secretary of commerce, got the president to invite the presidents of Ford, GM, and Chrysler on the trip. But their objectives were different from the administration's and they trashed the president at every stop.

The campaign had gone poorly for months. No one could make a decision. Skinner and Teeter looked at each other as equals, never agreeing and never deciding. By August it was clear that Jim Baker had to come back soon to take over the campaign, and even then it might be too late. The arrows were closing in on Sam Skinner.

The big difference between this experience and that of other chiefs was that Sam fully expected it, and may even have welcomed it. But like all others, he was not prepared. As early as January 1992, the president told a friend, "These last two months have been the worst of my presidency, and the last year has been the worst of my political career." It would never get any better.

On the morning of August 13, 1992, the president called me in at about 8 A.M. He said we would be announcing Jim Baker later that day as chief of staff, and asked me to prepare a statement introducing Jim and praising Sam. Sam would be going to the Republican National Committee.

"Does he know yet?" I asked.

"No," the president said, "I'm going to tell him in a few minutes."

"Do you want me to prepare the way, or say anything to him?" I asked, wanting to be helpful but not really wanting the assignment.

"No," the president said, "I will talk to him. It will be all right."

No sooner had I returned to my office than Sam walked in, closed the door, and pulled up a chair in front of my desk. "It's going to happen, buddy," he said. "Baker is coming over."

I wasn't sure how to react because it didn't seem to me that Sam could have had time to see the president since I did. "What will all the roles be?" I asked generally.

"Baker doesn't want to be chief of staff," Sam said. "He will be here to run the campaign. That's fine with me. Two different roles."

My secretary, Claire Pickart, poked her head in. "Mr. Skinner, the president would like to see you."

"OK, buddy," Sam said, "here it goes." Sam had a Boy Scout quality about him, epitomized by calling people "buddy," that was endearing. People liked him, and no one accused him of malicious motives, or arrogance, or being power mad, or any of the normal traits that are picked up and immortalized in backstairs gossip. He just never quite understood the White House rituals, and from his first day to his last, the momentary pressures were so great that he never had time to learn.

Fifteen minutes later he came back into my office, closed the door, and started pacing the floor. "It happened," he said. Tears were welling up in his eyes, his face was growing red. He was stunned. Like Regan and Sununu before him, the fact of what had happened was so remote to his experience that he just never considered it. "Baker is going to be chief of staff," he said. Everyone in town knew that. Baker would never come back without full power and authority in the White House. And everyone in town knew Baker was coming back.

When a chief of staff is in that final frenzy, when all the nerves are exposed and raw, when all the defenses have been smashed by too many mistakes, too many stories, too many arrows, the chief stands alone with his private anguish. There is nothing left to do but walk out the back door and drive out through the big iron gates forever. Sure, there are other jobs in the campaign, or the cabinet, or an embassy, but the White House days are over and it is a terrible wound to suffer. The ritual is over. It is painful to watch.

CHAPTER NINE

Spin and Other Yarns

"The truth cleverly told is the cleverest lie of all."
—THOMAS HARDY

A journalism professor once told me, "There are two kinds of truth: the kind you can prove in court, and the kind any fool can plainly see." It has always astonished me how many times the government tries to establish courtly truth without establishing the kind that any fool can plainly see.

By the same token, the press often works from the other direction. They quickly adopt the obvious truth without bothering to prove it. Thus the government and the media once again find themselves talking past each other on the issue of truth.

This is significant because telling the truth, or lying, has become the primary factor in determining how the press judges presidents and press secretaries, and vice versa. A president perceived as honest can get away with a multitude of errors, but a president perceived as dishonest will have every mistake magnified. The jury in deciding all this, of course, is the White House press corps, which sets itself up as defender of the truth and prosecutor of all liars. Sometimes a one-time-only lie, committed by a first offender, if there is such a person, is treated the most harshly because it betrays an established trust. Presidents Jimmy Carter, Jerry Ford, Ronald Reagan, and George Bush were in this "first offender" category, all basically honest men who valued this virtue and tried to keep it in all their undertakings. Presidents Lyndon Johnson, Richard Nixon, and Bill Clinton might be classified otherwise. I believe that LBJ started the great mistrust of government by the media when he, and his administration, obfuscated so often about Vietnam, our casualties and our intentions. Richard Nixon in Watergate took "misleading" to a new level of mendacity. Bill Clinton has made "evasion" commonplace, a sort of ready response to any predicament, political or personal. Newspaper columnists in America today routinely describe case after case of President Clinton saying one thing and denying it days later, until we begin to ask ourselves: What is true and what isn't? Raising taxes, gays in the military, Gennifer Flowers, Haiti policy, use of force in Bosnia, ethics in government, the travel office firings, Paula Corbin Jones, Hillary's commodities trading, Whitewater— the explanations and reexplanations seem never to end.

The ultimate sham in this upside-down treatment of truth is the case in which lying becomes a form of honesty, declared so by the news media, and then celebrated. Let's call this the Ed Rollins Conundrum. Rollins, a Republican political consultant in Washington, told the press that he had paid black ministers in the New Jersey governor's election of 1993 to keep people away from the polls, thus holding down the traditionally Democratic vote. When the press noted this remarkably unsportsmanlike conduct, Rollins immediately said he was lying. The Washington press, which had always valued Rollins as a man willing to say irrational and intemperate things about public officials (a trait they called "candid"), crawled to his defense. Stories began appearing that referred to the "poor, sad" case of Ed Rollins, and then he started getting credit for candor again, as in "He lied, but he admitted it." Soon he was back on the speaking circuit, political campaign contracts were rolling in, he had expanded his company to international dimensions, and he was interviewed by CNN's Larry King for nearly an hour. Most significantly, he had made lying an asset, indeed a point of some stature that was playing quite well. *The New York Times* reported in June 1994 that Ed Rollins had returned to New Jersey to tell black ministers, "I have been in politics for a very, very long time. I have made statements before that have been stupid. I have made statements that I'm sure are inaccurate. I have never made a statement ever in my life that has been as hurtful and undone everything that I've tried and spent my entire life to be all about." In other words, he had lied before but never as successfully as this time.

In the late 1980s, however, the White House press corps was intent on setting a higher standard. They knew that Reagan and Bush were honest and honorable men, which made them doubly difficult to berate. So they poked in every corner for evidence of untruth. The problem, of course, is that "untruth" abounds everywhere in the White House and it comes in many forms, some barely recognizable, and almost all cloaked in the colorful robes of "national security," "preventing leaks," or "preserving the president's options."

When Ronald Reagan brought me to the press briefing room on January 12, 1987, to announce my appointment as his new assistant for press relations, a very rare event occurred: The announcement was greeted by applause, with some reporters even standing. No one could remember that ever happening before, in any situation, and I was truly overwhelmed. I stepped to the microphone following the president, said how honored I was to be given the job, thanked the president, declined to take any questions, and started to walk off. How foolish of me to think that declining to take questions meant they wouldn't be asked. And when you're on television, as I was at that moment, you can't refuse to answer for fear of appearing to be a dolt, especially after you've just received a standing ovation.

"Marlin," Sam Donaldson said from his end seat on my left, "I just have one question. Will you ever lie to us?"

This is the most obvious question to ask a new press secretary, yet I was stunned. I felt like a lover who had just shared sex, only to be asked if I cared. I turned to walk off, and Sam persisted. He yelled, "Will you?"

I stepped back to the microphone and said evenly, "No."

It was a test Sam had learned in the Carter administration. During the 1976 presidential campaign, following the organized lying of Watergate, President Carter had promised the country that he would never lie to them. The standard had always been there, but this was the first president forced to define it. The press watched his administration carefully for evidence of failure. Finally it happened. During the Iranian hostage crisis, when fifty-two Americans were held for 444 days in the American embassy in Tehran, President Carter's press secretary, Jody Powell, denied that the president had sent messages to the ayatollah when in fact he had.

Jody had a very tough time of it in the briefing room after that. But he made the best of it, declaring later that lying is sometimes justified when lives are at stake in national security situations. That's not a great explanation, but it is thoughtful and makes you stop and think about the issue. The White House press corps knows that there are many verbal dodges a press secretary can make to preserve the integrity of national security matters without lying. Jody is still held accountable by the press. Fifteen years after the Carter administration ended, Jody still has to answer the question: "Is it ever acceptable to lie to the press?" In my appearances with him, I always answer no, but try to be as supportive as possible. It is not because I think lying is ever justified, but because I know how many times, and under what extreme pressures, a press secretary must fight off the twin threats of bad information and tainted sources, coupled with just a pinch of media trickery, in order to ensure truth and accuracy in information.

My first, and most intense, challenge in this area was defending the president and the administration during the Iran-Contra investigations. But I was successful in maintaining honesty as a basis for my relationship with the press throughout the period. Who would have guessed, then, that the biggest test of truth I ever faced would arise almost overnight, early in the Bush administration. This small episode involving a Panamanian coup attempt shows just how fragile information can be, how wrong it can be, and why a press secretary can never take the integrity of information for granted, even if it comes from the Oval Office.

On October 3, 1989, I called my daily press briefing for 9:30 A.M. in order to finish before the official state visit of President Salinas of Mexico, which would involve an arrival ceremony on the South Lawn and formal meetings with the president the rest of the morning. After Salinas, Soviet defense minister Dmitriy Yazov was visiting in the afternoon. It was a relatively routine day. At 11 A.M. I went to the small secretarial office outside the Oval to wait for President Bush to finish his meeting with Salinas. A large television set, part of the office for the entire ten years I worked in the White House, was on, barely audible. The CNN commentator was explaining that a possible coup attempt was under way in Panama against the dictator and indicted international drug smuggler, Manuel Noriega. I was astounded. We had no advance knowledge of this—no presidential briefings.

Brent Scowcroft, the president's national security adviser, was talking to the Pentagon on the phone located on top of the TV. CNN was saying that the bridge in Panama City connecting the Panamanian Defense Forces (PDF) and the city was open, and their pictures showed it. This meant that Noriega's forces would soon be arriving to save him. Noriega was apparently being held, or at least threatened in some fashion, on one side of the bridge and his rescuers in the PDF were on the other.

"How about the bridge?" Brent asks. "CNN says the bridge is open."

I can't hear the other end of the conversation. After a second,

Brent asks again, "Can we signal the PDF that we're on their side—
that there's no doubt where we stand?"

Another pause.

"Have we secured the causeway?"

Bernard Aronson, assistant secretary of state for Latin America,
is standing beside Brent and watching the TV. "Can we go on radio?"
he asks. It's clear we don't know much about all this but we want to
help, at least to the point of signaling our support for the coup plotters, whoever they might be. This is always dangerous, of course, because America might be called upon to back it up, and that definitely
had not been decided, or even discussed with the president.

Governor Sununu, the president's chief of staff, walks in, listens
to the conversation and offers, "Noriega may bring troops in by air.
Can he?"

"We don't really know where Noriega is, do we?" Brent says,
then pauses. "The U.S. has helicopters and A-37s in the air . . . for
surveillance."

Suddenly, Sununu raises his hands in front of his face, simulat-
ing a guillotine blade, stiffens his body, and chops the air downward
as he declares: "Block the causeway. Send the signal."

"It is blocked," Brent says.

"No it's not," Sununu says. "It's on CNN."

"Troops are there to block it if necessary," Brent says.

"I mean get the troops and tanks up on the bridge where the PDF
can see them," Sununu says.

"They can see them," Brent says.

"Then why can't CNN show them?" Sununu demands.

"Ask CNN," Brent responds.

At 11:30 A.M., the president was scheduled to see the former
chairman of the Joint Chiefs of Staff, Admiral William J. Crowe Jr.,
who was retiring after forty-seven years of naval service and four
years as chairman. Ironically, during that time, he had opposed at
least two attempts by President Reagan to take action against Noriega in Panama. Admiral Crowe was not an activist chairman, opposing most military actions, including the reflagging of Kuwaiti oil
tankers in 1987. In Panama, he felt America did not know how to
fight in an urban setting, and in 1987 he argued that the 10,000
American dependents and civilians in the Canal Zone should be removed before any action was considered. By 1989 much of that had
been accomplished. But by the time of Crowe's retirement, Presi-

dent Bush was ready for a new chairman and did not ask him to stay for another term. Nevertheless, General Scowcroft wanted the admiral to have a well-deserved farewell meeting with the president, so he remained on the schedule for 11:30 A.M. Then the president had a luncheon with federal agency administrators. Scowcroft scheduled a briefing on Panama for the president by Secretary of Defense Richard Cheney for 1:30 P.M.

Secretary Cheney, handling his first significant military crisis for the president, came to the Oval Office with very little information on events in Panama. He readily admitted as much, even though the United States had a huge military base in the country. Cheney said that General Cisneros, the deputy U.S. commander at the base, had met with the rebel leaders and they claimed to have Noriega. They said Noriega was safely in their hands and they would not give him up. More incredibly, the rebels wanted to retire him to a mountain home.

"How did Cisneros see these guys?" the president asked.

"I guess he just walked into the *commandancia*," Cheney said. "He's a ballsy guy."

"If he just walked in, where were the rebel troops?" the president asked. "Wasn't he stopped? Isn't there any fighting around the compound?"

"I guess not," Cheney said.

"Is General Thurman protecting U.S. lives there?" the president asked. General Maxwell Thurman had just gone to Panama to take charge of the U.S. base. General Cisneros was number two in command.

The president was clearly taken aback at how little information we had. Finally he said, "Here's what's needed. The rebels have to say 'We have Noriega. We have the government. We need support for democracy. We need U.S. help to preserve order in the city.' If all these things happen, then we can help."

"OK," Cheney said, "I'll ask for five things: One, Cisneros should reestablish contact with the rebels. Two, find out the rebel intentions about Noriega. Three, will rebels accept extradition or expulsion of Noriega? Four, will the rebels ask for our help? And five, tell Thurman to prepare to use military force."

The president approved. "I've reached the point where I'm ready to consider military force," he said.

"The reaction in Latin America will be bad," Brent said.

"I think we should go in and get him out," the president said. "We'll have a bad time of it for a while, but then it's over." The meeting broke at 2:30 P.M.

As the group left the office, I stayed behind to remind the president that he had a photo opportunity with the White House press pool at the beginning of his 2:30 P.M. meeting with General Yazov.

"At this photo op," the president asked, "can I say that the rebels have Noriega? That they seem to be in control?"

This was standard practice, for the president to rehearse a line or two before each meeting that he would give to the press pool. That way I could raise any objections, or alert him to special questions the press might ask.

In this case, I was very nervous. "No," I said. "Cheney's report leaves all kinds of holes. We don't know where Noriega is. We know hardly anything. I recommend you say we're monitoring events, on top of activities, but there is still much confusion in the area. It's only 2:30 P.M. We have three or four hours to comment on this and still make the evening news. We need more information."

The president agreed. The pool report filed by Toby McIntosh of the Bureau of National Affairs quoted the president as saying, "The U.S. is in very close touch. Beyond that I would simply add to the rumors if I commented further. We are watching the situation. The number one priority is the lives of Americans. There are rumors around that it is an American operation. That is not true."

Asked about possible help to the PDF, the president said, "That is part of the confusion. We have no argument with the Panamanian Defense Forces. Our argument has been that Mr. Noriega has aborted the democratic will of the people of Panama."

The president could change subjects and meetings with amazing speed. Within two minutes, General Yazov was seated beside him, and the president was saying of the Soviet Union, "Nobody today is talking about an arms race. We're talking arms reductions. It's time to go ahead. You have to crawl before you walk, but we are moving."

"We are very close," Yazov replied, "on air-launched cruise missiles, bomber counting rules, and verification. All have been moved to the forefront. Goodwill on both sides means verification can very easily be achieved. You have American inspectors everywhere today, base visits, bomber inspections, open skies."

"Let's keep pushing," the president said.

Yazov got up to leave just before 3 P.M., leaving by the formal front door of the Oval Office that opens into the hallway. The others in the meeting, including Secretary Baker, Scowcroft, Gates, and I, started out the side door that leads through the secretarial office connecting the Oval to the Cabinet Room. As I reached for the door, Assistant Secretary Aronson burst past me, almost shouting.

"Mr. President!" he said. "It's over! Noriega's troops have taken the compound. Noriega is free and rebels are being rounded up."

"That sure doesn't square with what we just heard," the president said. "Are you sure?"

"Yes, sir," Aronson said.

With that the group walked into the Cabinet Room to start a meeting on aid to Poland. The military situation was over. For the president, it lasted only a few hours, but the credibility war was just beginning and it would last for days.

The press had been perched outside my door for hours, watching events in Panama on CNN and waiting for a presidential response from me. When word spread that the coup attempt was over, the steam went out of the press like air from a slashed tire. The real news value was in a possible U.S. intervention. The only question left was why had we not intervened? The truth was, of course, that we knew too little, too late, to have done anything. Also, we were not ready. As I reluctantly pushed the door open, Helen Thomas screamed the first question, "Has the coup failed?"

"We believe it has," I said. "We don't have a lot more information than you have, but it does appear at least that his forces are back in control. As I say, we don't have direct knowledge. We don't know where Noriega is, where he's gone, whether or not he was injured. So it certainly is far from authoritative in terms of our judgment, but that's the best we have at the moment."

I was trying to use all the information we had to sound authoritative, but still qualify everything. The first question was easy. The second would undoubtedly go to the issue of our involvement. That seemed relatively easy too. I had been in every meeting the president had on this subject. I had heard everything he had heard. Never was there any mention of U.S. involvement. Indeed, most of our discussions were about the conditions under which we might offer some kind of help. The president had even said in his photo opportunity that America was not involved.

Brit Hume had replaced Sam Donaldson for ABC News during the Bush administration. They are totally different in personality, character, and approach. But they had two great similarities: high intellect and sound news judgment. Brit was nearly fifty, as was Sam during his White House years, mature and experienced. Brit had started as a reporter for Jack Anderson in the heady days of the 1960s after Jack took over Drew Pearson's column. He learned how to investigate, how to look behind the story to examine motives, and how to question every government rationale by his own scales. He was an excellent reporter who feared no one, asked the tough questions, and was deceptively gentle because he looked so young. His hair had a boyish cut, hanging like bangs across his forehead, and most people guessed he was in his thirties. He wasted no time in getting to the key question. "Was the U.S. called on to help?" he asked. "Did we offer military help?"

"We were not asked to help," I said. "We have considered this a matter of internal conflict between various factions of the PDF. Our Southern Command there in Panama took steps to protect U.S. citizens and property and our treaty rights, but we did not take any action that would constitute direct involvement."

My briefing the next day lasted almost an hour, mostly on Panama. The first question: Would I categorically say the United States was not involved in the coup attempt?

"Well," I said, "it's pretty hard to be categorical in a situation where you have a military base with several thousand troops there, right in the middle, indeed right next door to a Panamanian military base. And you have the government located in such a small space. There are obviously communications between people and so forth. But we were not involved in the planning of this or the discussion of this or the execution. And President Bush made that fairly clear yesterday, and if there were differences in those answers that [we gave], I think they result more from just differences in the questions they received."

I was dancing. Dancing is when a spokesman isn't quite sure of his facts, but wants to sound authoritative, has to protect the president, and tries to give an explanation that will hold up under critical examination. That usually means to state one clear fact, then qualify it forty-seven different ways.

Roman Popadiuk, my deputy, and I fought this question all day. We both felt in our guts that something was wrong. The press had a whiff of something we didn't have, but we didn't know what. In addition, this was my first such crisis with President Bush. I had assumed that if you sat in every meeting with the president, if you talked with him between meetings, and if you stayed in touch with the National Security Council staff, you would have all the information. That was a bad assumption.

At 6:10 P.M. on October 4, the day after the coup attempt, *Marine One* was preparing to lift off from the South Grounds to take the president to Chantilly, Virginia, to attend a fund-raiser for Marshall Coleman, Republican candidate for governor. As I was putting on my coat, Roman popped into my office, winded from running across the street from the Old Executive Office Building where most NSC offices are located. "Wait," he said, "I have to tell you. We can't tell anyone." That was a warning not to tell the press.

"Gates called me into his office just minutes ago," Roman said. Robert Gates was deputy national security adviser and later director of the Central Intelligence Agency. "He closed the doors and checked the windows." Everyone in the White House does that when they have a secret, because the CIA briefs everyone that some country is eavesdropping through the windows at almost all times. "He says no one knew about this, not Brent, the president, or himself. He says Giroldi, the coup leader, met with the CIA station chief in Panama on Sunday night. Giroldi told him about the coup, asked that we block the causeway and the Bridge of the Americas, and he asked for refuge for his family."

"Jesus Christ!" I exclaimed. "We've been saying we only had rumblings, third-party talks with Giroldi's wife, and we didn't know whether to believe her or not. Now you tell me we talked to the head of the coup?"

Roman said nothing.

"Why wasn't the president told?" I asked.

"Gates says they didn't know," Roman said.

I ran for the chopper. On the return flight from Chantilly about an hour later, Joe Hagin, Andy Card, and I sat on the bench seat that runs along the wall of the helicopter, beside the presidential seat. Our knees were almost in the president's lap. As we reached altitude, the president asked, "Marlin, what's happening? Anything new on Panama?"

"Mr. President," I said, "I was told tonight that we talked to the head of the coup on Sunday night."

"Who talked to him?" the president asked.

"The CIA station chief," I said.

"Well if he did, I sure didn't know about it," the president said. "I'll call Brent."

Oh no, I'm in trouble again. Now Brent would be upset that I told the president.

"Don't quote my facts too directly, Mr. President," I said. "I may be wrong. Just ask about CIA involvement."

When the chopper landed at the White House, I hurried out the back door. The president and Mrs. Bush went in the diplomatic reception entrance. I ran through the Rose Garden, jumped a small hedge near the sidewalk, raced to my office, then on to Brent's office in the far corner of the West Wing. He was gone, but probably still in his car. His secretary got him on the line.

"Brent," I said, "this is a heads-up. The president asked me about any new information on Panama and I told him the CIA may have talked to the coup leader. He's going to call you."

Brent had intended to tell the president before he left, but didn't get a chance.

I hung up and raced back to the motorcade, which was forming on the South Grounds where the helicopter had been only moments before. Our day wasn't over. The president was going to the Ramada Renaissance Hotel for a benefit appearance on behalf of the Challenger Space Center Foundation.

In the hotel basement, the motorcade emptied. The president got out of his limousine and called me over. As we walked through the back halls of the hotel kitchen, past the garbage cans and the stale desserts, the president put his arm around my shoulders and half whispered, half talked.

"I talked to Brent," he said. "He says it's just the CIA talking to lower members of the coup, nothing of significance to report."

"OK," I said, wondering why Brent would play down the meeting and not acknowledge it was Giroldi the CIA met with. I let the matter ride for nearly a week. But the press was on me every day as more details would seep out of Panama about the coup.

On Tuesday, October 10, I happened to be outside the Oval again with Scowcroft and Gates. I mentioned to them that not knowing about the Giroldi-CIA meeting had ruined my credibility because I had claimed we had no advance knowledge of the coup.

"But we didn't know," Brent said.

"Yes we did," Gates interrupted. "It was in the PDB"—the "President's Daily Briefing," a written report on world affairs that the CIA gives the president each morning, usually accompanied by an oral briefing.

"I didn't see it," Brent said.

I walked away, wondering what really happened. It was clear that everyone was covering something, some little piece of their fanny that was exposed from not coordinating properly, not reading the right reports, not making the right phone call, not telling the president, not demanding better information, not something. I used to joke with fellow staff members that in the White House everybody lies to everybody most of the time, meaning that nobody ever told you everything they knew about anything. It wasn't lying really. But if you are a press secretary, whose every statement must withstand the media honesty test, you soon learn to question everything you are told in the White House.

Even so, the press seldom uses the "lie" word against a government official because it's so serious. In my six years as press secretary, it was used against me only once and it related to this Panamanian coup incident.

The Wall Street Journal had published a lengthy story on the coup, obviously fed by the CIA station chief in Panama. Basically, he was angry that the U.S. government had dropped the ball on his coup attempt, which he undoubtedly had nurtured, so he fed the whole story of U.S. ineptness to the *Journal.* He was right, of course. Apparently his reports to CIA headquarters never got transferred to State or Defense, and therefore never fed directly to the president. The CIA's daily written report to the president apparently did mention the contact, but in such an elliptical way that no one caught the significance.

In my briefing of October 10, the press was in full cry. They had us on incompetence and lying, a deadly combination for a politician.

Nick Benton was the White House correspondent for Lyndon LaRouche's many publications and productions. LaRouche was a far-right cultist who later went to jail for tax problems. But he had several publications spouting his views, and his correspondents were assigned to several federal agencies. Benton was middle-aged, mild-mannered, slightly tweedy, and a true believer. LaRouche was hated by the press for his shady activities and high-handed ways, including accosting people in airports with his literature. In a way I was fortunate that the charge against me came from Benton, and not from a mainstream news organization.

"*The Wall Street Journal,*" Benton started, "yesterday repeated its assertions that, at the least, there were third-party contacts between Giroldi and U.S.—and officials who then discussed the potential coup with U.S. officials at least two weeks before Sunday. And they said that those officials passed this word on to Washington over the weekend or some such language and that—are you still maintaining the assertion that there was no contact directly with the U.S. or indirectly with the U.S.—that the U.S. government, including the CIA, had no knowledge of this before Sunday?"

"The question is," he continued, "were you aware that these were lies?"

There it was, the "lie" word. My nerves froze. Everyone in the room fell silent, waiting to see how I would respond. Larry Speakes, my predecessor, had been accused of lying and he blew up, attacking the press for making false charges. But I didn't think that tactic worked. Speakes looked cornered and defensive. It seemed to me the best response might be to throw myself on the mercy of the court.

I patiently explained what we did in protecting lives in Panama, in blocking off the causeway, and then admitted that we simply did not know that this action also had been requested by the coup leader. Indeed, the president did not know it.

Then I begged for mercy. "I think you're right that maybe I shouldn't have said anything. Maybe I shouldn't have told you anything last Wednesday. But I've always tried to do otherwise. I've always tried to tell you what I knew, what we knew—the status of things. I tried to be open and honest with all the information we had, and I was. The fact that there was more information that came out later that showed that we didn't have it, that's unfortunate."

"Well," Benton said, "that you didn't have it, but certainly Secretary Cheney knew exactly why those troops were put out on those roads, and may not have told you."

"I'll leave it the way I said it," I said, choosing at this point to eat the problem. Besides, I had to defend Cheney, who obviously didn't know where his troops had been or why. In fact, that information had never gotten to the secretary of defense. Furthermore, every aspect of the administration's communications system had screwed up. I could not defend my own credibility on this matter without admitting that the president, the secretaries of state and defense, and the national security adviser had no idea what was happening in Panama. In addition, everything I told the press was exactly what the president had been told.

At one point, Brit Hume asked, "The president did or didn't know there had been direct contacts?"

I said I would have to check the facts. I did not want to publicly admit our failures. The press took me around the block about six times on this issue. My guiding principle was that it was better for me to be accused of lying than for the president and Cheney to be accused of incompetence. It is the netherworld of government that we were all innocent and yet guilty at the same time.

Fortunately, everyone in the administration saw very clearly what had happened. The president demanded a better communications system. Cheney sent shock waves through the Pentagon and the new chairman of the Joint Chiefs of Staff, General Colin Powell, stiffened the chain of command. General Scowcroft and Bob Gates established the Deputies Committee, chaired by Gates and consisting of the "number two" people in all the national security agencies, that would meet continuously during security crises. It was a system designed to pull information through the system rapidly and accurately, and feed it directly to the president. It worked flawlessly in the later invasion of Panama and in Desert Storm. In many ways, we were lucky to have had the Panama coup fiasco occur so early in the administration.

This episode also sealed our fate with CBS News. President Bush and Dan Rather, the CBS anchor, had become mortal enemies as a result of their live interview during the 1988 presidential campaign. Rather is a self-proclaimed liberal whose weekly radio show on CBS openly condemns conservative policies and ideas. He clearly hoped to damage Bush in the TV interview, rehearsing all day, taping a prosecutorial lead-in about Iran-Contra, and turning over much of his regular newscast to others so he could concentrate on the interview. He immediately went on the attack about Iran-Contra, and Bush countered, asking Rather if he would like his entire career judged by the time he walked off the set during a newscast and left the network dark for seven minutes. Rather was stunned, looked in shock, and came back with shrill and ugly questions. The consensus afterward was that Bush had won big, destroying Rather and establishing himself as a tough competitor. Rather, of course, hated Bush after that.

On October 3, the day of the Panama coup, Rather tried to surreptitiously broadcast his news show from the White House lawn as a way to tie President Bush to the failed coup attempt. We had always rejected any attempt by any television show to use the White House as a set. The president simply felt so strongly about the dignity of the White House that we decided early in the administration on this policy.

Rather tried to clear twenty CBS technicians into the White House that afternoon, without giving a reason. It was obvious what he was up to. We asked a friendly CBS correspondent, who admitted it, so we denied access to Rather.

On October 11, the day after my stormy briefing about lying, Rather referred to the White House "cover-up," "changed story," and "stonewalling" on Panama. My favorite story about Rather's ludicrous attitude relates to how he began his newscast on the riots in Detroit by saying: "In this Reagan/Bush era of budget cuts, riots erupted in Detroit tonight." He would hold on-air conversations with his correspondents that always began: "Didn't the White House blow this, Lesley?" And no correspondent who wanted to keep his or her job ever disagreed with Dan Rather on the air. Robert Lichtner, who measures media coverage in Washington, reported in 1992 that 87 percent of all CBS stories were critical of the administration, compared to 57 percent at NBC and 39 percent at ABC. In any case, no one in the White House ever believed CBS would be fair to the administration.

During the Bush presidency, we offered many interviews to CBS correspondents Bob Schieffer, Charles Kuralt, Randall Pinkston, Harry Smith, and others. All we wanted was someone who would be civil. But CBS management always said, "No, only Dan Rather interviews the president."

During the 1992 campaign, CBS finally changed its policy. It agreed to a Rose Garden interview with the president by the CBS *Morning News* team of Harry Smith and Paula Zahn. It would be a "town meeting" format, last an hour, and be the first such production with CBS during the Bush years. Sure enough, at the last minute, Rather sent his personal producer and production crew to Washington to take over the show. As the show was about to end, I discovered Susan Zirinsky, Rather's producer, crouched behind some Rose Garden hedges, shouting into her two-way radio: "Ask him about Iran-Contra. Iran-Contra!" That confirmed everyone's feelings about the depth of Dan Rather's hatred for the president.

Lying to oneself, or self-delusion, is another serious problem for the White House. The pressures of governing, and the various political and pragmatic problems associated with so many different viewpoints, often force people to put round solutions into square holes, and then believe with all their hearts that they work. But any fool can plainly see that they don't.

I now live, at least part-time, in a little fishing and crabbing village on the Chesapeake Bay, Deale, Maryland. It's everything Washington is not, yet only thirty minutes from the city. I found it one desperate Sunday in the mid-1980s, looking for a haven from the White House that was close enough for a fast return to the city in an emergency, yet remote enough to give all my senses a break from the tension of performing in front of a press corps. Deale has no city hall, no sidewalk, and no clothing store selling slickers and white pants to boaters. It is blue-collar, commercial fishing. There are half a dozen boats at the Happy Harbor Inn that will help you catch bluefish for $250, seven or eight marinas for Washington sailors who buy thirty-four-foot Catalinas, wear blue jeans, and are probably looking for the same solace as I.

Deale reminds me of Kansas, a quiet place where you notice the roadsides, the wildflowers and twisted trees, where homemade markers spring up where friends have died in car crashes on the way home from the Elks Club. People care for each other. When Thomas "Muskrat" Greene, who lived for years on a houseboat at the Happy Harbor, died at age fifty-four, the commercial fishermen took up a collection for his cremation. Muskrat was renowned for eating oysters, even making it into the *Guinness Book of World Records* for devouring 2.2 pounds in two minutes, forty-three seconds. Thirty to forty boats escorted his ashes to Holland Point in the Chesapeake Bay, where he was cast upon the waters over the biggest oyster beds in the bay. His houseboat is still docked at the Inn.

I once learned a good lesson about self-delusion in Deale, which gave me one of the few plausible explanations I could fathom for the White House thinking it could get away with breaking the president's pledge of "no new taxes." I was eating a picnic table of crabs one evening at Skipper's Pier, an old, red-painted bar, restaurant, and gas pump that hangs off the end of Drum Point, where a three-piece band plays on Saturday afternoon to the admiring audience of Captain Billy, who owns the place, two crab boat fishermen and their girlfriends, one family from Baltimore with two kids, two local drunks, a couple of young bleached blonde girls, and one busy waitress—all of them, even the band, wearing blue jeans and thongs. I asked for dessert. The waitress, an attractive woman of twenty in a blue T-shirt that said "SKIPPER'S" on the front with a caricature of Captain Billy on the back, said they had carrot cake, chocolate cake, and ice cream.

I have been eating carrot cake all my life. It's the best, with that white sugar frosting, and the crushed walnuts that give it texture. Best of all, you can never really taste any carrots. The waitress, Paula, came back as dusk was vanishing and the lights were coming on across Rockhold Creek, and slid a piece of pumpkin pie in front of me.

"Wait," I said, "this isn't carrot cake."

"Yes, it is," she said.

"No," I said, raising my voice, "this isn't even cake. It's pie. Look, it has crust. It was baked in a pie tin. It looks like pie. It's not carrot cake even if carrot cake was baked in a pie tin!"

I felt I had destroyed her with the force of my argument.

"It is carrot cake," she said, "but if you don't want it, I'll take it back."

"Fine," I said. "I will not join the charade."

It was a small fight for mankind, but I wondered why Paula had clung so tenaciously to a conclusion that was obviously wrong. I concluded that she had been told it was carrot cake and, rather than fight the political pressures of her world, had deluded herself into thinking that indeed it was. That seems to be what the White House staff did in 1990 when we deluded ourselves into thinking that calling a tax increase by another name, revenue enhancement, would fool the world. On that fateful day when the brief presidential statement about the administration and Congress's budget deal reached the eyes of the first reporter in the White House briefing room, perhaps the biggest mistake of the administration was made. We agreed to raise taxes. Our political world exploded. The American people felt the president had lied about his 1988 Republican convention pledge, "Read my lips, no new taxes."

On the morning of September 26, 1990, I was called from my office and asked to join the budget negotiators meeting in the Family Dining Room, just off the State Dining Room, on the main floor of the White House. The negotiators, including Democratic and Republican leaders of Congress and White House economic and budget advisers, had been meeting for weeks at various locations, including some at the officers club at Andrews Air Force Base. It was an example of how far these negotiators were straying from reality that they thought Andrews would give them a special privacy, as if phones wouldn't reach that far. The haggling went back and forth for weeks, which our negotiators loved. It was the ultimate "insiders" game, and these were inside players. No messy press, or raucous congressional hearings, or loud markup rooms, just the power boys in a back room. It was Dick Darman heaven.

The public debate was over federal spending and how to cut the deficit, but the private debate was about political power. The Democrats, who controlled Congress, were not going to agree to any spending cuts unless the Republicans agreed to a tax increase. That way the Republicans could claim a spending victory, and the Democrats could claim a tax victory, or more precisely, the Democrats could take the tax cut issue away from the Republicans. Every day, the Democrats, particularly Congressman Richard Gephardt of Missouri, who had presidential ambitions, leaked some new tidbit from the negotiations that made it look as if the Democrats were winning. And they were. I would complain about our side giving away the public game by allowing these leaks to go unchallenged, by not telling the public what we were trying to achieve. Roger Porter, assistant to the president for policy and a negotiator, would say no, "I want to be able to look across the table and demand that Gephardt stop leaking." He wanted to honor the blackout. Porter was an academic, a student of the game, a staffer who had worked for three presidents but never really understood the combination of special interests, public opinion, and party politics that dictate so many decisions in Washington. Dick Darman did understand the game, but he only knew one way to play it, on the inside, where he could design Machiavellian moves involving the pitting of one congressman versus another, and in doing so, establish his own role and reputation. In one way or another, our entire team had bought into the inside game, infatuated and seduced by the chance to play ball with the powerful leaders of Congress. Worse, they had convinced the president that the dreaded deficit was so threatening that all political sense had to be sacrificed.

When I walked into the Family Dining Room, pushing the heavy, twenty-foot doors open ahead of me, everyone stopped talking, as if a priest had just joined the dinner party. The president, sitting in the middle of my side of the table, leaned back, turned in his chair, and held out a piece of paper for me to read. On the other side of the table were Senate Majority Leader George Mitchell, Speaker of the House Tom Foley, House Ways and Means Committee chairman Dan Rostenkowski, and other committee chairmen. On our side, flanking the president, were Chief of Staff John Sununu, Secretary of the Treasury Nicholas Brady, Roger Porter, Office of Management and

Budget director Richard Darman, and the Republican congressional leadership. I read the brief paragraph. It announced that the negotiators had reached an agreement to cut spending to reduce the deficit, and the administration agreed that "tax revenue increases" would be necessary.

I looked up at the Democrats. They were incredible. To a man, they gave two kinds of looks. One was of the cat who ate the canary. The other was frozen fear, as if I might blow their cover and expose their victory. They said absolutely nothing.

The president said, "Marlin, we have agreed to issue this before the members of Congress leave the White House. Can you take care of that?"

"Yes, sir," I said. It was then I knew the game was over. The Democrats had taken us to the cleaners. They had obviously demanded that the statement be issued before they left, because they knew that if anyone with political smarts and balls saw that statement they might talk the president out of it. I wasn't too smart or too ballsy, but I decided to give it a try.

I needed to get away from the negotiators and make my case. I left the room, but turned around just outside the grand doors, as they remained open. I stared directly at Governor Sununu, trying to get his attention without arousing anyone else. The Democratic side of the table could not see me, but the Republicans could. The president was talking to Mitchell. My eyes must have raised the hair on Sununu's neck, because he finally glanced my way. He got up and came out of the room. I could see the anger building in his eyes with each step, no doubt because I had not yet moved to release the statement.

"What do you want?" he demanded.

"Sir," I said. "This says we support raising taxes. This breaks the pledge."

"No it doesn't," he said curtly. "It says 'increased revenues.' "

"Nobody will be fooled," I said.

"It says 'revenue increase,' " he repeated as he turned to go back into the room. "Issue it."

The president and all his budget advisers had bought the Richard Darman idea that cutting the deficit was the only way to improve the economy. The president knew that it's very hard to win reelection during a recession. So he decided to roll the dice on a budget deal that would cut spending and the deficit in return for breaking his pledge on "no new taxes." The Democratic leadership of Congress had made it clear that their price for spending cuts and a better economy was a political victory for their party and Republicans accepting blame for a tax increase. The Democrats outfoxed us on two points. They understood better than we did just how much political damage would result from breaking the tax pledge. They also understood better than we did that cutting the deficit has little or no political value unless it works well and fast, resulting in more jobs and a feeling of general prosperity. That usually never happens, and when it does, it takes years.

As it turned out, one of the few people on the Republican team who understood this trap was Congressman Newt Gingrich. After the deal was reached, and the congressional leadership gathered in the Cabinet Room before going to the Rose Garden for the formal announcement, the president asked if everyone in the room was going to support the agreement. There were no voices of dissent. But when the group got up to leave for the Rose Garden, Congressman Gingrich went another direction and did not stay for the ceremony. Newt had earlier recommended a different course of action: Abandon the budget negotiations, keep the tax pledge, insist that Congress cut spending, and make a political fight out of it. It's clear now that we should have followed his advice.

At a minimum, we should have hit the tax pledge head on, explained the budget agreement as a courageous act of conscience in which the president was determined to fight the deficit, to slay the dragon, even at his own political expense. Instead, we tried to deny the undeniable and hoped no one would notice that the pledge was broken.

It was just another piece of carrot cake, and the American people refused to accept it.

Another information problem in the White House is verification. The flow of information is so great that one small break in the chain can mislead the multitudes. In addition, so many people bring a judgment to bear on the quality of information that one mistake in judgment can leave the rest in the dark. One of my earliest examples of this phenomenon related to the American hostages being held in Lebanon.

In the late 1980s, America still had a handful of citizens being held in unknown locations in Lebanon. Every few months some effort would be made by the terrorists to use their hostages, either to get publicity for their cause or to get the release of their compatriots being held in Israel or Europe. Rumors were daily fare. But when the press would come to me with a rumor of some American's release, I would always check it out with the National Security Council. Usually it was just a report, a rumor, carried on Beirut radio. Sometimes it was a CIA report issued in Lebanon in an attempt to break something loose, to get more information, or to test local reactions.

One day Ann Devroy said *The Washington Post* had a tip that a hostage was about to be released and asked if I would check it out. Usually, there was a grain of truth in any tip that came to me from *The Washington Post.* They have so many reporters in Washington and around the world, and so many sources, that it is folly for a press secretary to ever totally deny a *Post* story or tip. There is always some truth to it.

In government, however, bureaucrats have a disturbing way of denying entire stories if one fact or piece of the story is wrong. Similarly, government officials, especially those at the top, are prone to deny the existence of any information they don't know about. In both cases, they appear to be lying when these denials are given to a skeptical press.

I took Ann Devroy's tip to General Scowcroft.

"Brent, do we have an imminent hostage release? Ann Devroy says they have a tip that somebody is coming out."

"No," Brent said. "I don't know of any release. These rumors happen all the time."

I returned to my office and called Roman. "Brent says there is nothing to this," I said. "But Devroy is seldom wrong. Can you just check around and see what you can find out?"

Roman had a thousand sources. He knew the people at the working level, six levels from the top, the people who read all the MEM-CONs (MEMorandums of CONversation) at State or CIA, the people who sat in the back of the meetings and carried the briefcases. These were the people who knew the truth, what had actually been said in the meetings and embassy cables.

I called the operations room at the State Department.

"I just got a tip about a hostage release," I told the voice on the phone. "Do you have any operations under way to get ready for a release?"

"Yes," the voice said, "we dispatched an Air Force plane to Rhine-Main Air Force Base in Frankfurt, West Germany, yesterday to get ready for a release."

"What's on this plane?" I asked.

"The full package. CIA debriefers. Psychologists. Military doctors and nurses. Immigration. This is a standard group whenever we think someone is coming out."

"Who's coming out?"

"We don't know."

I called the Pentagon and asked Pete Williams, assistant secretary of defense for public affairs, to check it out. Pete was a close aide to Secretary Cheney and the best in the business. I always considered it one of the greatest strengths of the Bush administration that, with Margaret Tutwiler as State spokesperson and Pete Williams at Defense, we had the best at knowing and reading their bosses, at understanding public opinion, at working with their bureaucracies, and at understanding the press. Pete soon came back to me with a confirmation of everything I had been told at State.

Then Roman called. He had checked all his sources and came up with the rescue plane going to Germany, the name of the hostage, and the source of the report as coming from our CIA listening posts in the region.

I went back to Brent and laid out my information. I wanted him to know that I checked these things out, and that I had sources that knew their stuff. I wanted to teach him about the fragility of information, how misinformation or being uninformed can so easily be turned into a lie. On the first day of the Bush administration, I asked for a meeting with Brent to discuss the NSC and public information. He came to my office, a gesture that told me he was interested and approachable. I remarked to Brent that I had worked for President Bush before and he had a "real penchant for secrecy."

Brent stared at me, paused, then said, "So do I."

I laughed out loud. Brent had been a member of the Tower Board, with former senator John Tower and former secretary of state Edmund Muskie, that had investigated the policy aspects of Iran-Contra. Their report had urged more openness, a civilian national security adviser, better note taking at meetings, formal NSC meetings to discuss issues, better consultations with Congress, and less secrecy. So I was surprised by Brent's comment.

"In any case," I said, "I want to work with you, and I want you to trust me. I want you to know that I won't betray your secrets."

"Good," he said. "I was in the Ford administration and there was real tension with the press office." I took that to mean they couldn't be trusted to hold information.

So as I presented my information to Brent about the hostage release, I wanted to be careful not to be accusatory, or to appear arrogant and trying to embarrass him. I wanted him to know my problems, how it would have appeared if I had told Ann Devroy that there was no hostage release and how, when the truth came out, both Brent and I would have been accused by Ann of lying. Brent said he just didn't know. I understood that, but I wanted to impress upon him that the worst time to ever deny anything is when you don't know something. That's why good press secretaries want to know everything. I also wanted to show Brent that knowing all the facts didn't mean we would make them all public. I suggested that we tell Ann that she was right, there had been a rumor of release in the region, and we had taken normal preparations in case a release should occur, but we honestly didn't know if it would really happen, and we couldn't discuss the details of our preparations. Brent agreed. This position allowed me to be honest about Ann's tip, but still refuse to tell her about the actual preparations, such as flying the plane to Germany. State and Defense wanted to protect that information because it might signal how much we knew about the hostage takers, their methods, or their status.

Brent Scowcroft respected this process. A breakdown in information had been prevented from escalating into a public lie. That lesson was slow coming in the Clinton administration. On several occasions, George Stephanopoulos or Dee Dee Myers would rush out in the morning with an explanation that had to be retracted or amplified later. This was true in the initial military operation in Haiti, the role of the first lady in buying commodities futures, the role of the president in Whitewater, and the president's involvement with Paula Corbin Jones, who later sued him for sexual harassment. They learned the hard way that bad or incomplete information is often interpreted by the press as a lie.

Another big lie, peculiar to the White House, is spin. No other institution can perfect spin like the White House because the process requires fortress-like credibility and incredible gall. No matter how great the siege of the White House, people still want to believe the president and those who speak for him. Unlike Sisyphus, who had to roll the stone up the hill, the White House stone is always rolling down. The momentum of an issue is always with them in the beginning. Truth is the assumption at the beginning. Spin is the weaving of basic truth into the fabric of a lie, the production of a cover garment that protects, or obscures, or deflects public examination.

David Gergen, who helped engineer my move to the White House, was known as the "spin master" even then, mostly because he had been a speechwriter and loved words, and also because he could never stop talking. He overexplained every issue, sometimes leading to conclusions other than the ones intended. He also had a special knack for engaging a reporter in discussion, ascertaining the reporter's attitude on an issue, and, in midconversation, turning his explanation to fit the reporter's bias. This produced a number of stories favorable to Gergen, some favorable to the president, but a good many that suggested the White House staff was trying to save the president from himself. That did not sit well with Mrs. Reagan, who in 1983 told Jim Baker, then chief of staff, that Gergen's leaking was hurting the president and the spin master had to go. Baker took Gergen to lunch, explained the facts of life, and told the spinner to find another platform. A few months later he became editor of *U.S. News & World Report*, the perfect perch for a rhetorical whiz.

More than a decade later, Gergen was back in the White House of Bill Clinton, a man who appreciated spin and had used it often. It was fitting that when it came time for Gergen to once again move on, this time in the company of the president's chief of staff, Thomas F. "Mac" McLarty, the departure announcement in the Oval Office amounted to a coronation of spin, the awarding of the Oscar for fabrication and gentle explanation, five speeches by the participants that were made of golden thread and the smoothest weave.

Here's how spin works:

The president took the basic truth that Mac McLarty is an old friend and a nice guy and spun it to: Mac knows me and will be a private counselor, so I can better utilize his enormous talent. Never mind that the White House was mismanaged, embarrassing, and creating problems for the president.

Mac McLarty took the basic truth of his personal relationship with the president and spun it to: I wanted out of the chief's job so I could be a counselor and better serve the president. Never mind that every political adviser to the president had recommended McLarty's departure, and Bob Woodward's book, *The Agenda*, had documented staff confusion and incompetence.

Dave Gergen took the basic truth of his fondness for government, any government, and spun it to: I have always wanted to serve in international affairs and help the secretary of state. Never mind that Gergen already had announced his imminent departure from the

White House, but he hadn't found a job, and the remaining White House staff wanted him out.

Leon Panetta and Alice Rivlin took the basic truth that changes were being made and spun it to: We all wanted these new jobs. Never mind the staff chaos, travel office firings, bathrobes stolen from an aircraft carrier, subpoenas of seven staff members for improper activity related to Whitewater, the staff taking a helicopter to play golf, one suicide, and two top aides who walked through the revolving door during their first year, Roy Neel and Howard Paster, with such fat pockets that even cynical Washington was in disbelief.

It was after this ceremony, held in the Oval Office no less, when the Clinton administration truly distinguished itself from other presidencies in terms of spin. Dave Gergen went to the North Lawn of the White House for an interview on CNN. Panetta and McLarty appeared together on *Larry King Live* that night, and all the participants appeared on morning network television shows. This is the brilliance of the Clinton team's spin: They never quit. They never give truth a chance to catch up.

The abuse of truth infects the media as well. The press has a very unique set of codes for truth, not written anywhere, and practiced very unevenly, that dictate their methods and their stories. For the most part, I found that reporters seek truth in their articles or broadcast reports. They may be biased because of their advocacy, their environment, the personalities involved, bad sources, or a hundred other factors. But reporters seldom report information they know is wrong.

The code, however, says it's OK to set traps, use misinformation, and adopt almost any other sleight of hand trick *to get* the story. In the White House this usually takes one of three forms: television producers who will promise you any ground rule to secure an interview or get a piece of tape, correspondents who will play the "gotcha" game to get information, and reporters who base their quest for information on tricking their sources.

As we approached the last week of an eight-year Reagan presidency, the CBS *60 Minutes* program was trying every way possible to get a final interview with the president. It started with a call from one of their field producers. I waited a decent interval and declined the request, simply because it would not be in the best interest of the president. *60 Minutes* had made its reputation as an advocacy show that always tried to destroy institutions, especially government.

Every show was good-versus-evil. The show was liberal, conservatives were evil. Ronald Reagan, as a successful conservative who had
survived quite nicely for two terms without paying much heed to
anybody in the press, and to almost no liberals, was especially evil.
I had no doubt that their last attempt would be to show the president
as some feeble-minded old goat who had stumbled through the presidency.

Mike Wallace called to appeal. Mike Wallace has been destroying
people on television for years. As a small boy on the farm, when we
got our first Admiral TV set, I would watch Mike Wallace late at
night as he insulted his talk show guests, drove women to cry, and
performed his pioneering version of talk show extremism. It amazed
me, years later, to find that he was actually respected by his colleagues and a successful *60 Minutes* veteran. But I can't say my
childhood dislike for him ever really vanished. On this occasion, he
said he wanted to give the president a sentimental and sympathetic
last interview, that they wanted to look back at the accomplishments of eight years, and talk about the president's personal reflec-
tions. Sounds great, but what trash it was. First of all, that's not what
they wanted to talk about at all. Second, it was fully in line with the
cardinal understanding of television production: Tell any tale to get
the subject on camera. Once the camera is on, the subject is snared,
as surely as having a hook in his cheek. If you walk out of an interview, you look guilty of whatever sin the show is professing. If you
get angry, you look guilty. If you get tired, you look guilty. If you give
inconsistent answers, you look guilty.

That's why most people today, especially government officials or
corporate officials who have staff who study these matters, refuse *60
Minutes* interviews. It's also why *60 Minutes* so often turns to the
"stakeout" camera outside your home or office. If you won't grant
the interview, an unsteady shot of you running to your car will make
you look just as guilty. Now they are even using hidden cameras to
get interviews.

I said no to Mike Wallace. Then Don Hewitt called. The origina-
tor of the show and winner of every award possible for television pro-
gramming, he was powerful, rich, and untouchable at CBS, and had
taught his field producers every trick in the book to get interviews.
He begged, pleaded, and said this would be the show that established
Ronald Reagan's role in history. I declined.

Then Mike Wallace played his trump card: He called Mrs. Reagan. He had known the first lady for years. Wallace and Mrs. Rea-

gan's mother had known each other from the time when they had both worked in Chicago radio. Mrs. Reagan was very fond of him, and extended that affection to Chris Wallace, who was covering the White House. Often Chris would come up with information about the president's plans that I could never source, finding out later it came from Mrs. Reagan. She listened patiently to Mike, who pushed all the buttons about how great the president looked, how terrific he was on television, how this would be a chance to build the historical record, and how it would only be forty-five minutes on camera. That's the ultimate television lie. Producers will promise you a two-minute interview to get the cameras turned on. Then they have you, trapped like a rabbit in a gopher trap.

Mrs. Reagan agreed, and called Kenneth Duberstein, the president's last chief of staff, to give him instructions. As only Mrs. Reagan could do, she then told Ken to make sure nothing went wrong. I told Ken he was dead meat. Mike Wallace would ask mostly about Iran-Contra. He would never stop at forty-five minutes. He would ask technical questions to stump the president. He would ask the same question several ways to show inconsistency. All of this happened, of course.

As the interview passed the one-hour mark, Ken asked if I would pull the plug.

"There is no way to stop the interview without embarrassing the president," I said.

"Pull the plug," he suggested.

"You mean have the lights in the Oval Office go dark?" I exclaimed. "That would make the president look like a convict slipping out in the shadows."

"Tell the producer," he said.

"We did," I said, "at forty-five minutes, at sixty minutes. There is nothing we can do."

"Yes there is. Tell Don Hewitt," he said.

"We told Don Hewitt at forty-five minutes. You think he cares what we want? Hell no! All he wants is more film," I said.

"I'll tell him," Ken said. He walked over to Hewitt, tapped him on the shoulder, and told him to end it. Hewitt said fine, and continued for another ten minutes.

In 1994, President Reagan wrote an eloquent and optimistic letter to the American people announcing that he had Alzheimer's disease. Many people suggested that the president, although he had been out of office for six years, might have been suffering from Alzheimer's when he was still president. But it's impossible to believe that after seeing, or reading, the more than one-hour grilling of the president by Mike Wallace in the last days of his presidency.

Reporters sometimes use misleading information to create news. Standing alone at the podium, unable to consult staff, and showing every flinch or reaction, the press secretary is particularly vulnerable to overreaction, or accepting misleading "facts" he hears from the press and commenting on them. The reporter's questions, of course, are never reported. But the response is considered news if it changes the president's position, if it indicates some kind of action that affects people, or if it is outrageous and therefore interesting.

The master at threading an explosive question into a briefing was James Alan Miklaszewski, NBC News. It didn't surprise me to see President Clinton, during his trip to Russia in the spring of 1994, grant James an interview and then walk out. The cameras showed the president storming off the set, untangling himself from the lapel microphone wires, ducking beneath the tripod lights, and telling Jim in an obviously angry tone: "You had two questions, Jim. You had two questions."

Jim had been granted a quick interview on the summit, two questions about the meeting with Russian president Boris Yeltsin, but instead he asked about Whitewater and presidential scandal. I was proud of President Clinton for walking out, though. I would not have advised it because he made himself look thin-skinned, and the film, which was picked up by *Nightline*, showed how sensitive he was to Whitewater.

Another favorite trick of reporters is to misquote another politician attacking the president and ask for a response. For example, if Senator Robert Dole of Kansas, the Republican leader in the Senate, left the White House after a meeting with the president and told the press waiting in the driveway, "We'll have a lot of trouble passing this budget by recess," the reporter might ask me the question this way: "Dole says your budget won't pass. Why can't you even get your own party to support it?"

This presents a special problem. The press secretary can't be accusatory by saying the reporter manufactured the question. Such a charge would bring the entire room to the reporter's defense. Rather, the entire question must be dissected in such a way that the true Dole comment surfaces and is answered.

If I know the original Dole comment, I simply repeat it, saying, "I think this is what Senator Dole said, and we agree that the budget will be tough to pass by recess, but the senator and the White House are going to try." This kind of response lets the press know that I caught the reporter in the act, but I respect the press by not accusing him of lying, and that I know how to turn this question to my advantage.

Just as often, however, I will not have heard the Dole comment. In those cases, only instinct and tolerance would save me. Usually I said, "I don't believe the senator would say that. But even if he did, we still hope to pass the budget as soon as possible."

What the reporter wants, of course, is for me to lash out at Senator Dole. It would then be reported as: "White House Angry with Dole's Leadership."

The national news magazines, *Time* and *Newsweek*, seem to have the most difficulty with truth in photographs, perhaps because their cover photos are so crucial to their sales, and perhaps because the competitive edge between them is so small.

The Washington Post reported this situation in 1994:

> *Time* has taken a bit of a beating for electronically darkening the police mug shot of O. J. Simpson on this week's cover. Among those expressing disdain was *Newsweek* Editor in Chief Richard Smith, who declared: "We don't mess around with news pictures."
>
> *Time* is happy to point out, therefore, that *Newsweek* took liberties last year with the official police photo of Los Angeles patrolman Laurence Powell. On its April 26, 1993 cover, after Powell had been convicted in the Rodney King beating, *Newsweek* changed the color photo to black-and-white and enlarged it, to give it the stark, grainy texture of a newspaper picture.
>
> "I'm shocked—shocked—that *Newsweek* would mislead people when they say they don't alter cover photos," said *Time* spokesman Robert Pondiscio. "It's a flat out lie."

In December 1991, *Time*'s White House correspondent, Dan Goodgame, came to me with a confidential request, "*Time* has selected President Bush as Man of the Year for his leadership in Desert Storm. We would like an interview and a cover-photo session." On the surface, this seemed like a wonderful opportunity, at last some recognition of the president's leadership, with a nice picture that would be part of presidential history. But not so fast, dog breath. Closer examination disclosed a few flaws: First, the story was going to be written by Goodgame and Michael Duffy, who were writing a book at the time on the Bush presidency. It was scheduled to come out in the election year, and it was bound to be critical. In my many discussions with these two correspondents, both of whom are charming and interesting personalities, it was clear that Goodgame believed in an activist federal government, and Duffy had concluded that our domestic policy was lacking. Even though I suspected he was right, I could not encourage this kind of story. In addition, this would be a highly personalized report in which all the failures of the administration would be directly attributed to the president.

When I presented the *Time* request to the president, he immediately saw the possibilities for disaster, but we agreed to the interview as the best way to influence the story. The picture seemed like the least of my worries.

In late December, just before their final deadline, Goodgame asked for a one-hour photo session with the famed photographer Gregory Heisler. He further asked for a special room and four hours of setup time to get the camera and lights at just the right angles. We scheduled the shoot for the Map Room, so named because Franklin Roosevelt set up his maps of World War II in this room, just off the basement lobby in the main mansion. When the day of the photo session arrived, my staff helped Heisler set up. They kept me posted throughout the morning that the setup was going well, the photographer was very thorough, every light and camera position was marked on the floor with tape, every angle of the photographs was predetermined, and every position of the president had been rehearsed. No snags thus far.

As I walked with the president from the Oval to the Map Room, he joked about this being another futile effort. "They'll probably conclude that I lost the war."

"No, it will be fine," I reassured him. "There will be some criticism of domestic policy, but overall it will be fine. It's still the Man of the Year, after all."

When we walked into the setup, I was struck by the precision of the layout. Every camera had to be in just the right place, and the president was very carefully posed at three different angles. Even when Heisler asked the president to turn his head, it was at the exact same height and posture as the previous pose. I was a little impatient, but not suspicious. I supposed this was how all New York artsy hot-shot photographers worked. So when the first copy of the Man of the Year issue was tossed onto my desk, it was as close to a self-induced heart attack as I would ever come.

"Those bastards!" I screamed. "They lied to me! This whole thing was a setup!"

There was silence as my staff gathered to give me support. They knew that I was fully responsible for allowing this to happen, for arranging the interview and the photo.

"Those dirty rotten bastards!" I screamed again. "How could they do this to me?" showing again how we all tend to personalize disaster. The cover photo showed President George Herbert Walker Bush with two faces. The story was just as bad, giving the president credit for Desert Storm but also presenting his other face, the one that had "done nothing" in domestic policy. They even renamed the issue: "Men of the Year."

CHAPTER TEN

Drugstore Cowboy

It was the worst mistake of my career, calculated and wrong. In the early months of the Bush administration, Mikhail Gorbachev proposed a number of formulas for reducing the arms race. He continued the rhetoric of perestroika and kept public pressure on the United States to match his offers. In his speech to the United Nations on December 8, 1988, Gorbachev proposed a unilateral reduction in conventional forces in Eastern Europe. In reality, of course, the Soviet Union had so many more troops and tanks in the Warsaw Pact, most of them lined up along the East German border, that the unilateral reduction, and any mutual reduction, would still leave the Soviets with a sizable advantage. We demanded "parity," which meant a reduction to equal numbers.

Secretary of State James Baker visited Moscow in early May 1989 and won what we thought was a major achievement, another promised reduction in the nuclear arsenal. Baker also pressed Gorbachev for a reduction in weapons aid to Nicaragua. The United States had exhausted millions of dollars in helping the rebel Contras fight the ruling, communist-supported Sandinistas, who were under the command of Daniel Ortega, president of Nicaragua. If Gorbachev was sincere about easing East-West tensions, stopping that aid would be one of the clearest signals of his intentions, and one we could measure. Privately, Gorbachev suggested he might be able to do that, but he could not announce such a decision at that time.

In the meantime, President Bush had undertaken an across-the-board review of the administration's foreign policy, under the direction of General Scowcroft. In fact, it was a rather informal review that grew more specific each time the president talked about it in

public, but it did give his new foreign policy team time to analyze
the world situation. When it became clear that the press and the
public were expecting some kind of climax to this effort—perhaps a
report to the nation, a speech or a press conference—we put together
a series of four speeches by the president that would constitute the
conclusion of the review. The first of these was given May 12, 1989,
at Texas A&M University in College Station, Texas, a firmly patriotic institution in which patience with communism was as short as
the students' burr haircuts. The president called for ending the hostility of the cold war years and "the integration of the Soviet Union
into the community of nations." But coming on the heels of Gorbachev's specific arms proposals, the Bush speech fell flat.

The Los Angeles Times summation seemed accurate:

> Gorbachev had demonstrated skill in maintaining the initia-
> tive on arms control, repeatedly taking Washington by surprise.
> In that context, Bush was correct in his address Friday to press
> Gorbachev for further tangible steps, including acceptance of
> open aerial surveillance of troop movements, free immigration
> and renunciation of the Brezhnev Doctrine that had asserted a
> Soviet right to intervene in Communist nations. Bush was also
> wise to recognize with new clarity the value of the social and eco-
> nomic changes taking place in the Soviet Union. Nevertheless,
> the American President's address left the impression that his for-
> eign policy is still being formed, a status that limits his ability to
> give vigorous leadership to the alliance, and a circumstance that
> inevitably makes it seem that Washington is always reacting to
> Moscow, not charting its own course.

Secretary Baker and the president had started putting references in
all their speeches and press statements to the effect that we wanted
to see "deeds, not words" from the Soviet Union, especially in terms
of cutting off Soviet aid to Nicaragua. But the rest of America was
rushing headlong into its infatuation with Gorbachev, and the press
wasn't even printing our admonitions to demand more than promises. I started looking for a way to break through the fog. I knew that
one sharp statement, well timed, could catch public opinion and
turn it.

On the Monday after the president's speech, I raised this problem
with my staff.

"How do we break through?" I asked my deputies. "The public

thinks Gorbachev is a white knight, but he hasn't followed through on any of his promises. And his unilateral actions sound terrific but have no real impact."

"Why don't we just say so?" volunteered Alixe Glen, my deputy since the beginning of the Bush administration.

"I don't want to challenge Gorbachev, or offer a judgment on the specific proposals. I just want to wake people up," I said.

"No, Marlin," Roman advised. "Just let it go." Always the foreign policy professional, Roman thought the war of words was just part of the geopolitical dance. As far as he was concerned, it would all be worked out in negotiations and endless meetings between faceless bureaucrats. But that was reality. I wanted to change perceptions, the political perception that Gorbachev was ahead of the West in arms reductions and a lessening of tensions.

"How about this?" I said, leaning back in my swivel chair. "We need a metaphor—a word or phrase that will make people question the Soviet statements."

"No, Marlin," Roman repeated. "Leave this to Baker."

"How about 'drugstore cowboy,' " I suggested.

"Are you serious?" Roman asked.

"Sure," I said, for the sake of argument. "It's an old Kansas term, out of the Wild West. I can't remember exactly what it means. Something about bragging."

"No, Marlin," Alixe said, laughing, thinking I would never actually follow through on such an idea.

"OK," I said, "I guess you're right."

But the next day, *The New York Times*'s R. W. Apple reported a new poll showing that "Mikhail Gorbachev's aggressive and inventive diplomacy has so transformed this country's view of the Soviet Union that two out of three Americans say Moscow no longer poses an immediate military threat to the U.S. and nearly three out of four consider nuclear war unlikely."

However, the poll also showed that 48 percent of the 1,073 respondents said they thought the Gorbachev proposal had more to do with gaining a military advantage, while only 34 percent said the primary Soviet motivation was reducing tensions. As R. W. "Johnny" Apple pointed out, people still didn't quite trust Gorbachev.

As my staff gathered on May 16 to prepare for the morning briefing, I couldn't get the poll out of my mind. Maybe the timing was right for a strong comment. The press was sure to ask for a response. Maybe the public was ready for a small dose of reality.

"Natalie," I said to my secretary, Natalie Wozniak, "let's get the dictionary and look up the term 'drugstore cowboy.' "

"Are you still on that kick?" Alixe said. "Forget it."

"No, really, just look it up."

Natalie got the dictionary from the outer office and sat back down on the couch, surrounded by our entire staff, with bodies on the floor, on tables, and leaning against the fireplace. She started to read: " 'Drugstore cowboy' refers to someone who makes promises he can't keep."

"Yes," I said, "that's it exactly."

She continued. "It's a term widely used to characterize young men who would hang around small-town drugstores at the turn of the century."

"Yes," I said, "Gorbachev makes promises he doesn't keep. It would make just the headline to turn the debate. It doesn't denigrate his proposals. It's just a more colorful way to say 'deeds, not words.' "

"No, Marlin," Roman said. "Don't use it."

"OK, Roman," I said reluctantly. "Call the briefing."

We were about ten minutes into the briefing when Owen Ull-mann, of Knight-Ridder Newspapers, asked the question that touched all my hot buttons.

"Marlin," he said, "since the election, Gorbachev gave conventional arms cuts in New York, plutonium factories, his latest offer handed to Baker; now this. And the president's been calling for deeds, not words, but what deeds has George Bush responded with? I mean, you've criticized Gorbachev here, but he's made a whole series of proposals. I don't recall that Bush has responded with deeds, but just words."

Owen knew that to turn the challenge against the president would stir me to anger. I could feel the blood pressure rising. Like an early-warning system, my face was flushing, but I could not stop. It seemed that everything was right: the poll, the question, the challenge to the president. I would be careful, but I was going for it. I could feel Roman and Alixe staring holes in the side of my face, begging me to look at them so they could shake me off the course they knew I was about to take. I did not look at them.

Instead, I began, "I think that's the essence of the PR game that he's playing here, and that is that the United States has been very careful and methodical in its examination of our relationship with the Soviet Union. On the basis of that, we have opened the door to any number of possibilities that could result from an improved relationship. And the president has said that he is willing to change the way the United States had viewed the Soviet Union for the last forty years. And out of that could come any number of kinds of initiatives. We contrast that, which is an admittedly cautious approach, to the one of throwing out in a kind of a drugstore cowboy fashion, one arms-control proposal after another—all of which, upon examination, proved to be either very little change from existing situations involving promises that have been made in the past, involving reductions that are not meaningful in terms of our strategic relationship with the Soviet Union, or reductions that are not meaningful in terms of the NATO relationship or the Warsaw Pact."

"Does that apply to the ones I just mentioned," Owen asked, "such as the conventional arms cuts?"

"The conventional arms cuts is a good example," I responded. "When they outnumber us with the sizable quantities that they do, we are saying arms reductions are welcome and we would like to see conventional cuts. But on the other hand, we've got to be talking about reductions that lead to parity, and that's what we want to see, or at least to negotiate."

The phrase had been passed over rather quietly, arousing no immediate reaction. No snickers, no oohs and ahs, none of the telltale audible gasps when the press corps thinks you have just screwed up badly.

Then, about five questions later, Owen came back to the "drugstore cowboy."

"What's a drugstore cowboy?" he asked directly.

"Have to go back to my Kansas ancestors to get that," I said.

Then the briefing moved on to Panama and South Africa. As I rushed out of the briefing room and back toward my office, Alixe caught my glance and rolled her eyes. She knew I was in deep doo-doo, as Vice President Bush once said.

The staff filed in behind me, saying nothing, waiting for my reaction, my own recognition that I had overstepped my bounds. I just stood behind my desk, looking at their faces and knowing that every one of them was fearful for me. They knew the recriminations that were coming.

I sank into my chair, propped my feet on my desk, and asked, "What's going to happen?"

"First," Alixe said, "you have a gaggle of reporters outside the door wanting to talk privately to you. You better figure out what you're going to say."

"Then," Roman said, "you had better tell the president. The wires are running the story now. State will be reading it in minutes. And Gorbachev and Gerasimov will have it soon. I'll tell Scowcroft. But first, go see the president about this."

It was beginning to sink in. Like a terrible crime, or perhaps a football injury on the playing field, no one wanted to say the offending words. My staff talked around it, as if to say "drugstore cowboy" would deepen the wound or make it contagious. But the press were not afraid, they were hungry. Someone outside the door shouted, "Bring out the drugstore cowboy!" My heart began to sink. Fear always brought a physical reaction, a rubbery weakness in the knees that I could never understand. It just never made sense that an intellectual problem could actually weaken your muscles, but it did. My arms were growing tired and I let them hang over the arms of my chair.

"Will the president be upset, do you think?" I asked.

"The president, and maybe even Baker, may not be upset," Roman said, "but the Soviets will be. The liberals who love Gorbachev will go crazy. And you're going to get big headlines." At that, Roman began to laugh, breaking the tension. "Big headlines."

"I'm going to the Oval."

As I opened my door, they started to shout. Helen's screechy voice was first, or maybe I just always heard it first: "Where'd you get that 'drugstore cowboy'?"

"What is a drugstore cowboy?" someone screamed.

"Is Gerasimov an urban cowboy?" another voice said.

I hurried past, saying nothing in response, but feeling my courage slip away as I took those twenty steps to the Oval. I still had some reservoir of feeling that I had accomplished my objective, that the debate had been turned, and now the nation would focus on the reality and substance of Gorbachev's proposals. But if that happened, it would be weeks before anyone recognized the success. No, this was not a comment I should defend. I would tell the president what I said, why I said it, then admit it was a mistake.

"Is the president available?" I asked his secretary.

"He's at his desk," she said.

I walked up to his door and pressed my eye against the peephole that was normally used to see if guests were preparing to leave the Oval. President Bush was writing at his desk. I turned the knob and slowly pushed the door open.

"Marlin," the president said in greeting, "come in. How are the overnights?" At least he was in a good mood.

"Mr. President," I said, walking toward his desk. "I think I made a mistake. I was looking for a phrase to replace 'deeds not words' in describing Soviet intentions, so I told the press that Gorbachev throws out arms control proposals like a drugstore cowboy."

The president had resumed writing. I said nothing, waiting, standing, suddenly alone in an Oval Office that seemed as big as the Superdome. President Bush was not a man of anger. Disappointment was his emotion. Silence was his weapon. Anger, I have found, can often be dismissed as temporary or just an emotional outburst. But disappointment and silence live forever. You never really know how deep the feeling is, or how long it will last, or how permanent the scar will be. In this case, the president was disappointed.

The administration was only five months old. I had worked hard every day to prove my trustworthiness, to prove I could withstand any amount of heat and still say the right thing. Now all that work was gone. I remembered my high school journalism teacher, Mrs. Dorothy Elliott, who said that a great newspaper builds its reputation every day, yet one bad story will destroy it. I had written that one bad phrase.

The president finally looked up. "What kind of reaction are you getting?"

"The press love it, of course," I said, "because it's colorful and I'm in trouble. We haven't heard from anyone else yet."

"It may not be so bad," the president said. "Let's wait and see what happens."

"Mr. President," I said, "I'm terribly sorry. I'll do whatever it takes to help make this right. Apologize to Gorbachev. Whatever. And if it gets bad, I'll resign immediately."

"I don't think that will be necessary," he said, and returned to his writing. That was the Bush dismissal. Whenever he started writing notes, or quit looking at you, it was clear that he wanted you to leave. The most successful staff recognized that moment instantly. I turned and rushed out of the room.

As I headed back to my office, the full impact of the personal situation hit me. I had just done damage to the presidency, and to the nation's relationship with the Soviet Union. I knew better than most that all foreign relations are personal. I knew I might have to resign. I thought my career was over. Real fear set in, as I realized that every honorable objective I sought in using the phrase "drugstore cowboy" had been reversed. I sat down next to the *Buckaroo* statue in the hallway, hearing the press rumbling just inside my office door, and I could not move. I remembered being eleven years old.

It was a .22-caliber rifle, handed down from one generation of farm family to another so that its genesis was unknown. It had a rusty barrel held in a bulky wood stock that had been knife-carved and sanded by hand. It was crude, unbalanced, and heavy. I took it from the corner of our stairway that led to the earthen basement, always cold and damp, a source of rust for all things metal. The bullets were in a box on the shelf above the gun. I shoved four or five in my pocket, more than enough for a single-shot rifle, and slipped one into the bolt-action chamber. I walked to the front door that opened from the kitchen, took aim through the screen door that was always torn from a child's fist or an errant baseball, and held the barrel steady on a brown cider jug that had been left in the yard.

As I walked out, the door slammed behind me, pulled by the simple, black, half-inch spring strung from a nail on the door to another on the jamb. I walked slowly down the broken concrete steps. Outside the small, fenced yard, I turned toward the chicken house about thirty yards away. It was small, with a dirt floor and about six roosts for the fifty or so chickens that were the backbone of subsistence farming: eggs and dinners. Over 100 new chicks were introduced every year, purchased from the local hatchery and delivered in cardboard boxes, and opened with great delight as the small yellow creatures tumbled over each other to explore their new world. Only half would survive the cold nights, the badgers and coyotes, and the electrical failures that would extinguish the lights, scaring them into corner heaps and certain suffocation. But today the house was barren, except for one scraggly rooster and a few hens pecking aimlessly in the dirt.

Lying in the doorway was Bozo, his huge mongrel head resting between his paws, eyes opening only occasionally at the screech of a blackbird, snoozing in the shade. I walked to a point about forty feet from the door, being careful not to disturb him, to arouse neither his curiosity nor his anger. As I raised the gun to my shoulder, he slowly lifted his head and shook it to lift the veil of drowsiness. His ears perked. As I sighted along the barrel, my eye focused on his wet nose and I began to wonder why he was so mean, willing to bite anyone but my younger brother, Gary, who had named him. In the early

1950s, Bozo was an affectionate name taken from a popular and nationally known circus clown. No one knows why Gary named it so, but the fun-loving name clearly did not fit the personality of the animal. He was a killer of chickens, and only this morning a killer of my brother's new Easter rabbits that had been penned in a chicken-wire cage roughly constructed by my father. He was an egg-sucking dog, perhaps the meanest epitaph given to a farm dog and a designation that surely meant his demise by some circumstance. We had tried giving him away, scaring him away, and pelting him with rocks. More drastic means were always vetoed by my nine-year-old brother, who would cry and scream that we were hurting Bozo. But this morning he had made his fatal mistake with the rabbits. They were Gary's, one white and one pink, purchased at the local grocery store, and warmly held in his arms ever since coming home the day before. They did not survive the night and Gary was finally through with Bozo.

Now was the time. I pulled the trigger. A little puff of smoke appeared at the end of the gun, but in the clearing I could see the blood spurt from the top of Bozo's nose. Then fear struck. He was not dead. He shook his head. Foam began gurgling from his mouth and he struggled to rise, first on his front feet. My God, I thought, I have hurt this animal, almost as big as I was, and he was going to come after me.

I held the gun tightly, even though I was crying and knew I could not get another bullet out of my pocket in time to reload. I was scared and started calling for Mom. As I ran for the house, Bozo was fully standing and beginning a guttural growl that I would hear for many years. About twenty yards from the house, I turned and caught a glimpse of him in full pursuit, blood flying, fur rigid and long, and teeth bare.

"Open the door, Mom!" I cried. "Open the door!" I could barely make out her form in the doorway. Then, in exaggerated motions, her arm reached for the screen, and it began to open. I raced through the doorway and the screen slammed behind me. An instant later, Bozo's full body struck the screen. There was no slowing or hesitation. Every fiber of his being was reaching out for the source of his pain. As he crashed, Mom slammed the inside door closed in case the screen didn't hold.

We went to the window, searching frantically for his presence. I leaned the gun against the wall, peered outside, and saw him clearly, pacing in front of the door. He was still bleeding, but it had slowed.

The wound was just above the tip of his nose. The bullet had passed cleanly through. Finally, he sat in front of the door, pawing at his nose as if trying to wipe away an itch, not comprehending what had happened, but knowing that a mortal enemy had tried to hurt him. He would wait for revenge.

"When will Dad be home?" I asked.

"Not till later," Mom said. "He's in the field. We'll open the door and warn him when he drives in."

I went to the living room to sit down. Thankfully, my brother was at Grandpa Seaton's home some three miles away and wasn't coming back that night. What had I done? Why was I so anxious to take this dog's life? He had just killed a few chickens, after all. Now I had an enemy for life, a stalker who might follow me anywhere, who might wait for me at the school bus stop, or in a field, or in a dark corner of the barn during haying time.

"Mom," I said, "I should finish the job."

She was weeping.

"Maybe you should," she said. So I went to the gun leaning against the wall and picked it up. It was now foreign to me, heavy and bulky, and somehow longer than before. I was trembling.

"Where is he now, Mom?" I asked.

"He has moved around the house," she said. "He's under the spirea bushes by the dining room."

I went to that side of the house and looked out the window, but I couldn't see him. There was blood on the ground so I knew he was there, waiting. I went back to the kitchen and opened the front door. The screen was bowed in three or four inches, with small blood stains in the wire, trapped there in the instant that Bozo had landed.

I raised the gun again to aim at the brown jug, fearing my nerves were weak, and wanting to reassure myself of conviction and ability. My cheek rested on the cold steel, just beside the bolt. But I could not find the jug. I could not hold the gun still enough. It had a life of its own, a part of my trembling body, careening wildly in my hands, with no direction or control. Fear was in me and I could see it at the end of the barrel as I searched hopelessly for the target.

"I can't do it, Mom," I said. "I just can't do it." But I had already done it, and the pain aches within me to this day. Bozo survived, and sometime during the night gathered the strength to stagger away from our farm forever. I never forgot how quickly my sure sense of courage, duty, and honor had turned to fear, failure, and dishonor.

Now it had happened again, with the drugstore cowboy, on May 16, 1989, only this time I was forty-six years old.

Finally, I worked up the courage to open the door of my office and face the press. Then, just as I was about to turn the knob, I could hear them shuffling away, like a herd of cattle growing restless in a storm, so I paused until I could feel them moving down the hall and back to the briefing room, then I entered. Roman and Alixe were waiting for me.

"How'd it go?" Roman asked.

"The president was calm," I said. "I don't think he liked it. He certainly would never have said it."

"Did he say that?" Alixe asked.

"No, I just know it," I said. "What's the press saying?"

"It's not good, Marlin," Roman began. "They think you made a mistake. It was too personal. You can't call a head of state a name. It's going to be headlines and editorials."

"Did any of them give me credit for turning the debate, for focusing on Gorbachev's actions?" I asked defensively.

"No," Roman said. "They weren't gloating. They just didn't understand why you did it. I think they wonder if maybe you were put up to it."

Listening to the press in my outer office provided the best intelligence available about press attitudes. Sometimes, after a big story broke, the ten or fifteen reporters who gathered there would start conjecturing on the reasons for a presidential action, and a story would be self-generated. But more often, it was a chance for my staff to quietly sit in the corner of the room and monitor attitudes.

When George Stephanopoulos took over briefing duties in 1993, and occupied the press secretary's office at the beginning of the Clinton administration, he cut off press access to the outer office. George had redefined the briefing role, giving himself the title of communications director. He tried to do both jobs. They are quite different roles, however. The communications position is primarily one of planning and meeting with other staffers about the president's activities and agenda. The fact is, other members of the staff don't want to come to your office if they have to pass through a dozen screaming reporters, so George made the office "off-limits" to press. Not only did this cause a loud and angry protest that soured press relations for months, it also cut the press staff off from a vital intelligence source. Often in the first few months of the Clinton administration, George or Dee Dee Myers, who carried the press secretary title but functionally served as a deputy to Stephanopoulos, made mistakes that could have been corrected or avoided if they had had a good read on press reaction. The best example is when the Clinton White House fired the career government employees who ran the White House travel office, a dedicated group of workers who had traveled around the world many times with the press corps, had gotten them rooms in remote corners of the world, had carried their luggage, and had made special arrangements of every kind for the press's erratic travel needs. When the Clinton staff professed total surprise at the press's hostile reaction to firing these people so loyal Arkansas followers could have the jobs and the airline contracts that go with them, it was clear the White House had a tin ear about how the Washington press view political patronage and an equal deafness to their feelings about the personnel in the travel office. A few loitering reporters outside the press secretary's office would probably have alerted the White House to both mistakes, and fast. There is nothing like a few shouting reporters to alert you to the need for damage control.

Damage control was my concern after "drugstore cowboy."

"Roman," I asked, "do you think the Soviets will protest or respond?"

"Not formally," he said. "They won't officially dignify the comment. But I bet Gerasimov has some smart crack about you tomorrow." Gerasimov gave only infrequent briefings, but he was getting more regular at informal briefings with the press. I could see his role, and his confidence, grow each day on the wires. We had become long-distance correspondents through the news media. During the cold war years, the Soviets seldom used the media for international leverage, mainly because they had no free press of their own. Nobody believed *Pravda* or *Izvestia* because they were tools of the state, and the Soviets didn't know how to use the press. But Gorbachev was learning the art of Western media manipulation, and in Gennadi Gerasimov, a diplomat who had lived in New York and worked at the United Nations, he had the perfect associate to help lead the Soviets into the new world of public relations.

"Let's ride it out," I suggested, "and see where we are tomorrow. If the Soviets say anything official, I will publicly apologize immediately. I'll probably have to do that tomorrow at the briefing anyway."

The next day, May 17, 1989, may have been the height of the new

Soviet experimentation with public diplomacy. The lead stories in *The Washington Post* were: Gorbachev was visiting China, and in a speech to Chinese academics in the Great Hall of the People, he called on the United States to withdraw troops from South Korea. A second story from the same trip declared Gorbachev's intention to cut Red Army strength in the Far East by 120,000 men and retire sixteen battleships in order to relieve tension in the region. In one day's work, Gorbachev had very skillfully fired an effective salvo at America by announcing a troop reduction and increasing the pressure on America to also reduce forces. At the same time, he forged a new peace offensive with China, thereby scaring the bejesus out of American military planners. He had our heads spinning.

On the same page, of course, was the story of Fitzwater challenging Gorbachev to end his aid to Nicaragua, and to make good on his arms-control promises instead of acting like a "drugstore cowboy." Actually, the stories were quite fair and balanced. My comments, coming on the heels of Gorbachev's China announcements, were actually welcomed by some in the White House. Indeed, were it not for my visit with the president, I might never have heard any criticism at all. Although that can be misleading. Once again, the axiom was holding that if someone in the White House is in trouble, or has committed some terrible mistake, it is never mentioned to his or her face.

The press, however, had no such reservations. Reporters were openly calling me the drugstore cowboy, and I took it good-naturedly. After the first day of no Soviet response, that threat passed. After the first night of television news, when my comments were treated only lightly, and then in the context of the other Gorbachev statements, that threat too passed. The fear, of course, that builds up in a press secretary's mind during these situations is that all the network anchors will simultaneously call for your resignation. That, of course, would never happen.

The rest of the five-day news cycle that follows any major news event is deadly for this kind of mistake. The first two days belong to the hard-news side of the media. The next three days belong to editorial writers, columnists, talk-show hosts, groupthink shows like *The McLaughlin Group*, and finally the news magazines. All of these elements make their living on analysis, which means being judgmental. All of them will say you're crazy and should be fired before sunrise. In my case, most of them did.

Richard Cohen, a *Washington Post* columnist, called me reck-

lessly glib and said, "The White House confirmed that Mikhail Gorbachev had promised to halt military aid to Nicaragua. To this development, White House spokesman Marlin Fitzwater reacted like a
bride getting yet another Lazy Susan. He belittled it and called Gorbachev a 'drugstore cowboy.' It was not reported whether Fitzwater's
head spun around at the time."

The *Post* also ran an editorial entitled "Fitzwater Diplomacy"
that cut me to pieces. Perhaps the most disastrous press relations aspect of this episode for me was that Stephen Rosenfeld, the *Post*'s
foreign policy editorial writer, became a permanent enemy. I have
only met him once in my life, a handshake at a cocktail party celebrating *The McLaughlin Group*'s ten years on the air. He decided
that I simply was not qualified for the job, and wrote several more
critical editorials aimed at me during the remainder of the administration. In my twenty-seven years in government, he's the only reporter I ever felt truly disliked me, or at least let it show in his copy,
and I wouldn't recognize him on the street today. There may have
been many others who didn't like me, but at least I couldn't tell from
their reporting.

I made two huge miscalculations in "drugstore cowboy." First,
the term is too personal. The press immediately shortened it to:
"Fitzwater calls Gorbachev a drugstore cowboy." I should have
known that would happen. Had I truly come to terms with that one
single fact, I would not have used the phrase. I had long lived by the
belief that a press secretary, representing the president, does not
have the right to call anybody names. Yet in spite of Alixe and
Roman's best efforts, I was so intent on turning the national debate
that I missed the obvious.

Second, I misjudged the context. The actual sentence in which
"drugstore cowboy" was used was never printed. The arms-control
context was always omitted. In fact, within days most writers, like
Cohen, were repeating the phrase as a response to the pledge to end
Nicaraguan aid. I should have known this would happen also.

I present this episode in my life to show the fragility of information, and how it can be handled by the media. I think it's also in-
structive to point out that this reaction is not the media's fault; it
was my fault for being too glib in the first place.

The issue slowly died away until President Bush met with French
president François Mitterrand in Boston. The French president visited our president's Kennebunkport, Maine, home, then they gave
speeches in Boston and held a joint press conference. Mitterrand

gave long rambling answers that few cared about. Sometimes joint press conferences with him would cover only two or three questions. In this case, Sandy Gilmour, of NBC News, chose to use one of those questions to ask if Mitterrand thought Gorbachev was a "drugstore cowboy."

I stood at the edge of the stage, trembling with anger and resentment, as Gilmour started his question. I could see no reason for asking it except to embarrass me. Mitterrand smiled and said he wasn't familiar with the term, but went on to praise Gorbachev. President Bush looked down at me from his position on the stage, and I whispered, "Don't defend me." He asked for the next question.

For months after that people sent me a news photo clipped from a Canadian magazine of five young men, wearing 1950s-style blue jeans, work shirts, and hats cocked over their eyes, leaning against a drugstore window. The cutline read: "Drugstore Cowboys, Blind River, Ontario, 1955." That is the same year I was entering high school in Abilene, Kansas, hanging out at Callahan's drugstore, and looking for all the world like a drugstore cowboy.

The Soviets, by the way, never said a word about the incident. But I deeply regret it because I believe history will record Mikhail Gorbachev as one of the greatest world leaders of this century.

CHAPTER ELEVEN

Malta Media

S itting in a small, cold, gray office well below the deck of the USS *Belknap*, floating in unusually rough seas for Malta harbor, and alone with his thoughts just as he wanted, President George Bush in December 1989 charted the course of post-cold war relations with Russia, in tone and in substance. It was more than a year before the end of the communist empire. By the middle of President Clinton's term, in 1995, that course was still being followed.

The Malta summit provided to me the best evidence of George Bush's vision, a practical view of how the post–cold war world would work and America's role in it. He knew the Soviet Union was changing in a way that could forever alter East-West relations, and he spent long hours pondering a new role for the USSR, a new role for NATO, and a changed relationship with Germany. At the same time, he had a world vision of the United States as a growing economic power in association with Canada, Mexico, and the Latin American countries. By the end of his administration, much of this outline would be taking shape in a new world order.

I don't write about the Panama invasion and the Persian Gulf War in this book, partially because they deserve, and will get, longer treatment in other books. They were both models of decision making in most respects. Certainly they demonstrated a decisive president who determined his purpose and his will early in the situation, and never wavered in his conviction. But they were relatively clear-cut in terms of the options presented.

I prefer to dwell on the Malta summit because it shows the president sorting through a complex situation, with no clear-cut resolution, with very little precedent in history, and with a very definite view of America's role in world affairs. That view stands in stark contrast today with President Clinton, who has opted to express American will primarily through the United Nations and other multilateral institutions. President Bush always saw America in the lead, deciding its own interests, then persuading others to join or follow.

The "vision thing," as he called it, bothered President Bush a lot. The press had labeled him as too practical or pragmatic a politician to have vision. A big part of that analysis was due to the fact that he was always compared to Ronald Reagan, whose vision was more visible, rooted in romanticism and dreams of "morning in America." Even people who thought SDI (Star Wars) was nuts were taken with the Reagan imagination. He could see the shield in space that would catch incoming missiles and fling them harmlessly into oblivion. Indeed, Reagan's staff twice intercepted a Reagan written speech insert about the prospect of an alien force threatening the earth from space, thereby bringing all the countries of the world together in a Steven Spielberg defense of mankind.

One weekend at Camp David the Reagans invited me to watch movies with them on Saturday night. We sat in the living room of the president's cottage, Aspen, with the president's doctor and military aide, eating popcorn, and watching a double feature. The first movie was a Western featuring Randolph Scott, who got the girl and captured the bad guys. The second was about a British jockey who had fallen from his horse, nearly died, but came back against all odds to win the biggest crown in racing. When they ended, the president and Mrs. Reagan were in tears.

"I love these kinds of movies," the president said. He was a romantic.

A few years later, President Bush invited me to the same Aspen lodge for movies. The first was a Sylvester Stallone action thriller with the most imaginative of special effects and far-out technology. The second was *Field of Dreams,* about a baseball team featuring Shoeless Joe Jackson that comes back from the dead to play ball in an Iowa cornfield. The president loved the action thriller but said he didn't care so much for the *Dreams* picture. "Just too far-fetched," he said.

The minute the president made that remark, I thought: This is the difference between Reagan and Bush. Both are men of vision who look to the future, but one looks through the gauzy lens of his dreams, the other through the viewfinder of a telescope. Unfortunately, the Bush vision was seldom recognized, even though it was on full display in Malta.

President Bush had secretly proposed the Malta meeting to Gorbachev in the summer of 1989, when both sides were sparring with speeches and arms-reduction proposals. Gorbachev seemed to sense an urgency about his country's future, knowing that he must make significant reductions in his military ambitions in order to satisfy the country's economic necessities. The Soviet Union was falling far behind the industrialized world in its standard of living. Gorbachev had initiated his glasnost, or "new openness," with a focus on political reform. But he needed economic reform and the money he could save from arms reductions.

President Bush saw this situation as one of great delicacy. He sensed that the Soviet Union was looking for a new relationship with the West, but needed time and support to make the changes. Gorbachev was driving a team of runaway horses. Bush had to decide how to react if Gorbachev got control of his horses, or if they turned over the wagon and ran headlong for the far horizon. He decided he wanted a private talk, and proposed meeting on U.S. and Soviet ships in the port of Malta. Gorbachev quickly agreed, but both men needed some time for planning and preparation. They agreed to meet late in the year, probably in December, and not to tell anyone in advance. They both joked on the telephone about their ability to keep a secret, especially a summit meeting. President Bush took this a little more personally than did Gorbachev. After all, the Soviet Union was built on secrecy. The United States seemed to never be able to keep a secret. Yet President Bush loved secrets and he vowed to himself to keep this one, to show a doubting Gorbachev that he could.

World events of 1989 were most dramatic, ranging from the various arms-control proposals by both the United States and Soviet Union to the demonstrations and crackdown in Tiananmen Square in China. The American people were clamoring for an East-West summit and starting to ask why George Bush was so timid. R. W. "Johnny" Apple, the New York Times political writer, wrote a front-page article stating this proposition and it burned every high-level foreign policy official in government. Sometimes the press will strike a nerve just at the moment of greatest sensitivity, or point out a trend that others feel but no one has articulated, and it moves the entire government. Sometimes one article will do it. Apple's article struck such a nerve. The president respected Apple, and he openly referred to this article in meetings, making everyone aware of the public pressures that were building.

Johnny Apple was a legend in Washington journalism twenty years ago, even before he became a foreign correspondent and then Washington bureau chief of the *Times*. In the days of Johnson and Nixon he rode the press bus, drank late into the night, argued wildly with would-be politicians, learned how political leaders are made in the small towns of America, and then wrote the most colorful of stories. After returning from Europe, with a similar reputation for saucy reporting nurtured in the great wine cellars of the Continent, he brought a new glow to *New York Times* political reporting.

Johnny is the old and the new of the *Times*. He loves journalism and the good gray lady. He also started when the *Times* was peopled with sparkling wits, distinguished gentlemen writers, crusty old ferrets of the news, and columnists who wrote about world affairs and then advised presidents on how to govern.

In the early 1970s, when I was at the Environmental Protection Agency, the environment was covered by Gladwin Hill and Ned Kenworthy, the "gentlemen of the *Times*," as we knew them. They were monuments to me. I loved their class, their dignity, their sense of belonging to journalism, and their writing. Johnny Apple brings those qualities to the new world of *Times* journalism that features computers, blue jeans, earth shoes, long hair, and second degrees in law. It's a rare figure in Washington today who has enough self-confidence to be a "character." Yet Apple grumps and groans around Washington wearing red-and-white-checkered shirts, a bow tie, and seersucker suits, never much worrying about whether his large frame and ruddy complexion fit the mold. It was not surprising to me that Johnny had caught the crest of the wave in U.S.-Soviet relations in 1989 and asked just where the Bush ship was sailing.

President Bush was acutely attuned to the press, but sometimes his stubbornness would force a rebellion or, as happened late in his term concerning the economy, disbelief. In this case, the president had charted a course based on international considerations and was not about to change it to satisfy the cries of public opinion. But he was watching it carefully, and one of the best ways was to listen to my press briefings on his intercom, which transmitted my daily briefings to various offices in the White House. Every day he heard someone ask, "When is Bush going to meet with Gorbachev?"

The president understood press relations enough to know that he didn't want, or need, to risk his credibility with reporters on this issue. He called me back to his private study, and praised my handling of the briefings.

"I know what you're facing out there," he said. "Rough. I heard Hoffman ask about a summit. You said the right thing. But I want to tell you something." Then he stopped and looked me straight in the eye, his face deadly serious. He was sizing me up, about to make a judgment as to whether I could keep a secret.

His eyes never wandered as he spoke. "You have to keep this to yourself. No one knows but Baker and Scowcroft."

Now I was a little nervous, not because only Baker and Scowcroft knew, but because Sununu and others didn't. "Yes," I said. "I understand."

"I'm going to meet with Gorbachev later in the year. We don't have a date yet. And we can't announce it. I wanted you to know so that you don't get in trouble—deny or something—during the briefings."

"That's great!" I blurted, elated that we were going to show the critics wrong. The president allowed himself a little smile, then became stern again.

"You can't tell anyone," he said, "and you'll have to work out what to say to the press." I left the Oval feeling exhilaration. We were going to have a summit. The president was on top of public attitudes. He was managing this process behind the scenes with Gorbachev. And he was sensitive to my needs, respecting me enough to bring me in on the secret, giving me the confidence to deal effectively with the press.

My lines quickly formed. Whenever asked about a summit, I would say, "We don't have anything to announce. It could happen at any time. President Bush and President Gorbachev will meet when they are ready." I never said "Nothing has been scheduled," or "I don't know," or "They haven't discussed it." When the summit finally was announced, several reporters went back to the transcripts to check my words. The president had kept me honest.

When the time finally came to make the announcement, General Scowcroft was making the arrangements with his Soviet counterparts so our press releases would be simultaneous. With an eight-hour time difference, this was difficult. The day before the announcement, David Hoffman of *The Washington Post* wrote that the summit was set. Someone had leaked.

When the president saw the *Post* and the Hoffman story, he went through the roof.

"Who did this, Marlin?" he shouted. "This violates my promise to Gorbachev!"

"I don't know, sir," I said, "and we'll never know. But it doesn't matter. We kept the secret for six months, and tomorrow's the official announcement. This probably came from an embassy, or someone in Moscow, or maybe one of their foreign correspondents picked it up and gave it to David."

We never discovered the leak. Most leaks never are discovered, and most don't matter anyway. They embarrass but seldom matter, like this one. Nevertheless, the president never gave David Hoffman another interview, or even called on him at press conferences. Once, he answered a question from David without realizing who he was, and complained about the mistake for days afterward. Later in the administration, David was transferred to the State Department beat. He was replaced by Ann Devroy, an equally tough reporter who knew how to work sources just like David Hoffman. I used to tell the president, and still believe, that no one can talk to David Hoffman or Ann Devroy without giving them information they want.

In preparing for the summit, I wanted to give the president my views on Gorbachev as a negotiator. I had watched him, at the table, in three previous summits and found him enormously cunning in conforming his style and personality to his political objectives. I also knew Gorbachev read the Western press, and might challenge the president rather dramatically to see if he was as "timid" as the press indicated. After all, I had seen him challenge President Reagan (even suggesting Reagan couldn't think for himself). I wanted President Bush to be ready for that kind of intimidation, if only to make sure the president wouldn't turn the table over. But I didn't want to offend Scowcroft or Baker by intruding on their territory, nor did I want to pretend that I was a foreign policy expert.

I told all this to the president. He said he would like to see my comments, and suggested that he send me a note asking for them. Thus my professional relationships could be maintained. President Bush understood these bureaucratic intricacies better than anyone I ever met. He knew that in my situation it was OK to respond to a request for information, but offensive to offer it. We both had spent many years playing the bureaucracy game.

In the preparations for the summit, it became clear that Bush and Scowcroft were on the same intellectual track. Probably not since

Nixon and Kissinger had two foreign policy experts been so similar in temperament, experience, and thinking. They were both true gentlemen of the old school who respected loyalty and dignity, who understood historical fact and tradition as guiding lights of foreign policy, and who savored the personal dimensions of understanding between leaders as understanding between countries.

General Scowcroft was a diminutive man of sixty-four, balding and gray, who wore light gray suits that were functional and an occasional blue shirt suggesting he might have a wild night left in his fighter pilot's soul. He had spent years studying the Soviets. He outlined the Gorbachev situation as one with three possible futures.

In the first future, perestroika would succeed. This scenario assumed that the somewhat limited changes being made in Moscow would change Soviet economic conditions. The political situation internally would then stabilize, with Gorbachev reaching some understanding with the Baltic states and their yearning for freedom. Finally, the Soviets would become less military-oriented and threatening to the United States. But Scowcroft judged this future unlikely.

The second future involved a violent change of government. Perhaps a coup, or uprising in the Baltics, or military pressure, but some internal force that would overthrow Gorbachev and lead to radical instability. Scowcroft thought this possible, but still unlikely.

The third future predicted Gorbachev would pull it off, but that things would not work out very well. Perestroika would force some changes, and some of the economic conditions would improve. The Russian people would endure and feel a little better about themselves, and a process of continual restructuring would occur in which the Soviet Union tried to adapt to world economic circumstances. This was the "slow decline" scenario, because Scowcroft concluded that true reform was impossible and, as he said, "It is only a matter of time—even if it is a long time—until the USSR as we know it ceases to exist."

General Scowcroft thought the third scenario was the most likely. As it turned out, of course, he was extremely close to winning the soothsayer award: Scenarios two and three occurred within a year.

President Bush worried most about the second future. As CIA director, and as a vice president who had gone to the funeral of several Soviet leaders during the 1980s, he saw the real possibilities of an overthrow. He also felt America's greatest influence would be in scenario three, where the slow decline of the Soviet Union could be guided in ways that lessened world tensions. In meeting after meeting, he posed these questions to his advisers: How can we help? What can we do to help their economy, but not increase their military threat? Can we tie those together? Bush believed that Gorbachev, under any scenario, was redefining the Soviet Union, and the United States needed to move now to give direction to that new definition. He calculated that Gorbachev was in a difficult position, wanting aid from the West but unable to ask without suffering ridicule from his hard-liners. Sometimes, during staff briefings, the president's face would harden, he would slide down in his chair, and the old Yankee lines around his eyes told me he was working this problem out.

On November 30, 1989, the president held a National Security Council meeting with the vice president, Secretary of State Baker, Secretary of the Treasury Brady, Secretary of Defense Cheney, General Scowcroft, CIA director William Webster, Joint Chiefs chairman Powell, Deputy National Security Adviser Gates, two NSC Soviet authorities, Bob Blackwill and Condoleezza Rice, and me.

This was the last meeting before Malta. The president began: "I want to demonstrate our readiness to engage Gorbachev on changes in the Soviet Union. This is a chance to meet informally without the pressures of a full-blown summit. We are not going to negotiate arms control or the future of Europe. I want a clearer view of the barriers we face and a more precise understanding of our differences."

President Bush left the discussion to take a phone call he had placed earlier to French president Mitterrand. He soon returned, saying, "Mitterrand will help with Lebanon. He's encouraging about Malta. I rooted the Luxembourg guy out of bed this morning to talk about Malta. He says the most concern about private agreements will come from [British prime minister Margaret] Thatcher." The president was touching bases with the NATO countries before the Gorbachev meeting, an overture they respected highly.

"I also talked to [Canadian prime minister Brian] Mulroney," he said. "He says Gorbachev wants a get-acquainted session. Brian spent five hours with Gorbachev. He says Gorbachev wants our help without it looking like we're helping."

"We should help the Soviets," the president said. "Get them involved in the world economy. We have some people who don't want to help in any way. They are wrong. We're not going to let Howie Phillips decide these matters." Phillips and Richard Viguerie, right-wing political operators, had always been critics of the president. With the Republicans in power, any self-proclaimed Republican who would speak out against the president was made an instant celebrity. Phillips and Viguerie played the renegade card quite effectively, and the president tended to use their names interchangeably with the devil himself. After the 1992 elections, when all Republicans became out-of-power critics, Phillips and Viguerie faded back into the woodwork.

The president mentioned that he had also called Prime Minister Giulio Andreotti of Italy that morning. "He said Gorbachev is very defensive about Central America. I also called Margaret [Thatcher] and I asked her what kind of Soviet action would it take before we could respond by reducing our forces."

"She was silent," the president said. "Then she said, 'Never. Even if they eliminated all their forces, they could always build them up again.' " This brought the room to silence, as the enthusiasm for change in East-West relations was once again tempered by the strong will of Margaret Thatcher and her memories of World War II. It was a good place to end the meeting.

When we disembarked from *Air Force One*, the president's Boeing 747, at the Malta airport, a logistical problem occurred: *Marine One*, the president's helicopter, was waiting but would not start. I always thought it was a good omen to have such a physical reminder that not everything in life can be controlled, or work according to plan. We got off and moved to *Nighthawk II*, the designated backup chopper, and flew into Malta for a diplomatic meeting with the prime minister of our host country, Edward Fenech-Adami, who was very pleased by the world attention.

"Malta was my idea," the president said. "My brother came back from your national day with a glowing report of your hospitality. We are not here to upstage Gorbachev. Our problems are too serious for PR. We want to know how much change he can accommodate."

The president always had a unique ability to let foreign leaders glow in the U.S. limelight. He understood American power so well, and had such self-confidence, that he always found a way to step back and let others take credit, or draw smaller countries into his circle of power, to make them feel good about the United States. In this case, he turned to General Scowcroft during his meeting with the leader of this small island nation, and said, "Brent, anything new in the Philippines? I think the prime minister would be very interested." He would be now, but I doubt if Mr. Fenech-Adami had ever given it two seconds' thought before the president brought it up.

While flying to Malta, the president was called on the plane by Vice President Quayle and Bob Gates, the deputy national security adviser, later to become director of the CIA. They outlined a coup attempt in the Philippines against the legitimate government of Mrs. Corazon Aquino, who had asked the United States for assistance in putting it down. American officials never had much confidence in Mrs. Aquino's ability to lead the country, especially in her power to control the tough and seasoned members of her cabinet. A coup was always thought inevitable.

Gates had convened the Deputies Committee, organized after the first disastrous coup attempt in Panama, and was pulling together information from all sources for the president. They recommended, with some imagination, that the president reject direct intervention, but instead fly some low-overhead "high maneuver" aircraft that would give the coup plotters the idea that America was about to come storming to Mrs. Aquino's rescue. It worked. With U.S. fighter aircraft screaming off the runway at the nearby Subic Bay airfield, then diving and buzzing highways and homes in the path of the advancing coup, the message was clear.

The president and Prime Minister Fenech-Adami were meeting in a cavernous stone-walled room of the presidential castle that had a medieval flavor of high ceilings, heavy, rough-hewn wood doorjambs and fireplaces, and iron chandeliers. Brent returned to the room, walked dramatically across the barren floors, and reported to both leaders, furthering the impression of giving the prime minister a personal report.

"President Aquino believes the tide has turned," Brent said. "The government troops are rallying to her. There are some pockets of resistance. We are flying cover, but will stop shortly. We have had no air action."

"We offered air cover in response to her request," the president injected. "We do not intend to get involved in a slogging war in the Philippines." In discussing any military conflict, the president's language tended to revert back to World War II, in this case to the "slogging" war in the Philippines. MacArthur may have slogged. If we had intervened, it would have been at 600 miles per hour with air-to-ground missiles. Nevertheless, "slogging" was probably a good image for the president to have. I have always feared the day when military intervention becomes too clean, too high-tech, and too easy.

The logistical plan for the Malta meeting, as laid out by the president personally, was to have two warships in the harbor. Bush and Gorbachev would stay on their respective ships, and alternate meetings on each ship. President Bush was a Navy man, the youngest fighter pilot in the Navy when he joined in 1942. He flew TBM Avengers, sometimes with the cockpit canopy slid back and hard wind in his face, off of the most primitive carrier decks, and was dramatically shot down off the coast of Chichi Jima, where he was rescued by an American submarine. He knew warships. He knew they have tight, cramped quarters with small conference rooms and sparse accommodations, just the kind of excuse he could use to limit the delegation size without bruising egos. He wanted a small party, a conversation with Gorbachev, and no staff. He knew, of course, that the staff contingent would grow, but he hadn't counted on Gorbachev's dislike of the sea and tight places. The Soviet chairman brought his warship all right, but it was the Soviet equivalent of "the Love Boat," a Russian cruise liner, the *Gorky*. Gorbachev's concession was to bring a Soviet cruiser, the *Slava*, and park it near the *Belknap*. But he visited it only once. Instead he stayed on the *Gorky*, and according to his staff, even then didn't get too close to the portholes. The *Gorky*'s spacious ballrooms, bars, guest suites, well-stocked dining rooms, and fine mahogany conference rooms would do just fine for the Soviet meetings. One other new wrinkle that nobody had counted on was the most violent Malta harbor storm in the last twenty years.

Gale-force winds around Malta continued through the day on December 2. In Marsaxlokk Bay, where the USS *Belknap* and the Soviet cruiser *Slava* were anchored, the winds were between thirty-five and forty knots from the northeast with gusts as high as forty-nine knots.

That night, the commanding officer of the *Belknap* ordered his crew to slip the stern anchor, and hold the engines steaming toward the bow anchor as a means of better holding her position. If the winds calmed, the stern anchor would be reattached.

Slava was holding her position with the help of tugs on the bow and stern. The wind had caused three- or four-foot swells inside the sheltered harbor. Seas outside the harbor were sixteen feet and building. Boating to and from *Belknap* had been limited to officials involved in the bilateral meetings. For President Bush, it was a dream come true. He was getting his privacy, and he was commander in chief of the American Navy, on his private ship with the feel of cold steel beneath his feet, and he was about to redirect the entire cold war relationship with the Soviet Union. He walked bare-headed about the ship, entering the captain's area on the bridge, with the control panel's red and blue lights barely illuminating the area, while the ship's officers stood silent, drinking coffee and discussing the weather. The president climbed into the captain's chair, which was elevated and rotated 360 degrees, leaned back, and enjoyed the roll of his beloved sea as it tossed the ship. His mind was deep inside the American presidency and what he was about to do.

The *Belknap*'s commander had given up his stateroom for the president. It was a small three-room suite with blue carpet, leather lounge chair, blue couch, and mahogany desk, all standard issue. In addition to the commander's private mementos—including a brass submarine mounted on wood, pictures of an Irish setter and a picture of partially submerged submarines under full steam—there was a coffeemaker, three telephones, and small U.S. and Soviet flags in a wooden holder. A new brass plaque on the door read "President Bush NTD 02-78-2."

The president called for a last briefing in the wardroom at 3:30 P.M. He had been giving this summit a lot of private thought. He wanted it to establish a new relationship with the Soviets; if the cold war truly ended, this would be the foundation for post-cold war relations. If the Soviets proceeded along the two scenarios he considered most likely, the United States would do all it could to encourage reform; and if Gorbachev were overthrown, at least America would have tried. He also wanted this meeting to show that he was strong and was his own man despite living in the wake of Ronald Reagan for eight years.

In addition to those of us staying on the ship—the president, Scowcroft, Sununu, Baker, and me—the briefing included Robert Blackwill and Condoleezza Rice of the NSC staff, Margaret Tutwiler, Bob Zoellick, and Reginald Bartholomew from the State Department, and Lieutenant General Howard Graves from the Joint Chiefs. The president wasted no time. He wanted to go through his presentation. The reason soon became clear. He had solidified in his own mind some strong commitments to the Soviets, and he wanted to see how this group would react.

"I'm going to start off by calling for the next summit," he said. "Set a date." He was no doubt tired from traveling all night. But he was also stern, as if putting on his game face for the big contest. There could be no mistakes.

"What's wrong with saying I'm gonna waive Jackson-Vanik [the law that prohibited certain trade as long as the Soviet emigration laws wouldn't let people leave their country]," he said, not as a question. "Let's not be negative. I want to be positive. I want to do it, so let's say it." Then he stopped, collected his words, and delivered the lines as if he were looking straight at Gorbachev: "I want to waive Jackson-Vanik. So as soon as you get your law—and a trade agreement—I'll waive it. I propose we start *now* to negotiate a trade agreement. Soon as we get a trade agreement, then I'll waive Jackson-Vanik, and then you'll get most favored nation trading status."

Someone at the table spoke up to add that he could say that the Soviets have made great progress and reforms were very encouraging. The president snapped back, "I can fill in the bullshit portion, just give me the facts." I loved that line because that's what staff always do. They advise you on how to say things, or give you helpful little asides, when what you need are numbers, history, and facts to back up your arguments. After that day, I always told my own staff: "I'll handle the bullshit; just give me the facts."

"I want substantive and positive proposals that will further the relationship," the president said in closing the meeting. "We are going to have a new relationship."

The first meeting was scheduled the next morning on the *Gorky*. At 8:30 A.M., the president went out on the *Belknap*'s bridge to view the sea. It was still churning badly, under dull gray skies and heavy winds. "This doesn't look bad," he said. "Let's take the launch to the *Gorky*."

As we climbed up the gangway on the side of the *Gorky*, I worried that there might be some disconnect between the two leaders. Gorbachev was clearly a different kind of Soviet leader, relaxed, Western in dress, humorous, and outgoing—but he wasn't exactly casual. In four summits, I had never seen him without a tie. It may have been pushing it to think he would enjoy donning a Navy pea coat and sitting on the deck of a destroyer. The *Gorky* was a long way from battleship gray. It had red carpets throughout, floor-to-ceiling mirrors in most rooms and hallways, and gold chandeliers in the dining and meeting areas. Coming onto the ship, we could see the mirrors through an open door.

Gorbachev greeted us warmly. He grasped my hand, then stepped back, gave me a Jack Benny double take, and asked, "Marlin, you lose thirty pounds?"

I had just lost forty-five pounds on an all-liquid diet, drinking five glasses of nutrients a day for two months. It was a marvelously fast plan, but left me looking a little drawn, and with a new case of gallstones. I explained the diet plan to Gorbachev.

"Is that a program?" he asked, meaning, I guess, was it a legitimate, doctor-sponsored plan?

"Program?" I asked.

"Yeah," he said.

"Yeah," I said.

"Oh, that's good," he replied.

It was a small touch, but important to me. He had signaled open and warm friendship, asking about my health and joking, calling me by my first name, and never mentioning the drugstore cowboy incident. Also, I was the only holdover from the Reagan administration, and the only American he had met with in previous summits.

The meeting started at 10:05 A.M. with both leaders in expansive moods, the Soviets on one side of the table and the U.S. team on the other. As the host, Chairman Gorbachev started with introductions. President Bush waited till he had finished, then said, "I know the whole cast of characters."

"Yes," Gorbachev said, laughing. "But Marshal Akhromeyev is in civilian clothes. In the United States he wore his uniform to scare the U.S." Field Marshal Akhromeyev was a hero of the Stalingrad defense against Hitler's army in World War II. He had served under Stalin, Brezhnev, and the others as a loyal communist, and he was having some trouble with perestroika. I sat beside him at several dinners. He seemed interested and approving of better relations, and lessening the military tensions between East and West. Nevertheless, he was a proud communist, and you could see in his eyes that he was not certain about changing the ideology of his country, economically or socially. It turned out later that he supported the coup against Gorbachev. When the coup failed, he committed suicide.

Gorbachev continued his welcome. "I appreciate your initiative in suggesting this meeting," he said. "A lot is happening. We have to find different ways of dialogue—commensurate with the pace of change. More working contacts. This is prelude to official summit. I like meeting, not formal too much. We need more than exchanges of letters. We need to talk. This meeting is more than just a symbol. Our people will look to us to get down to business."

Because Gorbachev didn't speak English, all this came through a translator who was very good, but occasionally dropped some pronouns.

The Gorbachev comments were just what President Bush wanted to hear. "There have been so many dramatic changes in the world since we suggested this meeting," the president said. "I would like to go over in that corner at some point and talk."

"Good," Gorbachev laughed. "They'll get tired of us and we'll get tired of them," referring to the staff. This was typical Bush. He always wanted to get leaders alone. He trusted his own instincts and he wanted to test Gorbachev's, without the reporting apparatus around him.

"I know you are the host," the president said, "but I would like to start first. I would like to put some ideas on the table." Gorbachev quickly agreed. For a president who shunned the dramatic, who resisted the staged show, Bush seemed to have an unerring feel for presence and timing with foreign leaders. He wanted to lay out his plan first, to set the tone and stage for the meeting before Gorbachev could say anything negative, to show Gorbachev that he had come to Malta to form a new relationship.

"First," the president said, "the world will be a better place if perestroika succeeds. Most serious people in the U.S. don't feel negative to perestroika. There are differences in the analytic community, but you are dealing with an administration that wants to see the success of perestroika. I propose to spell out some positive initiatives, not in a negotiating sense, but a broad framework for working together."

He began by proposing a summit for the last two weeks of June 1990. Then he moved through his agenda, ending his offer to waive Jackson-Vanik by clenching his fist and saying for all in the room to hear: "I will push the American side to move fast. I want it done."

The president moved through the economic agenda, then he tackled Central America, calling it "the single most disruptive factor in our relationship." He continued, "I am raising this in the most direct fashion," and then he used a simile, which he seldom did in general discussion, so it must have been planned in his mind. "It is like a giant thorn in the bottom of one's foot, when we're trying to walk smoothly," he said.

Then the president began reeling off one Central American country after another, comments on the U.S. relationship, or some personal conversation with the head of the country. President Bush felt a special affinity for Central America, and probably gave the region more serious attention than any president in decades. He talked about Castro, Cristiani of El Salvador, Perez of Venezuela, Ortega of Nicaragua, Arias of Costa Rica, and others. Gorbachev was impressed.

Bush ended his discussion of conventional weapons in Europe by saying, "I'm committed to a CFE [Conventional Forces in Europe] treaty. I'd like a goal of having a CFE summit in Vienna in 1990 to sign a treaty." The president was hardening his position on almost every point. With hindsight, there was a very obvious and chartable progression in his thinking from the first Washington briefings a month earlier. By the time he sat down at the table, his mind was set. The president finished talking one hour and ten minutes later. It was an incredible performance, sustained and eloquent, and coming from a man normally so impatient with words that he seldom used verbs.

Gorbachev collected his papers, and let the silence build as everyone waited for his response. He slowly looked Bush in the eye and said, "This shows that the Bush administration has decided what to do." President Bush was very pleased, and handed over a personal letter from their mutual and old friend, Ronald Reagan.

I was waiting to see which of the many Gorbachev personalities would emerge in this summit, and we were rewarded by his most charming performance to date—a somewhat subdued leader fighting high historical odds, searching for a new course for his country, and quite philosophical about his prospects and the Soviet station in the world. Add to that the sweetener of having just heard the message he wanted, the words of a new American president willing to explore a new East-West relationship based on economic growth, and the result was a quiet, thoughtful dialogue. Gorbachev appeared a little insecure, looking for a blanket of cover from the Americans, but confident as always. His approach was different from all past summits.

"How to evaluate history," he began. "We cannot make it. It has happened. But it is our duty to examine it and analyze it." Ironically, President Bush is not a reflective, philosophical man either. Yet this is exactly the kind of talk he wanted to hear: Gorbachev's views on the future and the history of his country.

"We are at an historic watershed," Gorbachev said. "We have to address completely new problems. Shall we address them as in the past, on the basis of old approaches?"

Gorbachev was using one small symbol of his new Western ex-

posure: a new leather-bound three-by-five notebook had replaced the
grade-school green spiral notebook of his trip to Washington in 1988.
But he used it in the same way, rolling pages of handwritten-in-blue-
ink notes over the top as he spoke, slicing the air with his hands, and
gesturing broadly, although in more fluid, less threatening motions.

"We had forty-five years of peace," Gorbachev said. "But the
arms race is not good. You must deal with it. The emphasis on confrontation due to ideology is wrong. But it is good that we have
stopped and we now have an agreement on this."

"The man in the street is aware of these changes," he continued.
"They have an impact on policy making—in the U.S. and in Soviet
Union. We face a problem of survival. Environment. Technology.
Resources. People are aware of these problems."

Then he grew especially quiet, laying down the leather notebook
and folding his hands in front of him, elbows on the table. His voice
had softened to little more than a whisper. He looked only at the
president, straight ahead. "Some people think Eastern Europe is
cracking, falling apart," he said. "This means policy of cold war was
right. Only thing U.S. has to do now is keep the basket open and
gather the fruit. That would be very dangerous and I am glad to see
that you do not agree with that. It's clear that President Bush has his
own understanding that is consistent with our times."

He paused. "I note that you have spoken out for perestroika, but
it is for the Soviet Union. We would like to hear more—some specific steps that confirm and we now have heard those plans—those
steps."

Gorbachev leaned back in his chair, having completed the personal part of his message, having thanked the president for American help in a very dignified and politically correct way. Even then,
his real enemies were sitting on his own side of the table.

"There is a major regrouping in the world now," he said. "We
will have to deal with a Europe of increasing integration, with Japan
becoming another major factor, and China, which neither of us
should try to exploit against each other. India is balanced. I welcome
Gandhi's position of good relations with both the U.S. and Soviet
Union.

"What is our manner of action and inaction," he continued, referring to our bilateral relations. "We have been thinking. We believe the U.S. and Soviets are doomed to cooperate. But we must
abandon looking at each other as the enemy. We both factor in military size. Am I suggesting some type of U.S.-Soviet condominium?

No. I think it is reality. Patterns of cooperation have evolved. There must be an understanding of this new reality. We want the U.S. to be a confident country that takes on—that tackles—its problems."

Gorbachev was painting a new U.S.-Soviet relationship in which it was in both countries' interests to help each other—to help solve each other's problems. Then he whispered, "The key is how we build that bridge across our problems."

Once again he leaned back in his chair, and let his words of shared help float across the table. Suddenly, his hands flew out in front of him, fingers fully extended, and he exclaimed, "This is most important. Nothing else compares!"

With that he picked up his leather notebook, flipped through the pages and said, "Now, let me turn to your specific points."

Before he could start, President Bush interrupted. "I hope you have noticed that we have not responded in recent months in a provocative way. I am cautious, but I am not timid. I wanted to send a signal by not jumping up and down on the Berlin Wall that I understand the changes."

President Bush acted with reservation when the Berlin Wall fell. It was a November day in 1989 when the first hole was punched in the Berlin Wall. People began chipping at it with hammers and chisels, until the wall of concrete, brick, stones, and wire began to crumble. But it was too fast and too physical. The wall as a symbol of repression was much higher and stronger than the visible one. It had built up in our minds for forty years and it was inconceivable that it could be destroyed so fast. Yet that was not the dominant factor in the minds of either the press or the president on that day.

When the wire stories began coming in that people were breaking down the wall, I saw it the same way the White House press corps did: as a big news story to be handled immediately. I took the wire stories in to the president, who was sitting in his study off the Oval watching on CNN as people climbed the wall and toppled over to the other side. He read the wires slowly, as if making an independent determination of their truth.

"Do you want to make a statement?" I asked.

"Why?" the president said. He knew me well enough to know that my question was really a recommendation.

"Why?" I repeated. "This is an incredibly historic day. People will want to know what it means. They need some presidential assurance that the world is OK."

The president just looked at me. He understood the historic

point, of course, but his vision was taking him into a future of German reunification, diminished communism, and a new world order to be established.

"Listen, Marlin," he said, "I'm not going to dance on the Berlin Wall. The last thing I want to do is brag about winning the cold war, or bringing the wall down. It won't help us in Eastern Europe to be bragging about this."

"I understand that, sir," I said, "but we have to show that we understand the historical significance of this. You don't have to brag." I paused to let him formulate a message in his mind, then added, "We can just bring the pool into the Oval Office, you will sit at your desk, and the whole thing will be very dignified and presidential."

"OK," he said, "when do we do it?"

"As soon as you're ready," I said. "How about three-thirty?" It was November 9, 1989.

The White House press corps, of course, is not dignified and doesn't give a damn about things appearing presidential. The fourteen-person pool—with cameras, tripods, blue jeans, sandals, and all manner of garb—trooped into the Oval. As soon as they were told the president would sit at his desk, they crowded around it so closely that some reporters were in the picture. Lesley Stahl of CBS was the network television correspondent. She positioned herself right beside the president's chair. I asked her to move back. She moved one step. A cameraman said, "Lesley, you're in the picture." She moved back one more step. Nobody, if they ever wanted to draw a breath again, was going to get between Lesley and the president.

When the press was set, and I went back to the study to escort the president out, he had been joined by Secretary of State Baker and General Scowcroft. They were talking about new opportunities for East-West relations, the challenge to NATO and how America would have to give it new meaning and direction, and speculating on the pace of German reunification and how America might push that forward. The president was getting excited and his mood improved considerably. I thought he was in an excellent frame of mind to do the press conference.

I gave him some talking points on the logistics of the wall coming down: when, at what location, reaction from some world leaders, etc. He read them and started walking toward the Oval. He opened the door and all the lights came on. He walked to his desk, sat down, and said a few words about the historic moment.

But from the beginning, he seemed uninspired. As he continued, the president did the one thing that made every Bush staffer start to sweat. He started sliding down in his chair. It was the absolutely ironclad signal that he didn't like what he was doing, didn't want to be there, and was probably going to show it.

Soon he was talking in a monotone, his head bowed and hands folded across his chest. I started thinking of tricks to get him to sit up—like handing him a note, but reaching in from an off-camera position so he would have to lean forward in his chair to get it. George Bush just could never hide his feelings. If he was happy or excited, his arms would flail and his eyes would dance around a smile that twisted all over his face. But if he was reluctant, or distracted, the lines in his face would deepen and his eyes would glaze over in seconds. He was now in full glaze.

Finally, Lesley stepped forward one half step, which put her about two feet from the president, and turned sideways, as if addressing both the president and the cameras at the same time, and said, "In what you just said . . . you don't seem elated."

"I am not an emotional kind of guy," the president said.

"Well, how elated are you?" she asked.

"I'm very pleased," he said, and tried to explain that he was pursuing various diplomatic courses in this period of "dynamic change."

I soon called "Lights," the signal that the press conference was over. The TV cameras were supposed to turn off their lights. Sometimes they did. Sometimes they didn't. But it was also a signal for the president to stop answering questions, or better yet, say thanks and leave the room. Sometimes he did. Sometimes he didn't. It is a truism of White House journalism that no reporter will leave a room as long as the president is still talking. Both George Bush and Ronald Reagan were told that all they had to do to end a press conference was stop talking and walk out. Yet they never could.

After the president went back to the study, I hurried to my office and called Lesley, who had just arrived at her CBS cubbyhole in the back of the briefing room.

"Lesley," I said, "I just wanted to tell you the president's motivation today. He is worried that if America appears gloating, it will be resented by Gorbachev or others in Eastern Europe. He feels everyone will recognize the triumph of Western values and capitalism over the tyranny of communism, so he doesn't have to brag. He is planning for the future."

"Well, why didn't he say that?" she asked.

"He didn't feel that would be appropriate," I said, recognizing that she was right. That's exactly what he should have done.

"I don't think so," she said. "I don't think he realizes what has happened. People are dancing in the streets. It's a celebration of freedom. We have pictures from all over the world. People are celebrating the end of the cold war, and President Bush acts like he's asleep."

This was another case, like the Tiananmen Square demonstrations in Beijing, China, where television sets the tone or mood of response for America. A president has two options: lead that response and set the tone through a strong public presentation, or reflect that tone in some symbolic way. Only disaster awaits the modern president who does not recognize the television tone of events, or worse, rejects it. Most assuredly, he will be judged as out of touch or out of his head. In this case, Lesley went on the air and said the president seemed distracted and disinterested. Others picked it up and reported the same reaction.

The president was furious with the press, but he didn't want to do anything publicly to change it. He had a curious code of media discipline that said: "If I am doing the right thing, I can take any punishment." For eight years he suffered being called a wimp for his loyalty to President Reagan. In this case he was willing to suffer again. The only payoff he would get came at Malta, when he leaned across the table to Gorbachev and asked if he had noticed that America had not reacted in a provocative way. Gorbachev did appreciate it.

"I welcome your steps," Gorbachev said. "I see a political will on the part of your government. Times under Reagan, we felt things stopped moving. Geneva, no movement. So at Black Sea, I got idea for a meeting in a few weeks at Reykjavik. Some in both countries were scared. But it was an intellectual breakthrough. Now is another breakthrough. I was waiting to see the U.S. will. Now you have shown it."

Gorbachev then reiterated the theme that had motivated Bush in the first place to be sensitive to the Soviet sense of face, of their self-image, of their own morality. "I am against Western values," Gorbachev said. Everyone at the table bristled, thinking this might turn to a criticism of democracy. But Gorbachev was objecting to the term "Western values." He said the economic problems of the Soviet Union, and the need for perestroika, did not mean that "Western values" had won. "Western values are universal values," he said. Gorbachev was trying to be subtle, in a critical way. His concern was that he was being portrayed as the loser, or the USSR was being portrayed as without values, when people spoke of the victory for Western values. He wanted the president to know that portraying him or the country as without values was not helpful in getting Soviet citizens to adopt his changes. Gorbachev had first raised this issue in New York in December 1988 when he met with Reagan for the last time and Bush for the first. Bush had never forgotten. And it had motivated much of his response to the fall of the Berlin Wall. That's why he didn't want to "dance on the wall."

Secretary Baker interjected, "Why don't we use the term 'democratic values'?"

Gorbachev showed some enthusiasm for this term because it was more politically specific and didn't have the effect of suggesting that the Soviets didn't have good values.

"We are ready to work with you," Gorbachev said, "steadily, and without surprise." With that, they began to discuss each of the president's seventeen points.

We set out for the USS *Belknap* after the meeting, scheduled to review the morning session and have lunch with advisers, then return to the *Gorky* for dinner. But as the launch, a relatively small thirty- or thirty-five-foot wooden boat, highly varnished and spotlessly clean, pulled away from the pier, it was soon clear that the rolling waves and whipping winds were actually dangerous. The boat was having trouble keeping course, even though the trip was only a few hundred yards. Water was spraying in over the bow and the stern, and all of us were advised to stay low and hang on. As the president moved up to the captain's side, he almost lost his balance. I started imagining a quite different story, one about Bush, Baker, Scowcroft, Sununu, Fitzwater, and Valdez, the President's photographer, lost at sea.

A small dock was rigged alongside the *Belknap*, perhaps twenty feet below the deck, where the boat would moor, and then we would climb a narrow stair up the side of the destroyer. The launch was supposed to pull into the mooring, someone would throw a bow line to a waiting seaman, then the captain would maneuver the stern or bow into the dock so it was parallel with the ship and could be tied up at both ends. We made two passes at the dock, located on the starboard side of the ship, but the captain couldn't get the stern of the boat to move into the ship. The waves were so large that the tiny launch would be picked up several feet, dropped several feet, and each time washed away from the ship. In addition, each time we moved into the ship, the waves would slam us against the destroyer's hull. After the second slam against the destroyer, I realized that we were in an old wooden showboat that could well break apart with a couple more slams. By this time, every face was worried.

Finally, the captain decided to try landing on the other side of the ship, where a similar dock had been constructed. On the port side, we again made two passes. The wind and waves were reacting differently on this side, but the result was the same. Finally, on the fifth attempt, the captain said he was going to establish one line from the stern of the boat. The front end of the boat would swing out toward the open sea, but he thought we could get off. When we reached the deck of the *Belknap*, the ship's commander said, "This is the worst storm in port that I've seen in twenty-four years." He didn't have any doubters in our party.

Unfortunately, the pictures of our landing attempt led reporters to dub the meeting a "sinking summit." This made it all the more important that I have a good briefing that evening—to get our story out about the summit's successes.

After 4 P.M., the president and the captain happened to walk by my cabin on their way to the deck to check the weather. They had to decide whether we could get back across the harbor for the Gorbachev dinner on the *Gorky*. The president walked out to the edge of the ship, grabbed the cable handrail in that particular area, and exclaimed with great enthusiasm, "Let's go!"

This had to be the captain's worst moment, his greatest fear. "It's a near impossibility, sir," he said, surveying the waves, which were still rising up like small buildings, blotting out the shore and throwing spray in every direction. It was dark and getting darker. I knew that no Navy captain would say no to his commander in chief unless the reality of the situation was very dangerous, probably ten times more dangerous than necessary to make that decision. I was relieved by his courage in telling the president we could not go to the *Gorky*.

I was supposed to brief the press with Gorbachev's spokesman, Gennadi Gerasimov, in the early evening before the dinner. This was important to me, because it was our glowing opportunity to take credit for the Bush seventeen-point plan, and to show that the president had taken the lead in defining a new Soviet relationship. But there was no way off the ship, and the ship-to-shore lines were so filled with static due to the storm that I couldn't even give Roman an adequate briefing on the day's meeting. Also, because the president had protected the security of the briefing, we had no written copies in advance. It was up to me, and I was stuck.

Finally, I got through to Roman at the press filing center, a grand Malta hotel made of heavy stone and set alongside the harbor. It was a most beautiful setting and building when awash in sunshine, as it was most of the year. But in a storm, it was disaster. The roof leaked. The joints were loose from baking in the sun by the Mediterranean Sea. Insulation was scarce and it was cold as a cave. The press was restless, some were angry, and all were wondering how they were going to get a story. The essential rule to remember in a situation like this is that something will be written, the vacuum will be filled.

First, I asked Roman to call Gennadi and cancel our joint briefing, on the grounds that the symbolism of a one-sided briefing would be contrary to the objectives of the summit. We were there in partnership. Roman said the press was all over him, and the Soviet press staff was already spinning a story praising Gorbachev's leadership. I told him I would call back.

The president and his four staff members gathered early on the boat for dinner, in the captain's dining room. I told the group that we were having trouble getting the word out about the morning meeting. Baker said he had just talked to Margaret Tutwiler at the hotel and she said the Soviets were giving private briefings. I left the table to call ashore.

When Roman came on the line, he was frantic. The press were crazed, accosting all the staff in hallways, running from the Soviets to the Americans, trying to piece things together. So I gave him my notes. First, we tried to go through the seventeen points so he would have the president's plan.

I gave him everything I had, which in my notes totaled seventeen points, and several quotes by both Bush and Gorbachev that summed up the atmosphere and attitude of the meeting. But the phone line was so scratchy, it was hard to tell what was getting through.

When I finished, Roman said, "I only have fourteen points."

"That's impossible!" I shouted into the phone. "I gave you all seventeen."

"Go through them again," Roman said.

I read the first words or key phrases from each point, and Roman checked them off. Again I couldn't quite tell what had been missed.

"I still only have fourteen," Roman said.

"Look, Roman," I said in exasperation, "you've got them all. You've just numbered them wrong. There have to be seventeen, because seventeen is what we gave Gorbachev. So take whatever you have and make seventeen points out of it, OK?"

"OK," Roman said.

"Now," I said, "call Margaret and tell her to call *The Washington Post, New York Times,* and *Wall Street Journal.* She can call them to her room, bring in Paul Wolfowitz, Bob Blackwill, and Bob Zoellick from the State and NSC staffs, and piece it all together. You tell everyone else. I don't care how you do it."

"Everyone else" meant thousands of reporters from every country in the world. Roman would grab a few U.S. reporters in the hallway and talk "on background" because he wasn't certain enough of what happened to allow quotes. But just as he would finish three or four points, a herd of Japanese reporters would spot the hallway gathering and rush up with their cameras. When the first flash went off, Roman would stop, call out, "No pictures," and wait for a response. The U.S. reporters, growing close to deadlines and angry anyway, would lash out at the Japanese, telling them to turn off the cameras and shut up.

Roman would start again, as a dozen new people joined the group. The original group would start moaning and griping, but Roman would surge on. Again and again, a TV camera crew would stumble upon the group and turn its camera lights on. When this happened, Roman would repeat the same process as with the Japanese still cameras.

The word spread fast that Roman was briefing and the crowd soon grew to more than 100. Roman said that was it, and fled for his life to an office where he could close the door and try to figure out who had the story and who didn't.

At the same time, Laura Melillo was meeting with Wendy Walker, CNN's White House producer, to discuss television interviews with U.S. officials. It came across Laura's hand-held radio that Roman was briefing again, and everyone should hurry to another lobby. At that moment, Laura looked up to see CNN's twenty-foot satellite dish, tethered on the portico of the hotel, simply slide into view at the left side of the dining room window, move along the veranda as if on a stage, and then exit on the right.

"My God!" Laura exclaimed. "Did you see that? I think your dish just blew away!" It did.

Back on the *Belknap,* I made one insurance call, to Brit Hume of ABC News. I wanted television coverage and I knew Brit understood the issues and would piece this story together even if my description was vague or broken up by the storm. I reached him at the hotel using our ship-to-shore radio, so it was hard to tell who else might have been listening, but it didn't matter anyway. I gave him all seventeen points.

At that point, I figured Roman had given a private briefing to the wire services. They're the most important because a wire story at least ensures that everybody in the world gets access to the basic facts. Margaret had covered the big newspapers. I was satisfied we had gotten the story out. In a way, the storm had helped because it left almost no room for critics.

I returned to the dining room for the most memorable and enjoyable dinner of my career: four hours with the president, Baker, Scowcroft, and Sununu. We talked about every policy and personality of government, assorted world leaders, the president's plans for a new Soviet relationship, and all of the talk well oiled by several bottles of the ship's best wine. The absolute best part was that no one could get to us. The storm raged. We were exquisitely alone.

After another day of meetings in which Bush and Gorbachev explored the possibilities for perestroika and European affairs, it was agreed that the next summit would be held in June 1990 and they would try to sign a START treaty at that time. This sort of deadlining is crucial in foreign affairs because it makes negotiators for both sides work toward a deadline that is real and public. No one wants to tell the two superpower leaders that the treaty won't be ready, unless, of course, the issues are simply too difficult, in which case the summit would probably be delayed.

Gerasimov and I had done our dual briefing act in two previous summits, Moscow and Washington, and they had worked relatively well. If there were deep disagreements, the joint briefings tended to keep them submerged, and they certainly symbolized a new unity. At Malta, Gorbachev was looking for unity and world support, and he asked President Bush to share a joint press conference with him. The president instantly agreed. It was quite successful in portraying the new relationship, with pictures shown around the world of the two men together, answering the same questions, laughing and comfortable with each other. The press conference was held in the music room of the ship, on a stage usually reserved for the band, on the sixth deck, with room for 450. The press filled about half the room, and technicians roamed around with their equipment in the back. It was such a warm performance by the two leaders that afterward the room took on a sort of class-reunion atmosphere. The two leaders left the stage to talk with the first ladies. Foreign secretaries and U.S. officials were warmly shaking hands and talking about next steps. For most, this had been their first meeting, and many more were expected.

Gerasimov was the only one not happy. He felt I had sandbagged him by getting an agreement not to brief the night before, then putting out our story by telephone. He told the expanded pool after the press conference that he was "very displeased" by my efforts. "It is for you to pronounce moral judgments," he said. "I had a very big temptation to go into the press center to brief alone and get all of the publicity. But because I was not to do that I refrained."

It was an unfortunate situation. But Gennadi had privately briefed his press, and that's really all we did. Plus, our story was the one Gorbachev wanted out. Nevertheless, Gerasimov felt betrayed and our relationship was never quite as warm again. He was replaced by Gorbachev soon after this, reportedly because he was getting too much Western publicity. I don't know if that's true, but he was very good, and the perfect spokesman to bring the Soviet Union out of isolation. He was very smart. As we prepared for the next summit, Gerasimov sent a delegation of his deputies to Washington to study the White House press operation. After I had explained my staff structure, the daily briefings, how to collect information, and how to relate to the president, they said they had one last question: "How can we get those telephones like you used on Malta?"

CHAPTER TWELVE

The Deathwatch

Nothing preys on a press secretary's mind like the president's death or illness, an assassination attempt, even a stumble while jogging, because it focuses all the pressures of the White House and the media on one person and every word spoken. Nothing dictates the daily pattern of existence for the White House press corps more than this same set of factors. They talk about it under their breath, in a low whisper, out the sides of their mouths and with heads slightly turned, "The deathwatch." It's an embarrassing reason for being, and like so many of the media's unwritten rules of competition, appreciated only by those who labor in the profession—those who think the champion reporter is the first one on the scene, the first one to get words on the air, the first wire service to ring the five bells at ticker machines all over the world to signal that a national emergency has just occurred. They don't like to talk about this either. It's not high-minded enough. The American people don't really care about these grubbly little competitive battles. It's an inside game that the media play with themselves and they couch it in the grandest of terms: "the continuity of the presidency."

This is another cold war idea that spawned a raft of artificial rules and traditions about how the press covers the presidency. First, there is the idea that in the few minutes between a president's death and a vice president being sworn in, the nuclear button will be pushed somewhere in the world, missiles will come flying from all corners of the globe, and God help us if Helen Thomas is not there to see them land.

Second, the theory goes that if a president is stricken, there are so many repercussions throughout the world and so many people will be living in abject fear and panic that only instantaneous news reporting can save the nation from jumping off its balcony. Similarly, if an assassination occurs, instant and massive coverage is needed to prevent conspiratorial accusations from undermining at least the mental strength of the country.

My rationale is much simpler: Maintaining "the deathwatch" is the most direct way to compete. As the technology of live television, computer networks, and portable telephones has made it more difficult to compete on the basis of news, the personal fights between correspondents to be the first to the phone intensify. In the White House briefing room today, they still tell the story of the Kennedy assassination, when Jack Bell of the Associated Press and Merriman Smith of United Press International were riding in the same car in the presidential motorcade. When the shots rang out, the story goes, the distinguished Mr. Smith dove for the telephone, called in a few sentences to report the shooting, then yanked the phone out of its holder and threw it out the window. Thirty-three years later, the White House still provides two separate motorcade cars for AP and UPI so they can't destroy each other's phones. Never mind that every third person in America today has a mobile telephone, and every journalist has one. Never mind that nearly every one of the fourteen journalists in a presidential pool can instantaneously get the story out by some means, probably on live television. Never mind that nearly every motorcade is covered by helicopters, à la O. J. Simpson's low-speed car chase through Los Angeles in 1994. The culture of the press corps does not change easily.

Terry Hunt, White House bureau chief for the Associated Press, is a rational family man with a beautiful wife and child, a house in the suburbs, a number of tweed sport coats, and sensible shoes. Yet if President Bush went jogging at 6 A.M. on a cold Maine morning, with temperatures plummeting to three degrees below zero—and he sometimes did—Terry Hunt would be leading the pack in pursuit, trotting along the beach wearing a plaid hat with ear flaps and all the L. L. Bean sweaters he could muster. This proves that both the president and Terry were a little bit nuts, but at least the president enjoyed it. Terry was on the deathwatch.

Press secretaries, at least those who want to survive, accommodate all these fears and build elaborate communications systems so that a reporter is never more than minutes from a telephone, and never loses visual contact with the president. I once saw Helen Thomas, at age seventy, sitting in the back of a military truck bouncing across the Saudi Arabian landscape in pursuit of the president. When she spotted President Bush coming out of a bunker nearly fifty yards away, she moved to the back of the camouflaged truck bed and jumped. Someone caught her arm in time to help steady her. Her knees bent and her head started down, but at the last second she regained her balance, stumbled forward a step or two, steadied herself, then took off running toward the bunker. Three young Marines stood and stared in amazement. I started running after her, sure she was going to kill herself in the 110-degree sun, caught her by the elbow and ran with her for a few more steps before I could get her to slow down. I was exhausted. But I knew she would run till she dropped if I didn't give her some cover, some reason why she did not need to hear the president say "Very interesting" as he emerged from the bunker.

There is an internal barometer of performance in Helen that dictates how she covers the news, and what it means to be a journalist—no short cuts, no getting it secondhand. She is from the old school that has to "be there." Rightly or wrongly, I tried to follow her standard, to always be with the president, at his heels in every campaign stop, in or outside every holding room before a speech, and in my seat on *Air Force One* on every trip. Late in the administration I passed up a few trips, but it was always with great guilt. Was this commitment rational? Of course not.

In this climate of twenty-four-hour-a-day dedication to the presidency, there is always an element of burnout in every reporter, and in the press staff who must worry about the president's activities day and night. They are the staff who get up at 3 A.M. if the president gets up at five. I once tried to explain to President Bush that if he jogged at 6 A.M., the press had been up since 3 A.M. They have to gather at the White House, go through metal detectors, have all cameras and equipment sniffed by the Secret Service bomb dogs, and then wait. The Secret Service always makes them wait because the Service hates the press. The Secret Service is there to protect the president. The press are in their way, whining and complaining. The president's response to all this was: "They don't have to come." They do, of course. It's their job and their calling.

The one respite from this entire system, the one refuge for the press and the president, is Camp David. It is 200 acres in the Catoctin Mountains near Thurmont, Maryland, built by Franklin Delano Roosevelt as a release from Washington that was close enough he could return in an emergency. It has double security fences around the perimeter with plenty of barbed wire, and Marine guards everywhere. Presidents like it because the press can't get in. The press like it because the president can't get out, at least not without being spotted. And if the press secretary will assure them that some system has been established to tell them of any presidential movement, they can sleep happily.

On Sunday, May 4, 1991, President and Mrs. Bush were enjoying a beautiful spring weekend at the camp. New leaves were filling out the aspen trees, the bushes and underbrush made every turn in the wandering pathways an adventure, and the sun was sending beams through the tree limbs illuminating dust and bugs floating gently through the afternoon. For me, it was also a lazy spring day to be enjoyed away from the presidency.

Melinda Andrews, whom I had met in the White House during the Reagan administration, and I made plans to go to the Gold Cup, an annual steeplechase race held near Middleburg, Virginia. The Gold Cup course is laid out across a rolling hillside, the jumps and hedges are prepared with immaculate care, and the horses from nearby Virginia stables are trucked in to compete, often family against family in the cloistered world of hunt country gentry. These people lead their horses around the stables, and sit and talk beside their Rolls-Royces or their pickup trucks—depending on whether the husband and wife came together or separately. They wear wonderful plaids and herringbone sport coats with enough threads hanging out to suggest the same outfit was worn to feed the horses. This world is closed, and operates barely cognizant of the other Gold Cup world.

That other world is made up of the pretenders—people like me. We go to Gold Cup to dress up like rich barons and wear straw hats and pretty sun dresses. We find an old tweed coat in the back of our closet, adorn it with a silk handkerchief draped casually from the breast pocket, don an old pair of Wellington boots, and pretend we are Zelda and Scott Fitzgerald for the day. Washington lobbyists set up tents with fried chicken and bars to entertain their guests, students from Virginia colleges gather to dream of someday owning the place, and bureaucrats take picnics to eat on a blanket so far from the track that the races are little more than noise. But by the fourth or fifth race, all the classes have merged, except, of course, for the aristocrats. The rest drink beer like crazy, visit all the tents, and shout at old friends spotted in the distance. Every few minutes we turn to watch the horses go by, not knowing their names or their riders, and not caring. We are part of the spectacle, and it is glorious.

Early in the afternoon, after the third or fourth race, I suggested to Melinda that we should head home to beat the traffic. Never mind that the actual race for the Gold Cup was at least another hour away. The beer was making me a little dizzy, especially while trying to walk under a heavy straw hat with twelve-inch brim. It was a thirty- or thirty-five-mile drive back to Washington, and I didn't want to hurry. I also knew my limits on beer. So we took one last walk through the social cauldron, then edged the car through the hayfields and out to the road home. Just as I pulled onto the asphalt for the three-mile drive to Route 66, which went directly to Washington, my beeper went off. It was a constant ping that would not stop until I read the message: "CALL HERRICK. CAMP DAVID. EMERGENCY."

"Oh no," I said to Melinda. "This is the worst. Where's a phone?"

"Should we go back?" she asked.

"In that crowd? We probably couldn't even find a phone," I said. "Let's go to The Plains. Can't be more than two or three miles. Find a gas station." My mind was whirling. What kind of emergency? Most likely the president had decided to leave the camp to play golf and didn't want to take the press. John Herrick, who was the press staff person on duty at the camp that weekend, might consider that an emergency, especially if he could imagine the tongue-lashing Helen Thomas would give him for letting the president make a se-cret movement. Maybe it was an accident of some kind. The presi-dent was always installing new recreational equipment at the camp. Maybe somebody was hit by an arrow at the archery range, or a clay pigeon went astray, or a Marine guard went a little bonkers from being cooped up in the woods and started shooting his gun. That had happened once, but nobody was hurt. Or maybe the president died. Christ. I stepped on the gas.

"Not so fast, Marlin," Melinda said. "You've had quite a few drinks. There's the town. We're almost there."

There were only about three stores in The Plains, Virginia: a sandwich shop that looked like it had been closed for about three years, a gas station, some other buildings closed on Saturdays and so obscure that it was difficult to tell what they were, and one restau-rant, the Rail Stop. I parked on the street, jerked the door open, and ran for the restaurant. There were quite a few cars outside, no doubt from the Gold Cup, and inside it was crowded. Eight or ten tables, filled with people in leather boots and jodhpurs, a few families, and several pretenders at the bar, all eating hamburgers and French fries as near as I could tell. I asked the bartender for a phone and he pointed to the back.

It was noisy. My head was hurting. And the phone was just outside the men's room in a hallway so narrow that I had to move aside whenever someone went into the bathroom. I cupped my hand over my ear, turned to the wall, and called the White House operator. She put me through immediately to Herrick at the camp infirmary.

"Marlin, we've got a situation here," he said. "The president collapsed on the jogging track. They're checking his heart now. They're taking him to Bethesda Naval Hospital."

"Is it a heart attack?" I asked.

"The doctor says he doesn't think so. Something about an irregular heartbeat."

"What happened?"

"He was jogging in the woods, on the path, when he ran out of breath," John said. "The agents brought him to Eucalyptus, the infirmary. Dr. Nash is checking him out. What do I do?"

"First," I said, "no matter where the president goes, you stay with him. When you know for sure where you're going, call Roman and tell him to meet you there. I'm going directly to the White House. If you see any press, tell them all information will come from the White House."

"Do I call the press?" he asked.

"I'm going to dictate a statement to you now," I said. "Call it out to the wire services just before you get on the helicopter." I wanted three things in place immediately: a statement on the president's condition that would reassure the nation, at least saying he was alive; an internal communications network that put my own people in the chain of information directly from the doctors; and a point of information dissemination away from the hospital where I could maintain control. The White House was the best. God, I wished I hadn't had so many beers.

"Have you got a pencil?" I asked. "Take this down. Wait, someone's coming out of the head." It was a father, opening the door while trying to zip his six-year-old son's pants. "OK, John, are you ready?"

"You fill in the blanks," I said, "starting with this. At approximately 'blank' P.M. while jogging at Camp David, President Bush suffered a shortness of breath. He was taken to the Camp David medical facility and was examined by Dr. Michael Nash, one of the president's physicians, and determined to have 'blank.' Dr. Nash says the president is in stable condition but will require further examination at Bethesda Naval Hospital. The president departed Camp David for Bethesda Naval Hospital aboard *Marine One* at 'blank.' The president is in a stable and safe condition.

"John," I continued, "get Dr. Nash to fill in the blank with the medical term for what happened. This will be immediately analyzed by every doctor in the country, so it has to be technically accurate. Also, if we tell people it was not a heart attack, we have to say exactly what it was, and the more technical the term the better."

"OK," he said. "I'll check it with Dr. Nash."

John Herrick was a star on our staff. He was twenty-five, but mature and experienced. A Midwesterner who had graduated from Dartmouth, he worked in the president's 1988 campaign as a press advance man, so he knew how the press operated and he appreciated their deadlines and competitive problems. He was level-headed and smart, loyal, fresh-faced, and honest. He lost his temper sometimes, but it was always on behalf of his duty or responsibility, and he was not afraid to make a decision. We had three young staffers, John, Michael Busch, and Sean Walsh, all of whom deserved those adjectives. They rotated weekend assignments at Camp David with the president, again so I would have a way to announce events from the camp. This was often necessary because it seemed that some international crisis was always happening on weekends.

"I'll call you as soon as I get to the White House," I said, and hung up. I tried to call Chief of Staff John Sununu but there was no answer. One of the most fascinating aspects of being a part of the presidency, a part of history, is the uncanny self-awareness of your role that sometimes occurs, as if you are in a painting, or playing a cameo role in a film. As I walked out through the Rail Stop, a few people recognized me and stared. Most said nothing. But all would watch television later and marvel that they were unknowingly part of the ten-minute tabloid that announced the president's illness to the world. I even imagined a plaque outside that men's room: "Inside they pee, outside the president is safe. It happened here."

I ran for the car. Melinda had a map on her lap and said it showed the closest way was Route 66 directly to Washington. I told her the plan and asked her to keep an eye out for a telephone along the highway in case I got another page and had to call in. I also wanted to make another call to Sununu. I headed down Route 66 at about eighty miles per hour, sure I would be stopped, but thinking maybe I could ask for a police escort to the White House. It never happened. I did stop once to call Sununu. The White House operator told me he was on his way to Bethesda. That was good, because it meant somebody would be in charge to handle all the notifications.

Back at Camp David, the president was getting ready to leave. Governor Sununu called the camp and talked to the doctors, then to John Herrick.

"What's going on there?" he asked.

"We're getting ready to leave," John said. "I have a statement from Marlin that I'm just getting ready to call out."

"Read it to me," he said. John read it slowly.

"Whoa. Whoa," Sununu said. "We don't want to say atrial fibrillation. We don't need to get people scared of a heart attack."

"Marlin says everyone will think it's a heart attack," John said. "The best way to stop speculation is to say exactly what it is."

"Read it to me again," he said. As John was about halfway through the statement, the agents shouted, "Go!" John looked up to see the president coming out of the infirmary, with the doctor holding one arm and a nurse holding an intravenous bottle as he walked. His shirt was open, and a heart monitor was attached to his chest with suction cups. John was taken aback. The president looked terrible. Herrick jumped into the nearest car. He realized that Mrs. Bush's seat in the limo was taken by the doctor and the nurse, so he motioned her to get in with him for the short ride to the Camp David landing zone. Mrs. Bush, as usual, was calm. She worried about the president's appearance and Herrick gave her his Camp David windbreaker to give to the president. She later put it around the president's shoulders when he walked from the helicopter to the hospital.

On *Marine One*, the president immediately asked Herrick for his briefcase, opened it, and took out some letters. This was far more reassuring than the sight of nurses holding IVs.

The president turned again to John. "What have we told the press?"

"Nothing yet," John said.

"You mean I'm flying to the hospital and nobody knows?" he said. "That's not right."

"I have a statement," John said. "Marlin said to release it before we left but I didn't get a chance." He didn't mention reading it to Sununu. Herrick paraphrased the statement for the president, who nodded his head approvingly. Mrs. Bush, sitting in her usual seat directly in front of the president, said John should release it soon. Later, Mrs. Bush assured me that John had done his best and the president praised Herrick's calmness and maturity under the circumstances.

Once inside the hospital, John Herrick immediately went to a telephone, called the White House, and set up a conference call to the wire services. Saturday afternoon at the wires is pretty slow-pace. The weekend reporters are often at the beginning or the end of their careers, interns, or at least people who don't want to be there. None of them would even know John Herrick. But when the White House operator called, that gave him verification of identity. Even so, they assumed it would be a routine call about a presidential movement, perhaps notification for a pool to form.

"I have a statement," John said. He paused while they set up their computers to take it down. He didn't recognize any of the AP, UPI, and Reuters names on the phone. As he finished the first sentence, he could hear the typing. Even the line about the doctors examining him didn't get a stir. But when he got to the line "The president departed Camp David for Bethesda Naval Hospital . . . ," they started shouting. "What? What is this? Back up! Start over! Start the whole thing over." By the time John finished rereading the statement, bells were going off in newsrooms all across America. The AP correspondent pushed a button the moment John finished, and the story flashed electronically from coast to coast.

John hung up without comment, and called CBS News because they were in charge of weekend television pools and would have to get pool cameras out to the hospital. The minute his contact picked up the phone he said, "We already know. We got it. We're on the way!" All hell was breaking loose, but we were ready.

By the time I got to the White House, the word was out. Several members of my staff had already arrived, and they called the rest with instructions to come in immediately. Press were running down the driveway. By this time, I was sober as a judge. We had missed the evening news, so I knew I would have to hold a briefing that evening, on-camera, in prime time, with questions and answers. I started working the phones to the hospital, talking with Roman, then Sununu, then the doctors. The president's personal physician, Dr. Burton Lee, had a weekend home in Charlottesville, Virginia, and was still hours away from Bethesda. Dr. Nash was young, sincere, and helpful. He was a little scared of giving out information, but he knew I had been through this before. Sununu was off the wall, trying to control everything, arguing we should say nothing, and running from one medical person to another asking questions. Twice while I was talking to Roman, Sununu walked into the room, grabbed the phone out of Roman's hand, and demanded to know what I was talking about. I always patiently explained the reason for everything I was saying: trying to calm people's fears, trying to hold down conjecture, trying to be forthcoming so the press wouldn't think we were hiding something. The history of presidential illness is replete with cover-up stories, from Roosevelt's paralysis to Kennedy's back medication to Eisenhower's heart attack. I had helped Larry Speakes get all the information out about President Reagan's colon cancer and skin cancer, which he did successfully but with some difficulty. I was determined to do it right for President Bush. Sununu had to be reminded several times of the political ramifications if the public felt we were lying about the president's health. Finally, he agreed.

In the midst of all this, I realized how important demeanor and appearance would be in explaining the president's illness—no riding jackets or straw hats. So I sent Sean to my house in Virginia to get a white shirt, conservative tie, and blue blazer. I figured that if it turned out I was at the White House for days without going home, I could buy a few new shirts and wear the blazer every day. I figured that might happen if they had to operate, or if the president did have a heart attack.

By 8:30 p.m. I was ready. I drafted a two-page statement that covered the basics: presidential condition, medication, tests so far, names of doctors, contact with the vice president, and at least two sentences to assure the American people. The first was that the president was "relaxed, comfortable, and having dinner with Mrs. Bush." That was the lead of the statement.

I didn't put the most important sentence—about not having a heart attack—in the statement because I didn't want to take the chance that Sununu would take it out. I knew I would be asked about a heart attack. I asked the doctors privately, three times, if there was any chance this could be a heart attack. They said no. So I wrote in pencil at the top of my prepared text: "No evidence at this time of a heart attack." I left myself some wiggle room, but I wanted to give people this assurance.

The fourth question at the briefing was: "Is a heart attack definitely being ruled out?" I was ready. My strategy worked perfectly.

President and Mrs. Bush and Governor Sununu watched my briefing from the hospital. The first question asked was: "Marlin, how long was he running when this happened? And did he fall, or was there any outward sign?"

I said he had been running for several minutes, but I didn't have the exact time. Several minutes later a reporter asked: "Marlin, you've treated this all very coolly and calmly with no sense of panic . . . Are you saying that there is not a great deal of concern about the president's—either this episode or his health in the hours to come?"

Before I could finish the answer, Andy Card emerged from the press office and handed me a note. It was torn off the corner of a budget cover, written in bold, black ink: "The POTUS [President of the United States] just called. He was running/walking for 35–40 minutes."

I took the note, somewhat reluctantly. These notes usually meant I had made a mistake. Also, with the cameras on, it's hard to take a note in front of the whole world and then not explain it. But this one was most helpful, and very clever of the president.

"The president just called in to say that he was running or walking about thirty-five to forty minutes," I said. The room erupted in laughter, and you could feel the tension release. "Now," I continued, "this doesn't mean you can all ask questions of the president and he'll call up and give you an answer." More laughter.

"Is he watching this on television?" Pat Griffith of the *Toledo Blade* asked.

"Yes, he is," I said. "He thinks you're doing a great job so far, Pat." More laughter. The briefing was essentially over.

Bob Schieffer of CBS News reported the briefing: "So the White House spokesman, Marlin Fitzwater, reports the latest details on the president's condition, and obviously the president himself was listening to all of this because he apparently called in at one point, according to Marlin Fitzwater, and gave him some additional details—saying that he had been running thirty-five to forty minutes. So apparently he's doing fairly well." Schieffer also interviewed Dr. Samuel Fox of the Georgetown University Medical Center, who said of the president's condition, "This can be quite benign."

I was pleased. The world had been notified, calmed, informed, and the president was getting better. But the media suspicions were alive, as CBS's final report by Eric Engberg suggested: "It appears Fitzwater is 'giving us the straight dope' as far as he knows it when he says it's going to be a short stay."

After the briefing, I hurried back to my office and took a call from the president, which made me feel much better. At least he sounded good, and it gave me something to say in the tick tock. I hated tick tock. It was the press's demand for a minute-by-minute accounting of events. The press was clamoring outside my door. They wanted every detail of the day, the kind of process details about the actions of staff that allow the public and press to judge their wisdom. Every president hates process stories because they are always judgmental. Similarly, it's in the tick tock that press secretaries are judged: Do you know what happened? Is it accurate and honest?

This tick tock immediately took a curious twist because of the late Myron "Mike" Waldman of *Newsday*. Mike was a middle-aged reporter who wore wire rim glasses, had a couple strands of seaweed draped across his bald head, and could never seem to get the knot in his tie all the way to his collar, as if the last two inches were just too great a push. He had a penchant for striped shirts in colors that didn't match, shoes that were utilitarian, and he was always sweating. He worked hard, racing all over town to cover general assignment stories, and he was widely known to members of Congress. He could be tenacious if you gave him short shrift, but most of the time he was a true gentleman, of the pencil-behind-the-ear school of journalism, who, day in and day out, plodded through the facts.

Mike asked when the atrial fibrillation episode ended. "Because it normally takes three or four hours," he said. "I've had two myself."

Oh no, I thought, this is the worst. Now we have an in-house expert who thinks his experience is the model, or at least the norm. "You've had two of these?" I said. "Well, then, you tell us how this all works." I figured the first step would be to get Mike's story on the table.

"Did they use a defibrillator on him at all?" Mike asked.

Oh no, now I had to match Mike treatment for treatment. I never heard of any defibrillator. I decided against starting down that road, since I didn't know much anyway. So we danced for an hour of tick tock around all the things I didn't know about hearts and fibrillation.

At 9:17 P.M. it was winding down when someone asked if I had talked to the president. "Yes," I said. "He said, 'Marlin, see if you can get me a two-week vacation out of this, would you?' "

My staff jotted down eight basic questions from the tick tock that we needed to answer that night. We conferred with the doctors, wrote it up in longhand, and tacked it onto the bulletin board. The first day of the crisis was over. The next day would be the really tough one: the second-guessing, the long-term predictions, and the political fallout.

The worst thing about being president is that you can never call in sick or take a day off. You can't allow adequate recuperation. You don't even like to admit sickness, because sickness is weakness and politicians can never be weak. Think of the Herculean efforts to hide FDR's paralysis and John Kennedy's back. LBJ even showed his gall bladder scar as a symbol of his strength and vitality. Ronald Reagan had the most frightening scare word there is: cancer. He was honest about it, and probably the most open of any president until then, but his staff was scared to death.

Sunday, May 5, 1991, started with a morning briefing. It was an update on the president's condition and a promise that I would not leave my post, would report every nuance as I got it, and would call them the moment anything happened. I put a lid on until 5 P.M., meaning I promised not to make news during that period, and promised another briefing at 5:30 P.M. We discussed the president's appearance, his conversations with Governor Sununu, telegrams from foreign leaders, and other extraneous matters. Then, from the back of the room came a new voice, a tall, blonde reporter whom I recognized as Susan Spencer of CBS News. She was their medical and science reporter, and started asking about blood thinners, heart monitors, and normal heart rhythms. Susan was an excellent reporter who became permanently assigned to the White House after the incident, and always did her homework on stories. Susan's presence reminded me again to be damn sure of my facts.

Susan came to present a different kind of problem concerning how presidential staff view reporters. All the political prejudices of the White House were against her. She worked for CBS, so she was viewed as a Dan Rather clone. Her husband is Tom Oliphant, a *Boston Globe* reporter who appears regularly on television talk shows as a self-proclaimed liberal. Since White House staff put every reporter in one political group or the other, Democrat or Republican, Susan was quickly labeled a radical liberal Democrat just on the basis of her associations. I couldn't get anyone to return her calls. Some staff members would watch Tom Oliphant attack the president on Sunday television, and then curse Susan all day Monday. She may have been quite liberal, but she didn't deserve the treatment her marriage earned her.

Just as I was finishing this informal briefing in my office, the president called. Nothing helps your reputation like picking up the phone in the presence of forty reporters and saying, "Good morning, Mr. President." But then, of course, we had to spend another thirty minutes discussing the phone conversation and all the things the president hadn't told me.

About midafternoon, some alarm bells started going off. I kept in constant touch with Roman at the hospital, and talked frequently with Dr. Lee, who had returned from Charlottesville late Saturday night. The president was taking digoxin and procainamide for the atrial fibrillation, but his heart had not returned to its normal rhythm. Dr. Lee was calm, reassured me that the president was fine, had not had a heart attack, and would recover fully. But normally, the heart stabilized in a few hours, as Mike Waldman had said. I explained that I had promised a five-thirty briefing, but I didn't want to do it if we had any doubts about the president's condition. He said the doctors would meet at four o'clock to review the situation.

In our second conversation of the day, I asked the "what if" question. Dr. Lee said that if the medicine didn't work, they might have to shock the president electrically to get his heart back on rhythm in a treatment known as "cardioversion." My blood pressure went up twenty points, I'm sure. My mental vision was the same as everyone in America would have: a doctor putting two big electric pads on the president's chest, yelling "Stand back!" and the president's body jumping a foot in the air. Dr. Lee assured me that I had watched too many Dr. Kildare movies in my youth, but that the president would have to go under general anesthesia during the procedure.

Oh no. Another scare word: anesthesia. Anesthesia means unconscious, and that means the Twenty-fifth Amendment, a process by which the vice president becomes acting president during the president's incapacitation. The Twenty-fifth Amendment, ratified in 1967, says: "Whenever the Vice President and a majority of either the principal officers of the executive departments or of such other body as Congress may by law provide, transmit to the President pro tempore of the Senate and the Speaker of the House of Representatives their written declaration that the President is unable to discharge the power and duties of his office, the Vice President shall immediately assume the powers and duties of the office as Acting President."

When this amendment was passed, it spawned a number of hypothetical accounts of presidents getting sick and vice presidents declaring them incapacitated, presidents acting a little weird and the cabinet declaring them incapacitated, or sick presidents being attacked by villains so they never recover, with the vice president getting to keep his new power. There are a thousand plots you can weave out of this story line.

In the real world, about a thousandth of this fiction lurks in the heart of the most serious and rational chief of staff, so there is always a great reluctance to give up power under the Twenty-fifth Amendment, and great eagerness to take it back. It has only happened twice in our history, both times on my watch. Much has been written about President Reagan turning power over to Vice President Bush on July 13, 1985. Chief of Staff Donald T. Regan had no precedent for this procedure, and as a pioneer he did an excellent job. He was reluctant, however, and it showed in our slow and sloppy release of the actual letters to Congress turning over power. It happened, but only after the press made loud demands at a Larry Speakes press briefing at the hospital.

Similarly, Mr. Regan had President Reagan sign the letters reclaiming power within a few hours of his surgery, and with very little examination or review by the doctors. Indeed, it was only Ronald Reagan's normally scratchy handwriting that kept people from noticing that he could barely write his name in reclaiming power.

Interestingly, during the afternoon of President Reagan's operation, Vice President Bush stayed at his official residence, partly because it was a Saturday, and partly because he wanted to symbolically show that he was not working, and therefore could not be accused of trying to usurp the president's powers in any way. He invited three old friends to join him for tennis. It was a hot afternoon, but the vice president enjoyed the heat. He once kept me on the court through a ninety-five-degree marathon in which he whipped me solidly, despite my plaintive calls for mercy and a nearby shade tree. On this afternoon, he lunged for an overhead shot, lost his balance and fell back, hitting his head on the concrete. He did not move. The vice president's physician rushed to the court with smelling salts, put a towel under Mr. Bush's head, and took his pulse. After a couple of minutes, the vice president opened his eyes, shook his head, and slowly raised his body to a sitting position. For at least two minutes that day, both the president and vice president were unconscious at the same time.

I don't believe Ronald Reagan or George Bush ever worried for one second about turning power over to their vice president. But in political Washington, the president's staff always fears the worst. The worst, of course, is losing power.

In my last conversation Sunday afternoon with Dr. Lee, before his 4 P.M. review meeting, he was not optimistic about the medicine working. Too many hours had passed. We had to start thinking about the Twenty-fifth Amendment. Actually, Sununu had put General Counsel C. Boyden Gray to work earlier in the day, pulling the necessary letters together for possible signature. President Bush had directed early in his administration that this process be established and organized so it could be handled smoothly if ever needed.

On April 18, 1989, the president met with Vice President Quayle, Chief of Staff Sununu, Counsel Boyden Gray, Chief of Staff to the First Lady Susan Porter Rose, Dr. Lee, Mrs. Bush, and a representative of the Secret Service. The president wanted everyone to be aware of the process. Essentially, under Section 3 of the Twenty-fifth Amendment, the president declares himself incapacitated and declares himself well. Under Section 4, if the president can't make these declarations, the cabinet does it.

The president wanted to make clear that in any discussions of illness, general health, or the Twenty-fifth Amendment, the chief of staff, counsel to the president, and first lady were to be a part of it—especially the first lady. A notification process was established for the cabinet in case of disability, and Mrs. Bush was specifically included in those discussions.

The final conclusion of the group, however, was the most interesting. They did not discuss the problem of borderline disability, that is, "What if the cabinet thinks the president is disabled but the president doesn't agree?" Dr. Lee wrote at the time, "It will be the position of this office, and all attendant medical staff, that we will be most hesitant to declare a disability when there is doubt. In this setting, we guarantee extensive consultation with all of the principals present at the meeting on the 18th."

It was clear that I had to cancel my 5:30 P.M. briefing because of the ongoing doctors' meeting at Bethesda. It stirred some anxiety among the press, mainly from the television networks, who were facing a 6 P.M. deadline. I called each of them to provide a private briefing on the president's condition, with the caveat that the doctors, at the time of their broadcasts, would be reviewing the situation.

Dr. Lee had said in our last conversation that because of the dosage of the medicine, and the time it was taken, the president would have to be awakened about 5 A.M. and given the cardioversion at about 6 A.M. To me, that meant America would wake up with a new president. The president would be given the anesthetic just before 6 A.M., with the Twenty-fifth Amendment letters having been signed. Vice President Quayle would be acting president, and America would wake up to the voice of Charlie Gibson on ABC saying: "Good morning, America. Dan Quayle is acting president this morning while President Bush is unconscious and receiving electric shock treatment to revive his heart." Holy Toledo! That's just not right.

I asked Boyden Gray for a copy of the letters transferring power to the vice president, unsigned of course, so I could familiarize myself with the amendment, and be ready to reproduce the documents. I also asked if he could join me for a private talk. Boyden has two very strong traits, honesty and ethical values, at least as applied to government service. His rules for White House conduct were strict, and probably even hurt our ability to campaign in 1992. But he also kept us out of trouble for four years and guided President Bush through the Iran-Contra traps being set by Independent Counsel Lawrence Walsh. I wanted his judgment on the president's illness, because I was about to start a huge fight with John Sununu that would probably go to the president for resolution.

I laid out the situation for Boyden as he sat in front of my desk with my four clocks in the background. It gave an eerie feeling to the discussion, an acute sense of how one's life is divided into segments of time, once lost, never to be regained.

"Boyden," I pleaded, "we can't let America wake up to a new president. People will be scared. There will be conspiracy theories. Jokes about the vice president. And worse, our integrity will be kaput. I believe we have to tell the world tonight what may happen during the night. Then everybody is ready. We transfer power smoothly. Everybody knows the exact condition of President Bush. And if he recovers so none of that is necessary, what damage has been done?"

Boyden looked at the floor, thought the options through, and agreed. "Have you told Sununu yet?" he asked.

"No," I said. "I wanted to get your opinion first. Also I wanted to be sure my arguments were sound, because Sununu will argue against it on political grounds—I just know it—and I want to be right."

"What are the political concerns?" he asked.

"He may not want to say it," I said, "but I don't think he wants people writing columns about what it would be like under President Quayle. And I can understand that. It doesn't help Bush or Quayle to encourage speculation about a Quayle administration, but the alternative is worse. I don't believe we can just turn over the government to someone else, in the middle of the night, without the American people knowing about it."

"I agree," he said.

I reached for the phone to call Sununu at Bethesda. I hoped that Boyden would stay and listen to the conversation, so he would know exactly what I said, but he returned to his office. I got Sununu on the line and started through my explanation. Three sentences in, he erupted:

"Who told you about this?" he demanded.

"I've been talking with Dr. Lee all day," I said.

"We don't know what's going to happen!" he shouted. "We're not going to say anything!"

"Well, we haven't said anything all day," I said. "I have to brief tonight on the president's condition. They know the doctors have been reviewing the matter."

"How do they know that?" he shouted accusingly.

"I told them," I said. "It's a fact. You're not living in a vacuum out there. Everybody knows everything."

"Look, the president's just fine," Sununu said.

"I know, John," I said, "but we have to account for this possibility. Let me type up a statement on what we would say and fax it to you."

"OK," he said, and hung up.

The fight was on and I needed a second opinion for moral support. I called Roman at the hospital.

"What did you say to Sununu?" Roman asked. "He stormed out of here shaking his head and heading for the president."

"That's what I want to talk to you about," I said. "Tell me what you think." I went through the entire argument for the third time. Perhaps I just wanted to convince myself. But I had to check my reasoning. Often, I had gone to bat for the press in White House meetings, claiming they would be outraged by some action, only to be overruled and then have the press say nothing. I needed a second opinion.

Roman agreed. I hung up, took out a yellow pad of legal-sized paper, and began to write. I started with the key paragraph about the president's possible cardioversion, but then decided that was too abrupt. I started over with a routine description of the president's medication, his visitors, and a doctor's report. The key paragraph was number five:

"We remain hopeful that the medication will return his heart to normal rhythm. If by morning that is not the case, the doctors will consider electrical cardioversion. This procedure is well known and relatively commonplace. The risk is minimal, particularly in a patient such as the president who has no demonstrable heart disease. Nevertheless, it would require general anesthesia, which could be expected to incapacitate the president for only a short period of time. The final decision on this will be made tomorrow morning. During the short time the president would be under anesthesia, the vice president would be acting president under the Twenty-fifth Amendment." That was the bomb. Even as I wrote it, I could see reporters running for telephones and a long night of rewrite men searching through Dan Quayle files.

I faxed the three-page statement to Sununu and Roman at Bethesda. Sununu called a few minutes later to argue against the statement. He saw no need to get people upset. He argued that the medicine would probably work and then we would have created apprehension around the world for no reason. But he agreed to talk to the president about it.

Then he turned to argue with Roman. Roman said I had been through this before with President Reagan's colon cancer, his skin cancer, and Mrs. Reagan's breast cancer. He argued that I knew how to read the public interest on this matter. But Sununu stormed out, heading for the president's suite. Roman went with him.

The president was propped up in bed watching the news on television. He was hooked up to the heart monitor and the IV, looking a little pale and tired. The governor quietly explained my recommendations and handed the draft statement to the president. Sununu could turn his temper off and on, and up and down, like a radio dial. He was gentle as a breeze in presenting my case to the president.

"Get me the phone," the president said.

My hand was only a few inches from the receiver when it rang. "Hello, Mr. President," I said. I wanted to ask how he felt, but figured this was no time for small talk.

"John says you want to put out this statement," the president said. "Why do we have to do this?"

"Sir," I began, "we just can't have people waking up in the morning and finding a new president. They won't know if you died, or what happened. If we don't tell people tonight, they will go to bed thinking you're getting better. Also, we'll have to notify foreign leaders."

I knew if I mentioned foreign leaders, he would understand the anxiety and the notification problems, and that it might take weeks to demolish all the conspiracy theories.

"I have all the Twenty-fifth Amendment documents ready if we have to do that," I said. "But I would hate to call up reporters in the middle of the night to say we're doing it."

"Let me read this again," he said. I listened, and heard the scratch of a pen. Finally, he came back on. "Marlin," he said, "this is OK. I marked out a few paragraphs. When will you do this?"

"It will probably take me an hour or more to get ready," I said. "I need to get a full doctor's report."

"OK," he said, and hung up. I scheduled the briefing for 9 P.M. The networks asked for 9:02 so they could make station breaks. This was my second prime-time-live press conference in two days—very high-risk for a press secretary. The president and 80 million people would be judging me. I tried to minimize the risks with a few simple ground rules. First, I would read a prepared statement. That makes you sound authoritative and confident, as opposed to any ad lib statements that might sound hesitant or uncertain. Second, I had to take enough questions to establish my credibility, but not enough to show the limits of my knowledge. I figured about ten questions would do it. My safety net was to call for a last question and leave if any of the questions were total stumpers, or somehow uncivil. Always cut your losses fast. Last, I would make a clean exit. I'd call for a last question, take it, then say thank you and walk off, no matter what questions were being shouted.

At the end of every press conference, Helen Thomas and Jim Miklaszewski shout questions. Usually it's something personal that will stir a president to anger. It's part of their shtick. Presidents Reagan and Bush would always turn back and, in doing so, look hesitant or indecisive to the viewers. I was determined to not let that happen.

The press conference went smoothly—until paragraph five. Then people in the back of the briefing room started running for telephones. The briefing room ground rules state that reporters, once in their seats, can't jump and run out of a briefing to file a story. This is supposed to protect competitive fairness, particularly among wire services. As in all other points of competition, the wires go to extreme lengths to win this competition. In these cases, they station two other correspondents in the back of the briefing room who are not bound by the briefing room rule. They immediately file the story while their number-one reporter sits serenely in the front row. Occasionally, over the years, a press secretary has felt moved to try to manage this process with other rules, but I found that the less involvement in the press's conduct the better.

It took about seven or eight questions to cover all the details of the illness, the medical tests, and the Twenty-fifth Amendment process. Then the "what if" questions started. The first question asking for speculation is a signal for a press secretary to stop. In this case the fifth question after my explanation of the Twenty-fifth Amendment was: "Marlin, my question is what if the president is unable to make that decision [on incapacitation] himself?" I began looking for a place to stop, and found it at 9:16 P.M. I hurried back to my office to organize the staff for the next morning. We would have to be at work by 4:30 A.M., and everyone had to be ready for a phone call during the night—from me. I told them to lay out their clothes that night.

At 5 A.M., Roman walked into Bethesda Naval Hospital expecting the worst, but he found the best. The president had responded to the medicine. His heart had moved back into normal rhythm for most of the night, although it had fibrillated a few times. The cardioversion was unnecessary. Indeed, the president was scheduled to return to the White House at 9 A.M. I scheduled a full press briefing by the president's medical team at the hospital at 9:30 A.M. My strategy was that, with the president in the White House, the White House correspondents would have to stay with him. That increased the possibility that the major news organizations would send medical correspondents, not political correspondents, to Bethesda. It was a measure of my respect for the White House press corps that if I could save the doctors from their biting and incisive political questioning, I would do it.

To solidify this plan, I scheduled my briefing at 8:30 A.M. at the White House to discuss the president's general condition, his return to work, and his new daily routine. There was one major problem, however. The doctors weren't sure why the atrial fibrillation had occurred, or why the medicine was not constant in holding his heart in normal rhythm. Their initial explanation, which I passed along to the press, was that the dosage is very delicate and the medicine must be taken in just the right amounts. That's true, of course, but there was still an element of worry involved.

At 9:30 A.M. Dr. Lee, Dr. Bruce Lloyd, chief of cardiology at Bethesda, Dr. Allan Ross, chief of cardiology at George Washington University Hospital, and Dr. Jacob Verghese, a heart specialist at George Washington Unversity Hospital, briefed the press. During the Reagan illnesses, the doctors briefed the press continuously and it was so open that it led to some chaos. The White House, to its credit, wanted everything to be made public in order to allay fears about the president's age and health. Larry Speakes, the press secretary, was a very effective organizer and administrator. He established an unprecedented degree of medical openness. But after the network anchors had given America several guided tours of the president's colon, both through charts and plastic models, it became clear some control was needed. In President Bush's illness, I tried to establish myself as the single source of information, at least until we could present all the doctors together. Also, we decided early that only the key body test results would be given out. That tended to hold down the speculation based on other obscure and highly variable test results.

The president resumed his work in the Oval Office, hooked up to a heart monitor that recorded every heartbeat, and fed the result electronically to the medical office in the White House residence. A doctor was never far away. The president appeared to be in good shape, but every once in a while his heartbeat would become irregular again.

During the doctors' briefing at the medical center, Dr. Lee announced the diagnosis of the cause of the fibrillation problem: the president had an overactive thyroid gland. Ann Devroy of *The Washington Post* reported that, according to doctors, "Bush's thyroid was 10 to 20 percent more active than it should be. The thyroid is a butterfly-shaped gland in the front of the neck that secretes a hormone that helps regulate the body's metabolism. Thyroid overactivity is a well-recognized cause of atrial fibrillation."

Once the thyroid condition was discovered, and a treatment prescribed that was commonly known to millions of Americans, everyone felt better. It was not a heart problem at all. Indeed, the president had a thyroid problem similar to one suffered by the first lady. Not only did that make it more understandable and acceptable, it was even a little romantic.

Maureen Dowd of *The New York Times* wrote: "Mr. Bush looked good. Not as glowing as he often does, but not bad for a man who just spent almost 39 hours in the hospital. He was wearing a dark business suit and a red tie. His manner was easy and smiling and dismissive of his problem, as he noted that he hoped to be back 'into the athletic thing' soon."

But there was one significant physical side effect: stamina. For years the president had been known for his hyperactivity. People even joked about "his hyper thyroid." He jogged in freezing rains and scorching sun. He would play tennis, golf, horseshoes, and jog—all in a single day. Most curious was golf. He would race around the Kennebunkport golf course, once finishing eighteen holes in less than an hour, often picking up his ball the minute it hit the green, and seldom keeping track of the score. The press watched in dismay as he moved like a wind-up toy through one event after another.

Most of that ended with the thyroid disease. It had, in fact, been his thyroid. He never liked to admit to reduced stamina, and the president's physical activity remained strong and vibrant, but nothing like it was before the fibrillation. To those of us who watched him carefully, the old zip was gone. And it was noticeable in the campaign of 1992.

The president's schedule soon moved back into a normal routine and after a few weeks no one ever asked about the thyroid or his heart. But the problem was not totally resolved.

On July 24, 1992, the president addressed the National League of Families of American Prisoners and Missing in Southeast Asia at a hotel in Arlington, Virginia, before going to Ohio for a day of campaigning. Speaking to this group is always difficult because no commitment by government can satisfy a wife who has lost her husband in war. But President Bush was their friend. He was a war hero himself, a naval aviator shot down over the Pacific, and a constant defender of the POW cause. Nevertheless, as the president spoke, a young man on the press platform, of all places, started shouting. The president was cool. He stepped back from the podium to let the man be heard. Then the shouter started again. The president then did a very uncharacteristic thing: He shouted for the man to "shut up and sit down." Everyone was a little surprised. The president finished his speech, but the press reported it as "losing his temper" in the midst of POW protests. In other words, the protester had won by controlling the story and making a relatively friendly group appear hostile.

As I was walking out the door, I brushed up against Dr. Lee. He looked up and said, "I don't think he feels well. He had a fibrillation this morning." I was shocked, and asked for an explanation. Dr. Lee said the president was OK, and that this sometimes happened due to variables in the medication. His heart had quickly returned to normal, so the president stayed with the day's plan. But when we reached Golden Gate Park in Brookville, Ohio, for a barbecue and noon political rally, the heat was reaching an unbearable 100 degrees. There was no wind, the grass was brown, and the dirt was loose and soft so it burned the soles of your shoes. A tent had been set up about 100 yards from the stage for the staff to use as a holding room. When we first arrived I went into the tent to talk to the president about the POW speech. He was talking to local politicians. He looked terrible, pale and tired. His handkerchief, a long monster he always carried in his back pocket, was hanging from his pants. His tie was undone and the sweat was rolling down his face. All this, and he hadn't even started to speak.

I asked the visitors to give us a few minutes to talk White House business. That was just a ruse to get the president a few minutes to collect himself. Dr. Lee asked how he felt and he said he was fine. But he didn't look it. I knew he was about to wade into a crowd of 5,000 people, in front of many cameras, and it would be at least an hour before he could escape. The only person who was with the president at every moment in a case like this was his photographer, David Valdez. Valdez had been looking at the president through his lens for years and was totally trusted by the Bush family. He knew every nuance of the president's face, eyes, and moods. I asked him if he noticed how the president looked. He said the president looked terrible, drained. I asked him to keep a particularly close eye on the president during his speech. "If you see anything funny—eye movement, limp arms, anything different, let me know and we'll get him off the stage."

Several times during the speech Valdez gave me a worried look, but he never said anything. As the president came off the stage, his executive assistant, Bill Farish, guided him through the crowd to the staff tent. The president's shirt was soaked, his eyes were sagging, and his voice was weak. He sat down on a metal folding chair, the only one in the tent, beside a folding wooden table, of the kind that had seen a thousand covered-dish dinners in church basements. He said nothing. I just looked at him and thought how sad it was that we drive our presidents to this, or that they drive themselves. This man was sick.

Fortunately, other events were unfolding. The Iraqi government had consistently refused to allow United Nations inspectors to enter facilities in Iraq that were suspected to hold information on weapons systems, including ballistic missiles. The president decided to cancel his weekend travel plans in order to review the situation at Camp David with his foreign policy team. I called a quick press conference in the press filing center for the pool, made the announcement, and took a few questions. It didn't last long, especially in the heat, and was over before the president finished his speech. But it had the effect of keeping the press busy enough that no one ever asked about the president's health.

I assumed that sooner or later a reporter would ask about the president's health, or he would have another, more serious, change of heartbeat. As it turned out, the president never had another incident that I knew about, but his body did slow down. The insane early morning runs were gone. Jogging became irregular and two miles instead of five. In addition, the old competitive juices that might have gotten the president into the 1992 campaign in the spring and summer seemed to have lost their edge. He desperately wanted to wait until after Labor Day to start the campaign. I think his body was a reluctant warrior.

Another key element of the deathwatch is attendance at presidential dinners, visits to the president's favorite restaurant—in George Bush's case, the Peking Gourmet in Arlington, Virginia—and sitting in vans for hours into the night as the president visits friends and relatives at their homes. I put all of these under the stakeout heading: waiting for the unexpected, like illness, or falling down, or saying something meaningful.

Foreign presidential trips were murder on the staff. We had to be up about three hours before the president to prepare for his events, and we had to stay up for a couple of hours after he went to bed, because that was the only time for planning and staff review. When the president was up, everybody was running. The one exception was a state dinner. The staff loved them because, for at least three hours, we knew where he was, what he was doing, and we knew he was trapped. It was very unlikely that a president would get sick and throw up on a prime minister.

On the president's visit to Japan in January 1992, everything was going wrong. Our new "joint chiefs of staff," Sam Skinner and Bob Teeter, had restructured the trip to fit domestic priorities: jobs through increased access to Japanese markets. This immediately made the trip contentious with the press because it had been politicized. It robbed the president of his strength: a foreign policy meeting that focused on world security. It also set objectives that could not be met: a significant change in Japanese market access. Worse, we decided to take along the chairmen of Ford, GM, and Chrysler to make the case for more U.S. auto sales. Unfortunately, their goals were different from ours. We wanted open markets and access. They wanted a percentage of the U.S. trade deficit with Japan earmarked for elimination, mostly through auto sales. Thus it seemed that the auto boys were less than supportive of the president. On top of all that, we were tired from a ten-day trip to South Korea, Singapore, and Australia before arriving in Japan.

As is customary, the first night in country was highlighted by a state dinner hosted by Japanese prime minister Kiichi Miyazawa at his residence. There is no more elegant and dignified setting in the world. No greater picture of discordance could be contrived than for a president to get sick in the Japanese premier's residence. Not even *Saturday Night Live* would try it.

In order to keep our press pool together in Japan, and to shorten the motorcade, we chartered a bus. When the president's motorcade pulled into the prime minister's residence and parked in front of the grand palace doors, the bus was moved to a nearby parking lot. Laura Melillo, the deputy press secretary accompanying the pool that evening, made a mental note of the location, nervous about getting the bus back into the motorcade at the end of the evening. Laura knew from experience that when a presidential motorcade starts to leave a site, the police are swarming. Everyone is a suspected threat, and it's hard to get near the motorcade, especially in a bus.

In addition, President Bush had a hang-up about motorcades. They seemed to represent all the waste and extravagance of government to him, and reminded him of the "elitist" charge so long thrown at him because of his wealthy upbringing in Greenwich, Connecticut. Sometimes when he was in a prankish mood, or we were attending a fat-cat fund-raiser by somebody's swimming pool, I would kid him about taking a limo to Greenwich Country Day School. He always fell in with the joke and poked fun at himself. But deep inside, I think it hurt him because of the implication that his success was not earned. In any case, he was always looking for ways to take cars out of the motorcade—eliminate the wire cars, take the communication people out, put all the staff in one van, all the press in one bus. In Japan, he got his wish.

The president and Mrs. Bush, accompanied by the prime minister and his wife, greeted each other, walked through the South

Vestibule to the Matsukaze Room for cocktails, then on to the Shakkyo Room for the receiving line.

Laura took the press pool to a holding room just off the vestibule near the entrance, within view of the motorcade. Next door was a room for Japanese press. Together, perhaps forty-five or fifty reporters began to settle in for a three-hour evening. But at about 7:15 P.M. Mary Tillotson, the CNN correspondent representing all television networks in the pool, rushed up to Laura. She said quietly, so as not to alarm the others, "One of the photographers shooting the receiving line says the president dropped out, that he looked sick."

"I'll check," Laura said.

This was the first alarm, as always, a tip from the press. Laura hurried to find the doctor or a Secret Service agent. By the time she cornered an agent who was authorized to talk—most of them will tell you nothing—the president and the prime minister were moving into the banquet hall for dinner. The agent said, "He's not feeling well, but he's in the dinner." In fact, the president had dropped out of the receiving line, was rushed into a nearby bathroom by his Secret Service protective detail, and on the way in started throwing up on himself. Dr. Lee was close by because the president had complained about flu symptoms even before leaving the Akasaka Palace, where he was staying. Dr. Lee examined him, warned the president that throwing up was the normal reaction to flu, and reminded him that most normal people stay home when they have the flu. The president protested and asked for a clean shirt, which one of the agents produced. Within minutes, he was back in the receiving line and heading into the banquet hall.

Laura didn't know at the time that the president had gotten sick. She returned to the holding room and told Mary Tillotson that she didn't know the exact condition of the president, but that "he is now in the banquet hall," and was clearly visible on Japanese television. HK Television of Japan had a lone camera set up on the balcony to record head-table toasts and speeches. Laura took an advance man and the still photographers to the balcony to check out the camera. She also wanted a chance to check out the president. He looked fine, at least from a great distance, and the HK people assured her that the balcony camera would not be manned during the entire dinner. Laura felt better about the Tillotson rumor after actually seeing the president. She returned to the pool, bringing them sandwiches and drinks from the kitchen.

As she was filling a plate with sushi and cucumber sandwiches, engines began to start up in the distance. White House press staff, so attuned to presidential movements and unscheduled departures, have a sixth sense about engines that suddenly start, about hallways that suddenly empty of Secret Service agents, about plainclothes policemen who materialize at unexpected times, and doctors and nurses spotted in unexpected places. We were never told, so we were always alert. Laura moved to the window and saw that the agents were moving the motorcade, turning it around for departure. Normally they would take a couple hours to do this. Laura's stomach started churning. She looked around. A medic was on the phone, apparently to a hospital. The constant traffic on her two-way radio went silent, and the radio admonition was given: "Keep communication to a minimum." That usually meant emergency.

Laura walked out of the room, then ran to the nearest agent.

"What's happening to the motorcade?" she asked. They only answer the precise question asked.

"We're preparing for departure," he said.

Laura remembered the press bus. She ran to the U.S. Information Agency employees from Japan who were helping with the press. "Get the bus in the motorcade," she ordered. "It's across the street."

The press, of course, were watching her every move. The press aide is always their barometer, usually their protector, and their only source of information. Michael Busch, who was assigned to the press pool in Panama some months later, actually commandeered the press bus in the middle of rioting, gunshots, and tear gas. He ordered it driven to the press area, rounded up lost reporters including Ann Devroy of the *Post*, and with a Panamanian driver led the entire group to safety. When Laura returned to the pool, Mary Tillotson and Michael Wines, of *The New York Times*, the print representative in the pool, wanted to know what was happening. Laura said she was trying to find out, and went to the staff room to get a "signal" phone.

One of the wonders of the presidency, and one of the costliest, most ridiculously unneeded aspects of the presidency, is the White House Communications Agency, a civilian name for the Army Signal Corps. At every place the president goes in the world, no matter what tree he climbs, a "signal" phone is there, specially wired and hooked up to a special "signal" operator stashed in a van or hotel room nearby. It's another relic of the cold war when everyone thought the president had to be minutes from the nuclear button. It sometimes took more than 1,000 White House Communications Agency people to "wire a city" for a presidential trip, at a cost of millions of dollars. But it could be handy. Laura rushed into the staff room, picked up the receiver, and asked for Marlin.

"We're keeping communications to a minimum," the signalman said.

"I don't care," Laura said, "get me Marlin Fitzwater."

I had skipped the dinner, asking Chief of Protocol Joseph Verner Reed to make some excuse. I was beat and figured I might fall asleep at the dinner. Instead, I went back to my room at the Okura Hotel, put on blue jeans and an Australian sweatshirt, and wandered down the hall to visit the first open door I could find. Mary Kate Grant, a speechwriter, was hosting one of those "sit on the floor, let it all hang out" bull sessions. I plopped down in a corner and began complaining about Lee Iacocca holding press conferences every ten minutes when someone came in and said I had a phone call. I considered not taking it, then got up and went next door to pick up a signal phone. Laura was shouting and gasping for breath.

"Settle down, Laura," I said. "What happened?"

Laura was racing through her words. She sounded in control, but on the verge. "The president is sick," she said. "They're taking him out."

"Have you seen him or talked to the doctors?"

"No," she said, "but they're moving the motorcade. And I just saw them take a gurney in."

At that moment, Deputy Chief of Staff Andy Card, the highest-ranking staff person on the trip, rushed up to Laura and shouted, "I need Marlin!" Andy was anticipating the press and public confusion.

"He's right here," Laura said.

"No. I need Marlin," Andy said, not believing that I could be on the phone at that very moment.

"Here, talk to him," Laura said, and handed Andy the phone.

"Marlin," Andy said, "the president's sick. We're going back to the residence or the hospital."

"Which is it?" I asked.

"I don't know," Andy said. "The doctors are with him now."

"Andy," I exclaimed, "call me from wherever you go! And get to a doctor!" I wanted Andy to get me a medical explanation in case I couldn't.

Laura came back on. "We're leaving," she said.

"I'm going to the filing center," I said. "All communications will come from here. Call me." The press filing center was in the basement of the Okura Hotel.

Laura hung up and ran back to the pool. The gurney was moving into the banquet hall and many of the press saw it. Reporters were grabbing cameras and rushing into the hall. The Japanese press were tumbling out of their room, pushing and shoving everyone. The U.S. press was doing the same. Japanese police were moving down the hallway, ordering everyone back. None of them spoke English. The U.S. press ignored them. The U.S. press in these situations always has an "I dare you to shoot me, fella" attitude. Photographers were hanging out the windows filming the motorcade, with engines running and staff or agents standing by every car. Win McNamee, a photographer for Reuters, got in a fistfight with a Japanese photographer. Laura grabbed him around the waist and started shouting, "Please remain calm!" The CNN camera began shooting her shouting. Laura yelled at Tillotson, "Turn off those lights!" Tillotson refused. Laura broke away from reporters and ran to find Andy Card. Bedlam was rampant. Only those with presidential staff pins were moving. Japanese police were pushing people against the wall.

"Andy," she said, "the press are going crazy. They saw the gurney. Have the president walk out if he can. If he's on the stretcher, that will be the picture." Of course, Laura didn't know that the HK balcony camera, running silently without attendance by crew, had already filmed the president of the United States throwing up in the lap of the Japanese prime minister. The film showed the president's head slowly collapse onto the prime minister's shoulder, his face turn as he got sick, then his body slide slowly to the floor. Mrs. Bush and Dr. Lee were beside him instantly on the floor. The president was unconscious. Dr. Lee, of course, knew exactly what the problem was: flu. He had already diagnosed it twice that night. He loosened the president's tie. A nurse mentioned his belt. There is no belt on tuxedo pants, so Dr. Lee unsnapped the president's pants and began to unzip the fly.

At that point, the president flickered an eyelid, raised his head to look down at his body, and exclaimed, "Burt, what the hell are you doing?" Both Burt—Dr. Lee—and Mrs. Bush laughed because they knew those words meant the president was all right. Mrs. Bush, showing the incredible poise which she always had, got up from the president's side, went back to the table, and helped clean up the prime minister.

Laura turned to an agent. "How's he coming out?" she asked.

"He's OK to walk," the agent said.

A pathway had been formed out of the banquet hall, with police holding people back on both sides and photographers shooting over their heads, through heads, and blindly just by holding their cameras up at arm's length and clicking.

The president emerged wearing an agent's raincoat to cover his stained tuxedo. He was pale, with hair mussed and matted over his forehead. He looked dewy, clammy, and white. Andy Card and the medic were walking with him. Laura was enormously relieved when she saw them put the president in his limo. That probably meant no hospital.

Laura turned to get the press into their bus. The police had them bottled up in a hallway. She grabbed the Secret Service agent assigned to help her, and together they convinced the police to make a hole in the crowd for the press. Once on the bus, the pool demanded to know where they were going.

"We're in the motorcade," Laura said. "We'll go wherever the president goes. Marlin is going to the filing center. He will release all information on the president's condition from there." Just then her radio traffic announced, "We're going to the Akasaka Palace." That certainly meant no hospital, and probably no serious illness. It also meant that security and press control could be maintained. This was the best news.

My other deputies, Roman Popadiuk, Judy Smith, Gary Foster, and Sean Walsh, were having a restaurant dinner as guests of the Kyodo News Service of Tokyo. Kyodo covers the White House in Washington, has a permanent bureau there, and Fumio Matueo, its chief correspondent, was a good friend of our staff. Roman was sitting on the floor, Japanese-style, when his pager went off. The message read: "POTUS BARFED IN DINNER." Roman returned to the table when a second pager went off, "POTUS LEAVING." Roman and Judy left immediately for the Okura Hotel filing center.

I had changed into a suit and tie, and ran down the hallway and through the basement to the press filing center. Press were beginning to stream in. My staff was gathering. I ordered the door to my office closed so I could talk on the phone, and told Sean to get ready for a live, on-camera press briefing as soon as I could get the facts. My first responsibility was to let the world know the president's condition, especially the people of America.

Roman came in with the prime minister's press secretary, Koji

Watanabe, who was very apologetic. He reported that HK television had filmed, unbeknownst to U.S. or Japanese authorities, the entire illness sequence. He said they might be able to suppress it if they tried. He asked if I wanted it suppressed.

I glanced at Roman and said no. "Do you agree, Roman?" I asked, just to see how my case sounded. "First of all, I don't believe they can suppress television film. It probably already has been fed to a hundred stations and electronically all over the world. Second, I don't want to be charged with covering this up. Our task is to be so open that people will believe us when we say he just has the flu. And that won't be easy."

"I agree," Roman said. I thanked Watanabe, who was very kind and considerate through the entire affair. Laura Parham, an assistant press secretary, rushed in to say that Andy Card and Dr. Lee were on the line.

Dr. Lee went through all the symptoms and his diagnosis. It was common, old, everyday flu. The president knew he was sick before he left for dinner, but felt he could make it. He didn't want to be discourteous to Prime Minister Miyazawa by canceling. His vital signs were normal. I took down all the vital statistics and every other tidbit I could get. My credibility was at stake and I wanted to be sure something wasn't being hidden. I hadn't been told before the dinner that the president was sick, so I was a little worried about being told everything now.

I hung up and started to write my statement in longhand. As a question would come up on some fact or time, Roman was dispatched to find the answer. Just as I was finishing, I glanced up at the TV set running CNN silently in the corner of my office. It showed the head table at the dinner. The entire sequence was played, from beginning to end. Then it was played again, just in case anybody missed the picture and the symbolism of an incredibly helpless American president sinking under the Japanese banquet table. "Jes-o-pete," I said to Roman, "that is powerful stuff."

I called Dr. Lee back. "Have you seen this film?" I asked. "Nobody is going to believe this flu business. The president looks like he's dying. What's his condition now?"

"He's sleeping," Dr. Lee said.

"Burt," I said, "we have got to be absolutely accurate here. Everyone will second-guess us. Medical history books will be looking at everything you did. This is a political year. The Democrats will say we're hiding an illness. And that goddamn film says something is worse than the flu."

"No it's not, Marlin," Burt said. He was very calm. "It's the standard garden-variety flu. And passing out is completely normal if you exert yourself while you're sick."

"You mean," I said, "that any normal person would have gone to bed, and because he didn't he got sick and passed out? That is normal?"

"Yes," Burt said.

I began the on-camera briefing at 9:17 P.M., less than one hour after the president had gotten sick. I figured we would have at least two briefings on this matter, so the first one should present a serious posture, if only out of deference to our hosts. The second one, probably the next morning, should be smiling and a little lighter to show the problem was past. My first words would be the most important. I wanted to say three things: The president is safe, he has the flu, and he's in his suite—the last point being the most symbolic, totally verifiable, and therefore the most important. Common sense would tell people that if the president was really sick, he would be in the hospital.

"President Bush is in his suite at the Akasaka Palace and is feeling fine, following a bout with the flu," I said. "The president's personal physician, Dr. Burton Lee, said the president is in good shape and probably will feel OK tomorrow."

The first question from Terry Hunt of AP went directly to the old cold war bugaboo about the nuclear button. "Did he ever lose consciousness?" Terry asked.

I wasn't sure and hadn't directly asked the doctor, but I suspected he was unconscious because Dr. Lee told me the story about the president raising up when his pants were unzipped. I fudged. "He was in what we might call a faint condition, in the sense that he slumped over at the table, was conscious, and was helped to the floor by the leader of his Secret Service detail," I said. The key phrase was "what we might call." The White House press, accustomed to my dodges and weaves, knew that this meant I didn't know for sure, I wasn't going to say he was unconscious, and they might want to use the word "faint." It was a classic case of that understanding that builds between a press secretary and the press corps that makes the whole thing work, that gets out the most information in the most honest way without forcing either side to extremes. But both sides have to trust each other. In this case, the press read me perfectly.

The next hurdle would be the next morning. A joint press conference with the president and the prime minister was scheduled for

10 A.M. I called Andy Card, who was staying at the Akasaka Palace with the president, to ask if the president would appear. He asked me to come over early. When I arrived at about 7:30 A.M. at the centuries-old palace in the middle of Tokyo, the sun was shining on the last dew of the morning. It was clear as a bird's chirp in the formal gardens behind the palace, and the floor-to-ceiling windows were open, with sheer silk curtains blowing into the guest bedroom across the staircase from the president. Andy was having breakfast in his room, which stretched for thirty yards across the palace grounds. It had twenty-foot ceilings, gold-leaf trim around the windows and ceiling, gold chandeliers, canopied bed, tufted brocade chairs, and a breakfast table piled high with toast and jellies. The walls were cream and elaborately gilded with urns, birds, and flowers. There was a lilac brocade chaise and small sitting area by a gray marble fireplace with peach-covered easy chairs. A three-foot-high bouquet of silk flowers were beside the bed, and your nose had to touch the petals before you realized they weren't real.

I ordered eggs and bacon to go with the toast and sat down. "How's the president?" I asked.

"He's OK," Andy said, "but he doesn't look good."

"Is everything on the up-and-up, Andy?" I asked. "Is it really just flu? No heart problem? No complications?"

"No, I don't think so," Andy said. "He never should have gone to that dinner. But you can't stop a president from something like that if he's determined to go."

"How is he this morning?" I asked.

"He's sleeping," Andy said.

We finished breakfast. If there is one room in the world I would like to visit again, it's this one. Easily the most beautiful, comfortable, and functional I have ever seen. After eating, I walked around the room, sat in every chair, and plopped down on the bed. Matchless. But time was passing and we still had no word on the president.

I had drafted an opening statement for the president from a basic text supplied by the National Security Council staff. General Scowcroft arrived, had some toast, and approved the statement. At 9:45 A.M., just fifteen minutes before the press conference was to begin downstairs, I suggested we go see the president to go over details. I also wanted to make sure he was up and going through with it.

As we walked into the president's bedroom, Dr. Lee was sitting quietly at a table, reading. The room was long, and so big that I had to momentarily glance around to find his bed. When I did, I was horrified. He was lying flat on his back, hands at his sides under the sheets and covers, with eyes closed and his face so white it blended with the sheets. He looked dead.

I walked toward him and asked, "How do you feel, Mr. President?" I didn't worry about waking him up because we only had ten minutes till show time and I had to know his status. He said nothing. I walked close to the bed and stared. He slowly turned his head toward me and said, "Good morning, Marlin, are you ready?"

"Yes, sir," I said, "whenever you are. Do you want to do this?"

"Yes," he said, and kicked one leg out from under the covers. I couldn't see how he could get dressed and organized in ten minutes, but I was too nervous to hang around and watch.

"I'm going on down, Mr. President," I said, "to make sure everything is OK. Brent wants to talk about a few things while you get dressed. I'll meet you downstairs."

By the time I left the room, the president was putting on his shirt and socks. He was the fastest dresser in the world, but to do it while recovering from the flu was a special challenge. Nevertheless, at exactly 10 A.M. the president and General Scowcroft walked into the holding room to greet the prime minister.

The president looked terrible, and so alone. Indeed, he was. Sununu was gone. The new chief of staff, Sam Skinner, had stayed home to get organized. Secretary of State Baker was occupied elsewhere in the world. When the president walked into the press conference, even the press was stunned, first by his appearance, then by the mere fact that he carried it off, answering their questions with the strength and knowledge that he always showed. But it was the beginning of the end. The illness was only a symbol of our poor planning and misjudgments in trying to make political hay out of the trip. For those of us around the president, it was plain that something had gone terribly wrong, and that the judgment of our new campaign team was open to question. But it was worse for the president, because it was on that trip that he lost confidence in the judgment of his new team, and he would never regain it.

CHAPTER THIRTEEN

First Ladies of the Press

The White House press corps—about seventy people on a daily basis—is a diverse lot. According to legend, there have always been women in the White House press corps. In fact, in the library of the National Press Club, Washington's premier press fraternity, you can read about one such female journalist, so intent on covering a story that she followed President John Quincy Adams down to the Potomac one summer afternoon, hid while he disrobed and waded into the river for a swim, then sat on his clothes and refused to budge until he gave her a satisfactory answer to her question. Having been on the receiving end of years of coy cajoles, shrill harangues, and vigilant interrogations from the legendary women of the White House press corps, I have no doubt the story is true.

Certainly, any American who has ever tuned in to the evening news or watched a presidential press conference in the past ten years has seen these women in action. You probably can recognize some of the bigger names—Andrea Mitchell, Lesley Stahl, Cokie Roberts, Helen Thomas—vying for camera time and giving presidents, cabinet members, and press secretaries constant headaches, indigestion, and gray hair. In addition to these perfectly coifed, designer-clad, camera-friendly celebrities, however, there exists a group of women reporters of an earlier vintage, who are not as well known but are just as dogged in their determination to press the president. In some ways they are the most persevering reporters of the lot. They know all the tricks of the trade, have mastered the vulnerabilities of the White House staff, and know how to manipulate the power structure of Washington in ways seasoned mainstream reporters never dreamed of. They are over sixty years old, report for newsletters or publications so obscure no one knows them, often carry Instamatic cameras, and seldom ask questions that the television networks give a hoot about. But at a recent televised press conference by President Clinton, the last three questioners were pillars of the "First Ladies' Club": Sarah McClendon of the McClendon News Service, Evelyn Y. Davis of *Highlights and Lowlights*, and Trude B. Feldman a freelancer for various publications.

The dean of the group is Sarah McClendon. This eighty-four-year-old with sparkling blue eyes, a mischievous smile, and an East Texas drawl, approaches press conferences with the singleness of purpose of a pit bull. A short woman, now hunched with age, she sits in the second-to-last row of the White House pressroom, almost hidden (save for a tuft of fuzzy, red hair) by rows of reporters' heads in front of her, until she decides to strike. When she does, she rises slowly from her seat, often with the aid of a cane, and begins barking her questions to the podium. And woe to the poor president or press secretary behind the podium if he isn't prepared.

Sarah once rose to ask me about a Pennsylvania company she said was being investigated for selling equipment later found to be in the hands of Saddam Hussein in Iraq. Sarah always had some obscure case in which the government had screwed up, or was insensitive, or had wasted taxpayer money. No one else in the press corps cared about these stories, and I usually tried to give a general answer and move on.

In this case, I had no idea what she was talking about but said I would look into it. The next week she came back and asked if I had any new information. I didn't. So she lectured me on the government's role in letting these capitalist swine help the enemy. I listened patiently, said I would look into it, and moved on.

Another week passed and Sarah came back at me. I went through the same song and dance again, but it was starting to get irritating. Also, some of the big-name reporters, who cared not a whit about the subject, were beginning to wonder why I couldn't come up with a reasonable answer. After the briefing that day, I asked my staff: "Do you suppose Sarah is on to something? What the hell is it with this company?"

Navy Commander Bill Harlow had been assigned to my staff to help explain military affairs, so I asked him to look into it. He came back in a few days to say that indeed, this company was under investigation, but because of grand jury rules I couldn't discuss the case. I was pleased. Now I could give Sarah an answer and look responsive. I could even praise her in front of her colleagues, always a good move. And I could use the grand jury rules to keep from saying any more about it. When Sarah came back at me the next week, I gave her the full spiel.

Unfortunately, within an hour after the briefing I was told I had violated a grand jury rule by even acknowledging the investigation. "Holy cow!" I thought, "I'm going to go to jail because of Sarah Mc-Clendon." The company in question was really angry, calling my office to complain that their stock had tumbled due to some earlier story, and my new statement would certainly cause another nose-dive. "Holy cow again!" I thought. "Now I've put a company out of business because of Sarah McClendon." It turned out, thankfully, that the company's stock went up three points the day of my answer to Sarah. But the whole episode was another reminder to always take the "First Ladies" seriously.

Sarah wasn't always so bold. In fact, when she first earned a White House press pass in 1944 and began covering the Roosevelt administration for *The Philadelphia Daily News*, she was terrified to ask questions. Aside from being painfully shy, she was often wit-ness to FDR's wrath. An angry Roosevelt often poked fun at the fourth estate, once forcing a particularly antagonistic reporter to stand in the corner of the Oval Office with a dunce cap on. Working conditions were different then. There was no press briefing room. When President Roosevelt decided he had something to say, the handful of reporters who made up the White House press corps were called into the Oval Office, and as FDR pontificated, they furiously scribbled their notes, using each others' backs as makeshift writing desks.

Sarah finally found the guts to ask her first question during a news conference held by President Eisenhower. By that time, the haphazard press conference format practiced by Roosevelt had been changed to a more orderly and controlled venue, held in the Indian Treaty Room of the Old Executive Office Building. The Indian Treaty Room is a drafty, highly ornamented two-story room, with marble floors, gilded moldings, and lousy acoustics. At this particu-lar press conference, Sarah arrived late and was relegated to the bal-cony, where protocol dictated that no one ask questions. After only a few minutes of remarks, Eisenhower prepared to leave. Sarah real-ized that in order to hold her own with the big boys, she had to take a chance. So, in a voice she prayed was loud enough to be heard, she asked:

"Mr. President, is this going to be the format for all of your press conferences, or are we going to be allowed to ask questions?"

All the male heads in the room turned around and the president squinted to see where this female voice was coming from. It worked. Sarah was on her way to making a name for herself.

As one of only five women correspondents in Washington at the time, she constantly challenged the predominantly male press establishment. She first applied to become a member of the male-only National Press Club in 1955. Although her application wasn't even acknowledged, she didn't give up. And when women were finally admitted as members in 1971, she was one of the first.

Sarah's modus operandi has always been to try to cut through the fog of governmental rhetoric and find answers to the questions small-town America cares about. Thus her questions are usually very specific and often very obscure. Even though some members of the press corps refuse to take her seriously, rolling their eyes and groaning out loud when she begins one of her rambling diatribes, I learned not to make that mistake, and so did President Bush. To prepare for the briefing sessions prior to a presidential news conference, I'd have everyone on my staff try to predict what the "Sarah Mc-Clendon" question would be. Sometimes this strategy worked, sometimes it didn't. She always managed to get under President Bush's skin. He liked her personally, appreciated her Texas ties and long association with *The El Paso Times*, and was deferential to her because of her age. But when she was ready to ask a question of the president, she was ready. If the president called on someone else, she started screaming her question. One day the president said, "Sarah, I won't take your question until you sit down and ask it in a dignified manner."

"You won't answer my question if I ask it in a dignified manner, Mr. President," she said.

"I'm not going to answer it now," the president said.

"Well, I'm going to keep on asking it," she said.

Soon the entire press corps, including me, was upset because all this valuable television time was being wasted, and some reporters began muttering: "Just answer her question, Mr. President." He did, but he didn't like it. Sarah had beat another president into submission.

Another "First Lady" with a White House press pass who, like Sarah McClendon, admits to overcoming shyness, is Evelyn Y. Davis. This

sixty-five-year-old with an elfin grin, a shock of red hair, and an an-
noying voice strikes terror in the hearts of corporate chief executive
officers all across America.

Evelyn earned her entrée to the White House in 1976 after developing a rather infamous reputation with the creation, twelve years
earlier, of *Highlights and Lowlights*, a newsletter to which only
CEOs can subscribe and which seems to be corporate America's answer to *The Hollywood Reporter*. Published out of her office in the
tony Watergate Office Building (she lives next door in the equally
swank Watergate Apartments), the newsletter is a combination gossip column, social calendar, and corporate commentary that uses
more exclamation points than a teenage girl's diary. Fortune 500
CEOs subscribe to *Highlights and Lowlights* at a cost of $290 per
copy and begrudgingly listen to Evelyn. Many will admit that it may
not help business to listen to this self-proclaimed "corporate gad-
fly," but it certainly can hurt business if they don't.

Evelyn Y. Davis—she admits the *Y* doesn't stand for anything—
grew up in Holland, as she says, "on the wrong side of the ocean but
the right side of the tracks." She had one brother, with whom she
was constantly competing for her father's attention. As a teenager,
she decided she wanted to be a player in the male-dominated corporate world, and she constantly pushed herself to make her father
proud. She emigrated to the United States after World War II and
landed in Washington, where she studied business administration at
George Washington University. With seed money from some secu-
rities left her by her father and, later, settlements from two divorces,
she started investing in the stock market.

Now Evelyn is a millionaire with holdings in about 120 blue-chip
companies, including American Express, General Motors, USAir,
and Procter & Gamble. "My stocks are my children," she says
proudly, and she takes great pains to carefully watch over her brood.

Many CEOs would characterize Evelyn as more of a meddling
mother, however. She attends around sixty annual stockholders'
meetings per year. She's certainly overcome the trepidation she felt
when she first stood at the microphone, shaking like a leaf, to ask a
question at an IBM shareholders' meeting. Now Evelyn is drawn to
those microphones like a bee to honey. Her long ramblings
prompted Citicorp to limit shareholder questions to three minutes.
She loves the spotlight. She once gave Lee Iacocca diet advice. She
once gave May Department Stores Company chairman David C. Far-
rell a $1,600 check and warned, "David, please make sure your man

is on time when he comes to hang my drapes. I'm a busy woman."
At the White House, after being snubbed by NBC White House correspondent Andrea Mitchell, Evelyn phoned General Electric CEO
Jack Welch to complain. She boasts that relations with Andrea were
much improved after the phone call.

Luckily for me, I was not a corporate CEO. My dealings with Evelyn were much less confrontational. At press conferences where the
rest of the pack of White House correspondents asked question after
question on the hot topic of the day, Evelyn always kept her questions on the subject she knew best—American business. And every
question to the president was designed to do one thing: promote herself.

In 1994 she bought a Chrysler Cirrus and turned it into a promo-
tional dream. She went to the presidents of Ford, Chrysler, and General Motors to announce that she was going to buy a car. Each
company gave her a special presentation on the model she wanted.
She got that in the papers. Then she picked Chrysler and got that in
the papers. Then she got the president of Chrysler to personally deliver the car to her Watergate apartment, which she got on TV. How
did she do this? By calling every carmaker, reporter, and flack in
Washington—probably at seven in the morning—and promoting her
moves. People give her what she wants just to get rid of her. Evelyn
knows the power of persistence.

I didn't really learn the secret of her success until she discovered
that I might mention her in this book. Suddenly, she was calling
every day to promote some new exploit about herself. She would
often call at about 7 A.M.

"Evelyn," I would say, "I'm asleep. Call me later."

She would keep on talking.

"Evelyn, I'll call you back later."

She would keep on talking.

"Evelyn, I'm going to hang up," I would say.

"No you're not," she said, and kept on talking. I could only imagine the corporate executives and government officials who had been
getting this wake-up call for years.

The story of Trude B. Feldman in the White House is beyond belief.
We know very little about her. She won't say her age, her hometown,
where she went to school, or anything specific about her family. She
tells us only what she needs for leverage. She disclosed that her
brother is a rabbi. Sometimes she claims special relationships that

don't always check out. Anyone Jewish may be claimed as a relative
if it suits her objectives. For years she told me that Max Kampleman,
the chief U.S. arms-control negotiator, was her cousin and "he
wanted her to have an interview with the president." Finally, I called
Kampleman and he said Trude had been using that scam for years to
get interviews. No relation at all.

She continually asked me for special information on Israel, saying that a state department official had told her she could have it.
One day I asked him why he granted her special access. He was surprised. He said he only talked to her because she claimed the White
House referred her to him.

Trude must be sixty-five, and continually claims ailments, but
she scampers around the White House like a church mouse, unwanted but so familiar that no one bothers to deal with her. In those
days she lived in a three-room apartment a couple of blocks from the
White House. The rest of the time, from nine in the morning until
the press office closes at 10:30 P.M., and on weekends she lived in the
basement of the press briefing room.

The basement houses the radio networks with their small sound
booths, the CNN booth (constructed there because there was no
room upstairs), and a few reporters' desks. In the back corner, behind
a stack of newspapers literally four feet high that covers her desk
and the one next to it, sits Trude. Every three months we sent the
trashmen to her desk to throw away all the papers. It's a fire hazard.
She would scream that we were trying to force her out of the
White House, collect a half dozen more papers until she felt comfortable, and then wait three more months for the process to be
repeated.

Trude has perfected her coverage of the White House based on
one simple principle: No one wants to be rude to an old lady. So she
works her way through the president's staff, calling them at home
for information, asking for personal favors such as rides, and, most
importantly, beseeching them to help her secure an interview with
the president. Because she works the State, Treasury, and Defense
Departments at the same time, there is always a network of fifteen
to thirty federal officials secretly tied together by one incredible underground telephone system manned by Trude.

The biggest mystery of Trude is how she gets people's telephone
numbers. Being unlisted means nothing to her. She talked regularly

with General Scowcroft, John Sununu, Andy Card, Bud McFarlane, John Poindexter—virtually anybody she wanted. Many people considered her behavior erratic, and were not eager to be in contact with her. She started many telephone conversations with claims of persecution and harassment by someone.

"Marlin," she would say, "why won't the president give me an interview? I know Sununu hates me because I'm Jewish. But I never did anything to him. It's your staff who hates me. They won't let me in any of the pools and I know Bar doesn't want that."

"OK Trude, what do you want me to do?" I asked.

"Tell the president that his Jewish friends are not his friends," she said. "They don't care about the president. They just care about themselves. I know King Hussein will want to see me when he comes. Why won't you let me go to his state dinner? It's that Anna Perez on Mrs. Bush's staff. She won't let me in anything. Marlin, you said I could be in every pool."

It soon became clear that the only way to survive this telephone torture was to hang up. But it's very hard to hang up on a short, pleading little old lady in a print floral dress, who keeps saying, "Please help me. Please help me." Sometimes, walking through the White House, I could just barely see her forehead peeking from behind a marble column. She would quickly draw back at my approach. If I questioned how she got in this strange location, she would simply turn and walk away.

She was a notorious reception crasher. All the embassies and trade associations in Washington were on the lookout for her at their parties, but as happened in the White House, it was easier to let her in than cause a confrontation. Some mornings I would find cookies or pieces of cake left on my desk with a note from Trude. I never knew how she got access in the middle of the night. But I worried that going to receptions around town was her only way to get food. I asked her about where she ate and did she cook, but it only made her angry. The most frustrating aspect of our relationship was simply that there didn't seem to be any way to help her, at least any way that she would tolerate.

In my tenure at the White House, two high-level staff meetings were called by Chiefs of Staff Howard Baker and John Sununu to decide what to do about Trude. Both sessions were motivated by true concern for Trude's welfare. Because of her clandestine life, most people didn't know where or how she lived. We had all heard stories of her stumbling through snowstorms at ten o'clock at night, and we had all seen her latching on to guests at presidential events begging for rides home.

General Scowcroft, President Bush's national security adviser, is the sweetest, kindest, most caring and considerate gentleman you can imagine. Trude zeroed in on him with unerring instincts for the perfect foil. She called him, shouted at him in the Rose Garden, and wrote him notes begging for invitations, interviews, and rides home at night. But she miscalculated in one respect: Where others had eventually slammed down the phone and told her never to call again, General Scowcroft actually cared enough to inquire about permanent help. He asked that the White House think of some way to help her. But at the staff meeting, no one could produce a course of action that she would accept, or that we could enforce, or that hadn't been tried before, so nothing changed.

We wanted to call her family, but she wouldn't tell us how, and no one seemed to know them. Once she left the White House for six months and went to California. She didn't tell us what she planned to do out there. But when she returned she would acknowledge nothing. She seemed calmer, but after a few weeks she was back to her old self.

At the end of the Reagan administration, so many cabinet officers and senior officials had complained about Trude that the president's physician became concerned. We informally agreed that Trude should not be allowed in the Oval Office, at least not in an interview setting where she would be alone with the president. She was just too unpredictable and still claimed everyone was after her. But when she realized the exclusion, she became more contentious than ever.

When President Reagan awarded the Medal of Freedom to former first lady Mrs. Lyndon Baines Johnson, Trude demanded to attend the ceremony as a guest, claiming she had covered the White House in the 1960s and was a personal friend of Lady Bird. We declined, but we let her in the special press pool to cover the event. After ceremonies in the East Room, President and Mrs. Reagan and Mrs. Johnson moved to the main foyer for a receiving line.

Trude, seeing her opportunity to greet Mrs. Johnson, ran across the East Room, through a back door in the Green Room, and was moving toward the Grand Foyer and the receiving line. Mark Weinberg of my staff saw what she was doing and moved to cut her off in the Green Room. When Trude saw Mark she tried to make a downfield fake and slipped on the marble floor, falling on her hip. Everyone gasped and moved away from her. The president's physician, Colonel John Hutton of the U.S. Army, was called. He asked to examine her and she agreed.

About two hours later Dr. Hutton appeared in my office.

"Trude won't leave," he said. "What can I do?"

"What do you mean?" I asked. "Where is she?"

"She's in my office," he said. "I examined her. She has a bruised hip. She claims to be in great pain. I told her I wanted to call an ambulance and have her taken to the hospital for X rays. She refused. I told her I couldn't let her leave without signing a release form, but I think she should have X rays. Now she says she won't leave and she won't sign anything."

"You mean," I said, "that she just wants to stay there, to sleep there."

"I guess so," he said.

I recommended we go to Helen Thomas. Helen was a tough reporter, but she had a kind heart and cared about people personally. She had known Trude for years, and I hoped that as a woman she could talk sense to her. She agreed, but when we started for Dr. Hutton's office, he called to say Trude had gone. "She just picked up her coat and walked out into the night," he said.

The most remarkable aspect of Trude was that she could write, smoothly and well, and she got published. Several Jewish publications, such as the *St. Louis Jewish Light*, carried her stories. She also wrote feature stories about the first family and sold them to the *Indianapolis Star*, the *Detroit Free Press*, the *Midland Reporter-Telegram*, and *McCall's* magazine. It was hard to believe that the same person who scrawled illegible handwritten notes to the president on the back of already-used typing paper could also write such stories. President Bush's files include dozens of notes from Trude, few of them with a complete sentence or a coherent train of thought, and most written in her distinctive longhand with great looping letters, like some threatening note from a suspected villain. Yet the published stories were superb, and they always praised the president. This final point, by the way, will cloud the judgment of any president.

The archives of presidential history must record the astonishing fact that both President Reagan and President Bush, on their last full day in office, January 19 of their terms, granted the last media interview of their presidencies to Trude B. Feldman.

Naomi Nover, about four feet eleven inches short and uncomfortably overweight, trudged up the White House driveway every day to attend the briefing. She moved slowly and not all her joints bent. But they had been climbing off of presidential buses and airplanes for many years. Sometimes she stoped about halfway down the driveway to rest and, setting her bag on the asphalt and bending only at the waist, searched for a Kleenex. The ever-present bag at the end of her arm moved like the pendulum of a clock, just inches off the ground. It was canvas, usually embossed with the name of the corporate donor, "Delta Airlines" or "Singapore—See Its Beauty."

There was a timeless quality about Naomi, not because she covered so many presidents, but because she had been a bookmark for all the rest of us who paraded through the White House. Sam Donaldson used to tease her unmercifully. Photographers would sometimes give her false directions to the motorcade. Whether she was driven to it, or came by it naturally, I cannot say, but she was also mean. She would scream at our press staff about some perceived slight, accusing the young women of imagined abuses, often reducing them to tears.

For years she carried a Brownie Instamatic camera, slung around her neck, resting on an enormous chest that started the downward flow of her body. She would stand on the tarmac of an exotic airport in, say, Istanbul, holding her bag in one hand and snapping away with the other. Then she would stand perfectly still, looking around for the press bus, and wait for someone to give her directions. We always assigned one staff person to keep an eye on her and help if necessary. It's not cheap to travel with the presidential party, and most news organizations complain incessantly about the costs. Not Naomi. She paid cash, in advance.

Naomi stories abound from years of presidential travel, and they tie journalists together like military campaigns. "Do you remember Naomi on the Philippines trip?" That's the one where she fell down in a rice paddy. "Do you remember Naomi when the press bus caught on fire?" That's the one where she got stuck between the seats and couldn't get out.

Or, the most famous of all, "Do you remember Naomi in China?" Everyone remembers. Gary Shuster, six feet six inches of irreverence, wrote for *The Detroit News* when President Reagan went to visit the terra-cotta statues of Chinese warriors unearthed near Xian, China. The president was invited by his hosts to climb down into the excavation for a closer look at the row upon row of pre-served statues. When Naomi started to enter the excavation, she was stopped by the guards, as were all of the press corps. Only the presi-dent was allowed. Gary Shuster, watching Naomi's attempt to get a closer picture, approached the guards. He took a dollar bill from his wallet and said, pointing to the picture of George Washington and then to Naomi, "She is very important in our country." The guard looked at the portrait on the dollar bill, then at Naomi, and ushered her into the excavation.

There was also a great sadness about Naomi and how the press related to her. She represented the halcyon years of journalism, those decades after the war when modern journalism was established and Barnet Nover, Naomi's deceased husband, was one of the premier journalists in the country. A Pulitzer Prize winner, Barnet was *The Denver Post*'s Washington bureau chief for twenty-five years. Naomi was always with him.

In 1988 Naomi gave the White House press corps a refrigerator in memory of Barnet. It was ceremoniously moved into the back of the White House briefing room, and was immediately filled with turkey sandwiches, soft drinks, and assorted processed foods. Naomi watched the refrigerator grow into disrepair over the years, until the door wouldn't quite close and rust had developed on the trays. It sad-dened her greatly, because to her it was a shrine, as surely as if a ten-foot statue of Barnet Nover stood on the site. Soon she became offended whenever someone slammed the door, or left an open bot-tle of ketchup to accidentally fall out. Finally the refrigerator was re-moved, and Naomi seemed older and more distant than ever. In 1995 she died in the hallway of the Dirksen Senate Office Building, still carrying her bag and her camera, on the job.

Finally, a love story. She appeared in my mind like an old tintype photograph of a Civil War sweetheart, fuzzy and out of focus, out of date in her period costumes, and as beautiful as only a memory can be. She called out to me over the years in the strangest places, when I was searching for the perfect wife, or mourning the death of my mother, or admiring a woman of great achievement and sensitivity. Her voice was clear, demanding, and loving. Yet as intimate as my feelings were for this extraordinary woman, she was not mine alone.

Indeed, every boy who grew up in the 1960s knew the voice and smile of Timmy's mother, June Lockhart. Lassie and Timmy were just television characters for me. But not Timmy's mother. I waited at the beginning of every show for her to emerge from that dilapidated farmhouse, wearing a crisp dress and apron, let the screen door slam behind her, and call for Lassie to come home. I dreamed of what she must be like off the set, getting into her car, driving home, living in the only settings I could imagine from my limited life. It was a strong image that survived many years of diversions.

Then, one day in 1987, my secretary, Natalie Wozniak, meekly stuck her head into my office to ask, "Do you know June Lockhart?"

"June Lockhart!" I exclaimed. "The movie star? Timmy's mother?"

"Yes," Natalie said. "She just called and wants to come to your briefing."

"Why?" I said. "Are you sure it's the movie star? She must be close to sixty by now."

"She says she's in town for a play and would like to meet you," Natalie said.

"No kidding?" I shouted. "Of course. I love her. I want to meet her before the briefing."

As I look back on that morning, it stands alone in the pantheon of great meetings that the White House affords its tenants. Movie stars and world leaders walk into your office as casually as your children. They appear for only a few minutes, yet leave a lasting picture in your mind. Reggie "Mr. October" Jackson, striding up to my desk, tossing me a baseball, and talking about Washington as if we had just spent the evening drinking together . . . Mother Teresa, so slight and frail, moving across the Oval Office to take a seat on the president's couch. Such a diminutive figure, you expected a weak voice, yet she spoke with no pleasantries or wasted breath: "I'm here to get $40 million from the U.S. government," she said sternly. The president and I sat up in our chairs like scolded schoolchildren . . . Greeting the Pope in the Vatican and feeling his large farmer hands, like my father's, touch me with a softness reserved only for angels . . . Following the queen of England into Buckingham Palace for lunch and thinking it wasn't really much different from visiting a very nice lady in Abilene. There was a very simple kindness about her that I had not expected . . . Walking into the West Lobby and hearing Ted Williams, perhaps the greatest baseball player of all time, shout across the room, "Fitzwater! There's Fitzwater! Come over here."

My God, he knew me. Then looking to my left and seeing Joe DiMaggio, and shaking his hand, so soft and gentle. My God, now I've shaken the hand of a man who made love to Marilyn Monroe . . . Ernest Borgnine sitting in the Red Room when he should have been out scaling a cliff or destroying an army . . . Peter Graves of *Mission Impossible* stopping by to say hello . . . Johnny Mathis, singing so strongly at the annual Christmas Pageant of Peace on the Mall, then coming to the president's Christmas party, standing in a corner waiting to be drawn into conversation, but being so shy that conversation was difficult . . . And heads of state like Prime Minister Major of the United Kingdom and Prime Minister Mulroney of Canada just stopping by to see the U.S. publicity machine in action . . . Jay Leno in the briefing room, slightly unprepared, thinking the press would always be friendly to a star, until they asked about his contract negotiations.

Over a ten-year period, thousands of celebrities and world figures walked through the press office. But none of that prepares you for meeting a childhood idol, someone you've dreamed about and wondered about in those moments of childhood when imaginary playmates were real.

Suddenly, there she was. Her hand outstretched. She was smiling that innocent, glowing, embracing smile. She was older, of course, but not exactly old. She was beautiful.

There have been a million dime novels that describe the "alabaster" skin of a young lover. It's a cliché. I often wondered what alabaster skin was really like, presumably pure white with no imperfections, smooth like a vase, yet soft as snow. June Lockhart, that day at least, had alabaster skin. I welcomed her to the White House, tried to maintain my composure, explained briefly that I had been a big fan of *Lassie,* and asked how she knew about my briefings. She smiled and said she had followed the briefings for years and just thought they were interesting. It was a very formal meeting, mostly because I was so scared and I didn't want to make a fool of myself. Natalie escorted her to the briefing room.

It was the first of many briefings she attended, always sitting demurely along the side of the room or standing in the back. When President Reagan was visiting in California, the staff and press stayed at the Century Plaza Hotel in Los Angeles. I continued to brief every day and June was usually there. We talked often, but she never said exactly why she had such a profound interest in the press corps. Jeremiah O'Leary, who had covered the White House for years

with *The Washington Star*, later *The Washington Times*, said he remembered seeing her at briefings during the Kennedy years.

   I kept asking reporters about her past relationships with the press
corps, and slowly another love story emerged. It seems that she had
been appearing in another play in Washington in the 1960s when she
met William Lawrence, the distinguished White House reporter for
The New York Times. Lawrence introduced her to the White House
press briefings, even taking her on presidential trips with the traveling press entourage. Their affair lasted several months, presumably
until the theater run was over and June returned to California. Memories of the relationship are very vague today, but the excitement
and passion of the times must have left June with a magnetic pull to
the briefing room. She became an honorary member of the press
corps throughout the Bush years, and still drops by for an occasional
briefing by the Clinton administration. I prefer to believe, however,
that she could not possibly be as attracted to George Stephanopoulos, Dee Dee Myers, or Mike McCurry as she was to me.

CHAPTER FOURTEEN

The Bermuda Campaign

S ometimes you can identify the exact point at which all the frustrations of life become just too much to bear, when everything is going wrong, and you think it's everybody else's fault. In the spring of 1992, Pat Buchanan had challenged the president's reelection in New Hampshire, Ross Perot had challenged us everywhere else, President Bush's opinion poll ratings were dropping like rain, and I just couldn't figure out what was wrong. It's like a great football team—perhaps the Buffalo Bills or the Dallas Cowboys—who have won the big ones but then fall apart. Nothing seems to work. Arguments and finger pointing take over. Then things get worse. I told all this to my friend in the situation room, Bill Sittman, at the end of May and he said, "Go to Bermuda. Get some perspective."

Chelston sits high above Grape Bay on Bermuda's east side, a relatively modest limestone home and guest house that looks down some three hundred yards, through orchards and gardens and vine-covered walls of long-deserted property lines, finally reaching the beach and the water's edge. There is a small yellow bath house that stores chaise longues, a few ice cubes if the previous guests have been thoughtful, towels and a shower. If you stand alone on this site with the purple bougainvillea at your back and the ocean noise filling your ears, filling every vacant space in your mind, it's possible to forget that, in the middle of a presidential campaign, you may have burned out.

I often thought of my mind as a tape recorder, absorbing information from any and every source, spitting it out to reporters who stored it in their tape recorders. I would rerecord again and again, as I had been doing for ten years. But one day the words seemed to jumble in my mind, with pieces of one word running into another, and strange sounds popping in as if the tape were in "fast forward." At some point, the tape had to break. My last chance to prevent this from happening was Bermuda. When the campaign team of Sam Skinner, Bob Teeter, and Fred Malek took over in January to build a Bush/Quayle '92 team, the personal rivalries and jealousies of the last twelve years seemed to dissipate any enthusiasm even before we started. Many of the big-name performers of the past had opted out. Roger Ailes, perhaps the only handler George Bush really listened to, said his public relations consulting business was bipartisan and he couldn't participate full-time. Craig Fuller, who had engineered so much of the 1988 campaign, had joined the Philip Morris Company and was unavailable. Lee Atwater, the 1988 political consultant and later Republican National Committee chairman, had died of a brain tumor. John Sununu, who helped steer the late stages of the 1988 primary and then the general election, had been forced out of the White House and discredited with most Republican leaders. Peggy Noonan, the gifted writer who penned the "kinder, gentler" portions of the 1988 campaign, decided she was a "best-selling author" and could no longer write speeches. Ed Rollins, the Reagan campaign consultant, was forced out of the National Congressional Campaign Committee by an angry President Bush. Rollins sent out a committee newsletter advising congressional candidates to shun the president. The old Reagan hands, like Dick Wirthlin, Stu Spencer, Lyn Nofziger, and others had never made their peace with the Bush people, and vice versa.

So we started the campaign with a chief of staff who had never run a national race and was demonstrating a peculiar inability to make decisions, a pollster who by definition changed his mind with every new piece of information, and a businessman who had few political instincts, no experience, no supporters, and no definable reason for being there. Throw in a campaign communications chief, James Lake, who wouldn't give up his private PR clients to avoid conflicts of interest, a political director, Mary Matalin, who was moonstruck over the Democrats' leading political operator, James Carville, and a press secretary who was burned out. The president should have fired us all. By May, President Bush's campaign had survived the New Hampshire primary challenge of Pat Buchanan and the candidacy of Ross Perot. But we still had no message, no campaign plan, no idea how to deal with Perot if he stayed in the race, no plan for the convention, and no answer to the basic question: Why should George Bush be reelected president?

It all started with "the funnel." Incumbent presidential bids had been run out of the White House often enough, but never under the growing ethics rules passed by Congress or the Federal Election Commission, and never under the intense scrutiny of a partisan press corps that wanted a Democratic victory. In addition, President Bush was an honest and honorable man who played by the rules. Thus it was that Boyden Gray, the president's counsel, was charged with seeing that the White House and the campaign operated within all election laws in this new joint venture. He was a stickler. At six feet four inches, Boyden had a regal, if stooped, presence. He came from old money, in tobacco, media, and other interests in the Carolinas, and a family of public servants in the law firms and administrations of Washington. He was rigid and eccentric, keeping a pet pig in his Georgetown home, driving a car modified to burn natural gas, and playing tennis regularly with Katharine Graham, chairwoman of the Washington Post Company. Most of us in the White House saw this latter pastime as the most eccentric of all.

Boyden started from the premise that the White House and the campaign could not talk to each other. This would avoid any conflict of interest that might arise from politicians and consultants having inside access to the White House staff. In true lawyerly fashion, he set up a third party to act as a conduit, in this case a White House staffer called "the funnel." We had funnels on the family farm to pour gas from the can to the tractor without spillage. I remember that a funnel, sitting on the barn floor, has a big round bottom and small pointed top. Our political funnel was supposed to be the same—someone to sit at a desk all day taking phone calls from the campaign and passing orders back and forth with rote precision. Being picked for this job was like being selected to be a leaf in the school play. The job carried the added instruction that "the funnel" could not be a participant in decision making because it would taint the ethics of mixing politics and government. Only a lawyer could think this would work. It didn't, of course, but it created six weeks of confusion and hostility before someone finally killed it. Actually, I'm not sure anyone killed it. But everyone quit using it, so that one day the funnel realized that nothing was flowing through its stem and it became a potted plant, rather like in a fairy tale.

The other disaster at the beginning of the campaign was my promotion. While the president was in Japan in January 1992, Sam Skinner gave an interview to *The Washington Post* in which he blamed most of the president's troubles on poor communications, "people weren't getting the message out." He suggested in print that Dave Demarest, the director of communications, would soon be replaced. Leon Panetta, when he became chief of staff to President Clinton in 1994, said almost the same thing about Press Secretary Dee Dee Myers, and blamed Clinton's problems on poor communications. Both chiefs learned a valuable lesson with these statements: No chief has the power to fire people without the president's blessing. Presidents who raise and spend $40 million to get elected, and who travel to every Holiday Inn in America for twelve months or more hugging babies, do not give up any power to their chiefs of staff. None. What chiefs of staff should say when they are appointed is the following: "The president has given me full and complete authority to do anything he wants me to do." Chiefs are hired hands just like everybody else. Dave Demarest and Dee Dee Myers were not fired. In fact, they both found friends they never knew they had.

In Dave's case, old friends called the president. Skinner's enemies talked about scapegoating. The staff was demoralized. The president wasn't too pleased with the public flogging.

Skinner knew the only answer was a quick replacement. But nobody seemed to want the job. Peggy Noonan was happy being a writer in New York, but said she might work for the campaign. Jim Lake, who had worked in the Reagan campaigns and was a partner in his own Washington public relations firm, wanted the job but wouldn't give up his firm. So he joined the campaign organization where that kind of conflict is not governed by law. Tom Griscom, now with R. J. Reynolds Tobacco, took one look at the job and said he wasn't ready to return to Washington. In between each new candidate to surface, Sam would ask me to take the job. I instantly, every time, declined. I liked being press secretary. I knew the job. And I knew that running the communications office was a thankless task similar to leading fifteen mules to water. It involved supervising the speechwriters, which alone made it an impossible position. I did not want it.

After Jim Lake had negotiated with the ethics counselors for the second time in two weeks, finding no suitable configuration of the job that would satisfy all parties, Skinner called me into his office.

"Marlin," he said, "you've gotten lazy. You know how to be press secretary. You don't want to work any harder. So you don't want to be communications director. But now I'm telling you, you have to take it."

Sam had pushed my button. I resented his comments. My competitive juices were flowing. He knew it. He thought I would say OK. But I had been taunted by the best reporters in America and I knew the right answer was to calmly say, "Let me think about it." I left his office and recounted to myself all the reasons why this would fail: The press would look at me differently because dealing with the press is a short-term function, while communications—mostly planning and scheduling—is long-term. There wasn't enough time in the day to do both jobs. Lastly, it was not clear that this campaign had any leadership. That seemed selfish so I eliminated the last reason. The money was the same. I weighed all of these quite rational reasons and then rejected them. I would do it, mostly because Sam said he had no alternatives, and I would do anything to help the president. I did ask for two conditions: the title "Counselor to the President," and the right to quit or be fired at any time from the communications job and go back to being press secretary.

"If you find somebody else to do the job, or you're unhappy with me, just say the word and I'm history," I told Sam, hoping he would find someone else. "The 'counselor' title is just for my résumé. It's not as good as money, but that's all there is. My real worry, Sam, is that I can't do both jobs. I have never thought anyone could, even back when Gergen wanted both jobs in the Reagan administration. They are separate and distinct functions. But I'll try if you want."

Sam was grateful. Basically, nothing changed. Demarest stayed to run the speechwriting and general communications office and I continued the daily press briefings. But the attitude of the press toward me did change. For years I had nurtured press relationships based on my role as an honest broker between the president and the press. Now that was shattered. Reporters saw me as the strategist, the propagandist, the counselor who could not be completely trusted to tell the truth because I had taken sides. They were like a loyal dog that has been inexplicably hit by its long-trusted master and ever after approaches with wariness and distrust. Going into a presidential campaign was not a good time to endanger that trust with reporters. Nevertheless, I vowed to give it my best shot.

In the wake of the funnel, the next management invention to coordinate between the White House and the campaign, which had now grown to almost 200 people, was the 6 P.M. meeting in the Old Executive Office Building. The purpose, in theory, was to bring to-

gether the leadership of the campaign organization with the senior
White House staff on a daily basis to decide the course of the presi-
dent's activities. But it never worked. In the first place, people
didn't show up at six. The designated participants were Skinner,
Campaign Chairman Bob Teeter, Campaign Manager Fred Malek,
Political Director Mary Matalin, Fred Steeper, the pollster, Cam
Findlay as aide to Skinner, and Dick Darman as the unofficial liaison to James A. Baker, the secretary of state. Room 180 of the Old
Executive Office Building is a standard-issue government conference
room with a twenty-foot mahogany conference table, twelve to fifteen brown leather chairs, and a few prints on the wall of the White
House in various positions. There was no sense of a campaign about
it, no posters or dirty coffee cups, no screaming volunteers. In spite
of eight months of these meetings from January until the Republican
convention, there never developed a camaraderie or sense of purpose
among the group. I don't think the people in the room really respected each other. They didn't want to be there. The rivalry between the White House and the campaign was so intense in terms of
who controlled the president's time and energy that the 6 P.M. meeting became torturous, like having to put on a pair of rubber over-
shoes for two hours a day, even in sunny weather.

The routine was the same. Fred Steeper would summarize his latest polling, which always showed disastrous news for the president.
Fred was a slight figure, a protégé of Teeter known to few of us before the campaign. He always seemed depressed, as must be natural
when you gather bad news every day. But he also was honest. In New
Hampshire, he told us that people just didn't want the president reelected. He told us Perot could beat us. He told us Clinton had
tapped into something among Americans and should be taken seriously. He told us that the position we had taken on every issue was
unpopular with the American people. Every issue. Worse, he kept
telling us that the president still hadn't given Americans a reason to
vote for him. We had no message.

We also had no plan. This was my first national campaign as an
insider, so I was reluctant to show my ignorance. But finally I started
asking about a campaign plan. Teeter and Malek kept saying they
had one.

"Then what is it?" It was a state-by-state analysis. "What's it say
about messages, themes, purpose, and vision?" It didn't.

So we would talk about the themes Clinton was using. Mostly

we ridiculed them when we should have been copying them. We couldn't decide if the economy was improving or getting worse.

The president would have meeting after meeting with his economic advisers in which he always asked one question: What's wrong with the economy? Secretary of the Treasury Nicholas Brady cited statistics showing the economy was recovering rather well. Mike Boskin, chairman of the Council of Economic Advisers, was shell-shocked by the second recessionary dip in 1992 and never seemed to have a straight answer. The president privately admitted to friends that he had lost confidence in his economic team.

The six o'clock group was totally in the dark about the economy. We talked about it as if in a trance, waiting for some economic genie to wave a wand and tell people the recession was over. The press kept reporting how bad people felt about the economy. As the campaign wore on, the president was so upset with the press that he thought the stories were made up. That, incidentally, is the greatest danger of allowing bitterness or anger about the press to dominate your thinking. You don't believe their stories. In our case, we distrusted the press and believed the traditional economic indicators, thus totally misreading the growing anxiety in the country about jobs, careers, corporate restructuring, and foreign competition. We believed it would be enough to talk about caring and about creating jobs, without actually developing an economic message of action.

All through the off-year elections of 1986, I traveled from city to city with Vice President Bush. He would dramatically whip his wallet out of his pocket, slam it on the podium in front of him, and shout: "Here's what it's all about! As my good friend [Ohio governor] Jim Rhoads says, people vote their wallet!" In 1992, I never heard him quote Governor Rhoads.

We never had an agenda for the six o'clock meeting. Anybody who wanted to could take charge of the meeting. If I needed a decision on press, such as which talk shows to accept, I would produce a two- or three-point agenda, pass it around the table, ask for views, then summarize the discussion and state what I thought we had decided. If there were no objections, I wrote a memo to the president asking his approval and arranged for the scheduling secretary to reserve time for the events. Soon everybody was copying my method in order to get decisions. Unfortunately, there still was no overall plan that drew these activities together.

In midspring, the futility of these meetings was affecting everyone. Teeter and Skinner decided that the group needed to meet weekly with the president so he could offer direction. Also, the president was hearing strange stories about disorganization at the campaign, and a lack of direction from the White House. So he also wanted a more active role, and scheduled a meeting every Thursday afternoon.

In the first Thursday meeting, the president turned the session over to Teeter, who immediately asked for a press report from me. I felt sandbagged. He had never mentioned a report to me before the meeting and I was unprepared. It was easy enough to talk about general press attitudes, editorials, and mood of the press, so that's what I did. What I really wanted to do was introduce the topic of televised town meetings and interview requests, but I didn't have my recommendations ready. I was furious.

The next Thursday I was prepared, but Teeter launched into a huge show-and-tell about how the campaign was organized and who was doing what. The third week, another show-and-tell about the communications organization. In three meetings, we still had not discussed message, theme, or a plan for winning. Finally, George W. Bush, the president's oldest son, came to Washington from his home in Dallas to attend the fourth meeting. I handed him a brief note, "When do we get a campaign plan?" About halfway through the meeting, he asked the question. "Soon," was the answer. A few weeks later we got a thick package of polls, state race analyses, and regional problem areas. That was supposed to be the plan. But it never said a word about the message: why George Bush should be reelected president.

As this organizational fiasco was unfolding, the press hit us with the now-famous "supermarket scanner" story. It hurt the president badly in terms of public perception, and it sounded an alarm for those of us planning presidential events. The president attended the annual meeting of the National Grocers Association in Orlando, Florida, on February 4 to talk about the economy and families. Before the speech, he toured their trade exhibition of new supermarket technology. Our advance team had some new people who thought it would be a great picture to have the president appear with a life-size statue of Daisy the Cow that was part of a milk exhibit. I was walking about fifty yards ahead of the president when I saw the cow. Always afraid of pictures that might hold the president up to ridicule, I grabbed the lead advance man and screamed at him to get the president away from that phony cow. Unfortunately, he guided the presidential party across the aisle to the National Cash Register company's checkout scanner exhibit.

"This is the scanner," the president asked, "the newest scanner?"

Bob Graham, the NCR representative on hand, said, "Of course, this looks like a typical scanner you'd see in a grocery store."

"Yeah," the president said.

"There's one big difference," said Graham, lifting off the scanner's top plate to reveal a scale underneath. He weighed and rang up a red apple.

Then Graham said he wanted to show the president the machine's "really quite amazing" new feature. He had the president scan a credit card with a universal product code that was ripped and jumbled into five pieces. The machine read it and rang up the correct sale.

"Isn't that something," the president said graciously.

Later, the president told his audience that he was "amazed by some of the technology."

Andrew Rosenthal, the *New York Times* reporter covering the Bush campaign, had stayed at the press filing center set up so reporters could hear the president's speech, then wrote his story and phoned it to his editors. A pool of reporters had accompanied the president on his tour and filed a report on the scanner episode for the reporters in the filing center to use in their stories. Rosenthal was writing his story from the pool report. He chose this opportunity to be clever.

His story appeared on the front page of *The New York Times* the next day under the headline: "Bush Encounters the Supermarket, Amazed." The Rosenthal story indicated the president didn't know how a scanner worked and was out of touch with American life. Other newspapers and TV and radio stations picked up the story, all suggesting the president was out of touch. It was one of those stories where the truth never catches up with the lie. No other reporter at the event wrote the story this way. Reporters started arguing about what actually happened. I urged all reporters to go view the pool videotapes of the episode. Then we contacted NCR and asked them to give interviews to reporters about what really happened. NCR also sent a letter to the president, confirming that it was brand new technology involved.

Andy Rosenthal and *The New York Times* defended their story, as they always do. But Andy's colleagues knew the truth. Andy spoke openly of his dislike for Reagan and Bush. It often happened that as we routinely handed out copies of the president's speeches on the press plane, Andy would grab his copy, glance through it, then parade up and down the aisle of the plane criticizing the speech, urging other reporters to share his view. Our staff, and most reporters, were bewildered by these performances because they were so obviously biased. At first we thought he just hated Bush. But it soon became clear that his attitude was often fed by his personal insecurities. We soon realized that his press plane performances were designed to be sure the story he planned to write was acceptable to his peers. As he strutted up and down the isle castigating the speech, we would hear the same words we read in the next day's paper.

Andy is the son of A. M. Rosenthal, former managing editor and now columnist for the *Times*. A. M. was a legend at the *Times*, and Andy often spoke privately of his difficulties in living up to Dad's reputation, especially at the *Times*, where nepotism has long been a problem. At the same time, Maureen Dowd, the other *Times* correspondent covering the White House, was receiving rave reviews for her writing flair and insightful reporting. She was a clever writer, and could take a mundane analysis, recast it with colorful metaphors, and produce an illuminating piece. Andy was no match for her talent, but he wanted to try. When he spoke of her stories, there was always a tinge of jealousy. Add to all this a dissolving marriage and you have a reporter who is very unsure of himself. Suddenly, Andy was handed the supermarket scanner story and his chance to give it a clever twist. He could not resist.

The morning the story appeared, the president sent me one of his famous morning notes on blue presidential stationery. I could just see him furiously typing away in his study off the Oval Office:

To: Czar Fitzwater
Re: Overnights
Once again my ire turns to Rosenthal. The NCR
people were explaining brand new technology to
me. Not simple checkout technology. Please tell
the little "——" that I am
tired of his editorializing every day in his 'news ???@#$$%^& *
coverage.
Feeling better now—forget it, but what a terrible little guy he
is turning out to be.
What is it about him?
Thanks for Listening,

GB

It was classic and sums up the frustration we all felt about a story that essentially was manufactured and against which we had little recourse. Perhaps the most interesting response came in a letter from Arthur Ochs ("Punch") Sulzberger, chairman of the board and chief executive officer of the *Times*, to the president:

". . . there was no question that Andrew Rosenthal's article on the supermarket electronic checkout system was 'just a teeny-weeny bit naughty.' Little did any of us expect that the story would be picked up by others, including some not too subtle political cartoonists.

"The purpose of the story was to have a little bit of fun, and if we had too much at the expense of the President, I apologize."

That kind of apology doesn't make a president feel much better, especially when it's not accompanied by a printed apology or retraction.

Other members of the White House press corps would sheepishly stop by my office to apologize on behalf of Andy, defending themselves by pointing out that no one else had run the story the way he did. Nevertheless, several newspapers ran a *Times* version two days later. *The New York Times* is one of the most powerful newspapers in America and few reporters have the strength to criticize it, but one did, and it took enormous courage. Going against your peers in journalism requires incredible fortitude and integrity. The press always defends its own.

On February 11, 1992, Christopher Connell of the Associated Press wrote the single most courageous story of my White House years. He not only defended a president; he blew the whistle on the *Times*. His dispatch was in the best wire service tradition of objectivity, not mentioning the *Times* until the fifteenth paragraph, never mentioning the writer of the story in question, but laying out the reality of the situation in clear terms: "It turns out the supermarket scanner that drew President Bush's attention at a grocers' convention last week really did have some unusual features," he wrote. "It can read labels—the so-called universal product codes—that are ripped up and jumbled."

Then Charles Osgood, on his CBS morning radio show, recounted the facts as reported by Connell, and ended his report by quoting NCR's Graham as saying "the whole thing is ludicrous." Osgood added, "He's right, and we were wrong. Fair is fair." Unfortunately, not many journalists showed the courage of Connell and Osgood.

This story left a general pall over the president's staff. Not only was it going to be a nasty campaign, we weren't ready to deal with it. Our internal systems were breaking down. People were bypassing the established processes and scheduling presidential events directly through Kathy Super, the scheduler. The White House advance office was feuding with the campaign advance office. The campaign acted like it was managing a congressional candidate, the White House staff acted like it was managing a governing president, and in fact nobody was managing anything. As often happens in the midst of chaos, an underground group began to develop, mostly out of concern for the president. We simply were afraid that public events would deteriorate to the point that it became noticeable to the press. We could not afford another supermarket scanner incident.

March 10, 1992—I called the press "lazy bastards." We had a morning campaign stop at Oklahoma Christian University when I made my most unchristian comment of the campaign. We had been on the road for four days, with bad stories every day about sparse and unenthusiastic crowds—and some were. It just seemed that people were turned off by the campaign—no real excitement. The press seemed more cynical than ever, trying to build up Pat Buchanan just to establish a conflict with us. The press hated Buchanan and his right-wing ideas. But they were willing to use him to irritate us. The day before Oklahoma, the president had a huge rally in Hialeah, Florida, with thousands of screaming Cubans from that community. But the press filing center was in a hotel miles away. Andy Rosenthal of the *Times* and Ann Devroy of *The Washington Post* chose not to attend the rally. They wrote that the Hialeah crowd was lackluster, largely because they had not been there to see it.

All this was grating on my nerves when our motorcade arrived at Oklahoma Christian. I immediately walked through the filing center to the event site behind the building. When I opened the door to go out, the crush of the noise and cheering almost forced me back inside. It was like a grenade of excitement had gone off, with nearly 20,000 people straining at the barriers, covering the hillside under a bright and warm winter day. It was spectacular. I walked back into the building to the press filing center, a lecture hall located not twenty feet from that magical crowd. There sat thirty to forty reporters, in an auditorium setting, listening to the president's speech on the public address system. I appeared at the top of the seats, which formed a well in front of the professor's podium, with Ron Kaufman, the White House political director. My blood pressure was surging upward. I can only remember my good friend Tim McNulty, of *The Chicago Tribune,* sitting in the front row and laughing as I started shouting.

"It's a great day!" I screamed. "Everyone out of the filing center. C'mon. Off your asses and outta here!" They thought I was laughing, but I was mad. Nevertheless, some inner trip wire told me to get out of there. I turned and walked down the hall. Kaufman was laughing and screaming, "Yes! You did it! Great!"

Judy Smith, my deputy, walked up to ask what all the commotion was about. I told her, still mad.

"Judy," I said, "we should turn off the public address system in the filing center. Make them go to the rally." She and Ron could now see that I was mad, and they didn't argue. Judy left to carry out my command.

Then I got a terrible piece of bad luck. Rita Beamish of the Associated Press and Kathleen DeLaski from ABC News saw me in the hallway and came over to complain. My worst nightmare. Rita wore her politics on her sleeve. She opposed every Republican program. She was pro-choice, pro-welfare, for bigger government, antimilitary, and a feminist. She was married to Paul Costello, who was former press secretary to Rosalyn Carter and Washington mayor Sharon Pratt Kelly, and a campaigner for Michael Dukakis. She tried to nail me every chance she got.

Kathleen DeLaski was new to the White House, number three in the ABC pecking order, a young and attractive reporter whom the network was grooming for the future. But she had two distracting habits: She seemed to repeat her questions three or four times and I couldn't tell if she didn't understand the answer or was just harassing me, and she seemed to try to embarrass me in front of my colleagues. At her first White House press conference, held at a housing construction site in nearby Maryland, she asked the president if he agreed with something I had said. He did, of course. But there was no real purpose to the question except to embarrass me.

DeLaski later became press spokeswoman for President Clinton's first secretary of defense, Les Aspin, no doubt getting a taste of her own medicine.

When I saw Rita and Kathleen in that Oklahoma Christian hallway, I blurted out, "I'm sick of you lazy bastards. Go out and cover the events."

They both spun on their heels. They knew they had me. Rita rushed into the filing center and announced to all who remained,

"Marlin called us 'lazy bastards.' " Within minutes, the story was speeding its way around the world. The press corps didn't write it as a hallway conversation with Rita Beamish; rather, it was another example of the frustration of the Bush campaign. In truth, it was.

The "lazy bastards" story consumed our day. I had apologized by noon, and was in full grovel by 6 P.M. That pretty much limited the story to one day. But it was still a day lost for the president and it depressed me even further.

I did receive one very interesting note of support, however, from Congressman Newt Gingrich of Georgia, now the Speaker of the House of Representatives. During the Bush years, Newt was always considered a loose cannon, mostly because of his glib criticisms of the president, and also because he constantly called members of the president's staff with public relations ideas on how to present our programs. Some were great. Some not. But it was clear that he was a very creative political thinker who was bringing a new zest to the Republican Party, if only because he was defining capitalism and conservatism as vehicles for solving social problems. I found that very exciting.

When Newt publicly criticized the president on the economy, the press corps came to me for a response. I tried to square the circle by saying that while the president didn't agree with Newt, he always appreciated his advice and counsel. I added that Newt is a very creative politician, a former history professor, and "is a sort of Plato of our time." I meant it as a compliment. But Newt sent word to Nick Calio, the president's legislative director, that he was offended. With that as history, I was glad to get a personal, handwritten note from Newt after my use of the term "lazy bastards."

Newt wrote: "I was proud of your last week's assault on the self-centered cynicism of the White House press corps—they live in a gilded cage and share a culture of acid contempt for us and our values. In a sense they represent the valet syndrome run wild (no man is great in the eyes of his valet). You tarred them and attracted attention to their behavior. Congratulations. Newt."

March 1992—Back in the White House for a few days of governing, several staffers came to me to ask for a meeting of everyone involved in the president's travel and communications. I agreed, as long as it was inclusive, involving all the relevant White House offices and the campaign. Nearly twenty people crammed into my office for the first meeting. It was the first time that speechwriters met with advance men, and public liaison people met with political people. Basically, we took the president's campaign schedule as decided by Skinner and Teeter, and tried to make sure the staging, the meetings, the letters of invitation, and the speeches all meshed. It was quite useful for a while, until everybody in the White House wanted to attend. The word got out that if you wanted to be a part of the process, to get ideas into presidential speeches, to get people invited to meetings, to know what was happening, go to Fitzwater's meeting. At one point, we had nearly thirty attendees sprawled on the floor in every direction, including most of the senior staff to the president.

I began to worry that we were developing an alternative power center that Skinner and Teeter would grow to resent. We tried every way to coordinate through them, but my fears were justified. Word started to spread that the real decisions about the president's activities were being made in the communications meeting. We did not want to take over the scheduling process. I wanted no part of any mutiny, and suddenly the whole apparatus seemed wrong. It was very uncomfortable to feel like a second staff was developing. After Sam Skinner made his first surprise drop-by at one of our meetings—walking over bodies, standing behind my desk, and then reversing most of our decisions—I abandoned them. I was severely depressed about our organization, and confessed to a few friends that I might be losing my perspective. I was blaming everyone else and they simply couldn't be that bad. Maybe the problem was me. My solution was to take a vacation, and to do it soon, before the campaign really got rolling. I wrote the chief of staff a memo asking for leave from March 31 to April 10, 1992, and made arrangements to go to Bermuda.

The guest house behind the consul general of Bermuda's home is a small, stone, four-room cottage, with floor-to-ceiling windows and shutters that bang in the night. Vines cling to the outer walls and drape themselves over the windows. The small porch on the front faces a courtyard and looks out across the great expanse of ocean. Behind the cottage is a ten-foot stone wall, covered with colorful flowers that catch the morning sun. If you sit on the porch with a good book, you are in a private world, locked between the volcanic stone of the island and the ocean. For three days I stayed on that porch, letting the sun soak up the worries and fears of Washington while I tried to sort out my priorities and rest. I had two goals: to get a firm grasp on my role in the campaign, and to develop a political mindset that would allow me to ignore the media contentiousness in the campaign and stay calm. I decided first to resign the communications position as soon as possible, but certainly by the time of the Republican National Convention in August. Second, I decided I could not change our campaign by trying to do other people's jobs. I wasn't qualified, didn't have the time, and it was enough to deal with the press.

On the afternoon of April 2, 1992, I took a leisurely stroll down the winding front drive of Chelston to Grape Bay Drive, then cut across the highway to the small neat white house of Alfred Birdsey. Alfred is a well-known Bermuda artist who paints in watercolor splashes of blue and green, with black outlines of boats and houses that define the colors. His studio was open. I went around to the back and hesitantly walked through the open door. There he sat, eighty years old, chatting with a friend in a straw hat like mine. It struck me that he looked like his paintings, thin and straight, with body lines somewhat crooked with age. He was very talkative and curious about my background. He said he liked President Bush. "Clinton is not a very sincere man," he said. I was relieved that people so far away could see through Clinton.

Birdsey showed me his new silk-screen process, a jury-rigged contraption made of one-inch-by-two-inch scraps of wood, some half-rusted springs, and brown wire. He had made it himself. The purity of his artistry extended even to his supplies. I lingered as long as possible, buying several watercolors, trying to soak up his Rockwellian honesty as a counterforce against the politics ahead. As I trudged back up the hill to Chelston, I was really starting to feel in control of myself again.

My telephone rang about 7 P.M., just as I was fixing a cocktail to accompany the sunset. It was Judy Smith, my deputy in the White House.

"Get your pink little cheeks back here!" she screamed, laughing into the phone.

"Not on your life," I responded.

She said Ann Devroy had called her and was writing a story for the *Post* about me and the staff. She said the story would appear Saturday, April 4, 1992. It was mostly about Skinner, Deputy Chief of Staff Henson Moore, and the assistant to the president for policy, Clayton Yeutter.

"It's terrible," Judy said. "She calls those guys the Marx Brothers. She says you blew up in a meeting with Henson Moore and said if he wanted to take over communications, fine, but leave you out. She also says you went to the president to talk about your problems, and then abruptly left for Bermuda."

"First, let's establish the truth," I said. "I did complain in the long-range scheduling meeting that at this point in the campaign we should be able to schedule four, six, and eight weeks in advance. We can't leave every decision till the week before. Second, I went on vacation because I needed one, haven't taken one in years, and the campaign will be tough. I simply needed the rest."

"OK, Marlin," Judy said, "now what's the real story?"

"That's it," I said. "I didn't complain to the president about anything. I didn't shout at Henson. On the other hand, this story is really about how messed up our decision making is, and that's true. It's also true I'm tired to the bone. But it sounds like someone is using me, and my vacation, to create a story that aims at Skinner, Moore, and Yeutter."

My respite was over. On Saturday morning I called my friend Melinda Andrews in Washington, asking her about the story. She said it was terrible, on page one, and read "The White House Is in Gridlock." "You threatened to resign," she said, "then left for Bermuda."

I called Judy Smith, who read me the entire story, and a two-sentence statement she had already drafted, saying I had not threatened to resign and everything was fine. She also said she had talked to Sam Skinner about the story and she thought he would like to have something about himself in the statement. I dictated two more lines for her to use: "The chief of staff and deputy chief of staff are doing an excellent job. We have a top management team in place."

"Make sure you clear this with Sam," I said. "This may be the first time in history that a press secretary has been asked to give a vote of confidence to a chief of staff. But I'll say whatever he wants me to say."

Judy cleared it with Skinner and issued it Saturday afternoon. By the 6 P.M. news, my Bermuda retreat was known around the world. I turned on the little TV set in the cottage and could barely pick up the CNN channel. The screen was white with snow and shaky, but the story was unmistakable. The CNN correspondent was in front of the White House. The screen showed pictures of me briefing at the podium, and me getting off *Air Force One* wearing a cowboy hat. Then the frame froze, as the reporter explained that I was disgruntled and thinking of resigning.

All I could think about was: What must the president think of all this? I may have to resign. Some of the president's advisers will be telling him I've become a liability. Skinner and Moore may never forgive me for this, and they could try to make resignation my only alternative. In any case, I now needed a second week's vacation—badly.

It's interesting to note how a story like this develops. One's first impulse is to blame the reporter. Then you blame your enemies for leaking. Then you blame those who are closest to you because they know the most—your inner feelings and all that. But in fact, and in most cases, it's just an alert reporter who smells a story and starts calling people. In this case, the reporter was one of the best in the business, Ann Devroy.

She had just returned from vacation herself, but still thought it a little strange that I would suddenly head off to Bermuda in the middle of a presidential campaign.

"You didn't take vacations," Ann said later. "You always went with the president, Reagan to California and Bush to Maine, and that was your vacation. So I decided to call a few people and ask."

Presidents and politicians tend to think that sources spew out stories in whole cloth. That seldom is the case. Usually it's piecemeal: "Marlin was frustrated." "Marlin felt decisions weren't being made." "I don't know anything about Marlin, but nobody is in charge around here." "It's not Marlin, it's the campaign." Pretty soon the whole story starts to unravel. In this case, Ann Devroy called a half dozen of my staff and colleagues. By the next day, a dozen more White House staff, and outside friends of the president, called her. It only took a couple of hours for the word to get out that Ann Devroy was writing a story about the president's staff. And everybody wanted in.

Why does this happen? One reason is that in Washington, unlike anywhere else in America, people talk to each other through the press. The media, by accepting anonymous sources, offers a chance for any member of the president's team to tell him he's wrong, crazy, and listening to the wackiest people. The press is like the IRS in this regard. They encourage the tattletale. My vacation was the perfect vehicle for everyone associated with the Bush campaign to tell the president what was wrong.

I first met Ann Devroy in 1983 in Santa Barbara, California. I was the new deputy press secretary and Ann was the number-three *Post* reporter at the White House, behind David Hoffman and Lou Can-

non. We both had the vacation assignment. I was roaming around
the hotel when she and her husband, *Baltimore Sun* reporter Mark
Matthews, asked if I would like to join them for a tour of the city.
We visited the mission where the city was founded, the fancy hotel
where Jack Kennedy had honeymooned, and other sites. It was a
splendid afternoon and we became friends. I'm so glad that afternoon
happened, because over the next ten years Ann Devroy and I would
spar and banter and clash over a thousand stories. She would search
me out at the beach, rout me out of bed, challenge my assertions,
and sometimes discover that I was successfully avoiding her. She
was right. I had long since learned that in some situations, such as
the night before a military invasion, the best thing to do is hide.
Sometimes it is simply impossible to talk with a reporter without di-
vulging information. Often I would say to Ann, "Ann, I simply can't
and won't talk about this." She would change the subject and come
at me from a different direction.

Thus my trilogy of advice for staying out of trouble would be
complete: Cave early and often, grovel if you have to, and you *can*
run and hide. Ann Devroy was always honest with me, and I worked
very hard to always be honest with her. She would get madder than
hell when I avoided her. But I think she understood why. At least she
understood the nature of our private war in which the press secretary
always fights with one arm behind his back, trying to serve two masters.

I often thanked the Lord we had become friends that warm afternoon in Santa Barbara.

The Bermuda story lasted only a day. When politicians talk about
stories having "legs," they mean some force in society or in the story
itself will keep it alive. Usually, this means the story requires a follow-up by lawyers, or the courts, or some event. Sometimes it means
that a special interest group, or the opposing political party, will provide reporters with more information that creates another story.
None of those factors seemed to be at play here. The ramifications
inside the White House, however, would continue for some time. I
decided to return to Washington on April 5 to face my colleagues
and, undoubtedly, the president.

Sitting in the Bermuda airport waiting for my flight, I was approached by a familiar face, Faith Whittlesley, director of public liaison in the Reagan White House and later ambassador to
Switzerland. We exchanged greetings, and in the next breath she
said, "Bush has to speak out on abortion. You have to help him."

"Bush is pro-life," I said.

"Yes, but he doesn't speak out enough," she said. "No passion."

"He talks about it all the time," I protested. "He's asked in all the press conferences."

"He must speak out against fetal tissue research," she said.

I was having trouble believing this conversation was happening. In the middle of an airport lobby, we were talking about fetal research. Whatever happened to lost luggage conversations?

"He does," I said. "He has threatened publicly to veto the bill allowing it."

"Yes, but he doesn't have passion," she said again.

"I'll tell him," I said.

As she turned to leave, picking up her bags, she said over her shoulder, "They carry the fetuses in buckets to do the research."

"Buckets of fetuses," I thought. "Another sign it is going to be a very long campaign."

Back in Washington, I received a call from the president's social secretary, Laurie Firestone, inviting me to dinner and a concert with the president on April 7. George W. and Republican National Committee chairman Rich Bond were the other guests. My heart sank. Here comes the ax. George W. is no doubt here, I thought, to ease the pain of firing me. Maybe Bond was invited to offer me a job at the committee. That would make a more dignified dismissal. At a minimum, they would want to know what the hell that Devroy story was all about.

I arrived in the president's family quarters in time for the evening news. He welcomed me back from vacation, George W. and Rich seemed very lighthearted, and the president ordered drinks. I ordered scotch on the rocks, just in case I needed fortification. After the news, we went into the family dining room for dinner, the same place I had had a private dinner with the president before the Panama invasion and a private lunch before the Iraq invasion. It was a special place for me. I don't know why the president chose to dine alone with me on those occasions, but I always cherished the idea that he would want to share those delicate and emotional moments with me. It would be a tragedy to be fired in the same place.

Susan Biddle, one of the president's photographers, came in to take pictures and the president invited her to stay. The dinner was quite pleasant, with the discussion centering on the campaign. The president wanted to stay on the high road. He believed we should respond to the gossip of the day about Hillary Rodham Clinton by staying above it—don't get drawn into Clinton's marital problems. But he didn't ask about my vacation.

At 8:30 P.M., we left for the Kennedy Center to hear Anne Murray sing. The president liked her voice and had ordered one of her records by calling an 800 number that he saw on CNN. She found out and invited him to her concert.

We decided to leave at intermission, mainly because the president didn't like to stay up late. He was usually in bed by 9:30 P.M. and up at 5:30 A.M. We arranged to meet her backstage before leaving. The Secret Service took us to a private room that was empty except for a piano. I was flabbergasted when President Bush walked over to the piano, pulled out the bench, and sat down. I thought it was a joke. Then he started playing a song, tentatively at first, then he got into it. He finished and we applauded. He was playing "Swanee River" and showing remarkable talent. The amazing part was that in my seven years with George Bush, I had never heard him, or anyone else, say that he could play the piano. Certainly, no one had ever seen him play. When Anne Murray came in during "Swanee River," he immediately stopped, greeted her, and talked for a few minutes before we left. As we piled into the limousine, I wanted desperately to ask about his piano playing but somehow I didn't get a chance. We arrived back at the White House, walked into the diplomatic reception room, and walked toward the family elevator. I thanked the president for dinner and the concert. He said something about it being good to have me back and headed for the elevator. That was it. I went back to my office before going to my car, wondering why no one had even mentioned the *Post* story. My conclusion was that the president was waiting to see if I wanted to raise the issue. When I didn't, he simply used the evening to let me know everything was all right. But it wasn't, of course.

After Bermuda, the campaign year came at me like a jumbled slide show, filled with rallies, hurried trips back to Washington, speeches that sounded frantic, and an occasional slide that was upside down so I wasn't sure where I was. I remember them now as dates—days in history when events happened and decisions were made, but they didn't always connect.

April 21, 1992—We were still searching for a message. The Room 180 campaign group had a special meeting in the Roosevelt Room of the White House at 5 P.M. to discuss strategy. Fred Steeper brought his latest polls, which showed the recession, or fear of recession, was responsible for 95 percent of the drop in the president's favorable rating. But the main problem was still Perot, who was beating on the president every day. Dick Darman said we should attack Perot hard, and now. Teeter felt that would only infuriate Perot and ensure that he stayed in the race. The president and Teeter had felt all along that Perot would drop out once he saw that victory was impossible. Teeter predicted a June dropout by Perot, and felt we must woo the Perot supporters. Steeper said the president's greatest asset was character, so we decided to stick with a focus on "caring about people and jobs" and on media events that emphasized the personality of the candidate.

When it became clear we didn't have a political answer to the country's economic concerns, I wished we had listened more closely to Lamar Alexander's education recommendations. They might have given us a theme. Soon after Lamar became secretary of education in 1991, he presented the president a plan for implementing the national education goals developed previously by the administration and the nation's governors. The Education Department had been looking for a way to implement the goals in its various programs, but Lamar gave them a special political dimension. The genius of his proposal, called "America 2000," was that it showed the president how to make himself "the Education President," which he had suggested in his 1988 campaign.

Lamar proposed that a new experimental school be built in every congressional district in America, utilizing new curriculum, computer technology, and new teaching methods. It involved local school districts, set up local advisory groups of one kind or another, and sought financial support from corporations in helping to build the schools. I thought it was politically brilliant. Every member of Congress would support a new school in his or her district. The local participation would get people from all over America involved in a "George Bush" initiative. It would be a strong symbol of domestic policy interest by a president known mostly for his foreign policy interest. And it would give the president a legitimate reason to make political visits to every region of the country. It was easy to see that Lamar Alexander had a special talent for political organization and strategy. He was also willing to dedicate enormous time and energy to the task. Lamar went ahead with the project, as approved by the president. Unfortunately, the White House never seized on the project to fully develop its political potential. It was another opportunity lost.

April 30, 1992—The White House operator called at 6:30 A.M. to say Jim Miklaszewski of NBC was calling about riots in Los Angeles following the acquittal of the police involved in beating Rodney King. I didn't take the call, but sat up, fully awake, trying to think of a plan. My idea was to issue an early statement by the president urging calm, a morning meeting between the president and Attorney General William Barr to decide the appropriate federal legal response, a statement by the Department of Justice on its civil rights investigation, and presidential remarks tying all this together at a speech later in the day already scheduled for Columbus, Ohio.

I arrived at the White House at 7:15 A.M. and immediately went to the Oval. The president and Sam Skinner were in the president's study. The president asked about a statement, and I outlined my plan. He reached for the phone to call Bill Barr, who said the federal civil rights investigation would be accelerated. I suggested we schedule an 11:30 A.M. meeting with Barr at the White House and cancel the Columbus trip, which was a physical fitness event with Arnold Schwarzenegger. We didn't need any pictures of the president in a jogging outfit on this day. The president also invited Dr. Louis Sullivan, secretary of health and human services, and the only African-American in the cabinet, to attend with any ideas he had about special programs that could be targeted for South Central Los Angeles.

I left the study at 7:45 A.M., dictated a brief statement expressing the "frustration and anguish" everyone who saw the videotapes of the beating must feel, and took it back to the president at 8 A.M. for approval. I read it to the senior staff at 8:10 A.M., where Connie Horner and William Kristol, both hard-line conservatives, objected to the "frustration and anguish" line on the grounds that it signaled opposition to the verdict. The president left it in. Kristol, who is a very creative conservative thinker and later became a leader in the Republican Party's 1994 rejuvenation, immediately leaked it to the "Evans and Novak" column that conservatives were opposed to the language.

There is an axiom of the modern presidency at play here: A president has to reflect the response of the nation or he will be judged out of touch. And just as significantly, it's often the press that determines that response. Thus when pro-democracy demonstrators rioted in Tiananmen Square in Beijing, China, the president knew there was little America could or should do in protest. Cutting off trade would eliminate much of the impetus for change in China. Name calling would only harden Chinese attitudes. But because of the emotional pictures on television, and the visceral response of the American people, we issued harsher and harsher White House statements on a daily basis.

Similarly, we didn't want to be judgmental in any way about the Rodney King court case because the federal government would probably have further legal involvement, which we did. A federal civil rights suit was brought by the Bush administration. But I felt the King beating tapes were so emotional, and the public reaction so revulsive, that we had to at least recognize the "anguish and frustration" of those who had viewed the tapes.

I returned to my office, issued the statement, and began dictating another to issue after the 11:30 A.M. meeting. It was just a framework that would have to be fleshed out at the meeting. Bill Barr worked on the statement, announcing that the Justice Department would step up its civil rights investigation, and the federal government would focus its housing, small business, and social programs on the problems of rebuilding the area. The president delivered the statement on-camera in the press briefing room at 12:02 P.M. and walked off without taking press questions. The president was perceived as strong, concerned, and leading.

The president set in motion a number of actions to help. These included a personal visit to Los Angeles, the sending of a special federal task force to the city, and, perhaps most important, bringing the political leaders of Southern California to Washington to meet with Democratic congressional leaders, Senator George Mitchell, House Speaker Tom Foley, and the relevant committee chairmen. Mitchell had already made it clear that his Democratic Congress was not going to pass anything that helped the president in an election year, and Republican bitterness about his "politics over the country" was strong. Mitchell had made it clear to the administration that no matter how bad the economy was, he would never let a capital gains tax cut pass the Senate, and he would never allow any economic stimulus program to pass unless it included a tax increase, thus giving Democrats a political victory. The president knew he had to establish a commitment between George Mitchell and the California leaders, meaning let the Democrats have the credit—if Los Angeles was to get any aid. Even so, the legislation to rebuild Los Angeles stalled and stalled, with very little of it passing. Mitchell's bitter partisanship was the genesis of congressional gridlock that did not start to dissipate until his retirement in 1994.

Monday, May 4, 1992—I stepped in it, as we say on the farm. And the "gotcha" press performed its usual "create a scandal" routine. In the course of my daily briefing, the press was pushing hard for specific programs that the administration would develop for Los Angeles. Our plan wasn't ready yet, but it was to include enterprise zones to lure business and jobs to the inner city and housing incentives to encourage home ownership. The liberal press corps, of course, wanted direct social programs like Jobs Corps and federal work programs. I told the press, "We believe that many of the root problems that resulted in the inner-city difficulties were started in the 1960s and '70s and [the programs] have failed. We believe that we do need additional efforts that are made in the area of people getting independence and the ability to get jobs and to earn their way out of whatever situation they're in; to give them hope, to give them homes, to give them a stake in the community. We believe that there needs to be a basic redirection of the inner-city programs that focus on giving people pride in what their abilities are, and to earn a living and to have a stake in the community."

All of that was meant as a tip-off to the kinds of programs we were considering, and to guide reporters away from rumors about Job Corps kinds of programs. Unfortunately, I chose a few of the hot-button words—the reference to the failures of the '60s and '70s.

Two days later *The Washington Post* leaped to the defense of the liberal legacy and escalated the incident to a full-scale political issue, seizing the opportunity to portray Republicans as uncaring and giving the Democratic presidential hopeful, Bill Clinton, an opening. The *Post* ran a full page of academic responses from historians and political scientists on the "Fitzwater Theory." It was such overkill that I broke into laughter as I read that James Q. Wilson, a UCLA public policy expert, said that "There is one sense in which Fitzwater may be right, and that is if he means that our welfare system has made it easier for children to grow up in fatherless families and for fathers to escape their responsibility and for there to be a divorce between income and work." I agreed with that idea, of course, but had never considered it in making my original comments. Mickey Kaus, author of *The End of Equality*, said, "Fitzwater has a point." Glenn Loury, Boston University professor of economics, said, "I understand Fitzwater's statement as political rhetoric." Nine other national authorities opined on the Fitzwater concept. I loved Stanley Crouch, author of *Notes of a Hanging Judge*, when he wrote, "No, I don't agree with Fitzwater but I don't disagree either." He could have been a spokesman.

The best parts were responses by Joe Califano, a distinguished aide to LBJ and former secretary of health, education, and welfare, and Jack Kemp, secretary of housing and urban development. Both are friends and I'm sure they were asking themselves the question, "Why the hell am I responding to Fitzwater?" But they did. Such is the lure of publicity for a politician.

Then, to top it off, the *Post* ran a picture of LBJ with a quote on the Great Society, a picture of President Bush with a quote on the role of government, and a picture of me with my '60s and '70s quote. "That's me," I thought, "in the company of presidents." Of course, I do believe I was right, and Speaker of the House Newt Gingrich is saying many of the same things in the 1990s. It does point up the problem, however, of having 80 to 100 reporters stationed at the White House all day long with nothing to report but every word a press secretary says, social philosopher or not.

This incident also dramatizes the philosophical change in American politics between 1992 and 1994. Liberalism was still politically correct, and any attack on the Great Society programs of the 1960s was immediately challenged and ridiculed. After the midyear elections of 1994, the political climate had moved so far to the right that Senator Phil Gramm and Speaker of the House Newt Gingrich could blast the social experiments of the '60s all day long, and the press knew it was politically correct to do it.

May 6, 1992—Another special strategy session was called for Room 180. Teeter introduced Robert Wellstein of the University of Michigan, who did statistical modeling for corporate clients. Wellstein polled people on specific questions, then fed the information into a statistical model that projected how they would respond to different situations. His greatest success was in interviewing people about cars and then telling General Motors what kind of cars they would buy. In our case, he interviewed 1,000 people, ran the data through his model, and concluded that "character" was the president's strongest asset. "He's likable. He's like *Father Knows Best*, Robert Young," Wellstein said. Once again, we found a way to avoid deciding on a message or an issue for the president to run on.

June 20, 1992—A friend of mine called her astrologer to ask about President Bush's chances of reelection. "I know what you want," the astrologer said, "and I already have it. President Bush will be fine after July. I did his chart, and Ross Perot's chart, although I don't have all the details on him. I did them both for Kathy Super last week." Kathy Super was the president's scheduling secretary, and had worked for the president for a dozen years. She undoubtedly had given the astrologer's feedback to the president. Now I had to worry about this getting to the press. After the revelations about Mrs. Reagan making decisions for her husband on the basis of an astrologer's advice, we didn't need this story to get out. It didn't. She was wrong anyway. Things got much worse after July.

June 21, 1992—*The Washington Post* broke a story that Ross Perot had hired a law firm in Washington to get any dirt they could on President Bush. I immediately called it "shocking intimidation." This was a big break. Everyone knew about Perot's paranoia and his vindictive efforts to destroy his enemies, but this was the first documentation. I was mobbed by reporters as we got off *Air Force One* at the first campaign stop. By this time the internal heat was rising and most of our political advisers were seeking a trash-and-burn reaction to Perot. I took the guidance and called him "Paranoid. Suffering from delusions and paranoia."

Roger Ailes called a few days later to say, "Keep the pressure on Perot. I'm afraid our folks will turn to mush. Say, 'Methinks he doth protest too much.' People believe that old cliché."

I added, "He's afraid of others because he works so hard at making others afraid of him." The press loved it. But Perot's vindictiveness grew even hotter.

July 20, 1992—The president called a meeting in the Oval with his economic advisers, Michael Boskin, Nicholas Brady, Dick Darman, Clayton Yeutter, and Skinner. Boskin said second-quarter economic growth would be lower than in the first quarter, maybe around 1.5 percent. The first quarter was 2.7 percent. The president's face went ashen. He slumped down in his chair. "This is the worst news I've ever heard," he said. "How do we handle this?"

Boskin suggested explaining the volatility of the numbers, comparing them to the 1982 recession, and suggesting they would go up and down.

Yeutter suggested explaining how this recession was different due to structural changes in corporations and their effect on Wall Street.

Brady said forget the numbers and talk about the recovery anyway. He was convinced the economy was recovering.

Darman said freeze spending, and promise to veto any appropriation bill that was one dime over current levels.

Faced with four different opinions, the president asked Boskin to answer a series of questions in writing that he could use with the press. The president had the same problem everyone did in pinning Boskin down. I helped prepare the questions. The last one was: "How can you be elected president in a recession with rising unemployment?" Boskin said he wasn't qualified to answer such a political question.

July 14, 1992—Sam Skinner called at 10:30 P.M. He was dejected. Things were going badly. He implied for the first time that he might quit. "I don't know if I'm helping," he said. "The campaign is trashing me. Yet they're not doing anything. Events are not getting scheduled. Contacts aren't being made. Teeter keeps blaming the White House."

"Talk to the president," I said. "Lay it on the line. Either you take over the campaign or bring [James A.] Baker in."

"I will tomorrow," he said. But I don't think he did. At least Sam recognized the problem: that somebody had to take charge and make decisions.

July 23, 1992—The preconvention low point. The campaign kept complaining that the White House couldn't even write a fact sheet on our programs. Normally, fact sheets are written by entry-level staffers. Somehow, due to the bureaucratic power structures of the White House, it was decreed that all fact sheets would be written by the Office of Policy Development, headed by Roger Porter. Unfortunately, Roger couldn't write his name in less than three pages. So Deputy Chief of Staff Henson Moore called a meeting in his office to discuss the matter with Roger. Attending were Clayton Yeutter, former secretary of agriculture and U.S. trade representative; Mike Farren, former undersecretary of commerce; Steve Provost, the president's speechwriter; and the president's press secretary. Our purpose was to teach political fact sheet writing to a tenured professor of government at Harvard University who had already written two books on the presidency.

Farren produced an outline of a fact sheet from Bob Teeter. "First, you state the problem, with as many figures as possible," Farren said.

"The whole problem, or the more narrow problem presented by the action?" Porter asked.

I threw up my hands and left.

It was shortly after this that Claire Pickart entered my office with another one of those peculiar phone calls: "Do you know someone named Buffalo Bob Smith?"

I broke into song: "It's Howdy Doody Time. It's Howdy Doody

Time." That's about all of the lyrics I could remember, but I certainly knew the countenance of Buffalo Bob Smith and his redheaded, freckly faced friend.

"He's on the phone," Claire said, "and wants to give you one brief idea."

"Put him on," I said. I wondered if I would recognize the voice.

"Marlin," he said, "this is Bob Smith. I know you're having a tough time up there. I have one word for you to use—to put in all the president's speeches—and it will magically make things right."

"What is it?" I asked.

"Cowabunga!" he said.

I was beginning to wish I hadn't taken the call.

"That's right," he said. "Use it and I know it will work. Good luck."

I sat down in my chair, put my feet on the desk, loosened my tie, and shouted to Claire: "I have ten dollars for anyone who can tell me what 'cowabunga' means." Then we started laughing. More staff wandered in, repeating the word "cowabunga." Claire, in her rich Tupelo, Mississippi, accent, started singing, "Cowabunga, cowabunga." Tears were rolling down my cheeks as I laughed and thought: What is this world coming to?

July 23, 1992—We were flying on the C-20 executive jet from Dayton, Ohio, to Columbia, Missouri, when former president Jerry Ford called President Bush to discuss the campaign. The president hung up and said Ford called to recommend replacing Vice President Quayle on the ticket. Ford said he did it with Vice President Nelson Rockefeller "after Rocky came to me in the Oval Office and said, " 'You can't get the nomination without the right wing, so I'll take myself out.' "

"I thought Rumsfield got ticketed with that one," the president said.

President Ford hesitated, then said, "No, Rockefeller came to me." Even after fifteen years, and in conversation with another president, President Ford played the game. He would not admit that he had given advance approval for his chief of staff, Donald Rumsfield, to urge Rockefeller to withdraw. He had.

In recounting the conversation, President Bush said, "I could never get away with taking Quayle off the ticket. But a lot of people are talking about it."

"Even the right wing is talking about it," I said. "Of course, they want Kemp."

"I could never take Kemp," he said. "Can you imagine how out of control he would be?" Kemp was a very creative and energetic housing secretary. But he wanted to be president. Indeed, he ran against Vice President Bush in the early skirmishes for the 1988 nomination. To help unify the party, President Bush named Kemp as his housing secretary. But in cabinet meetings he couldn't resist commenting on economic and foreign policies. Other cabinet members resented it. Worse, Jack always had a sort of "class clown" habit of smirking, or rolling his eyes, when others, including the president, said things he didn't agree with. Invariably, the Kemp position opposing the president would appear in an "Evans and Novak" column within days.

Usually Kemp's objections related to foreign policy, where Secretary of State James Baker normally charted a course more moderate than Jack supported. The most dramatic example occurred in the waning days of the Soviet empire, when Gorbachev was trying to hold the Soviet Union together at the same time he was giving its republics more political freedom. U.S. policy was to support this process, believing that a sudden breakup of the Soviet Union would mean civil war and a destabilization that could put nuclear weapons into unreliable hands. The first and most divisive application of this policy was in Lithuania. The United States had never formally recognized its absorption into the Soviet Union during World War II, but under existing circumstances, we were not quite ready to recognize its independence either. The new leader of Lithuania, Vytautas Landsbergis, was pressing Gorbachev for its independence, and was pressing the United States to aid in that process by also recognizing its independence. Secretary Baker and the president were walking a tightrope, trying to support the aspirations for freedom of the Lithuanians and at the same time support Gorbachev's democratic reforms. Jack Kemp had trouble walking such fine lines.

One day, as luck would have it, Jack was scheduled to accompany the president to a housing speech immediately after a cabinet meeting. The discussion had been about Lithuania and Kemp had stated his view that America should recognize the independence of the country and let Gorbachev's chips fall where they may. After the president adjourned the meeting, a disgusted Secretary Baker followed the president into the Oval Office to complain about Kemp's comments being contrary to U.S. policy. Secretary Kemp also moved from the Cabinet Room to the Oval, in preparation for an immediate departure on *Marine One* for the housing speech. When he heard

Baker's comments to the president, he stopped just inside the rear door to the Oval and told Baker he was wrong on Lithuania.

Secretary Baker, recognizing the kind of personal confrontation better avoided, started to leave by the front door. Kemp kept talking. Baker stopped as he held the door wide open, could contain himself no longer, then turned to shout across the Oval Office, "Fuck you, Kemp!" For a second, time stood still. Everyone froze: the president behind his desk, Scowcroft next to the president, Gates near the windows, and I near the rear door. Then Kemp reacted.

The Oval Office suite of furniture, two couches with end tables, a coffee table, and two wing-back chairs, was between Kemp and Baker. Baker started down the hallway, past my office, and toward the West Lobby. Kemp reacted like a quarterback who had just been victimized by unnecessary roughness. He started running through the furniture, sidestepping the couch, dodging the end table, and breaking into the clear near the door. He chased Baker down the hallway, catching him just outside my office door. They were nose to nose when General Scowcroft caught up to remind the secretary of housing and urban development that the president was ready to leave. These kinds of incidents did little to move Jack Kemp up the ladder of potential vice presidential candidates.

The president greatly valued loyalty in a vice president. He had made it the hallmark of his own vice presidency. And from my vantage point, he never gave any opening to those who wanted to replace Vice President Quayle. In a 1994 book by *Newsweek* magazine on the presidential campaign, author Thomas DeFrank recounts how several staff people talked about removing Quayle from the ticket. The book implies that the president was willing to listen. I don't believe he was. He never gave any private signals of encouragement that I saw. I even remember complaining to Andy Card that the president seemed awfully hard-line in not even considering such a move. The president's attitude on Quayle was dominated by three factors: Bush had personally picked him; Quayle had received a savage beating from the press; and the eight years that George Bush had spent as vice president. President Bush knew the tortures that Dan Quayle had been through. He would not desert him under any circumstances.

That night I went to Camp David with the president for the weekend. I stayed in Dogwood cottage, which had been the site of visits by Bebe Rebozo, Russian field marshal Akhromeyev, Soviet leader Leonid Brezhnev, and Henry Kissinger, among many others. I had a lot of trouble sleeping in the same bed once slept in by some of these leaders: Brezhnev and Ceausescu of Romania. In addition, a new poll out that day showed us down by thirty points.

August 11, 1992—Yitzhak Rabin, the newly elected prime minister of Israel, came to Kennebunkport, Maine, to meet with the president. It was no secret that the president and former prime minister Shamir had sometimes had difficult relations. But in fairness, I remember those occasions during the Persian Gulf War when President Bush had to call Shamir in the middle of the night to tell him that Iraqi Scud missiles were about to fall on Israel. The president offered more Patriot missiles to intercept the Scuds, but always had to plead with Shamir not to retaliate—not to turn the war against Iraq into an Israel-Arab conflict. Shamir always held back. These were incredibly tough moments for Bush and Shamir. While they never really "liked" each other, they recognized each other's leadership qualities. Both were tough men who knew their purposes in the war.

But President Bush saw Rabin's election as an historic opportunity to move the peace process forward, and he wanted to seize it. After their meeting in the president's spacious living room, in which they agreed on $10 million in housing loans to Israel, the two men walked the nearly 200 yards to the president's small, detached office cottage near the entrance to Walker's Point. The press were waiting. But in spite of the historic nature of this meeting, the press were abuzz with a *New York Post* story that morning suggesting that President Bush had had an affair some years before with a woman on his staff. This was just gossip, denied by everyone, and written off several years before by *The Washington Post*, which had declared it to be nothing more than gossip.

The press corps had been looking for a way to smear the president on this issue for some time. Gennifer Flowers had held a nationwide press conference to accuse Bill Clinton of a twelve-year extramarital affair. The press carried the story broadly. Clinton survived the scandal. But it left the press corps of two minds: those who wanted to get some dirt on Bush in order to at least level the playing field for Clinton, and those who wanted to attack Bush because they felt guilty for carrying the Clinton sleaze story. In both cases, we lost.

Sure enough, after a few perfunctory questions about U.S.-Israel relations, Mary Tillotson of CNN asked the president if he had had an affair. There was stone silence. The president's face hardened, then he simply said, "No. It's a lie." The Bush family attitude toward the media hardened that day to granite, and I didn't blame them. The occasion for this sleazy question by Mary Tillotson was a press conference at the president's home, attended by his wife, daughter, grandchildren, and his own mother. The grandchildren instinctively knew something terrible was wrong, as all children do when their parents are threatened, and they looked frightened. Granddaughter Noelle started crying and Mrs. Bush quietly led her away.

It was an ugly moment that seemed so unfair. I had known Mary Tillotson for many years, even when she was a Washington radio broadcaster doing traffic reports. She was aggressive and ambitious, clawing her way to success at CNN as the number-two White House correspondent. She talked incessantly, and would never stop asking questions—the kind of reporter who asks why after everything you say. She has a square jaw around otherwise small features, black hair, and a small mouth that always gave me the impression of a magpie sitting on a telephone wire. I was so stunned and so angry I simply could not talk after the press conference.

Ellen Warren, correspondent for the Knight-Ridder Newspapers, filed this pool report after the press conference on my reaction to the Tillotson question:

> Fitzwater was very tight-lipped on this issue. Asked by the pool whether Bush was familiar with the *Post* report, the press secretary said, "I have nothing for you." When a reporter suggested to Fitzwater that the question had to be asked and that the matter should not be held against the CNN reporter who posed it, Fitzwater showed no animation. His lips didn't move. His eyes didn't twinkle. Nothing.

Ellen got it right. At that moment I hated the press corps for being so cowardly. They said they had to ask because the *New York Post* ran an article, as if they had no independent will or judgment, as if *The New York Times* has to run a story about space aliens because the *National Star* does. Nonsense. In truth, they couldn't wait to embarrass the president. This was a totally media-generated story, based on an ostensible quote from a dead man named Lou Fields in a book called *The Power House*. There was never one piece of independent research or confirmation on the Fields assertion. But the Clinton campaign's political director, James Carville, sent fax after fax of the book reference to mainstream reporters. And they couldn't wait to get it in print.

A few days later in Washington, Mary Tillotson stopped by outside my office to say that Andy Rosenthal of *The New York Times* had told her that I intended to "put her out of business," meaning not talk to her.

"No," I said to Mary, "I hope you'll never notice any difference in treatment. You're a professional journalist. We'll treat you that way. But I want to tell you how I feel personally. I think what you did was sleazy and despicable. It was outrageous and disrespectful."

"If it wasn't me," she said, "it would have been somebody else. My office expected me to do it."

"That's no excuse," I said. "Every reporter has to have her own ethics, and make her own decisions. You made yours."

I turned to go back into my office. Mary started crying, then turned and walked away. The matter was never mentioned again.

There is an important principle for modern journalism involved here. Many media critics today say journalism is too negative, too interested in sleaze and personality dysfunctions, too eager to destroy the reputation of federal officials. I believe this results from the phenomenal growth of journalism in the last two decades, from satellite television with 500 cable channels, to tabloid television that focuses on the underbelly of society, to the supermarket tabloids. Yet in spite of these new markets for information, the major daily newspapers, major television networks, and others generally perform by the same standards as they have historically. But it's more difficult to guard their journalistic principles today, as they face competition from a growing group of less principled organs of information. Responsible journalists do not have to smear a president just because irresponsible journalists do.

August 13, 1992—The president called me to the Oval to say, "We want to announce Baker [to take over as chief of staff] at 10:15 A.M. I'll announce it in the briefing room, but not take any questions. Baker will make a speech at 11 A.M. at State. He will be chief of staff. Skinner will be National Republican Chairman, the old Laxalt job, and Margaret [Tutwiler] will come over with Baker. [Bob] Zoellick, [Dennis] Ross, and [Janet] Mullins will also come. Of course, I don't know if Skinner will take this." The president handed me an announcement statement, obviously written by Baker. It was exciting to think that the old Baker efficiency was coming back to the White House. He would have every detail of this thought through—the statement, the timing, the calls to make and the interviews to give. It was a great feeling of relief to know he was returning.

"I think Skinner will take it," I said. "He's talked about Baker coming over in some capacity. He expects something. He's also talked to Henson [Moore] and Clayton [Yeutter], but I don't know their reaction." It was clear they would both be replaced by the Baker staff.

The president's phone rang and he picked it up immediately, obviously an arranged call. "Marlin," the president said, "get on the other line." I walked over to the white couches in front of the fireplace, sat down, and picked up the phone on the end table.

"Marlin," Baker said, "has the president laid this out for you?"

"Yes," I said.

"Take a look at the statement," Baker said, knowing the president was on the line. Baker broke into his teasing sense of humor. "It has a lot of good things about me. You may want to tone it down."

"Sure," I said, laughing.

The president picked up on the joke. "See if it says anything good about me," he said.

"It gives him some credit," Baker joked into the phone.

"Marlin," Baker continued, "Margaret wants out of the press. You've worked so close with her. Can she take over communications?"

"That's great," I said. "I want out of communications."

"He's mostly out of it anyway," the president said.

Baker hung up and I read the statement carefully, suggesting we make only minor changes. James A. Baker would be coming back to the White House as chief of staff and director of the campaign. He would be my seventh chief of staff in nine years in the White House. He was my first, and would be my last.

September 4, 1992—James Baker took over the staff and immediately instituted a core campaign group meeting at 6 P.M. every evening in his office, including Margaret Tutwiler, Janet Mullins, Bob Zoellick, Dennis Ross, Dick Darman, Fred Steeper, Fred Malek, and Bob Teeter. Everyone attended. No one was late. We needed this leadership so badly back in May and June when we still had a chance. But the president delayed because he just didn't believe Clinton could be elected, and Baker wanted to push the Mideast peace process as far as possible before the end of the administration. The result was Baker taking over in September with a big hill to climb. But at least it felt like a campaign, with one leader, and decisions were being made.

Fred Steeper's polls showed we were winning in five or six states, four or five were undecided, and Clinton had the rest. His polling questions showed we needed "a dramatic economic program." More than 80 percent of those polled wanted cuts in the White House and congressional staffs. Most everyone thought we had no economic plan. While Fred was going through the numbers, I scribbled a note on a blue five-by-seven pad with the words "Agenda Five" at the top. Below, I listed:

  5 percent cut in White House and congressional salaries
  5 percent tax rate cut, across the board
50 percent cut in White House and congressional Staff
  5 years to reach a balanced budget

I handed it to Zoellick. He smiled. Zoellick is a serious-minded economics scholar who worked for Baker at Treasury, then went to State as undersecretary for economic policy. He was an incredibly hard worker, at his desk well into the night putting his ideas on a yellow legal-sized pad, willing to spend hours explaining administration policies to staff and reporters, and willing to provide the sound bites that explained a complicated economic theory in twenty seconds.

I handed it to Teeter. He smiled.

I handed it to Baker, who passed it to Margaret. Her face lit up. "This is it," she said.

Baker asked Zoellick to see what he could do with it. It turned out that Baker and Zoellick had already decided to produce an economic program for the campaign, based principally on existing administration proposals. Zoellick worked all weekend to produce the economic program entitled "Agenda for American Renewal." We scheduled a speech at the Detroit Economic Club to release it. Booklets would be printed. Our message was finally being formed. My ideas were only a very small contribution to the final program, but it felt great to at last have a campaign message.

August 27, 1992—Baker called me to his office, then led me across the hall to Bob Zoellick's office. "We've got to have a way to respond to Clinton," he said. "Nobody seems to be able to break through." He read me a wire story in which Clinton called the president a liar and Pinocchio.

"We need to emphasize the doublespeak aspect of Clinton," Zoellick said, "and use the Powell and Schwarzkopf statements. Clinton keeps saying Schwarzkopf wanted the war to go on. That's not true and someone needs to nail Clinton on it." Powell and Schwarzkopf had both given us a written statement that said Clinton was wrong.

"Sure," I said, "but the press will accuse me of being too political in the White House. Howie Kurtz ran a story in the *Post* a few weeks ago quoting Paul Begala as saying I am the most political press secretary in this century." Even the press who knew I had been a civil servant for seventeen years, and had never met Ronald Reagan till I got to the Oval Office, called me political. I figured, so be it.

"Can't you say this is personal?" Baker said. "You've been with Bush a long time and Clinton's called Bush a liar. You feel you have to speak out."

"OK," I said, and headed down to the briefing room and the wire service booths. "I have this wire story," I began, "that has Clinton calling Bush a Pinocchio and a liar. I've been with the president a long time and this is just outrageous. Clinton's record for honesty and veracity is such that he shouldn't be calling anyone a liar. And look how he ignores the Powell statement yesterday saying both he and Schwarzkopf advised the president to end the war. Either Clinton doesn't know this, or doesn't want to know. He's the king of doublespeak."

There was silence when I finished. Before anyone could ask a question, I turned and walked away. The wires all ran the story. It appeared on the evening news and in the next day's daily newspapers. Predictably, of course, George Will said on the Sunday *Brinkley* show that it was unprecedented for a government spokesman to be this political. Tom Wicker, a *New York Times* columnist, said he had never seen anything like it. Only ABC White House correspondent Brit Hume pointed out that Clinton had called Bush a liar and a Pinocchio. The establishment press corps was in bed with Clinton.

September 29, 1992—we weren't eager to debate. Clinton was good in a debate format, glib in rebuttal, and, most importantly, appeared willing to say anything without regard to truth. It's very dangerous to debate someone who will make any charge, claim any fact, and never seem to worry about the consequences. Furthermore, the Republican representative on the National Debate Commission, Frank Fahrenkopf, seemed to have bought into the commission as some holy crusade and, from our viewpoint, was playing right into Clinton's hands. The commission would propose debates. We would decline. It seemed to us that the commission was doing Clinton's bidding.

Thus I was quite surprised en route to our fourth city of the day, Clarksville, Tennessee, when President Bush called me to his cabin and handed over a two-page, typewritten statement. "I'm going to deliver this at the next stop," he said, which was Austin Peay State University in Clarksville. The statement announced a challenge of four debates on four Sundays, and two more between the vice presidential candidates. Knowing how much the president disliked debates, I thought he was joking. Before I could finish reading it a second time, the president said, "Steve [Provost, the speechwriter] has it. Do whatever you need to do."

I ran to the back of the plane to see Steve. "Yes, it's true," he said. "Here's the full speech and statement at the top."

I asked Mary Matalin, sitting nearby, "What do you think of this?"

"Ex-cell-ent," Mary said in trademark fashion.

"What's our spin?" I asked. "Why are we doing this?"

"How about, 'We told you we wanted debates,' " she said.

It was late afternoon, fourth stop of the day, the press were tired, and we didn't have much time to make sure this speech got on the air. It seemed the best way was to get CNN to carry it live. But they had almost no time, and I doubted if they had a satellite truck in Clarksville. When *Air Force One* landed, I hurried off the plane to make arrangements. Now my adrenaline was flowing. We were finally taking charge of ourselves, at least, and maybe the campaign. This story was bound to put Clinton on the defensive. It had to be a surprise, and hopefully one that would be thrown at him by the press in a public place. That meant no leaks from Clarksville so there could be no advance warning to the Clinton staff.

In the motorcade from the airport, I radioed Michael Busch and Judy Smith of my staff, telling them to meet me "on arrival." They had already arrived at the university with the press corps and were setting up the press filing center. The minute our cars stopped, I jumped out and ran to Michael, Judy, and Sean Walsh, who had joined them. We had approximately fifteen minutes to put this together. I told Sean to get me Wendy Walker, CNN's senior campaign producer. I told Michael and Judy that we were making a big announcement, and I needed to go to the television network editing rooms. Follow us, they said. We ran into the gymnasium where the event was to be held. Bands were playing. Thousands of kids were cheering, "Four more years!" Bush banners were everywhere. It was a perfect location for good television pictures. The three of us rushed to the top of the stairs, where I ran into my worst fear, Ann Devroy of *The Washington Post*. If she found out, it would immediately leak to Clinton. Devroy would either call James Carville with the Clinton staff, or call *Post* reporter David Maraniss, who was traveling with Clinton, to get a reaction. I did the only thing a truly brave press secretary could do. I ducked into the first open door along the hallway.

Sean saw me go in and brought Wendy to the room. "Wendy," I said, "the president is about to make the biggest announcement of the campaign. I recommend you take it live."

"What is it?" she asked.

"I can't say," I said. "We're too afraid of leaks. You just have to trust me." On the one hand, that was asking a lot because she had to get people and equipment in place to cover the speech, and ask her bosses in Atlanta for air time, which meant preempting something already scheduled. Those decisions are not made lightly. On the other hand, she had every reason to trust me because she knew that I knew that, if this announcement was not as big as I told her, I would never be trusted again. She said OK, and ran out the door, with just ten minutes to rearrange the entire CNN network. Wendy was the best television field producer. Now Wendy Walker Whitworth, she is in charge of the *Larry King Live* show. The other networks had good people, but none cut as many spots during a campaign day, or were prepared to carry every speech live, or feed as many different shows as CNN.

With five minutes to go, I was paged by Jim Baker. I ran to a phone in the president's holding room. As I darted past the president, he asked, "What is it?"

"Baker," I said, and kept moving.

"Marlin," Baker said, "here's the spin. We wanted debates, but Clinton's people wouldn't talk to us. We're not dealing with the commission, so we proposed a six-debate package. Now it's time for Clinton to talk to us, and we'll work out the details. Got it?"

"Right," I said, and hung up. The Clinton team was afraid of Baker. They had studied the Baker negotiations with Mondale in the 1984 campaign and they didn't want to negotiate with him again. That's why they loved the commission, which they could control. By the time I hung up, the president was walking to the podium.

I ran back to the press filing center, where reporters were milling around waiting for the speech to begin. They were listening on the public address system. I shouted from the back of the room, "The president is going to make a major announcement at the top of his speech!" Then I turned on my heels and left. Reporters started running for telephones and typewriters. I went down the hall and emerged in the gymnasium just as the president started to speak. He led with the announcement, and the gym was rocking with thunderous applause, as if good old Austin Peay U. had just won the NCAA championship. People were chanting, "Four more years!" and kids were carrying streamers and banners around the gym floor. The networks' pool camera was on the floor of the gym, and I noticed it was panning the crowd. I started cheering like crazy. Ann Compton of ABC News saw me and pointed her cameraman in my direction. I thrust out my arms, fists clenched, and screamed to high heaven. By God, if they filmed me, they were going to see wild enthusiasm. And they did.

It all worked perfectly. The White House press corps was impressed by the announcement. We had turned the tables on Clinton and seized the offense. At the time of Bush's speech, Clinton was speaking in Ohio. As he walked off the stage, reporters yelled at him about "four debates."

Clinton didn't believe it. "No comment," he said. "You people have tricked me into this before." The news accounts reported him as "stunned," "caught by surprise," and "on the defensive."

That night we went to Nashville, our fifth city of the day, and the president appeared on *Nashville Now*, a TNN talk show at 10 P.M. Already that day he had made eight speeches and five appearances at fund-raising receptions. But he was on the show with his old friend, country singer Jimmy Dean. The president was just tired enough to let his guard down, his adrenaline was flowing, and he did a classic impression of Jimmy Dean selling "pure country pork sausage." The perfect end to a great campaign day.

There weren't many great campaign days in October and November. We were always between ten and twenty polling points behind Clinton. The final bitterness with the press erupted when Iran-Contra independent counsel Lawrence E. Walsh added information to his indictment of former Reagan secretary of defense Caspar Weinberger just four days before the election. Worse, from our campaign viewpoint, he included in the indictment a reference to Vice President Bush's involvement that had been raised and refuted years before. Among the papers was a Weinberger memorandum saying that he thought Vice President Bush had been in favor of trading arms for hostages. This accusation was meaningless because it didn't matter whether Bush was for or against. It was a technical addition to the indictment totally designed to excite the press and influence the election. Walsh grew to hate Reagan and Bush, and by 1992 his vindictiveness was driving his entire investigation.

The press were beside themselves. This was just the kind of bomb that could destroy an election for the candidate, and they all jumped on board the bandwagon. The day after the indictment, not one newspaper reported that the allegation against Vice President Bush was meaningless. Fortunately, we had previously scheduled a one-hour interview with CNN's *Larry King Live* for the night the story broke. This gave us a televised forum to refute the charges.

We spent all afternoon collecting the backup material, including congressional hearing reports, which showed the Bush reference was old and meaningless. The president laid all this out in the first part of the show, then they started to take call-ins. Tammy Haddad, producer of *Larry King Live*, had arranged for George Stephanopoulos, Bill Clinton's top political aide, to call in. He accused the president of lying. I was standing in the wings when the call came through and I couldn't believe Larry King would set us up, but it happened. We were never able to totally refute the story, and our polls started going down. We were within one or two percentage points in a CNN poll the day the Weinberger information was released, and we never got that close again.

The Walsh indictments fed into the "Iraqgate" hysteria initiated by Democratic congressman Henry Gonzalez of Texas, chairman of the House Banking Committee, who officially requested an independent counsel to investigate the administration's policy toward Iraq before the Persian Gulf War. There was no justification for any charge of illegality, but pack journalism gave this conspiracy theory quite a ride. Now-vice president Gore falsely accused President Bush of a cover-up. CBS's Mike Wallace and *The New York Times*'s William Safire fed the fires of scandal. The entire matter was politically motivated and amounted to zero. Henry Gonzalez demonstrated his buffoonish qualities to the nation when he tried to conduct Whitewater hearings involving President Clinton in 1993. By then Iran-Contra was just a memory.

Election day was a blur. I honestly, deep down, thought we would win in spite of the polls. The Clinton campaign had been so arrogant, so dishonest, and so filled with scandals about philandering and draft dodging that I just didn't believe that in the privacy of the voting booth people would vote for Bill Clinton. But they did. In the middle of the afternoon, I went to the president's suite in the Houstonian Hotel in Houston. I had been going to this suite for seven years, in the midst of every kind of national and international emergency, in good times and bad, but it was never as bad as this.

The Bush family was spread about the room, watching the results. George W., elected governor of Texas in 1994, was walking around in gym shorts. Some members of the family were in bathrobes. I felt out of place and didn't stay long. The president's family was around him and I knew that was the best support he could have.

Later, I dressed and went down to the motorcade forming up in the basement of the Houstonian for the trip to the Houston Convention Center where the president's concession speech would be given. I felt terribly alone as the Bush family started getting into their cars. Once at the Convention Center, the president and his family moved through a tunnel leading to the staging area where they would appear. I was moving with them, jostled by well-wishers and other staff, when the president stopped the entourage. He turned to his family and said, "OK, let's go do this with style and dignity."

CHAPTER FIFTEEN

Through the White House, Warmly

As William Jefferson Clinton was taking his oath of office as our forty-second president on the front side of the Capitol, I slowly mustered the mental energy to climb out of the van, still part of a ghostly motorcade that would never again carry a president but that waited silently behind the Capitol for any emergency use. The echoes of the crowd and the speeches drifted through the columns and across the marble floors of the Capitol, but still were muted to those of us on the back side of the building. I listened carefully, trying to pinpoint the exact moment in the program, perhaps to hear the taking of the oath. It was amazingly still behind the Capitol, with police and officials walking aimlessly, just to kill time, a group of photographers gossiping behind a rope line, and the president's helicopter sitting alone in the parking lot, as if tethered to the Capitol by the walkway that stretched some thirty yards to the bottom of the steps.

I walked over to the bottom of the Capitol steps, joined by two members of my staff who had escorted our press pool to their position in the ceremony, and simply sat down to wait for the new president's inaugural speech to end. It was an empty feeling. I was a curiosity to those gathered near *Marine One*, someone to be left alone.

I lit up a grand cigar, faced the warm afternoon sun, and thought back to my last afternoon in this location, January 20, 1989, when I had walked down the Capitol steps with President Reagan as the retiring president, and back up the steps with the new president, George Bush. That day had been filled with anxiety about the transition: how to cast off all my study of Ronald Reagan, his reactions to people and events, his policies, his personal history, his attitudes toward every aspect of life, and how to learn all those same qualities about George Bush. They would be different men in different times and I knew that the slate must be wiped clean, that the sadness and melancholy of a departing administration must be replaced with the joy and enthusiasm of a new administration.

That morning I had joined President Reagan for a last look at the Oval Office he had occupied for eight years. It was a sunny day and the bulletproof glass turned the room yellow. I had never seen the Oval with the recessed lighting turned off. This morning, only the natural light came in, and I realized it was because no one was there to turn the lights on. No secretary. No staff. It gave the room an eerie effect, as if in twilight. When the president came in from the colonnade, it was like a movie, with the star returning in shadows for one last look at the ranch. I thought his old friends should be there—Randolph Scott, Bill Holden, and the others.

He walked around the Oval, touching items of furniture for the last time. He sat at his desk, barren of pictures or any sign of daily routine, and read aloud the inscription on the brass plate telling how U.S. whalers had saved the British ship HMS *Resolute* after it had been abandoned in the Arctic. Queen Victoria had the desk carved from the hull of the *Resolute* and gave it to President Rutherford B. Hayes. He read it as if he had never read it before. I marveled again at the sense of wonder in Ronald Reagan, his ability to absorb the small joys in life and make them part of his general optimism.

Then he pulled open the center drawer, finding to his delight the only item left in the desk, a small notepad with the caricature of a turkey printed at the top with the phrase: "Don't let the turkeys get you down." He wrote a note to President Bush, wishing him well, and placed the pad back in the drawer.

Chief of Staff Kenneth Duberstein and National Security Adviser Colin Powell arrived and the three of us stood silently as the president took his last measure of the room. As the president started toward the door, Colin reported that "the world is quiet today, Mr. President."

"Oh," the president said, "who do I give this to?" He took his wallet from his pocket and pulled out the card with the nuclear code numbers for starting the process of activating the armed forces.

"After the swearing-in," Colin said, "the military aide will take it."

The president restored the card to his wallet. Then he walked to the door, turned to his small audience of three, gave his two-fingered salute to the forehead, and walked out. It was more dramatic than any movie he ever made.

I couldn't imagine what it would be like to reenter that same room in the afternoon with the new president. I thought about it all through the oath-taking and the inaugural speech, trying to reframe my mind to accommodate the new team. After the address by President Bush, I rushed through the Capitol ahead of the presidents to be at the bottom of the steps when the Reagans walked to *Marine One* for the last time.

I saw President Reagan's executive assistant, Jim Kuhn, standing by the helicopter steps and I wanted to join him, as I had hundreds of times in locations around the world. But the time had come to step back and change horses. Suddenly, the Reagans and the Bushes emerged from the Capitol and started down the steps. Secretary of the Treasury and soon-to-be Secretary of State James A. Baker and his wife Susan were close behind. Baker and I were making the same transition.

The group walked to the bottom of the steps and shook hands. The first ladies embraced. Then the Reagans turned and walked to *Marine One.* No one moved as the helicopter roared its engines, raised slowly from the parking lot, then gently faded upward and away from the Capitol. President Bush continued to wave good-bye. Then he and Mrs. Bush turned to retrace their steps up to the Capitol where the new president would sign the traditional congressional log book and lunch with the leadership.

As the Bushes started up the steps, Jim and Susan Baker fell in step behind them. As they reached the fourth or fifth step, I moved to join them, and a very curious thing happened. Bush, Baker, and Fitzwater all started to cry. We just couldn't help it. Our lives had been so intertwined with Ronald Reagan's. And now our lives were tied for another four years. I realized that the new president was struggling with the same emotions I was: loss and discovery. They don't often go together. It's not often that life provides you expectation and excitement to simultaneously crowd out sadness and loss. I felt guilty for feeling so happy and just could not stop the tears. President Bush pulled out his ever-present white handkerchief and wiped his eyes. Baker fought back the tears in a losing battle. He put his arm around my shoulder and said what I was thinking, "We've been through a lot with him."

As we got to the top of the steps I broke off to find a deserted corner to compose myself. The president and Baker had it tougher. They had to meet the congressional leaders. I wondered how the press would report our tears, but little was said.

As President Bush's motorcade made its way down Pennsylvania Avenue that day, President and Mrs. Bush got out and walked the last few blocks. I was a hundred yards or so behind them, and I knew I shouldn't have done it because staff should always stay in the shadows, but I climbed out of my van and walked as well. Between the president and me were all sorts of people, Secret Service agents, police, staff, and parade watchers who wandered into the street, so I figured no one would notice me, except for Courtney, my fifteen-year-old daughter. I got her seats on the parade route so I knew where she was sitting. Courtney and Bradley had visited often in the White House, answering my phones and watching television. But I had not spent as much time with them as I had hoped. It had been a great sadness in my life. I wanted Courtney to see her dad in the inaugural parade. As I passed the president's reviewing stand, I saw her across the street and caught her eye. She looked very proud.

Later, I waited for the new president to come into the Oval Office for the first time. As vice president for eight years, he had been there often. But I wanted to see him discover President Reagan's note. Remarkably, the Oval now appeared bright and expectant, full of light and enthusiasm. President Bush's mood was the same, and he also examined the contents of the office as if he had never seen them before. He sat down at the desk and immediately pulled open the drawer, discovering the note. He read it to himself and smiled. "What a sweet man," he said to no one.

All of this flashed before me as I sat on the Capitol steps in 1993, now knowing the terrible sense of rejection that goes with losing the presidency. At least now I would complete the ending, take the walk to the helicopter, and the final flight on *Air Force One*. There was no going back this time.

Tim McBride, President Bush's personal assistant, said we should get aboard *Marine One*. "The president doesn't want anyone outside," he said, "and they're about to come." I doubted that the president had said any such thing, but it was still a good idea. The final pictures of the president leaving the Capitol should not be cluttered with staff. I climbed aboard and was soon joined by Tim, the president's military physician, and a Secret Service agent. With the front and rear doors open, and a rigid Marine at each site, we waited. Finally, the Bushes and Clintons emerged from the Capitol and started down the steps. At the bottom, the ritual from four years earlier was repeated, and then the Bushes were walking toward us.

They were walking proud, holding hands, and striding. Mrs. Bush's pearls were shining in the sun. I wanted so badly to jump down the helicopter steps, come to attention, and salute them aboard. Tim, it turned out, had the same urge, could not contain himself, and rushed down the steps, coming to attention as the Bushes approached the chopper. I wanted to follow him, but held back. For nearly ten years I had followed the rule that nobody goes aboard *Marine One* ahead of the president, and everybody gets off before he does. It seemed very strange to be waiting inside as the president slid into his seat, leaned in to the window, and began waving. No one said a word.

As the chopper raised itself away from the Capitol and started down the mall toward the White House, I thought of all the presidents who had made one last pass over the executive mansion before heading on to Texas, or Georgia, or California. They all strained to see every detail, to tuck away the memories. I realized that I was searching the grounds, the building, even the parking lot, to see if I recognized anyone. But it was like leaving college after graduation. Everyone was gone. The White House was just a building, a monument, a house for our presidents. No one I knew lived there anymore.

Then *Marine One* started to bank around the White House, passing so close I could see in my old office window. It was dark. But suddenly, as if with X-ray vision, I could recognize a few friends, my extended family of reporters waiting patiently in the briefing room for the new president to come claim his prize. I could see Helen Thomas as if she were sitting beside me, hunched over her computer in that little UPI cubicle, throwing old news clippings of the Bush years into a waste can, and starting new files on Bill Clinton. She shoved her glasses back on her nose, and made some cryptic comment in response to a distant conversation she could hear in the back of the room. She was ready to take on the newcomers.

As *Marine One* circled back to Andrews Air Force Base, Mrs. Bush uttered the first words I could hear, and they were exactly the same, I was told, as Mrs. Nixon's nearly twenty years earlier. "It's so sad," she said.

I had expected the three-hour flight to Houston on *Air Force One* to be tearful and traumatic, but it wasn't. President Bush had picked the manifest carefully. First, no press. I had weakly objected, but the president was firm. Frankly, I was glad. It was over. To hell with them. The president had picked his old friends to go home with him, many of whom had never worked in the White House; so there was a somewhat festive mood associated with greeting people who hadn't seen each other in years. People stood around in clusters talking about the congressional years, the CIA days, various campaigns, and how presidential candidates had been selected. Almost no one spoke of the 1992 campaign. After all, these were really the first stone cold hours of realization that it was over.

My compartment on *Air Force One* contained four seats, occupied that day by General Scowcroft, Margaret Tutwiler, David Bates, and myself. Bates had been with President Bush for years, as driver, assistant, and friend. He was emotionally exhausted and morose. Margaret was planning, or working, or keeping herself disciplined and organized as always. General Scowcroft and I were a mess. We had been with the president since day one of the administration, in every personal situation. The general and the president were close in age and outlook on life, both men of great dignity and sense of duty. They were each other's best friend. I remembered once when General Scowcroft had a hernia operation, he was back in the office working almost immediately. The healing process took longer than it should have, and the general took to sleeping in his office early in the morning. He had this insane notion that he required only three or four hours of sleep a night. At age sixty-seven, he would work till nine or ten at night, go home to care for his ailing wife, go jogging at midnight, then return to his office at five or six in the morning. Often I would drop by his office on the way home, about seven, and he would be taking a nap. After the hernia, he began looking pale and drawn, even sounding weak, so I took to checking on him every morning as well. One day he was asleep at 7 A.M. on his couch. The next day the same. So I went to the president.

"Mr. President," I said, "I'm not trying to intrude, but I think General Scowcroft needs some time off. He's sleeping on his couch in the mornings and he looks terrible. I don't think he will ever take proper care of himself unless you order him to do it."

"Thanks, Marlin," the president said. "He's going to see his sister next week and stay a few extra days for vacation. I've talked to him about it." Once again, the president had already recognized the problem.

On the way home to Houston, it seemed like such a great tragedy that these two old friends should be separated, never again to wander into each other's offices to discuss geopolitical affairs, to kid each other about their mistakes or their newspaper quotes that weren't quite right, to speculate on the actions of other heads of state, and to say things like "Let's call Helmut and see what he says about reunification." In many ways, the sudden end of a presidency is like a death in the family, or at least a divorce, because the separation is so final, so absolute, and leaves all parties feeling so hopeless. It takes weeks, or months, to see yourself in a different venue.

I leaned back in those plush leather seats of *Air Force One*, the likes of which are not duplicated on any commercial airline, in any class. My seat tilted back to three or four angles, and swiveled 360 degrees, allowing me to prop my feet on the fold-down desk, put on my earphones, and watch the nineteen-inch TV built into the upper corner of the room. The console at my fingertips on the wall included dimmers for the lights, stereo channel selection and volume control, television controls, curtain movements, and a telephone— not hard to get out of touch with reality in this setup. I figured the best way to fight the sadness was to sleep, but it would not happen. I could not stop the memories, the flood of vignettes of the last four years, an overwhelming kaleidoscope of events that were sweet and warm. As we flew to Houston, I remembered . . .

In the spring of 1992, when the president's campaign was stumbling, the Gridiron Club had its annual dinner at the Capital Hilton Hotel. The club is comprised of sixty journalists, mostly print, who throw a formal dinner every year for the same purpose and in the same manner, nearly 1,000 guests sitting cheek by jowl at long tables. It's a white-tie affair, which means a $58 rental fee just for starters, and lasts for nearly five hours as the members perform badly written skits and sing original songs that sometimes rhyme, making fun of the current status of Republicans and Democrats. Then a leading Republican and Democrat respond, and finally, after the president has endured hours of barbs, jokes, and songs at his expense, he is expected to give a speech that is witty, endearing, self-deprecating, and full of good humor. In reality, of course, by the time eleven or twelve o'clock arrives, he doesn't really want to give the speech and thinks all journalists are from the far end of the horse.

The head table is a real trip. It includes the president, vice president, cabinet, and military leaders from all branches of the service, who traditionally rise as the Marine Corps band plays their service songs during the evening. It's always clear that some attendees can't remember what branch of the service they were in, most can't remember their songs, and don't want to remember their military careers anyway. But it's tradition, so we all stand up. I attended about fifteen of these dinners, sitting at the head table for the last six. They were actually great fun, except for that vague feeling that we government officials were like puppets, either being ordered to perform for our media masters, forced to be the butt of jokes, or at least put in a sort of plantation atmosphere in which the journalists owned the cotton. I think they liked it better than we did.

Dave Demarest, President Bush's communications director, suggested that the president turn his speech into a comedy routine based on Johnny Carson's "Karnak the Great, the mystical soothsayer from the East who can recite the answers even before he hears the questions." Ed McMahon, of course, was the setup man who handed Johnny the envelopes containing the questions. I was designated for this illustrious role. It was an ingenious idea because it suited the president's humor. He liked to tease. He could take a ribbing himself. And it gave him someone to play off of, me.

I fiddled with the script, but didn't get to practice with the president until the day before the show. He called me to the Oval. I sat in the chair at the side of his desk, and he sat in his formal chair as if reading a national security directive. Demarest, the author, sat in front of the desk and served as our audience. Can you imagine humor in this situation? But after three or four lines, always followed by Demarest's dutiful laughter, the president was starting to enjoy calling me a "snack-sneaking snowball." Soon it didn't matter how bad the questions and answers were, the president was nearly falling out of his chair after delivering put-down lines like "Marlin, my full-figured flack." The president's name for this spoof was "Tarmac the Magnificent." After the president nailed me a couple of times, I decided to take a chance on responding.

"Tarmac seems full of himself," I responded in jest. That drove the president crazy with laughter.

"Sidekick thinks bald is beautiful," the president said. I was on the floor. It was a perfectly wonderful skit and we both loved it. Whether we could pull it off at the dinner was another matter.

The next night, I went up to the president's private quarters early for a final run-through of the script. Mrs. Bush was getting dressed as the president and I started on the jokes. Once again we got laughing so hard I was rolling on the couch. Mrs. Bush came out of the bedroom to admonish us. "You two are having so much fun, I bet you forget all your lines," she said. By then the president was making up lines like "Marlin, you sufferin' saucer of succotash." I had no idea what that meant, but it was so outlandish that coming from the president of the United States made it uproariously funny.

At the end of the evening, when it came time for the president to speak, the president of the Gridiron Club announced that President Bush had lost his voice and the press secretary, Marlin Fitzwater, would fill in for him. As I walked to the microphone, there was booing and hissing from the audience. I started my introduction by apologizing for the president, who had slipped away from the table to a curtain behind me, where he put on a bejeweled cape à la Johnny Carson. As I started talking to give the president time to get robed, half the audience was getting hostile and half knew that something was afoot. I quickly moved to the introduction of Tarmac, and the president emerged. The audience went crazy. From that point on, we had them. It was a momentous performance. I was calling the president "full of himself," "hot tonight," and "too political." He was calling me a "blubbering snow cone." We ended the skit, walked out the door, through the hotel to the president's limousine, and repeated our best lines all the way back to the White House.

A "nor'easter" hit the coast of Maine in late October 1991. The president's home was right in its path. The house sits at the tip of Walker's Point, a promontory of rocks that jut out into the Atlantic at the most exposed point off Kennebunkport. It's a beautiful site when the waves are gentle, with drifting sea gulls dipping sporadically into the whitecaps, and the rocks around the house wrapping their arms snugly around the property. But in a storm it looks, and is, dangerous. The house is terribly exposed, and the huge boulders look like pebbles as the water washes effortlessly over them.

When news of the storm reached the White House, everyone watched television for word of the Bush home. It was not good. After a sudden change of wind, a series of huge waves rolled over the tip of the point, and hit the house at seemingly its strongest point. The water struck the end of the living room, marked by the floor-to-ceiling stone fireplace, gushed through the structure and out the back side which was mostly glass, taking everything in the house with it. The Secret Service filmed most of it, and sent the tape the next day to the president, who was visiting in Texas. We watched in the bedroom of their hotel suite as the giant wave reached up over the rocks, over the side of the home, appeared over the chimney of the fireplace, then disappeared into the house. Finally we could see the walls of the entire structure bloat outward as the fury and pressure of the water sought release through windows and doors. Then it was gone. And everything inside the main floor of the house went with it: chairs, pictures, tables, china, everything—including the entire back side of the house. I was sitting on the floor, in a corner, trying to hide and keep from crying. It was so shocking that no one moved. I just got up and left, feeling this moment of grief for the Bushes was too private to share.

By the time we arrived in Maine a few days later to inspect the damage, some of the major debris had been removed, but the aftermath was painful. It was muddy, and large pools of water had collected in all the low areas. The president, Mrs. Bush, Andy Card, and I walked from the road out to the house. From the front, the house looked intact. But timbers were strewn everywhere. Windows missing. Grass matted in mud. Then we walked around to the back, to the ocean side. It was staggering. There were no walls. The entire back of the house was gone, open as if it were a dollhouse waiting for some child to put in the furniture. I turned and looked out to sea, as if trying to spot the couch where Prime Minister Mulroney had told Irish stories, the table where Jordan's King Hussein had begged for understanding, the chair where French president Mitterrand had finally taken off his tie. But the ocean had moved them to an undersea room so big they would never be found.

I felt sick. I watched the president to be sure he was all right. Actually, I think he was in shock, at least in some emotional sanctum where I didn't want to intrude. He prowled the area, looking for lost items. There were few. But in a swampy area near the house he found a framed picture of his father, glass broken, picture yellowed and wet with seawater. He held it, stared at it, and carried it with him. Finally, Dave Valdez, the president's photographer, asked if he could take it to be restored.

When the president went into the house to walk through rooms, nothing was left but the mint green carpet in the living room. It was soaked with mud, weeds, and brine. He tugged at it and asked for help. Together, he and several of his staff dragged it out to the yard, draped it over a fence, and he began to squeeze it and beat it to get the water out. It was hopeless. It could never be saved. But he worked at it for hours because that's all there was.

Finally, I brought the press corps up to the house to see and film the damage. Some of them were moved, but others were amazingly

detached, walking around as if viewing storm damage in some remote part of the country. None of them would write about it with
the emotion I thought it deserved, I guess because one person can
never truly understand another person's loss. When George Bush
visited the aftermath of Hurricane Andrew in South Florida, he
knew the loss those families felt. He knew the Federal Emergency
Management Agency grants and loans didn't mean a damn thing. He
ordered in the Army to set up tents and bring in trailer houses, to
give the people something to hold on to, to touch . . . a carpet to beat.

We were in Kennebunkport in August 1991, four months after the
end of the Persian Gulf War. The president invited me, Robert Gates,
who was soon to be director of the CIA, and Andy Card to go fishing
for bluefish on *Fidelity*, his nineteen-foot cigarette boat. He loved
that boat and fishing more than anything. Once, when he was vice
president, we boarded *Fidelity* at about ten at night at Portsmouth,
New Hampshire, for a three-hour run up the coast to Kennebunkport. He kept it full-throttle all the way, water spraying over
the bow, taking every wave with a thud and burst of speed. It was
great fun for the first hour, then my back started hurting, my legs
began to tire from flexing with the waves, and my fanny ached from
bouncing on the back bench. But his face was glued into the wind,
hair plastered back so he looked like the hood ornament of a 1956
Oldsmobile, and his windbreaker had long since failed to do its job.
As we neared Walker's Point, close enough to see the lights of the
house, he found a bit more power in the twin engines and we raced
into the cove at full speed. I asked why. He said it was the closest he
could come to duplicating the race of the wind from an open-cock-
pit airplane, the TBM Avenger he flew during World War II.
    Fishing was a different story. He liked to slowly troll the ocean.
"Throw a line in," he would say. "Let's see what's out there." Sometimes the pole would rest on his shoulder like a carbine, with the
line trailing out behind the boat. On this August day, the sun was
bright as we pulled away from his dock and headed out to sea along
the coast. A few hundred yards away we passed a large white house
overlooking the inlet. Dozens of kids were on the deck, drinking and
playing music. One of them spotted us. They started shouting and
doing "the wave," standing shoulder to shoulder along the porch,
arms in the air, swaying from side to side.
    "Let's return it," the president said. All four of us stood side by
side in the boat, arms outstretched, and returned the wave.

While we trolled for blues, we talked about Saddam Hussein's continued defiance of the UN and what we might have to do about it. But suddenly we got into a school of fish, and from then on it was all fishing. The president drove and we pulled out about ten apiece. When we got back to the house, he carried the buckets of fish up on the rocks, pulled a long, thin knife out of the tackle box, and cleaned them for dinner. We just stood and watched.

The only time I was ever physically afraid for the president or myself was in meeting with Syrian president Hafez al-Assad in Geneva, Switzerland, in November 1990. We had just completed a visit to the American troops in Saudi Arabia. Our forces were starting the big buildup from 200,000 to 400,000 troops, and the reality of war against Iraq seemed imminent. President Bush had been assembling the largest military coalition since World War II, and getting Syria to join was an important objective. Syria was officially designated a terrorist nation. It was a friend of Iraq. The names Assad and Syria had been linked to nearly all of the major terrorist acts against Americans for the past decade, including, of course, the hostages being held in Lebanon.

This meeting was essentially a payoff for Assad, who demanded it as a price for participating in the coalition. Our primary objective was not only to secure participation, but to get a commitment to fight. It had been assumed that Syria might send a token force to Saudi Arabia, but it was not clear that they would actually fight another Arab country.

The meeting was to start about 7 P.M. at the Geneva airport. With *Air Force One* parked only a few hundred yards from the meeting site, there was a strange feeling of danger in entering a building already occupied by Assad's guards. I could not get out of my mind the sight of the ski-masked terrorists at the Munich Olympics, or the pilot leaning out of the cockpit of a hijacked airliner, or the downing of Pan Am 103. These were people who killed without discrimination, anyone to make their point. It was an official fear that I had not felt since the first Soviet summit in Washington when the cold war was still raging. There was nothing predictable about it—what would be said, how would the security forces act? Pervading the atmosphere was a sense that on a different day, on a deserted street, these were people who could kill and we would never understand the reasons.

We met in a small room, with eight chairs situated so that the presidents would be side by side, facing their aides. This meant that both men had to turn in their chairs, or at least strain their necks, in order to talk directly. This had a very peculiar effect on Assad, because he has a long neck and an oval face that resembles a hooded cobra. With dark eyes, a small chin, and huge forehead, when he turned to President Bush it was like a snake preparing to strike, a very disconcerting posture indeed. In addition, he tended to talk in circles, in conversations that lasted for hours, introducing one subject then withdrawing into another, then returning to the original dialogue. His body would weave as he changed subjects and this tended to intensify the menacing aspects of his countenance. President Bush seemed to ignore all this, of course, but he did want to counter this meandering kind of conversation with directness. He wanted there to be no doubt about his position.

"We do not seek to harm Syria's vital interests in any way and we do understand your security concerns," President Bush began. "But I would like to make four key points.

"Saddam Hussein must leave Kuwait. There will be no rewards. Partial solutions are no solution at all.

"Sanctions. There is no evidence that sanctions by themselves will make him do a 180-degree turn and get out.

"He's adding new troops. I'm very concerned about his biological, chemical, and nuclear weapons capabilities.

"We will have in place very soon a credible, superb military option. We have massive air power against which he could not stand for ten minutes. Soon we will have our best tank force in place—the best.

"Mr. President," Bush continued, "I don't want to use that. I don't want to kill one Iraqi child. But I am determined that Saddam must get out. If not, I will use it."

Assad listened intently, looking straight into President Bush's eyes, no doubt taking stock of the man and the American commitment. He moved not a muscle. President Bush was as direct as possible, knowing the signal he was sending.

"Now we're going to the UN," President Bush said. "The Soviet Union will be with us. The Chinese will support us or abstain, we think. I would hope that you could support this. It would be a good signal that the man [Saddam] must leave peacefully. I would also like to hear your views on sanctions, and what happens if Saddam withdraws. My view is that a return to the status quo is unacceptable."

Then President Bush moved through the rest of his agenda: moving the Middle East peace process, resolution of the civil strife in Lebanon, human rights, and terrorism. This was difficult, because the president had to be unmistakably tough against Syrian terrorism, yet not bring the conversation to a halt.

"I am grateful to you for helping get our hostages out," he began. "They are on my mind every night. We still say our prayers in the Bush family. I know this is a sensitive matter with you. But I want you to know this is not some bureaucratic concern. It starts with me and Jim Baker. We believe terrorism still remains in Syria and Syrian-controlled areas, and you still plan attacks on U.S. interests."

The president spoke for twenty-five minutes before Assad began his presentation. He started with a smile, adjusting his glasses, and thanking the president for his limited time, a humorous reference to his desire for a meeting of several hours and our request for a one-hour limitation. "You must have traveled through several time zones, natural and political," he said of our Middle Eastern tour. "In 1974, I met Kissinger. We did a review of the horizon. When he finished, he said, 'I have digressed.' You have been very brief. A military man is normally brief. I am a literary man and will make exception and be brief."

Assad was sometimes hard to follow, but he was interesting, using metaphors and dropping American names like Kissinger. He had a high tenor voice with a slight rasp. But it had clarity. One could almost imagine him singing first tenor in a church choir.

It was clear all of Syria's attitudes toward the United States and the Middle East were shaped by Israel. "We know the U.S. backs Israel and will not stop. But whether good or bad relations, we will keep calling on the U.S. as a superpower to help. Israel is strongest country in this area. It is exploiting the Gulf to get more aid, new weapons, to defend itself against imminent Iraqi aggression.

"This relates to our destiny," he said.

President Bush interrupted. "Do you worry this all adds up to an attack on Syria by Israel?"

"This is axiomatic," Assad said. "Who else will Israel attack? They want to expand. These are stable convictions to us. All Arabs know Israel wants to expand from the Tigris to the Euphrates.'

"Iraq is less dangerous to us than Israel," he said.

The other hot button was terrorism. Assad professed total innocence. "Terrorism is a crime," he said, "but there is a line between charges and crimes. According to the U.S. definition, history is full of Palestinian terrorists—the pilgrims who want independence, or changed governments. How can Palestinians be terrorists for fighting for independence within their own land? How can you implicate us for Pan Am 103 when there is no evidence?"

President Bush interrupted again. "Let's define it then," he said. "It's blowing up school buses. It's throwing an old man off his ship [*Achille Lauro*]. It's killing a man on the basis of his passport. These are terrorism no matter when they happen."

"We feel U.S.-Syrian relations are going backward," Assad said. "Talk of terrorism without proof. Aid to Israel. These are bad."

"I wouldn't be sitting here if I thought things are going backward," President Bush said.

The conversation ranged across the landscape, but always through Israel, as the two men discussed their differences. Finally, as it approached 10 P.M., President Bush moved to his key point, Syrian troops in the coalition. He wanted it to be the last point.

"Suppose we send troops across Kuwait to attack his armor," President Bush said. "Will this be just American boys?"

"We have not discussed this yet," President Assad said, "in Syria or with Egypt."

President Bush was happy with a lack of commitment because it meant Syria had not decided against sending its troops into battle.

"Could you tell the press this issue has not been finalized yet?" President Bush asked. "It would be very helpful, sending a much stronger signal to Saddam, and helping the U.S. feel we're not in this alone."

Assad agreed, then made a final point of his own. "Iraq does not know our position on this matter," he said. "We are for: no partial solution, no rewards, and restoration of the Kuwaiti government."

When the meeting ended, we emerged as if in a trance, so immersed in the dialogue, straining to hear every word correctly, and interpret every nuance, that for a time the physical surroundings had been blocked out. But then we stood and shook hands all around. Suddenly, Secret Service and Syrian agents flooded into the room and the old fears returned.

As we walked out of the building toward *Air Force One*, it was dark and cold. Everyone was eager to get on the plane, back in familiar surroundings, and out of Geneva. It was not an orderly group. In the darkness of the tarmac, it was hard to see the Swiss airport guards who were around the plane. Suddenly, they started stopping the president's staff, demanding identification, and pushing the

press corps away from the plane. Joseph Verner Reed, our chief of
protocol, was muscled aside, to which he took great offense, and
shouted to the six-foot-five-inch Swiss guard to "Unhand me." Apparently not accustomed to the Old World civilities of our distinguished chief of protocol, the guard simply elbowed him in the
stomach and shoulder. I grabbed Joseph and ran for the stairway. It
turned out that everyone had been manhandled to some degree by
the Swiss guards, for no apparent reason. We left Geneva with some
anger toward our politically neutral Swiss friends, after having had a
very productive conversation with our terrorist enemies.

Strange that I should dwell on the Gridiron dinner, fishing, storm
damage, and Assad during this last flight. But in these experiences,
each in a different way, there was a personal bonding I would miss,
a closeness and respect for a professional colleague I would probably
never know again. George Bush is a very complex and multidimen-
sional person. Yet because he compartmentalize so many aspects of
his life, including his friends, few people see the full range of his tal-
ents.

As the plane made its final approach to the Houston airport, the
first signs of private life appeared. A small motorcade of red and yellow sedans was waiting. The "Welcome Home" signs were all homemade. No bands. And inside, no hurry to line up and get off the
plane.

After President and Mrs. Bush greeted their old friends, the motorcade of three or four cars moved slowly out to the highway for the
final leg home. Only Andy Card and I were representing the staff.
Andy Maner, who had worked for me in the press office during the
campaign, was going to be the president's new press secretary in his
Houston office. Andy was twenty-three, tall, thin and as fresh-
scrubbed as a small-town Michigan boy should be. He loved the
Bushes and was eager for this new experience.

If Mr. Smith Goes to Washington had a sequel called Mr. Smith
Goes Home, this would have been it. The motorcade pulled up in
front of a standard two-story colonial home of the kind seen in every
town in America—black shutters, white frame, center hall. The
Bushes had rented the house from old friends. Not big. Not ostentatious. And the twenty or thirty friends who gathered on their front
lawn to greet them could just as easily have been going to a church
supper.

Andy Card and I stood out on the street while the president

milled about in the crowd. We just looked at each other, admired the maple trees in the front yard, speculated about neighborhood attitudes, and watched the focal point of our lives for the last decade prepare to take his leave. Finally, he motioned for Andy Maner to come to him. The former president of the United States put his arm around Andy's shoulder and said, "Let's go inside a minute." The transition was now complete. There were no more briefings to call.

Index

Index